COMMUNITY TREATMENT
of Juvenile
Offenders

SOLOMON KOBRIN
MALCOLM W. KLEIN

COMMUNITY TREATMENT of Juvenile Offenders

THE DSO EXPERIMENTS

Written with

Elaine M. Corry
Carl L. Heck
Frank R. Hellum
John Peterson
Katherine Teilmann Van Dusen

SAGE PUBLICATIONS
Beverly Hills / London / New Delhi

For information address:

SAGE Publications, Inc.
275 South Beverly Drive
Beverly Hills, California 90212

SAGE Publications India Pvt. Ltd.
C-236 Defence Colony
New Delhi 110 024, India

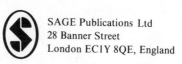

SAGE Publications Ltd
28 Banner Street
London EC1Y 8QE, England

Printed in the United States of America

Library of Congress Cataloging in Publication Data

Kobrin, Solomon.
    Community treatment of juvenile offenders.
    Includes bibliographical references and index
    1. Status offenders—United States. 2. Community-based
corrections—United States. 3. Juvenile justice,
Administration of—United States—Evaluation. 4. Juvenile
delinquency—United States—Prevention. I. Klein,
Malcolm W. II. Title.
HV9104.K64 1983   364.3'6'0973   83-13758
ISBN 0-8039-2108-X

FIRST PRINTING

For Charlotte,
and for
Laurie and Leigh

CONTENTS

TABLES AND FIGURES

PREFACE

The deinstitutionalization of status offenders constituted one component of a rather concentrated and pervasive national effort to alter the trends of delinquency during the 1960s and 1970s, an effort that is still continuing. By reviewing attempts at deinstitutionalization of status offenders, we open a window on the broader trends of diversion, prevention, and community treatment that have permeated this period and that have, paradoxically, helped set the stage for the more archaic, retributive flavor of juvenile justice in the 1980s. [1]

Summarized in this report are the highlights of our extensive study of a national, federally funded program, replicated in eight locations, to foster and encourage the deinstitutionalization of status offenders (hereinafter referred to as the DSO program). Status offenders are juveniles whose acts would not be criminal if committed by adults, acts such as incorrigibility, truancy, runaway, and similar strictly *juvenile* offenses.

We present first the history of federal efforts to assist state and local jurisdictions in their delinquency control activities, out of which the program emerged. Program objectives are then described. Their clarity and specificity are examined, as well as problems of their theoretical and conceptual grounding. The impact of goal-specificity issues on program structure and design are considered, together with effects on the organization and conduct of the evaluation study. Attention is then given to the state and local sites funded to conduct and test the effectiveness of their deinstitutionalization efforts, with consideration of the criteria used in their selection. This is followed by an account of youth served and the program's success in reaching the targeted offender population. The final chapter provides an overview and some implications.

The Juvenile Justice and Delinquency Prevention Act of 1974 opened a new era of federal concern with the problem of delinquency control and the rising movement for reform of juvenile justice. During the prior decade, federal action on delinquency was restricted to relatively small budget support of state and local demonstration projects. The 1974 act asserted a need for a comprehensive, sustained, and liberally financed approach. To this end, Congress created the Office of Juvenile Justice and Delinquency Prevention (OJJDP) as a semiautonomous agency within the Law Enforcement Assistance Administration. Based on extensive hearings that solicited the views of leaders in the youth services field and others, the language of the act specified the shortcomings of existing delinquency control practices and defined the remedies that states and localities would be encouraged to develop with federal funding assistance. [2]

Serious deficits of the juvenile justice system, according to the act, include excessive use of secure confinement in detention centers and juvenile institutions, compounded in many jurisdictions by indiscriminate mixing of serious and minor offenders in these facilities, as well as juvenile and adult inmates (see Saari, 1978). The act encouraged programs to divert minor juvenile offenders from formal police and court processing, to substitute nonsecure, community-based facilities for secure confinement, and to assist in the development of local youth services that reabsorb delinquent youth into the normal life of the community. A mid-1970s assessment of interstate differences in status offender arrests and detentions details the need for action (Smith et al., 1980). Included in the set of "advanced techniques" for the prevention of juvenile delinquency to be fostered was the avoidance of the use of juvenile detention or correctional facilities for juveniles "who are charged with or have committed offenses that would not be criminal if committed by an adult," that is, status offenses.

In addition to providing grants to states prepared to undertake comprehensive programs of this character, OJJDP was mandated to engage in four other activities:

(a) Develop a "special emphasis program" of direct grants to states and localities for programs consistent with the purpose of the act.
(b) Furnish technical assistance to participants in grant programs.
(c) Coordinate activities of other federal agencies that bear on youth and delinquency problems.
(d) Compile statistical and other information related to the treatment and control of juvenile offenders, but also conduct, encourage, and support research and evaluation studies to determine the results and effectiveness of juvenile delinquency programs, particularly special emphasis programs funded under the aegis of the act. This function was to be administered by the research branch of OJJDP, the National Institute for Juvenile Justice and Delinquency Prevention (NIJJDP).

Under its special emphasis program, OJJDP undertook as its initial effort to place in the field a program for the deinstitutionalization of status offenders. In light of the act's mandate that the effectiveness of its program be evaluated, the deinstitutionalization of status offenders program (DSO) was developed jointly by the Special Emphasis Program staff and the staff of NIJJDP.

As is true in the first efforts of all novel programs, difficulties were encountered that were bound to restrict the reach of program evaluation. From its inception, the evaluation effort became embroiled in the problem of specifying its objectives. The act had defined as a desirable and "ad-

vanced technique" the deinstitutionalization of status offenders, in effect
directing OJJDP to undertake an effort to reduce the use of secure confinement and to encourage the development of alternative, community-
based treatment facilities for dealing with the problems of status offenders.

As elaborated by the Special Emphasis Program staff, the directive
was seen as supported by two quite distinct justifications. The first was
drawn from labeling theory, which holds that for minor or first offenders
the experience of formal processing by police, courts, and correctional
agencies induces the young person to see him- or herself as a delinquent,
increasing the likelihood of subsequent offenses. The second justification
stemmed from ideas of equity and justice embedded in legal doctrine,
holding that it is both unwarranted and inhumane to subject persons to
secure confinement as a response to the noncriminal behavior represented by status offenses.[3] The program could therefore be seen as concerned primarily with deinstitutionalizing status offenders, that is, with
diverting them from detention and correctional institutions and, having
done so, with bringing about a reduction in their subsequent offense behavior by providing the backup of community-based remedial services.
These purposes could reasonably be regarded as setting the evaluation agenda.

However, the act also charged NIJJDP with the task of determining,
through evaluation studies, the results and effectiveness of OJJDP programs in the control and prevention of delinquency. In light of the first
directive, to which the Special Emphasis Program staff was responsive,
the evaluation objective was reasonably confined to an assessment of
status offense cases in the test sites funded and the discovery of effective
implementation models for dissemination to state and local jurisdictions.
Calling for a research and development approach, the second and dis-
junctive directive implied a need to field programs that were designed as
quasi-experiments in order to determine their effectiveness in the control
and prevention of delinquency.

The incongruence of the two approaches to the evaluation of the DSO
program could not reconciled entirely. Each has its proponents on the
OJJDP staff. The Special Emphasis Program staff, resting its case on the
clear language of the act, found itself in full accord with the doctrine that
the deinstitutionalization of status offenders in fact represented an "advanced technique" of delinquency control and prevention. Members of
the NIJJDP staff, committed to the doctrine of scientific skepticism and
directed by equally clear provisions of the act to "determine the effectiveness" of the proposed advanced technique of delinquency prevention,
pressed for the selection of state and local programs designed to yield
valid and conclusive findings respecting effectiveness. In the end, as formulated in the guideline document soliciting program proposals for potential funding, something of a compromise was reached.

As will be seen in subsequent chapters of this volume, the effect of the compromise was to reduce the prospect of obtaining the conditions for as satisfactory a test of program effectiveness as would otherwise have been possible, and to produce less than a full account of program implementation experience.

The test of deinstitutionalization coupled with the provision of community-based youth services as a method of reducing the offense behavior of status offenders required a program structure having a number of important features. First, it would have been necessary to specify a theory or rationale that justifies the expected linkage between program input and the desired program outcome. Second, in placing a program in field test sites, it is important to exercise care in selecting only those that have made adequate provision for program implementation. For the DSO program, this would have required that (a) the target population be clearly and consistently differentiated from delinquent youth who include status offenses in their behavior repertoire; (b) effective assurance be obtained from juvenile justice personnel that such youth would be diverted from preadjudication detention and postadjudication commitment to correctional institutions; (c) a network of youth service agencies be in place and prepared to accept and serve status offender cases referred to them; and (d) provision be made for the use of a research design establishing a comparison or control group not exposed to a DSO type of program. A final requirement was the availability, in the jurisdictions of program proposals accepted for funding, of the data resources needed to measure program impact on status offender behavior and firm assurance of evaluation access to these data.

However, because field test sites were not selected by these criteria, an examination of the effectiveness of the DSO program could not be assessed with complete rigor. Nonetheless, the evaluation findings on this matter, qualified as they must be, should prove useful at the very least in suggesting the likely limits of deinstitutionalization as the treatment of choice in dealing with status offenders. It should be kept in mind that these findings cannot be dismissed as pertaining only to *one* program; in fact, they are descriptive of *eight* independent programs in status offender treatment. The findings may also point to the need for much greater precision than is reflected in DSO-type programs in differentiating status offenders from essentially nondelinquent youth who commit status offenses from time to time, as well as from delinquent youth who intersperse their status offenses among more serious violations.

"Deinstitutionalization," note Handler et al. (1982: 105), "with its myriad of meanings was a national movement whose time had come; it swept the country." This volume is organized with a view, first, to describing the development of the national DSO program and, second, within the context furnished by its development, to assessing its effects with respect to the problems and prospects of status offender deinstitutionalization generally as well as to its delinquency control objective. We trust that these descriptions will provide the reader with a reasonably comprehensive picture of this very complex enterprise. But we also urge that readers refer to other materials resulting from this study.

Early in the history of the DSO project, it became clear that the constraints on both program implementation and evaluation design—due to the stances taken by OJJDP—would force a reconsideration of the ultimate value of the enterprise. The researchers, both national and local, suggested increasingly during their joint meetings that the ultimate value of DSO might be in its contributions to the social science and criminological literature, and the opportunity for graduate students to participate in those contributions. That prediction, we believe, is being confirmed. Just as this volume has been prepared in that spirit, we wish to acknowledge the efforts of our colleagues whose studies have appeared to date. Appendix A lists current publications; these will be joined by yet others as DSO data continue to serve the needs of research in juvenile justice.

NOTES

1. The interested reader can refer, for the historical context, to very useful reviews by Empey (1982), Zatz (1982a, 1982b), and Kornegay and Wolfle (1982). The most comprehensive bibliography on status offenders we have seen, containing over 1000 references, is included in Murray and Rubin (1982). For an even broader context, see the entire issue of the *American Behavioral Scientist* edited by Warren (1981).

2. The importance of the funding "carrot" was underscored in the analysis of Van Dusen and Klein (1981) of the subsequent California legislation. The absence in that case of funds to encourage the development of alternative youth services led, as expected, to little growth in status offender referrals to community agencies.

3. For a useful coverage of the ambiguities concerning criteria, relevant variables, and effects of juvenile detention, the reader is referred to Mulvey and Saunders (1982). Eloquent statements on the inhumaneness of status offender institutionalization are contained in Burkhart (1975), Watkin (1975), and Murphy (1974).

ACKNOWLEDGMENTS

The evaluation study of the National Status Offender Program could not have been accomplished without the dedicated assistance of a large and diverse corps of project employees, site evaluators, program directors, graduate student assistants, members of the Advisory Board, and a number of consultants, and, not least, the staff of the LEAA Office of Juvenile Justice and Delinquency Prevention.

Special acknowledgments for service beyond the call of duty go to the following members of the core project staff: Elaine M. Corry, Project Coordinator; Frank R. Hellum, Project Director; and Clarise Bronson, Senior Project Secretary. Richard Sundeen was a member of this group during the early stages of the study. Staff members with particular responsibility for data management included Lawrence McKeon and Lea Cunningham. Computer programming and the development of the data system were accomplished by Lynn Johnson, Dwight Greene, and Nicholas Statman, with consultant help from Charles Williams. Crucial to the implementation of the analysis design were Katherine Teilmann Van Dusen, William McGarvey, John Peterson, and Carl L. Heck.

In addition to John Peterson and Carl L. Heck, the following students devoted endless hours to providing assistance in specific phases of the study: Margaret A. Gordon, Kristine Kosak, James Jacob, Judith Gould, Robert Perez, and Tsuneko Eustice.

The task of generating the basic data of the study fell to seven site evaluators, whose heroic efforts to monitor, track, and record the flow of program clients through the services provided by their respective programs were indispensable to the conduct of the study. These included Maynard Erickson and Dean Rojek, Pima County, Arizona; Jack Isaacs and Roger Baron, Alameda County, California; Charles Logan, Connecticut; Frank Scarpitti and Susan Datesman, Delaware; Irving Spergel, Illinois; Stuart Deutsch and Jerry Banks, South Carolina; and Ann Schneider, Spokane and Clark Counties, Washington.

We wish to acknowledge as well the cooperation of the program directors at each site in providing in the most open and candid manner the information that formed the basis of the narrative descriptions of the programs, and in making available for interview their staff members and the personnel of justice and youth service agencies. Our thanks go to Boyd Dover, Pima County, Arizona; Jane Jennings and Robert Harrison, Alameda County, California; Deborah Leighton, Connecticut; Judy Drexler and James Kane, Delaware; William Dickerson, Illinois; George Grogan, South Carolina; Robert Axlund, Clark County, Washington; and Ray Lakewold and Sue Fish, Spokane County, Washington.

The study received valuable guidance in its early stages from an Advisory Board and a group of consultants. Constituting the Advisory Board were Albert J. Reiss, Jr., Lloyd Ohlin, and Howard Freeman. Consultants included LaMar Empey, who assisted the Office of Juvenile Justice as well as the project staff in the planning stages of the study; Daniel Glaser, who participated in the Advisory Board review of the evaluation study design; and Richard Berk, who provided important statistical and methodological counsel at several crucial points in the development of data analysis procedures. Special studies, to which we will refer later, were assiduously carried out under difficult data-availability circumstances by colleagues Robert M. Carter, Peter Gardiner, Jon Miller, and Susan Spelletich.

Finally, gratitude is owed to those staff members of the Office of Juvenile Justice whose support and assistance to the project went beyond the task of grant monitoring. Our thanks to Emily Martin, who was in charge of the agency's Special Emphasis Program, under whose aegis the National Status Offender Program was organized. Special thanks go to James Howell, Chief of the National Institute of Juvenile Justice and Delinquency Prevention, the research arm of the Office of Juvenile Justice, for his supportive understanding of the magnitude of the task represented by the effort to evaluate a national program in the uncharted terrain of the status offender problem.[1] We want above all to acknowledge our debt to Bonnie Lewin, project monitor through most of the life of the study. Without her unfailing appreciation of the conceptual and technical problems encountered in the study, her sturdy resolve to provide whatever OJJ support was required to meet these problems, and her trained grasp of the complexities of evaluation research, this study could not have been completed.

NOTE

1. Work reported in this volume was supported by grants 75-NI-99-0092, 76-JN-99-0014/1004, and 77-JN-99-0018 from the National Institute for Juvenile Justice and Delinquency Prevention (NIJJDP), Law Enforcement Assistance Administration, U.S. Department of Justice. Points of view or opinions in this document are those of the authors and do not necessarily represent the official position or policies of the U.S. Department of Justice.

All data collection forms and coding instructions are available from NIJJDP under the title *National Evaluation Design for Deinstitutionalization of Status Offenders Program*. Space limitations prohibit their inclusion in the present volume.

PART I

MANDATE
AND
CONTEXT

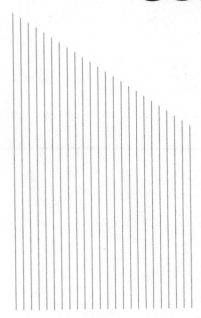

The Deinstitutionalization of Status Offenders

The Legislative Mandate

with Frank R. Hellum

P*assage of the Juvenile Justice* and Delinquency Prevention Act of 1974 marked the beginning of a major federal effort to prohibit the incarceration of juvenile status offenders in our jails, detention centers, correctional facilities, and other institutional settings. Status offenders are youths who have been charged with violations that would not be criminal if committed by an adult. These violations encompass such categories as incorrigibility, beyond control, truancy, runaway, and various acronymic designations based on the phrase "in need of supervision." In contrast to dependent or neglected children who may be regarded as immediate victims of either circumstance or the actions of parents or others, the status offender is viewed as having engaged in behavior that is subject to official sanctions. The behavior, however, is an offense only for those who occupy the age-based status of juvenile.

While this volume concentrates on this specific status offender population, it is clear that there is a broader context of concurrent youth programs within which DSO fits. Some of these fall under the Runaway Youth Act of 1974 and various education acts. For an extensive treatment of this context and the implementations of these programs, the interested reader should review Handler and Zatz (1982), a volume we see as directly complementary to ours, although less concerned with outcome issues.

The federal objective with regard to status offenders has been termed "deinstitutionalization" and implies at least a partial acceptance of a noninterventionist philosophy toward juvenile justice. In conceptualizing this objective it may be helpful to distinguish among three other related strategies: divestment, diversion, and decarceration.

The first of these, *divestment*, would require the removal of status offenses from the jurisdiction of the juvenile court system altogether and clearly represents the most extreme form of nonintervention. This strategy has also been labeled "decriminalization," but, since status offenses are noncriminal to begin with, use of this term may be somewhat confusing. A number of prestigious groups have endorsed removal of status violations from juvenile court jurisdiction (President's Commission, 1967; National Council on Crime and Delinquency, 1961); although not required by the provisions of the Juvenile Justice Act, a few states (for example, Alaska, Maine, and Washington) have recently revised their statutes to achieve either partial or total divestment of status violations.[1] Data from Washington suggest the likelihood of undesired if unintentional consequences of divestment, such as the relabeling of status offenses and delinquency offenses (Schneider, 1982).

Use of the term "*diversion*" is commonly applied to the employment of non-justice-centered resources in responding to juvenile offenders. Not only are these youths diverted "from" juvenile court processing, but they are also diverted "to" service and treatment alternatives available within the community. Without the availability of an alternative service capacity, diversion becomes the equivalent of a divestment strategy. In many respects diversion has been a traditional feature in the processing of juvenile violations. Juvenile courts have utilized both informal agreements and probationary provisions to require community-based services for juveniles as an alternative to further court action (Nejelski, 1976).

However, with regard to status offenders, recent emphasis has been given to "front-end" diversion in which police, schools, parents, and others have been encouraged to bypass the juvenile justice system completely and refer incidents involving status violations directly to the appropriate community-based service agency. Since diversion is likely to rely rather heavily on discretionary decision making, it usually amounts to a form of selective nonintervention. The full range of official options, including the coercive powers of the juvenile court, are left intact and are often available if diversion fails to produce a desired outcome or is viewed as inappropriate for the juvenile.

In contrast to diversion, the *decarceration* of status offenders does involve a reduction in the coercive powers of the juvenile justice system. This strategy is noninterventionist only in the sense that it limits or removes the authority of the juvenile court to detain a youth prior to, or following, adjudication of an alleged status offense violation. Saari (1981) has reported that, nationally, 30 percent of commitments have been for status offenses. Within these limitations, decarceration maintains the jurisdiction of the juvenile court over status offenders and allows intervention measures that are not accompanied by secure detention or correctional placement. However, if removal of the authority to incarcerate youth forcibly results in official inaction toward status violations, then decarceration may lead to a form of de facto divestment of such cases from the juvenile justice system. As will be discussed later, most juvenile courts are currently operating under statutory, administrative, or judicially imposed requirements for some form of decarceration of status offenders. But it is not uncommon in these jurisdictions to find "come back" provisions governing status offenders who violate court-ordered probation conditions. These provisions generally treat noncriminal acts in violation of a court order as delinquent offenses, which then permit detention and/or commitment of the status offender.

In light of these distinctions, then, the federal effort to foster the deinstitutionalization of status offenders can be described as an attempt to implement the strategies of both decarceration and diversion. While divestment also logically includes the decarceration of status offenders, it is neither a necessary nor a sufficient requirement for achieving compliance with federal provisions. As amended in 1977, the Federal Juvenile Justice and Delinquency Prevention Act of 1974 requires that the status offenders "shall not be placed in juvenile detention or correctional facilities" (223(a)(12)(A)), and provides for the termination of a state's eligibility for funding under the act if full compliance is not reached within a specified period of time (223 (c)). While the act recognizes the possibility of limited 24-hour detention, federal definitions suggest that "come back" statutes allowing detention or commitment of previously adjudicated status offenders for noncriminal behavior would be contrary to the decarceration objective (White, 1976). In lieu of detention and correctional placement, the act also mandates the use of "least restrictive" alternatives in providing services for status offenders (223(a)(12)(B)). The criteria used in defining these alternatives clearly reveal an intention to encourage the diversion of status offenders to community-based services and facilities.[2] Beyond these requirements, federal guidelines also prohibit alternative, *nonsecure* placement of status offenders in facilities that are similar, by virtue of either their size or function, to institutional settings traditionally used in providing custodial care for juvenile offenders. This objective offers the defining characteristic of federal efforts. *Deinstitutionalization* not only attempts to decarcerate and divert, but also seeks to block the re-creation of institutionalized treatment of status offenders at the community level.

The act thus had the double objective of removing from correctional institutions status offenders currently incarcerated and preventing their reentry, and terminating the practice of placing status offenders in secure detention. The intent of the act was to foster the replacement of incarceration and detention by the use of community-based youth services. But, as argued in a particularly perceptive analysis of the Connecticut DSO program, Logan and Rausch (1980: 8-14) indicate that the intent of the act may have been inadvertently subverted by its suggested remedies. Diversion and deinstitutionalization of status offenders, these evaluators suggest, cannot genuinely occur in the absence of divestment.

DEVELOPMENT OF FEDERAL LEADERSHIP

The history of federal involvement in the delinquency control field has been marked by two quite distinct phases. The first paralleled the rise and diffusion of the juvenile court movement, lasting from the early 1900s through the 1950s. It was governed by a traditional model of federalism in which all major decisions and substantive support for delinquency programs emanated from the state level. Federal leadership was limited to an advisory function in the formulation of policy toward youth. The second phase began with the efforts of the Kennedy administration to extend the New Deal philosophy of the 1930s to the social problems of the 1960s. It launched an era of active federalism in the field of delinquency. Leadership was assumed not only in the development of policy, but also in the commitment of resources for the implementation of policy.

Traditional Federalism

Over the course of this period every state succeeded in establishing a separate court system with jurisdiction over the behavior of youth, both criminal and noncriminal. The development of special statutes and special courts dealing with youthful misconduct rested on a theory of human development about the causes of juvenile delinquency, a related legal principle, and a corresponding philosophy of treatment. The attainment of adulthood, with its privileges and responsibilities, was seen as requiring a protracted period of development during which the young needed guidance, instruction, nurturance, control, and protection. When these needs were met, children were law-abiding; when they were not, children became delinquent. The prolongation of immaturity in modern society implied the raising of the legal age of criminal responsibility variously to the middle and late stages of the adolescent period. The associated philosophy of treatment held that the court should function as the parent of last resort in cases of extreme youthful misbehavior, intervening to provide for the developmental needs of the wayward. To accomplish this goal, courts assumed ultimate parental responsibility for the control of the child and undertook to supervise and correct his or her conduct. Attempts were made to furnish whatever additional services were, in the court's judgment, needed, available, and affordable.

The ideal prescriptions were not easily met. To process the flow of youthful offenders, new administrative structures had to be created and staffed, judges of requisite sensitivity and wisdom had to be selected, and treatment services had to be developed and routinized. Standards were also required to govern the selection and recruitment of personnel and to determine the character and quality of services designed to rehabilitate young law violators. In addition, it was necessary to encourage and maintain public support for the juvenile court and the philosophy on which it rested. Federal leadership was most in evidence with respect to this last set of issues during the rise and diffusion of the juvenile court movement.

These efforts took two forms. A White House Conference on Children and Youth was sponsored by the federal Executive Office and held every ten years beginning in 1909. The conference actively promoted a sense of national responsibility for the welfare of children, of whom delinquent children were viewed as a subset. The constituency of the decennial conferences was made up of professional welfare workers in communities around the country and those lay publics concerned with child welfare issues. Presidential sponsorship of the conferences lent legitimacy, prestige, and visibility to a growing national welfare movement.

The second form of federal involvement in delinquency prevention and control came with the establishment of the U.S. Children's Bureau in 1912. As a major feature of its mission, the bureau undertook to provide guidance in the development of the juvenile court movement by promulgating standards for court operations. In addition, it initiated the development of national statistics on juvenile delinquency by enlisting the cooperation of court jurisdictions throughout the United States.

Following the creation of the Children's Bureau, there was to be no major federal legislation in the juvenile justice field for the next half century. In light of the basic structure of federal-state relations, and given that states were assumed to retain exclusive jurisdiction in matters of criminal and juvenile justice, the federal role of adviser and standard setter appeared to be altogether appropriate. Until the end of the 1950s there was little expectation of more active federal participation in the efforts of states to cope with their delinquency problems.

Active Federalism

The advent of the 1960s marked a historic watershed in the federal role in the delinquency control problem. The preceding decade had witnessed an uninterrupted increase in reported arrests of juveniles and in the number of juvenile court cases, with a corresponding rise in public concern and anxiety. However, the politically quiescent years of the Eisenhower administration produced little inclination on the part of the federal establishment to break away from its traditional role in the delinquency field. It was not until the inauguration of President Kennedy that the federal government was brought into an emphatically activist posture in relation to the issue of delinquency.

Early in his brief tenure, President Kennedy established the President's Committee on Juvenile Delinquency and Youth Crime, consisting of the secretaries of the Departments of Labor and Health, Education and Welfare and the U.S. attorney general. They were charged with the task of coordinating the programs of their several agencies having some bearing on conditions productive of delinquency. The initiative was given legislative form by the enactment of the Juvenile Delinquency and Youth Offense Act of 1961. In addition to providing for the coordination of all delinquency-related federal programs, the act was designed to improve economic and social conditions among the disadvantaged segments of the population and to bring together at the local level the political, economic, educational, and social welfare institutions that affected the lives of youth. Congress appropriated what now seems a modest sum of $10 million annually for implementation of the legislation during its first three years (Empey, 1978: 326-527).

Apart from the vicissitudes of program outcome, the significant feature of this initial effort was the ground breaking it performed in redefining the place of the federal establishment in the nation's effort to deal with the problem of delinquency. Briefly, it introduced and legitimated the federal government as a source of both leadership and funds in the development of state and local community juvenile justice policy. Having thus been established, federal leadership in this field entered its current activist phase. It has been marked by a steady increase in the prominence of federal legislative and executive initiatives in moving both the thinking and the practice in juvenile justice toward new ground.

DECLINE OF THE THERAPEUTIC MODEL

As the juvenile court movement expanded and took hold during the period of traditional federalism, it was accompanied by an extensive refinement of the original developmental theory of delinquency. Professional interest in the field of delinquency control gradually began to focus on the intervening psychological processes linking abnormal development to delinquent behavior. From this perspective the delinquent act came to be viewed as merely symptomatic of an underlying psychological disorder. The initial developmental disturbance, especially from a Freudian view, would have occurred in very early childhood at a point too distant from the delinquent act to permit remediation. The professional practitioner, therefore, was left to apply the theories and techniques of an emerging therapeutic model to the proximal psychological causes of delinquent behavior.

By the 1950s the therapeutic model had come to dominate the field of delinquency prevention as well as efforts to deal with other forms of deviant behavior. However, as a vehicle for the implementation of social policy, the utility of the therapeutic model came to be questioned for a number of reasons. First, it is exclusively concerned with individual pathology and as a consequence can offer very little insight into the broader social and economic causes of delinquency. Second, the orientation toward individualized treatment has limited practical value in attempting to prevent or ameliorate delinquency on a broad scale. Preventive use of the therapeutic model requires the early diagnosis and prediction of delinquency in the general population. Such attempts have not only failed to survive close scientific scrutiny, but have also been subject to charges of class, race, and sex discrimination. Finally, the therapeutic model has traditionally been followed under the assumption that treatment is at worst a benign experience: While the clinical patient may not be cured through therapeutic intervention, those with psychological disorders will not have worsened as a result of treatment and those who might not have initially required attention will not be harmed by the experience. Beneath the political somnolence of the 1950s these limitations of the therapeutic model were not a major issue. However, alternative perspectives were emerging that would have considerable force in the ensuing decade for the theory and practice of delinquency prevention.

Challenges to the adequacy of the therapeutic model and its exclusive use in the delinquency field have been a penchant of sociologists in particular. In their view, the model obscured two types of important causal factors. The first concerned the social environment, that is, the positive inducements to delinquent behavior stemming from the prevailing economic and social conditions of life among the acutely disadvantaged populations of the urban metropolis (Shaw and McKay, 1969). Delinquent acts in response to inequities in the distribution of material, as well as personal, rewards could well reflect a rational form of adjustment rather than the pathological response assumed by the therapeutic model (Merton, 1968). Building upon these earlier sociological theories, two major publications appeared during the transition from traditional federalism and attempted to trace the linkage between social factors and delinquent behavior. The first of these offered the hypothesis of "status frustration," in which working-class youth are motivated to adopt a delinquent solution as a means of attaining their own definition of self-worth in a middle-class world that denigrates their working-class origins (Cohen, 1955). The second provided a statement of "opportunity theory," in which the blockage of access to both conventional and unconventional occupational goals led lower-class males to generate variant strains of a delinquent subculture (Cloward and Ohlin, 1960). It was on opportunity theory that the prevention program of the President's Committee of the early 1960s was founded.

The other domain of causal factors neglected by the therapeutic model concerned the response of the child to efforts aimed at the correction or treatment of delinquent behavior. The impact on the child of the categorizing and defining activity of the police, courts, and caseworkers came increasingly to be viewed as at least equally important in the genesis of delinquent careers as were the problems of pathology and personal deficiency (Lemert, 1951; Becker, 1963; Schur, 1971). Much of the delinquent behavior, particularly as it occurs early in delinquent careers, was seen as "natural" in the sense of childhood experimentation with the limits of prohibited behavior (Lemert, 1951). The deviant behavior of children initially acquires its meaning for the youth only as it is responded to and defined by adult authorities (Tannenbaum, 1938). In the case of delinquent behavior, the intervention of the police, incarceration in detention centers, and placement in correctional institutions were seen as carrying the potential for imposing on the young person a stigmatized conception of self. In contrast to the assumption of the therapeutic model, the malevolent impact of official processing was as likely to result from efforts to treat the delinquent offender as it was from efforts to punish him or her. Further undesirable consequences of the "labeling" process, especially for youthful, nonserious offenders, included enforced association with more sophisticated delinquents in jails and detention centers and rejection by conforming peers for reputed delinquent behavior. Consistently higher recidivism rates among those exposed to processing by the juvenile justice system and to institutional placements were adduced as evidence of the negative effects of labeling experiences.

These, then, were the major alternatives to the therapeutic model that were offered by sociology as the move toward active federalism gathered force. The revised federal stance required new theories if there was to be a movement toward a national delinquency policy. Hard empirical support for the sociological perspectives of that period were no more adequate than the "evidence" supporting the therapeutic model, prominent in the practice of psychology and psychiatric social work in the delinquency field. The sociological theories, however, offered a logic that simultaneously engaged the major emerging issues in juvenile justice and resonated with prevailing political policy. Under the Kennedy administration, opportunity theory was to become an intellectual linchpin in the early efforts to prevent delinquency. It would also serve as a basic strategy in the declaration of a war on poverty. Labeling theory would enter at a later point, first as the basis for critically appraising the system of juvenile justice, and eventually as a rationale for deinstitutionalization. While the therapeutic model would continue to reign at the level of individual practice, its position of prominence was destined to decline in the realm of policy determination.

THE DELINQUENCY PREVENTION OBJECTIVE

As previously noted, the shift toward active federal leadership in the delinquency field was initially given legislative force in the Juvenile Justice and Youth Offenses Act of 1961. The legislation was designed to furnish planning and seed money to cities that would attempt to coordinate the activities of youth service agencies and institutions in both the public and private sectors. The theory that explicitly guided the federal effort viewed delinquent behavior as a product principally of social conditions that blocked opportunity for the young in achieving occupational and other culturally valued goals. In focusing on the causal factors cited by opportunity theory, federal leadership moved beyond the practitioner's concern with treatment and attempted to implement a program of primary prevention. The objective of the program was to develop and direct existing resources in a unified attack on the basic causes of the delinquency problem (Marris and Rein, 1973).

The first federally supported programs in the early 1960s employed a combination of two basic strategies. The first involved the mobilization of youth service and welfare institutions in a coordinated approach to delinquency problems. The second encouraged the organization of residents in poverty areas to deal with the entire range of social problems influencing youth. Cities that participated in the federal effort tended to emphasize one or the other of these strategies. Mobilization for Youth in New

York City, for example, devoted its efforts largely to community organization and local political action. In Los Angeles, Chicago, New Haven,
Cleveland, and most other cities, program effort was directed principally
to the coordination task.

These early delinquency prevention programs were relatively short
lived, in very large part because, soon after inception, the core ideas of
opportunity enhancement, community action, and coordination of effort
were adopted by federal programs dealing with the more general problem of poverty. Indeed, the War on Poverty, initiated in the Kennedy
administration and expanded by President Johnson, was modeled on the
key elements of the Mobilization for Youth program in New York's lower
east side. As Empey (1978: 297-298) observes:

> Mobilization for Youth and the President's Committee (on Juvenile Delin-
> quency and Youth Crime) had scarcely gotten under way when opportunity
> theory became the rationale for social intervention on an even grander scale.
> A nationwide War on Poverty was declared. In October 1963, the President's
> Council of Economic Advisors asked David Hackett to submit a proposal for a
> series of programs, something like MFY, which would cost $500 million in the
> first year of operation. [After Kennedy's assassination one month later] . . .
> Lyndon Johnson decided to go ahead with it. . . . Most of the senior staff who
> had worked on the President's Committee now became leaders in the War on
> Poverty. They simply took many of the ideas originally outlined in the MFY
> proposal and transferred them to the new agency.

Having been established as the major objective of federal efforts, delinquency prevention was thus absorbed by the War on Poverty. This development clearly reflected the idea that delinquency was in the main a
result of the more fundamental problem of poverty, and as the latter was
ameliorated the former would come under control. The fact was, however, that whatever the accomplishments of the War on Poverty, reported
arrests for delinquency and juvenile court cases continued to escalate
and became a major political problem.

THE PRESIDENT'S COMMISSION

The unabated rise in crime rates generally during the 1960s led finally
to the establishment in 1965 of the President's Commission on Law Enforcement and the Administration of Justice. The commission was charged
with the task of conducting a searching reexamination of the problem of
crime and delinquency and of the operations of the nation's juvenile and
criminal justice systems. Published in 1967, the commission's report on

juvenile delinquency recommended programs addressed to two sets of concerns. The first included conditions in urban poverty areas that denied equality of opportunity to youth. The second involved the excessive intervention of the juvenile justice system in the lives of youthful offenders, particularly in regard to minor delinquencies and in noncriminal cases such as status violations. The report was critical as well of practices that denied due process to youths in juvenile court proceedings.

Accordingly, the President's Commission (1967: 66-77) offered two sets of recommendations. The prevention of delinquency, the report asserted, lay outside the powers of the juvenile justice system. To provide equality of opportunity to poverty-area youth, the needed reforms were a responsibility of the political, economic, and educational institutions of society. Specific proposals were directed toward the reduction of unemployment and provision of minimum incomes to strengthen the family unit, establishment of preschool educational enrichment, elimination of discrimination in job opportunities, linkage of schools to the world of work, and participation of young people in community decision making. These proposals and the underlying concern expressed by the commission indicated an acceptance of both opportunity theory and the delinquency prevention initiative that had already been undertaken at the federal level.

The recommendations relating to the commission's concern with juvenile justice are especially noteworthy in that they interject a labeling theory critique as a basis for advocating changes in the operation of the juvenile justice system. While a majority of the recommendations are directed toward establishing procedural regularity and due process within juvenile courts, major proposals are aimed at avoiding the unnecessary stigmatization of youth and the potential criminogenic influence of official processing. These latter proposals include the development of youth service bureaus and community-based services as alternatives to justice system involvement, screening of criminal and noncriminal cases with diversion to community services whenever feasible, elimination of secure correctional placement for status offenders, and prohibition of the comingling of juveniles with adult offenders. Citing the "uncertain gain" and the inevitable stigma of juvenile court processing for status offenses, the report went on to suggest that careful consideration be given to the complete removal of these cases from the jurisdiction of the juvenile justice system.

Not only was the report of the President's Commission significant in reinforcing federal efforts toward delinquency prevention, but it also added the reform of juvenile justice to the agenda of active federalism. In so doing, the labeling perspective entered as an alternative rationale to opportunity theory in selecting the course of future federal action.

The effect of the commission's recommendation on federal initiatives was not long in coming. In 1968 Congress enacted the Juvenile Delinquency Prevention and Control Act, administered by the Youth Development and Delinquency Prevention Administration (YDDPA) of the Department of Health, Education and Welfare. The principal thrust of the act was to assist in the development of youth programs in local communities through the allocation of modest federal grants. Only as a minor motif, the program was expected to foster reform in the juvenile justice system by encouraging a fuller use of diversion through the establishment of youth service bureaus.

THE YDDPA PERIOD

Between 1968 and 1972 were years of uncertainty regarding future steps. A more conservative administration had come into office, with a less sanguine view of the leadership role of the federal government in dealing with social problems. However, the urgency of the crime issue generally had already resulted in the 1968 establishment of the Law Enforcement Assistance Administration (LEAA). Located within the Department of Justice, LEAA's mandate was to assist the states, through the use of a block grant program, in reducing their crime problems. While there was uncertainty as to how the states might accomplish this aim, LEAA had taken as its central program interest the improvement of the law enforcement function. The issue of whether this extended to the juvenile justice system as well was resolved through the enactment of the Juvenile Delinquency Act of 1972. This legislation ratified an agreement between HEW and LEAA in which the YDDPA would confine its efforts to fostering community youth programs and LEAA would attempt to improve the delinquency prevention capabilities of the juvenile justice system. This division of effort amounted to a major recasting of the overall federal role as it had developed prior to the YDDPA period.

In confining LEAA programming efforts to the juvenile justice system there was a concentration of effort in precisely the area the President's Commission had viewed as fallow ground for delinquency prevention activity. However, with the dismantling of the War on Poverty initiative of the previous administration and the return to the more traditional form of federalism, the character of federal efforts to prevent delinquency shifted from the orientation of opportunity theory to an emphasis on efficiency and deterrence consistent with a law enforcement perspective. Any effort to increase the preventive reach of the juvenile justice system became the responsibility of the states and local communities.

The responsibility of YDDPA was similarly constrained by the requirement that its programming should focus exclusively on community efforts, principally the development of youth service bureaus. This effort would logically fulfill the recommendations for diversion proposed as part of an attempt to reform juvenile justice. However, in being closed off from the juvenile justice system, the efforts of YDDPA lacked a necessary mechanism for ensuring support for the development of community-based services for diversion purposes.

The break in continuity between the YDDPA period and previous federal leadership in the delinquency field was moderated by a single exception. The 1968 legislation that created YDDPA also gave to the Department of Health, Education and Welfare the task of developing a national approach to the problem of juvenile delinquency. This was implemented by organizing a series of conferences that attracted a continuing group of academic and program specialists in the delinquency field. They were asked to address anew the causal roots of delinquency and to suggest the policy innovations implied by their analysis. The document generated by these deliberations (Polk and Kobrin, 1972) highlighted the practices of schools and justice agencies that operate to alienate large numbers of youth, creating major barriers to the formation of legitimate identities. It recommended the development of a national youth policy—a "national strategy"—that would end the sharp segregation of adolescents into youth ghettos, link the young to the world of adult interests by establishing continuity between school and work, and confine the reach of the juvenile justice agencies to only the most serious and persistent youthful offenders (Empey, 1978: 534-535). This effort followed the reasoning underlying the previous federal concerns with delinquency prevention and the reform of the justice system. It also expanded the focus of labeling and opportunity theory to include the role of nonjustice institutions such as the schools in accounting for the delinquency of middle- as well as lower-class youth.

Briefly, then, the years following the report of the President's Commission, the YDDPA period, were marked on the one hand by a political climate of skepticism regarding the appropriateness of federal leadership in dealing with domestic social issues and, on the other hand, through the continued support of LEAA, the most massive federal intervention in the crime problem in the history of the country. While it was generally acknowledged that youth are heavily involved in the crime picture, there was a basic ambivalence in mounting a coordinated federal approach. The division of labor between LEAA and YDDPA resulted in a curious set of "catch-22" regulations. The delinquency prevention efforts of LEAA could only reach those youths who were already delinquent, and the YDDPA was prohibited from focusing reform efforts on the juvenile justice system. The modest level of federal activity in achieving the twin objectives developed prior to 1968 was to continue until the passage of the Juvenile Justice and Delinquency Prevention Act of 1974.

THE JUVENILE JUSTICE AND
DELINQUENCY PREVENTION ACT

Established in 1970, the U.S. Senate Subcommittee to Investigate Juvenile Delinquency provided legislative oversight specifically concerned with federal efforts in responding to delinquency-related issues. Chaired by Senator Birch Bayh, its initial attention was focused on the activities of the two major federal agencies having responsibility in this area, YDDPA and LEAA, both of which evidenced basic deficiencies in mounting delinquency-related programming. A fundamental problem in YDDPA was the absence of effective leadership. Although created in 1968 within HEW, the agency did not have an appointed director for more than a year and a half, and by 1971 had fallen seriously behind in achieving its original purposes. During this period the agency had been authorized by Congress to expend $150 million for juvenile delinquency programs; of this amount, $30 million was actually appropriated for operation of the agency, and only half, or $15 million, was eventually spent. On the other hand, the efforts of LEAA to deal with the delinquency problem were handicapped by the absence of a clearly defined legislative intent in the Omnibus Crime Control and Safe Streets Act of 1968, which created the agency. The original act did not provide even a reference to juvenile delinquency. The subcommittee, therefore, undertook during the period from 1971 through 1973 to design and promote legislation that would remedy this deficiency.

Over a four-year period the subcommittee conducted extensive hearings on these matters and eventually concluded that the bifurcation of federal effort had been ineffective in contributing to the prevention and control of juvenile delinquency. In its final analysis the Senate subcommittee cited three major problems: (1) the absence of centralized, national leadership in addressing the problems of juvenile delinquency; (2) an inability to coordinate the efforts of the various federal agencies with responsibilities toward youth; and (3) the inadequate level of funding available for the accomplishment of an effective federal program. The results of congressional hearings were succinctly summarized in the characterization of federal juvenile delinquency efforts as a "national disgrace and dilemma." On the basis of its extended hearings, the Senate subcommittee drafted the Juvenile Justice and Delinquency Prevention Act of 1974, endorsed with minor modifications by the appropriate House subcommittee.

The proposed act undertook to remedy the specific problems of prior federal delinquency programs identified by the Bayh subcommittee. The leadership issue was resolved by creating the Office of Juvenile Justice and Delinquency Prevention (OJJDP) as the single agency with primary responsibility in the area of juvenile delinquency and placing it administratively within LEAA. The administrator of OJJDP was to be appointed by the president with approval of the Senate, providing a high degree of policy control in implementing the act and in coordinating federal efforts. The willingness to invest adequate resources was particularly manifest in providing an authorization unprecedented in the annals of federal delinquency programming: rising from $75 million for fiscal year 1975 to $125 and $150 million in 1976 and 1977, respectively. The bulk of these monies was to be used in a program of grants to participating states under a formula requiring conformity to a set of specific provisions. These provisions defined the appropriate areas of programming at the state level and included requirements for the deinstitutionalization of status offenders as well as prohibitions on the comingling of juveniles with adult offenders. As the former principal member of the Bayh subcommittee staff, and later administrator of OJJDP, has described it:

> Formula grants are authorized for states that submit comprehensive juvenile delinquency plans as provided in the Act. Of these monies 75 percent must be expended on prevention, diversion and alternatives to incarceration including foster care and group homes; community based programs and services to strengthen the family unit; youth service bureaus; programs providing meaningful work and recreational opportunities for youth; expanded use of paraprofessional personnel and volunteers; programs to encourage youth to remain in school; youth initiated programs designed to assist youth who otherwise would not be reached by assistance programs; and, subsidies or other incentives to reduce commitments to training schools and to generally discourage the excessive use of secure incarceration and detention [Rector, 1975].

In addition to the formula grants program, the Office of Juvenile Justice engaged in four other major areas of activity. The first of these was the *special emphasis programs*, which involved direct grants to states and local communities for the implementation and testing of action programs that were consistent with the purposes of the act. The second was the provision of *technical assistance* to participants in both the formula and special emphasis grant programs. The third area concerned *concentration of federal effort* and was directed toward the coordination of federal juvenile programs. The fourth activity can be described as a general *research and information* function carried out by the National Institute for Juvenile Justice and Delinquency Prevention. The institute was created by the act as a specialized component of the Office of Juvenile Justice, mandated to perform four delinquency-related tasks: collection and dissemination of information, research and evaluation, development and review of standards, and training related to juvenile justice issues.

Clearly, then, the Juvenile Justice and Delinquency Prevention Act of 1974 emphatically reversed the historical uncertainty about the use of federal leadership in carrying through the policy objectives that emerged from the shift to active federalism during the 1960s. The assumption of national leadership, the coordination of federal effort, and the provision of fiscal muscle were firmly established in OJJDP. In addition, this agency was provided an internal structure and legislative guidelines for the general task of developing effective responses to the problem of delinquency. The 1977 amendments to the act sharpened and clarified the language of the original legislation, but did not substantially alter its major provisions. Moreover, the revisions provided for further authorization of funds amounting to $525 million through fiscal year 1980. A portion of all other LEAA block grant funds amounting to at least 19.5 percent was also required to be appropriated for juvenile delinquency programs. These features of the current act gave the federal establishment a strategic position in the future development of delinquency prevention and control policy.

THE LEGISLATIVE MANDATE: PROBLEMS AND PROSPECTS

When posed in relation to previous policy objectives in the delinquency area, the substantive thrust of the new federal legislation can be described as having two basic characteristics. First, the Juvenile Justice Act rejected very few, if any, of the objectives that had previously been undertaken in the area of juvenile delinquency. Second, however, the legislation established priorities in the pursuit of answers to the underlying problems of juvenile crime and youthful misconduct. Viewed in this manner, it becomes apparent that the federal legislative mandate resided in the priorities accorded a wide range of objectives, rather than in the endorsement of a single policy aim or a narrow set of objectives. It is also clear that relative to the two general policy directives emerging from the federal experience of the 1960s, the new mandate emphasized the goal of juvenile justice reform over that of delinquency prevention.[3] It should be noted, however, that the two issues may be fairly joined. Data from the famous Massachusetts Experiment indicate that which offenders become detained is a chancy affair, and that detention is determined in part by past detentions and is followed by greater recidivism (Ohlin et al., 1975).

As noted earlier, reform of juvenile justice as an area of federal concern was highlighted in the 1967 report of the President's Commission. The recommendations were directed to two levels of reform—diversion, or the removal of youth from juvenile court processing, and the establishment of procedural regularity for all remaining cases. With the exception of the emphasis on due process, diversion is consistent with the federal effort to encourage the development of national standards as pursued even during the period of traditional federalism. While providing opportunities for achieving both types of reform, the Juvenile Justice Act clearly emphasized diversion as the first order of business in modifying the system of juvenile justice. The federal initiative prescriptively endorsed the development of community-based alternatives as was attempted during the YDDPA period, but also provided for the utilization of these alternatives through prohibitions on the institutionalization of status offenders and for support for the diversion of minor criminal offenders as well.

In pursuing the objective of deinstitutionalization, the 1974 act in effect has given substantial impetus to a nationwide movement to end the use of detention and incarceration in correctional institutions for dealing with status offenders. Briefly summarized, Wisconsin and Alaska prohibited postadjudication commitment in 1971, with New Mexico following this lead in 1972. By 1973 three states—South Dakota, Texas, and Nevada—followed suit, as did five additional states in 1974: New Jersey, Massachusetts, Iowa, Maryland, and Illinois, with Maryland and New Jersey prohibiting preadjudication detention as well. In 1975, three more states prohibited detention, and three eliminated commitment. During the following three years, 17 additional states acted to restrict or eliminate the use of detention, and 25 to prohibit or reduce the use of postadjudication commitment. The trend continues as of the date of this writing.

This objective was achieved in some of the states by revising their administrative practices or regulations, or through executive or court order rather than by statutory change. Of the states that have deinstitutionalized status offenders, some (such as Maine and Alaska) have removed status offenses from court jurisdiction; others (such as Arkansas, Oregon, and Virginia) have limited their detention to a maximum of 72 hours; and some (such as Georgia) permit a court-ordered 48-hour extension to the 72-hour limit. Indiana prohibits secure detention only for runaways. Illinois permits postadjudication commitment only if parents are found to be unfit, and Texas may commit for the violation of probation.[4]

Thus most of the states have now moved either totally or partially down the road to legislative deinstitutionalization. In making eligibility for federal delinquency prevention funds contingent on progress toward total deinstitutionalization, the 1974 act offered the states a powerful incentive to continue their efforts in this direction. However, the very vitality of the movement tends to create problems of another order. Except for the still rare cases in which the juvenile court has been divested of jurisdiction over status offenses, courts face the task of dealing with these cases in a constructive and responsible manner. Recognizing this, the act also mandated the development of community-based alternatives to secure detention and incarceration. Unless such facilities are available in a jurisdiction on a scale corresponding to the volume of status offense cases, progress in deinstitutionalization is likely to be impeded.

Access to facilities of the required capacity and quality is only one of the problems confronting the status offender deinstitutionalization effort. A second problem likely to be encountered is opposition to the movement on the part of a substantial segment of the public. As embodied in the act, the conception of the status offender as a misbehaving, noncriminal offender is largely restricted to those whose professions and occupations have brought them into direct contact with the delinquency problem. There remains a large pool of public sentiment, reflected in existing state statutes, that defines status as well as youthful criminal offenders as constituting the delinquent population. Resistance to a discriminating and less "stern" treatment of status offenders may be expected in many jurisdictions.

Two further interlocking problems may be anticipated. The development and use of alternative community-based facilities implies a substantially reduced use of detention and incarceration facilities that are already in place, each with its complement of personnel with a vested interest in their jobs. Moreover, the continued need for secure facilities for young criminal offenders means that the diversion of status offenders to nonsecure facilities will leave the fixed costs of detention centers and correctional facilities unaltered. Hence it may well be the case that the development and use of alternative facilities will entail increased costs in many jurisdictions. Jurisdictions that may be ambivalent about the wisdom of deinstitutionalization may thus be persuaded that the trade-off between delinquency prevention and increased costs is unfavorable. The related cost problem concerns the possible need for an expansion of services for a segment of the status offender population, whose numbers cannot yet be estimated. It includes the incorrigibles or ungovernables and the chronic runaways who come to official attention after repeated episodes of misbehavior. They are likely to have come from distressed families and in some proportion to have developed severe behavior disorders. These problems are not readily remediable through brief intervention. They often require prolonged and costly treatment by skilled workers. An adequate response to this aspect of the deinstitutionalization problem requires a commitment by the local community to expand, often substantially, the resources allocated to the youth welfare function.

A fifth problem is likely to arise in jurisdictions operating under juvenile statutes that definitively prohibit the use of secure detention for status offenders. These statutes, most of which have been enacted in recent years, are often phased in long before there has been opportunity to develop alternative facilities. In these circumstances the police and the courts may be constrained to resolve the problem by refusing to deal with status offense cases, as shown by Van Dusen and Klein (1981). This may well result in a situation of massive neglect, with the unintended consequence in many cases of a possible escalation of minor misbehavior to serious delinquency. Alternatively, and equally problematic, if community sentiment insists on positive official intervention in all cases of delinquency, however minor, the resolution may take the form of upgrading the formal complaint from a status to a criminal charge, or downgrading a status offense to neglect /dependency in order to create eligibility for secure detention. Such "relabeling" is not only technically feasible, given the enormous discretion available in juvenile offense cases, it has been demonstrated in the case of California (Van Dusen and Klein, 1981).

Finally, in according priority to the deinstitutionalization of status offenders, the 1974 act has given decisive support to the therapeutic model of delinquency prevention. It assumed that some status offenders differ from many types of delinquent offenders in exhibiting severe developmental and associated psychological problems. In these cases remediation would require individual treatment of the several kinds embodied in the therapeutic model. While this approach may be unexceptionable where appropriate, it poses the danger of being legitimized as either the sole or the principal intervention strategy for the prevention of delinquency. This is particularly likely in view of the support it normally receives from prestigious professional groups engaged in the practice of individual therapy. As was noted earlier, the 1974 act was intended to encourage a range of intervention strategies, including "youth advocacy" approaches. These emphasize the importance of improving conditions known to be associated in the aggregate with delinquency, in particular those related to education, employment, and neighborhood subcultures. Because youth advocacy seeks institutional reform, occasionally of a radical character, it is programmatically diffuse and, unlike the therapeutic model, without an established body of practice.

Given this feature of the youth advocacy approach and the current salience of the deinstitutionalization drive, with its implicit revitalization of the therapeutic model, there exists a potential problem of imbalance among program approaches. Doctrinaire conceptions of the nature of the delinquency problem are frequently entertained, and with them a tendency to apply the limited remedies with which they are associated. Although neither the therapeutic nor the youth advocacy model necessarily fits all cases, the use of either in the program of any jurisdiction tends to subordinate or totally exclude the use of the other. As the emphasis on deinstitutionalization operates to enhance the relevance of the therapeutic model, the approach is likely to encounter informed and vocal opposition from supporters of the advocacy model. The resolution of such controversy will determine the survival of those elements of the 1974 act that go beyond the immediate interest in deinstitutionalization. Awareness of an imbalance in legislative support for the two approaches was already reflected in the JDDPA 1977 reauthorization bill (S.1218). Its language emphasized, among other things, youth advocacy, due process, and neighborhood courts. In one form or another each of the problems de-

scribed has become evident in the implementation of DSO, the first program "initiative" of the Office of Juvenile Justice.

In 1975, OJJ issued guidelines soliciting program proposals designed
to foster the deinstitutionalization of status offenders. In conjunction with
the program, OJJ established an evaluation study of the experience in
order to examine program achievements and the problems encountered
in the course of program implementation. The content of the solicitation,
the criteria for site selection, the administrative structure of both the program and evaluation components, and the characteristics of the programs funded will be presented in the next chapter. Following this, the
model represented by the programs that were included in the evaluation
study will be described. We will then move to considerations of effect
and success.

NOTES

1. Readers interested in the issues around divestment will find the debate well joined in
the articles constituting Parts 1 and 2 of a recent anthology published by the National
Council on Crime and Delinquency (Allinson, 1978). In addition, an influential lay group,
the National Council of Jewish Women, has provided a nonscholarly but effective statement of the needs for divestment (Watkin, 1975).

2. There is, indeed, ample documentation of the irrationality of much juvenile incarceration. Most thorough, perhaps, is the National Assessment of Juvenile Corrections, which
illustrates the poor fit between offense seriousness and likelihood of incarceration (see Vinter, 1976).

3. Useful background information and the statement of a more philosophically liberal
position taken by the National Council on Crime and Delinquency can be found in Hickey
(1977).

4. Further changes have occurred subsequent to this survey, which was taken in 1977.
Murray and Rubin (1983) have provided a recent update on state legislation and practice on
various aspects of status offenders and their handling.

chapter 2

The Deinstitutionalization Program and Evaluation Designs

with Frank R. Hellum

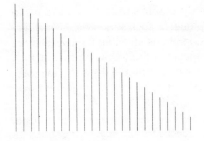

THE PROGRAM

President Ford signed the Juvenile Justice and Delinquency Prevention Act into law late in the summer of 1974. Its central feature was the offer of federal funds to states that agreed to undertake programs of delinquency prevention in conformity with the objectives stipulated in the act. Of these, a high priority was given to the removal of status offenders currently held in detention facilities and correctional institutions, and the prevention of their future entry into these facilities. This was to be accomplished by providing community-based alternatives through the use of existing youth agencies and the development of new services.

The act also made funds available, and in March of 1975 the Office of Juvenile Justice provided $8.5 million of these funds for use by public and private agencies to develop model programs for the deinstitutionalization of status offenders. Program proposals were invited nationwide, and a detailed set of guidelines was published and distributed. Federal support was to be limited to two years, with an expectation that the programs would then be continued with local resources.

To orient prospective grant applicants in developing their program proposals, four goals were specified:

- Establish procedures to utilize alternatives to secure detention at both the pre- and postadjudication stages.
- Remove status offenders incarcerated in correctional institutions.
- Provide community-based services as an alternative to detention and institutional placement and establish procedures that "hold service providers accountable on a per child basis."
- Evaluate the effectiveness of various program models in order to provide guidance for the future development of status offender deinstitutionalization programs (LEAA, 1975: 207).

It was assumed by OJJ that various program strategies would have to be adopted, but they had not conceptualized such strategies. All jurisdictions were expected to differ in the conditions affecting the feasibility of program implementation, but OJJ specified the following five factors, suggested by the authors of this volume as relevant to the effort to establish an ongoing deinstitutionalization effort:

(1) Not all communities were assumed to be equally tolerant of status offenders; therefore programs would be launched in situations of intolerance as well as tolerance. Saari (1981) has since noted independently that tolerance for community-based programming is lower where there is greater heterogeneity in social class, race, and education. She also reports "extraordinary variations in rates of institutionalization with some states placing 20 times more youth in institutions than others" (Saari, 1981: 45).
(2) Communities known to differ in the scope of available alternative program resources would be sought.
(3) Differences among communities exist in the discretion legally accorded to their courts to divert status offenders from detention and from correctional institutions, so jurisdictions varying in discretion would be sought.

A fundamental assumption of the status offender deinstitutionalization program held that its value lay in the avoidance of stigma associated with contact and processing by official agencies of juvenile justice. To test this assumption an effort was made to include:

(4) programs that varied in degree of sponsorship and management by official justice agencies so that it could be determined if the amount of justice
involvement might, in effect, subvert the stigma avoidance aim; and
(5) programs that varied in the use of treatment alternatives that maintain
the type of control over client behavior commonly found in official justice processing.

There were, thus, five dimensions of community and program variation that were considered important in selecting proposals for funding:
community tolerance of offender behavior; access to youth services resources; statutory provisions concerning status offenders; juvenile justice
control of programs; and program control of client behavior. If labeling
theory could be posited as the conceptual rationale for the program,
these five dimensions provided at least some rationale for selecting program approaches capable of testing that conceptual rationale.

SPECIFICATION OF PROGRAM
STRATEGIES AND ASSUMPTIONS

Program strategies were designated by OJJDP in general terms.
These included at a minimum the removal of status offenders from detention facilities and correctional institutions, and the prevention of their future placement in such facilities. In addition, where needed, programs
were to be designed to press for new legislation or the modification of
existing codes in the interest of fostering the diversion of status offenders.
In all instances programs eligible for funding would be expected to join
the twin objectives of reducing the use of locked facilities and expanding
community-based facilities, where capacity to provide services was to
be strengthened.

The proposal guidelines issued by OJJ also attempted to serve an
educational function by listing the assumptions on which the deinstitutionalization effort rested. As derived from the JJDP Act, three assertions
were offered, each stating a specific view of the character of the status
offender problem:

• The detention of status offenders and their incarceration in correctional institutions "is inappropriate and often destructive." Noncriminal youth stigmatized as delinquents are more likely to become delinquents.

• The adjustment problems of status offenders are "centered in the family and community and can best be treated through community-based services."
• Status offenders "can be treated more effectively and economically outside incarcerative settings" (LEAA, 1975: 208-209).

With respect to community resources, the stated assumption was that they "have the responsibility, interest, and capacity to respond in creative and responsible ways to the development and delivery of services which support more constructive juvenile behavior patterns" (LEAA, 1975: 209). Of substantial importance, however, was the fact that in discussing community resources, the OJJDP guidelines accepted the possibility that variant assumptions or theories entertained by proposal proponents regarding the causes of status offense behavior might modify the character of the services provided. It was evident that while the program took as its point of departure the conception of the status offense problem embodied in the 1974 act, the possibility of alternative conceptions was not excluded. As placed in the field, the OJJDP deinstitutionalization initiative thus remained marginally open to alternative conceptions of the problem and the acquisition of new knowledge. As will be seen later, a number of the funded programs did indeed modify the view of the status offense problem as presented in the guideline document.

Three features of the juvenile justice system were defined as favorable to the implementation of the program. Stated as assumptions, these were (1) its tendency to detain and incarcerate status offenders only as a last resort when less restrictive and more constructive community resources were not available or were unable to respond; (2) it was assumed that juvenile justice agencies would use their discretion to support alternatives to deinstitutionalization and detention; and (3) it was expected that the interest of juvenile justice agencies in making more efficient use of their resources would be served by deinstitutionalizing status offenders, particularly in dealing with the more serious juvenile offenders.

SELECTION OF PROGRAMS FOR FUNDING

Programs selected for funding represented the survivors of a multistage screening process. Of the several hundred initial concept papers received in response to the program announcement, a subset of their proponents were invited to submit preliminary grant applications. These were assessed in relation to a set of twelve criteria of varying valence, with each accorded a score value.

First to be eliminated from consideration were those that failed to attain a preset total score on two criteria: specificity of justice agency agreement to reduce the detention and incarceration of status offenders, and agreements from youth-serving agencies to participate in the program.

The survivors of this cut were then examined with reference to seven additional criteria:

- allocation of supplemental local funds to the program
- prospects of program continuity at the termination of federal funds
- the number and quality of youth-serving agencies prepared to provide services for status offenders
- the "quality" of the program, that is, its administrative and organizational coherence and the professional sophistication of its leadership
- provision for accountability in the expenditure of program funds
- the expected effectiveness of the program in winning public acceptance
- the evaluability of the program

Programs failing to score sufficiently high on these elements were also eliminated.

Finally, proposals surviving the earlier stages of selection were subjected to further screening on the basis of three additional criteria: the expected number of status offenders in the jurisdictions who would be benefited by the program; the prospect of inducing needed changes in the procedures and policies of juvenile justice agencies supportive of deinstitutionalization; and the capacity of the program to reach the jurisdiction's population of disadvantaged youth. Programs located in jurisdictions with large populations of status offenders were given the largest score values.

The task of selecting for funding a limited number of the proposals that survived the final cut posed serious problems. The scoring procedure provided no more than a general guide in identifying for exclusion the proposals for which reasonable grounds existed for disqualification. A procedure was developed by which final judgments could be reduced to quantifiable form; they were made by OJJ staff on the basis of subjective assessments of prospects each proposal offered for achieving program objectives. Many were of presumably equal merit in meeting the most stringent of the funding-eligibility criteria, and there were multiple candidates representative of specific locations on the range of variation sought. The scoring procedure thus met only part of the program selection problem.

The more serious difficulty concerned the issue of whether, given two equally meritorious proposals, preference should go to the one that was more advanced or the one more retarded in the degree to which the juvenile justice system in the jurisdiction had already developed deinstitutionalization activity. On the one hand, those that had entered on this path could more predictably make effective use of federal funds in advancing the cause of deinstitutionalization. Little time and effort would be needed to mobilize public support for the program, and the juvenile justice systems already had in place the policies and procedures necessary for the expansion of an existing program. Funding program proposals from such jurisdictions would have predictable payoffs in claiming OJJ effectiveness in the use of federal funds to deinstitutionalize status offenders. The certainty that increased numbers of noncriminal youth would be spared detention and incarceration was an attractive prospect.

On the other hand, the more pressing need was represented precisely by the jurisdictions in which there was less interest in, or more active opposition to, the exclusion of status offenders from detention or their removal from correctional institutions. Proposals from such jurisdictions came typically from public or private youth welfare agencies having only nominal commitment of support from some of their juvenile justice agencies. Yet it was evident that from a national standpoint these were the jurisdictions where the main problem lay. Status offenders were commonly detained, were indiscriminately mixed with delinquent offenders in juvenile detention centers and often in local jails, and commitments to correctional institutions tended to occur more frequently and for longer periods than for delinquent offenders. In such jurisdictions efforts to move toward deinstitutionalization would have to begin at the earliest stages. Community support would have to be mobilized and the cooperation of the juvenile justice system won. In view of the brief two-year span of federal funding support, the likelihood of reducing the detention and incarceration of status offenders, or the continuation of the program on local resources, appeared problematic.

The program proposals ultimately selected for funding represented an uneasy compromise between these conflicting interests and motives. In all, twelve programs were funded and were scheduled to begin operations during the first half of 1976. Of these, five were statewide (Illinois, Connecticut, Delaware, South Carolina, and Arkansas) and six encompassed county or city jurisdictions (Spokane and Clark counties in Washington State; Alameda and Eldorado counties in California; Pima County in Arizona; and Newark, Ohio). The twelfth program funded was the general effort of the National Assembly of Voluntary Health and Social Welfare Organizations to increase the interest of their affiliates in the status offender problem and to induce affiliates to increase the resources devoted to the problem. This latter was little more than a political plum, a measured "thank you" to those who had been supportive in the passage of the JJDP legislation.

As will be seen in the program model descriptions to be presented later, of the eight programs included in the national evaluation study, two were located in jurisdictions well advanced in the deinstitutionalization of status offenders, two were in jurisdictions heavily retarded in this respect, and the remaining four fell on various points of the continuum between these extremes. It can be argued, of course, that the congressional mandate would have been most fully implemented by selecting for funding only the programs located in the most backward jurisdictions, where it was routine practice to treat noncriminal youth as delinquent offenders.

However, the inclusion of advanced jurisdictions turned out to be advantageous in providing an opportunity to discover the problems, and some of their possible solutions, that emerge in deinstitutionalization programs that are more fully developed.

THE EVALUATION DESIGN AND CONSTRAINTS

For some years prior to the inception of the status offender program, the demand for the evaluation of all social programs came with increasing insistence from federal administrative and congressional sources. The demand was fueled by skepticism regarding the effectiveness of the New Frontier and Great Society social programs of the 1960s, directed in particular to the War on Poverty program of the Johnson years. The additional concern with the cost effectiveness of social programs suggested the use of evaluation of all federally funded programs as providing the only adequate grounds for their improvement, reconstruction, or elimination. It was consequently taken for granted that an evaluation study would be included in the planning stages of the status offender program. The task of organizing the study fell to the research arm of OJJ, the National Institute of Juvenile Justice and Delinquency Prevention.

During the 1975 planning year, NIJJDP provided a grant to the authors at the Social Science Research Institute of the University of Southern California to design an evaluation study of the status offender program. The research plan took as its primary study objective the task of ascertaining the effectiveness of the DSO program in achieving its delinquency prevention and control goals. In essence the following question was posed: To what extent, and under what community conditions, were DSO clients less prone to persist in status and /or delinquent offense behavior than were members of comparable groups of status offenders subjected to the traditional procedures of secure detention and commitment to correctional institutions? Additional questions to be addressed included those concerned with program effects on the social adjustment of program clients, on the procedures and personnel of the juvenile justice system, on leaders of the community institutions that affected the lives of youth, and on the community's youth service network. The design called as well for an examination of problems of program implementation, with special attention to strategies employed in their solution.

To answer the major question of program effect on the offense behavior of status offenders, the study design incorporated two principal elements. The first was the use of the strongest—that is, the most conclusive—experimental design permitted by the program proponents at each site. The recommended procedure for program client intake was a random assignment model. In this, youths eligible for program services by virtue of referral for a status offense would be assigned randomly to the status offender program or to traditional treatment, without respect to judgments regarding the "needs" of the client. If this procedure was not acceptable, provision was made for use of a number of weaker but possibly more acceptable experimental designs. OJJ had made proponent agreement to accept one of these designs an absolute requirement for funding eligibility. Unfortunately, this turned out to be a matter of form, not of substance, as OJJ staff itself was antagonistic to program adjustments suggested by evaluation needs.

The second principal element of the evaluation design was the development of a data base for analysis. This included information on socioeconomic, demographic, attitudinal, educational, and family status characteristics of each program client; the source of referral to the program; the formal complaint (if referred by police or court), together with a description of the behavior that occasioned the complaint; the record of both status and delinquent offenses; the community-based services to which the client was both initially and subsequently referred so far as this information was recoverable; and the record of client behavior and adjustment subsequent to admission to the program. In addition, data were to be obtained permitting characterization of each program jurisdiction with reference to elements assumed to facilitate or impede program implementation. This information was deemed essential in order to specify the conditions under which the program operated, and the degree of success with which various program models and components of each model were able to utilize or deal with each of these conditions. Thus the national evaluation study was designed as a comparative study with a view to specifying the contextual problems that must be taken into account if the deinstitutionalization of status offenders was to produce a demonstrable delinquency prevention outcome.

Information provided in the OJJ guidelines was only moderately explicit in presenting the character and thrust of the evaluation study of the national program. The major emphasis of the design was on amplifying the sparse current knowledge about status offenders and the status offense problem in order to furnish an empirical basis for the improvement of delinquency prevention programming. While not opposed to this objective, the presentation of evaluations aims in the instructional materials sent into the field by OJJ offered a slight shift in emphasis. Two evaluation study goals were specified: measurement of the success of the deinstitutionalization program; and assessment of the comparative effectiveness of the various program models to be funded. As for the first, programs were to be evaluated with respect to their success in reaching specified numerical goals in removing status offenders from detention centers, jails, and correctional institutions and preventing their reentry into such facilities. In addition, an effort was to be made to obtain data relevant to (a) changes in juvenile justice system processing of offenders, in particular their labeling, delabeling, and relabeling; (b) the effect of the program on juvenile justice system allocation of resources and personnel; and (c) unintended consequences of the program. As to the second evaluation goal, the comparative effectiveness of various program models, this was to be assessed with respect to (a) the comparative reduction in offense behavior among status violators served by the program; (b) change in their general social adjustment in family, school, and work settings; and (c) whatever additional criteria were deemed appropriate by the program director and the site evaluator in each program jurisdiction.

The guideline description of the evaluation study was also alert to the difficulties it was likely to encounter. Listed under this rubric were:

> absence of provision in the OJJ program for a long-time follow-up of program clients to obtain more conclusive evidence of program effect;

> the difficulty and cost of developing measurement instruments to serve evaluation research objectives;

> the likelihood that subsequent to their initiation, projects would alter their initial designs, reducing the validity of comparative effectiveness measurement; and

> the difficulty of establishing controlled experimental designs for the comparison of institutional and community-based treatment procedures for comparable status offender groups.

As to the last, anticipating the reluctance of program proponents to accept the need for building rigorous experimental design into their program intake procedures, the guideline document held out an attractive quid pro quo: "Special consideration will therefore be given to applicants who propose to incorporate control groups into their action programs" (LEAA, 1975: 16).

The experimental design issue was one facet of a wider problem, namely, the importance to be accorded program evaluability as a criterion for funding eligibility. We noted earlier that evaluability constituted one of the seven criteria for program fundability employed in the penultimate screening procedure. Evaluability in relation to the total possible score was accorded a weight of only 10 percent. Nevertheless, at the insistence of NIJJDP, the program staff requested the USC research staff to assist it in judging the evaluability of the approximately 70 program proposals that survived the first cut, and whose proponents might be invited to submit fully specified grant applications. These were assessed by us in relation to four criteria central to evaluation payoff potential: (1) placement with respect to the five dimensions along which programs were expected to vary; (2) availability of and access to juvenile justice data; (3) the number of clients the program was expected to serve and would thereby be available for evaluation purposes; and (4) receptivity to the requirements of the evaluation study, including in particular the use of some form of experimental design.

The level of concern within OJJ with enhancing evaluation productivity in the proposal selection process is suggested by the outcome of the evaluability assessment exercise. Of the 11 programs ultimately funded by OJJ (the National Assembly of Voluntary Associations proposal was not included in the assessment), only one had been recommended for funding on the basis of evaluability, with a second proposed as a possible substitute for the first. Two had been given secondary ranking (that is, others were more acceptable), one was given the lowest acceptable ranking, two were not included in the set reviewed, and four were rejected as posing virtually insuperable problems for evaluation. The outcome is presented in more convenient form below:

Assessment	Number of Proposals Ultimately Funded
recommended	2
secondary ranking	2
lowest acceptable ranking	1
rejected	4
omitted from review	2
total	11

To understand this outcome it is necessary again to refer to the presentation of evaluation goals in the guideline document. Two goals were defined: measurement of the success of the deinstitutionalization program in terms of the number of status offenders removed and diverted from secure detention and incarceration; and assessment of the comparative effectiveness of the various program models in reducing postprogram delinquent behavior on the part of program clients. In view of the scant account taken of program evaluability in the selection process, it is likely that this ordering represented a primary and a secondary concern of program personnel at OJJ. In effect, in presenting to the field the character of the evaluation to be conducted, OJJ reversed the priorities defined in the original USC evaluation design. There, the primary focus had been placed on the examination of the comparative effectiveness of various program models and justice system contexts in reducing status and delinquent offenses among program clients. Recognizing that "success" in deinstitutionalizing status offenders was heavily dependent on the way in which juvenile justice systems utilized their discretion in case definition and disposition, the evaluation was designed less to assess "success" than to bring to light the conditions related to variation in developing and utilizing community-based services in dealing with status offenders.

This reversal of priorities is probably traceable to the two basic aims of the deinstitutionalization initiative of OJJ. The first of these, increased utilization of alternative community-based facilities, was defined as socially valuable in itself and therefore not subject to test. The second was the improvement of knowledge about the characteristics of status offenders and the nature of the status offense problem in order to lay an empirical foundation for the use of deinstitutionalization as a delinquency prevention tool. While these aims are by no means mutually exclusive, each corresponds to a somewhat limited specialized interest, with program personnel inclined to emphasize the first, and research personnel the second. Indeed, the divergence of focus was given extreme expression at a meeting in which project proponents were briefed on evaluation aims. One participant stated that even if the evaluation study found that the deinstitutionalization of noncriminal young offenders did not reduce their delinquency, it remained a valid goal simply on the grounds of justice and humaneness. This is tantamount to the view that concern with program effectiveness is irrelevant.

The dialogue is perhaps captured in the following recorded exchange. The first two comments were made by local program personnel, reacting to the realities, as they saw them, of having to face their contractual agreements to participate in the national evaluation enterprise. The third is the statement of the "big gun," an LEAA administrator who reacted to the divergence of views in an unexpectedly strong fashion. Finally, the "coup de grace" was administered by an official from the federal Office of Management and Budget.

Local Program Administrator 1:	*What is needed is a local evaluation. Local evaluators say they are spending all their time and resources for USC. Very little is left for what needs to be done. All time and resources go into running around asking kids silly questions.*
Local Program Administrator 2:	*Is this a research project that you are funding? If it is then I'm sorry. Is it LEAA's intent to have this basically a research project? If so, this all falls in place. If on the other hand you are putting all your money into developing new techniques with research an auxiliary to it, by no means the most important part, it tells us something else. What's frightening at most of the sites—they feel strongly that this is basically a research project and everything is secondary to that. If that's true, the emphasis is misplaced. All the focus is on filling out forms . . .*
[Staff Notes:	*At this point everyone was talking (yelling) at once. Vote was taken to*

*determine whether to continue following
agenda or get evaluation problems in
general aired. Monday afternoon was
devoted to griping session, with each site
presenting its major problems. OJJ staff
told everyone to get all of the problems
out of the way Monday because
everything should be sweetness and light
when (the "big gun") arrived on
Tuesday.*]

LEAA Administrator: *I don't give a damn if every program here
fails as long as we learn something. I don't
expect them to. The money in these
programs is not important. This project
will help to decide what is best to do with
status offenders. It is crucial that we have
a good evaluation so we have something
to take to Congress that will influence
putting hundreds of millions of dollars
into programs. There must be
collaboration between program and
evaluation. Be careful that each site is not
developing their own separate project. If
programs are not sticking to strict
definition of status offenders, we will
have mush. Again, I don't care if every
program here fails as long as we learn
something.*

OMB Official: *LEAA has a bad reputation for funding
poor programs. Those days are over.
Without a good evaluation tied in, there
will be no programs funded.*

The same divergence of focus and interest existed in the OJJ staff itself. Through most of the planning year the NIJJDP and the Special Emphasis program groups in OJJ brought conflicting views to the issue of
primacy in program objectives. Trained in the canons of scientific investigation, the former had surveyed the research literature on the status offense problem by way of laying the groundwork for designing the status
offender program. Concerned with the gaps in knowledge disclosed by
the survey, and in the interest of implementing the congressional mandate in a systematic and rational manner, the NIJJDP staff were inclined
to give priority to the need to close the knowledge gap. In their view this
aim could best be accomplished by selecting for funding only those proposals that accepted the need for strong experimental design and that
indicated a willingness to assist in generating the substantial body of data

required. Essentially, then, the NIJJDP group viewed OJJ's status offender program initiative as an opportunity to build the knowledge base needed to deploy the deinstitutionalization approach for delinquency prevention purposes.

The Special Emphasis program staff, on the other hand, drawn largely from the practice field of social work, were more attuned to the task of demonstrating the feasibility of replacing detention and incarceration with community-based facilities as an appropriate means of dealing with the status offense problem. The 1974 Juvenile Justice and Delinquency Prevention Act had mandated deinstitutionalization on the *assumption* that it would in fact reduce delinquency, an assumption shared by the Special Emphasis program staff. The questions they were inclined to address in selecting programs for funding concerned the conditions of organization, administration, resources, and commitment calculated to promote and demonstrate the most progress in deinstitutionalizing status offenders. While the NIJJDP staff accepted this question as valid and important, they remained insistent on extending the evaluation to cover the entire gamut of empirical issues with which the status offense problem was encumbered. Among other things, the available research evidence strongly suggested a need for more definitive information in distinguishing status from delinquent offenders, in determining the incidence of neglect and dependency cases within the population treated as status offenders, and in ascertaining the age, gender, ethnic identity, family background, and offense pattern characteristics of those identified as status offenders whose response to various types of community-based treatment effectively reduced delinquent behavior. Put bluntly, the issue between the two components of OJJ was whether to treat the national status offender program solely as an opportunity to promote the status offender deinstitutionalization movement, or as an opportunity to generate the kind of discriminating information that would "fine tune" the movement as an instrument of delinquency prevention and youth welfare.

The issue is nicely typified by the net-widening issue, to which we will refer often in this volume. The Special Emphasis staff wanted to promote treatment of minor offenders "in need of treatment," with the offenders' status as legitimate targets of detention a secondary concern. The NIJJDP staff, and the evaluators monitored by them, were far more concerned with the issue of whether the treated clients did indeed meet the criteria of likely detention. The two staffs would evaluate very differently, for example, the fairly typical situation documented in the Pima County program by Rojek (1982):

For example, 20.6 percent of referrals came directly from parents, 10.5 percent from schools, and 11.5 percent from community agencies. Further, a new concept was invented, termed a "self-referral." Slightly over 10 percent of all diversion clients appeared of their own accord and requested a service. In most instances, these self-referrals were simply diversion agencies actively soliciting clients for their particular program. These new sources of referral may constitute a certain widening of the net that poses a grave danger to the diversion movement. Unless the program is carefully monitored, the community can use diversion agencies as a new dumping ground in place of the juvenile court. The potential for abuse by the local citizenry needs to be carefully assessed before conduits are built bypassing the police or juvenile court personnel.

The two evaluation aims remained a source of strain within OJJ during the program planning year and, in ways that will be noted, during program implementation as well. As has been indicated, the divergence in evaluation aims was eventually resolved largely by displacing the strain from the OJJ office to the field programs. Evaluability as a criterion of project selection for funding was accorded relatively low priority and, with the exception of one project, a weak "before /after" experimental design was substituted for the more rigorous random assignment design initially urged for adoption.

These problems were overlaid and rendered even more complex by the manner in which the national evaluation study was organized and structured. NIJJDP had already expressed its interest in addressing the unresolved empirical issues in the status offender problem through its close collaboration with the USC staff in designing the national evaluation study. The study was designed as a comparative examination of the conditions under which the deinstitutionalization of status offenders fostered a reduction of their offense behavior. This required the acquisition of uniform data elements to be obtained through the uniform administration of instruments across the set of diverse program sites, each varying with respect to data availability and access.

It was thus evident that for reasons of economy and efficiency the design grantee should also be retained to employ, train, and supervise the data collection staff at all program sites, and provide the required comparative analysis of program effect. However, LEAA regulations restricting the permissible dollar amount of a grant for sole-source funding foreclosed opportunity to assure the services of the USC group in conducting the research operation at all sites. Hence separate evaluation study grantees were procured on a competitive-bid basis in each of the eight program sites. Of the twelve projects funded, four had to be excluded from the evaluation study, as we had warned earlier in the site selection process: two (Eldorado County, California, and Newark, Ohio) had low numbers of status offenders; one (Arkansas) was insufficiently advanced in its deinstitutionalization planning and research capacity; and a separate outside evaluator was chosen to conduct the evaluation of one (National Assembly). Thus eight separate evaluation grants were made: a sole-source grant to the authors, and grants to seven different organiza-

tions to conduct the data collection operation at the eight program locations and, resources permitting, to pursue special site-specific evaluation
studies and their own research interests in the status offender problem.

The organizational structure implicit in the arrangement, although
necessary on fiscal and administrative grounds, was far from optimal. Its
principal difficulties lay in the splitting of responsibility and authority in
relations with site evaluators between NIJJDP and USC and in creating
communication barriers. As the funding agency, NIJJDP had sole authority with respect to the work of the site evaluators. As the organization
coordinating the evaluation study and conducting the comparative effectiveness analysis, USC was responsible for obtaining from site evaluators
an extensive body of data in uniform format and for maintaining quality
control of the data.

As a condition of its grants, each site evaluator agreed to provide to the
national evaluators at USC the full complement of data as prescribed in
the national evaluation design. This was clearly defined as their primary
task. They were encouraged in addition to use the site data that they
furnished to USC and to obtain whatever further data they wished for
use in evaluation or research studies of specific interest to them. They
were also expected to furnish information on program operations that
would serve the needs of program managers at their sites. However, as a
condition of their grants, site evaluators were obliged to accord highest
priority to the data requirements of the national evaluation study.

To meet the objectives of the national evaluation study, the authors
had to monitor continually and closely the data development work of the
site evaluators. This did not always work smoothly, especially in the early
days of instrument development. An assistant evaluation director at one
site exclaimed in desperation, "All these data elements, but where are
your hypotheses, what's your theory—I can't see how these variables
have to do with anything." "Then perhaps," retorted an equally frustrated USC evaluator, "you would be well advised to get someone on
your staff who knows some criminology!" In another instance, a site evaluator claimed that obtaining the required police data was next to impossible. Knowing that particular situation rather well, the national evaluators applied a rather heavy hand by dispatching a team of their own to
two police stations in that site. The team reported "three of us completed
17 cases, which included 44 offense incidents, in 45 minutes." The site
evaluator thereafter conformed to the data collection agreements.

The major axis of communication was between the eight site evaluators and USC. The lines of control and authority, on the other hand, ran
from the site evaluators to NIJJDP. The awkwardness of this arrangement
was eventually moderated by unusually supportive cooperation.

A further problematic feature of organizational structure had its source
in the Office of Juvenile Justice itself. The program and evaluation sides
of the deinstitutionalization program were handled by its Special Empha-

sis program staff and NIJJDP, respectively. Well into the first year of program operation this arrangement continued to interpose barriers to contact between the national evaluation staff at USC and the directors of program projects at the eight sites. Directors of site programs were responsible only to the Special Emphasis program staff. As a consequence, what may be termed a climate of "disconnectedness" was generated between site program staffs and both USC and the site evaluators. This occurred despite the fact that program directors were obliged by the terms of the program grants to provide assistance to site evaluators in the data collection operation. Communication difficulties stemming from the organizational structure of the OJJ deinstitutionalization initiative are best reflected by Figure 2.1.

Direct communication between pairs of units is indicated by the double-arrow lines in the figure. To obtain information about the structure and operations of site programs, USC was obliged to route messages through NIJJDP and thence to the Special Emphasis program staff at the OJJDP level. Indeed, until well into the second program year the USC group labored under an OJJ directive *forbidding* communication with the directors of site programs. An alternative route was through the site evaluators to program directors. But here there existed communication barriers of another kind. In addition to the chronic suspicion of evaluation researchers entertained by program personnel, site evaluators were burdened with the task of providing the voluminous data required for the

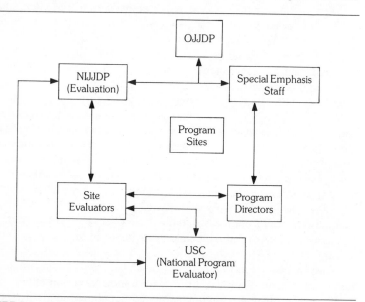

FIGURE 2.1   Organizational Structure of the OJJ Deinstitutionalization
              Initiative

national evaluation study. They were inclined for the most part to attend only to those features of program operations relevant to their data collection tasks. Their relations were further troubled by the demands imposed on program staffs to "paper" their client intake and service activities, that is, to complete the required data forms accurately and promptly.

Some feeling for the problems can be garnered from two experiences in one site. There were, first of all, occasional direct communications problems between national and site evaluators. At a national meeting of all evaluators, an assistant site evaluator inexplicably lay down on the floor in the middle of the circled tables. "Lying down on the job?" quipped another site evaluator. "No; they are!" replied the first, pointing directly at the national evaluation staff. Such symptoms of tension could be, and were, generally handled and resolved where direct lines of communication were open.

But where direct lines did not exist, as between the USC staff and program directors in the eight sites, indirect communications occasionally led to the application of the heavy hand of the OJJ monitors, as in this excerpt of a warning letter from OJJDP to the program director in the same site:

Although certain aspects of the national evaluation design had not been fully developed until recently, the need for access to official police and court records on individual status offenders has been continually emphasized from the beginning of the DSO program. In addition to its inclusion in the DSO program announcement, the necessity of access to police and court records was stressed at the meeting held in Kansas City last July with the DSO applicants and again, during the site visits to the individual projects last summer. Moreover, the ability to provide such access was a selection factor employed by the OJJDP in determining the final DSO grantees. In light of your Agency's stated commitment to participate in the evaluation, as indicated on Page 307 of your application: "This Agency has obtained commitments from courts and police for providing all types of statistical information," we are concerned now to be informed that you object to this aspect of the evaluation and further, that the local evaluators' intrusion into courts would strain your tenuous relationships. While we recognize that access to police and court records may be difficult in certain sites . . . it is our understanding that the local evaluators took this into consideration when choosing the particular sites to be evaluated. . . . Further, police and court records will only be collected on a portion of the status offenders (600 youth), and can be gathered at one point in time. Thus, according to the local evaluators, it will only be necessary to gain access to records in seven courts and 12 police districts. . . . Additionally, the data collectors will be thoroughly trained by the University of Southern California in the beginning of June. It is absolutely essential that access to police and court records is obtained. Your cooperation in this matter will obviously facilitate the local evaluators' entrance into police departments and juvenile courts. If access to police and court records is not possible, the . . . project cannot be included in the national evaluation. To exclude . . . from the national evaluation would seriously affect the scope of our overall evaluation of the DSO program. Since your program contains a wide variety of approaches to the treatment of status offenders, much valuable information would be lost. Additionally, your agency will be in violation of Special Condition #9 attached to your grant. This condition states: "The subgrantee agrees to participate fully in the national evaluation, in accordance with the design developed for the particular site."

As is frequently the case when formal organizational structure impedes task accomplishment, by the end of the second program year informal lines of communication had been developed between the national evaluation staff and the directors of site programs. USC staff had found it necessary to make frequent site visits to program locations to assist site evaluators with data collection and formatting problems. In the course of these visits opportunities arose both to observe program operations and on occasion to confer with program personnel. To supplement this source of information, as the funding period was drawing to a close several members of the national study staff spent several days at each program site obtaining interview data about structural and operational features of programs from program directors, their staff members, contracted service providers, and police and court personnel.

Three additional problems in conducting the national evaluation study deserve mention. They are offered here because there is every reason to believe they will be common to similarly structured national evaluations. First, the complexity of the task in organizing deinstitutionalization programs at multiple sites was initially little appreciated. Insufficient start-up time was provided for in the planning. As a result, a number of the programs did not become fully operational until well into their first funding year, drastically limiting the duration of the program "test" period. Failure to provide time to resolve start-up problems affected the evaluation study as well. Specifically, there was no opportunity prior to program initiation to field test the data collection instruments for their capacity to accommodate the enormous variation across sites in the character and quality of available data. The concern here was with both program service and client offense data. This became a serious problem in view of the need this imposed to modify data instruments simultaneously with the need to maintain data recording concurrently with program operations.

A second special problem was intrinsic to the scope and complexity of the data required to examine the comparative effectiveness issue across the range of program models and program components. In all, sixteen data sets were called for. In order to assure the uniformity of the information and to maintain quality control, these data were to be centrally processed and reduced to machine-readable form at the University of Southern California. Arrangements had been made with site evaluators to return to them their own site data, thus relieving them of the task of data processing. However, it shortly became evident that the time required for constructing an analytically useful data system capable of handling the massive volume of data was seriously underestimated. As a result, it proved difficult to provide site evaluators with the information they needed from time to time for purposes of monitoring their own progress in completing data collection and data correction tasks, in performing special analyses of interest to them, and in some instances of providing client flow information to their opposite numbers on the program side.

The third, and possibly the most serious, of these technical problems was the need to sacrifice data on program services. The evaluation design initially called for extensive detail on each youth served by the program with respect to the precise content, frequency, and duration of each of the sequences of services provided, as well as the professional level and treatment approach or intervention strategy of the personnel furnishing the service in each service episode. It quickly became apparent that the time and resources needed to record service history at this level of detail would be massively resisted by both service providers and site evaluators. The information was then supplemented by survey data describing in some detail the characteristics of the services provided by each program facility, permitting the recovery of service detail referenced in the *aggregate to all clients* serviced by that facility, but not specified to *individual* clients.

In sum, then, the program and evaluation designs were developed concurrently but not very collaboratively. Legislative ambiguities and mandates combined with divided value orientations in OJJ to yield less than optimal conditions for launching effective demonstration projects. All this combined with inconsistencies in approach to the national evaluation aims and with research complexities to yield an evaluation design seriously constrained from achieving its own aims, yet still sufficiently viable to make the attempt.

We move on next to an integrated description of status offending clients and of the eight DSO programs actually mounted, for they tell much about what can be achieved in this area and constitute an interesting cafeteria of alternative service models for various types of youngsters.

chapter 3

Characteristics
of Status Offenders

*with Frank R. Hellum
and Elaine M. Corry*

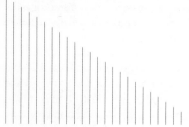

I*n the course of their operation*
over the two-year period of federal funding, the eight evaluated DSO
programs served approximately 16,000 youth. Slightly more than one-
sixth of the population was cycled through the program more than once,
yielding a case count of 19,524 (see Table 3.1).

In considering the material in this chapter, the reader should recall the
assumptions in the federal legislation, among many OJJDP staff, and
among many practitioners in the juvenile justice field that there is a common entity known as a *status offender* (as distinct from delinquent offenders). In later chapters, we will address this assumption more fully by
reference to past research and to analyses of the DSO data. For the purposes of *this* chapter, however, the issue may be suspended temporarily.

What we offer here is a descriptive analysis of the most comprehensive collection of status offending youngsters yet available. Despite the disparities in site-to-site definitions of acceptable status offender clients (some being highly restrictive and others highly inclusive), these data provide a very solid data base on selected characteristics of status offending youth in America.

In presenting the characteristics of the program clients, attention will be focused on their gender, age, ethnicity, community type, offense attributes, source of referral, and type of customary household. Beyond providing an accounting of the number and kinds of youth served by the national status offender program, these data offer an opportunity, first, to establish some of the parameters of a status offender population based on a large sample and, second, to assess some of the variation across jurisdictions in the types of juveniles defined as status offenders or regarded as eligible for treatment as status offenders. In addition, these descriptive materials provide an opportunity to examine some of the features of those who were referred for program services more than once, constituting a group whose status offenses were possibly more chronic. Finally, such materials allow the reader to assess the level of differential handling or "bias" applied to various types of status offending youths. A brief review of the evidence for such bias on the basis of gender, race, or economic status is contained in Zatz (1982a: 32).

GENDER

The data presented in Tables 3.1 and 3.2 support the general impression that females are overrepresented in the status offender population, constituting slightly over half of the total. Among the eight evaluated sites, the proportion of females ranged from a low of 44.6 percent in Delaware to a high of 69.2 percent in Connecticut, with a mean percentage of 53.6. Only in Delaware and South Carolina did the female proportion fall below 50 percent.

TABLE 3.1　New and Return Referrals, All Sites, by Gender

	Male		Female		Total	
	N	%	N	%	N	%
New referrals	7,459	46.4	8,617	53.6	16,076	100.0
Returns	1,305	37.8	2,143	62.2	3,448	100.0
Total cases	8,764	44.9	10,760	55.1	19,524	100.0
% return cases	14.9		19.9		17.7	

NOTE: Throughout the tables in this chapter, totals will differ somewhat as a function of missing data collected at each site. Missing data never exceed 5 percent, and seldom exceed 1 percent.

TABLE 3.2   New and Return Referrals, Each Site, by Gender

Program Site	Male N	Male %	Female N	Female %	Total N	Total %
Pima County, AZ						
New referrals	1,793	49.9	1,800	50.1	3,593	100.0
Returns	579	42.3	791	57.3	1,370	100.0
Total cases	2,372	47.8	2,591	52.2	4,963	100.0
% return cases	24.4		30.5		27.6	
Alameda County, CA						
New referrals	1,305	44.4	1,632	55.6	2,937	100.0
Returns	214	35.9	382	64.1	596	100.0
Total cases	1,519	43.0	2,014	57.0	3,533	100.0
% return cases	14.1		19.0		16.9	
Connecticut						
New referrals	128	30.8	287	69.2	415	100.0
Returns	10	20.8	38	79.2	48	100.0
Total cases	138	29.8	325	70.2	463	100.0
% return cases	7.2		11.7		10.4	
Delaware						
New referrals	867	55.4	697	44.6	1,564	100.0
Returns	76	48.1	82	51.9	158	100.0
Total cases	943	54.8	779	45.2	1,722	100.0
% return cases	8.1		10.5		9.2	
Illinois						
New referrals	1,003	38.3	1,614	61.7	2,617	100.0
Returns	240	32.3	504	67.7	744	100.0
Total cases	1,243	37.0	2,118	63.0	3,361	100.0
% return cases	19.3		23.8		22.1	
South Carolina						
New referrals	1,718	51.8	1,596	48.2	3,314	100.0
Returns	72	44.2	91	55.8	163	100.0
Total cases	1,790	51.5	1,687	48.5	3,477	100.0
% return cases	4.0		5.4		4.7	
Clark County, WA						
New referrals	283	40.8	411	59.2	694	100.0
Returns	46	35.1	85	64.9	131	100.0
Total cases	329	39.9	496	60.1	825	100.0
% return cases	14.0		17.1		15.9	
Spokane County, WA						
New referrals	362	38.4	580	61.6	942	100.0
Returns	68	28.6	170	71.4	238	100.0
Total cases	430	36.4	750	63.6	1,180	100.0
% return cases	15.8		22.7		20.2	

Females similarly predominated as a proportion of all program clients of both genders who reentered the program, constituting 19.9 percent versus 14.9 percent in the total case load. The imbalance is more striking when return referrals are compared for each gender group. For the entire program population, of re-referred cases, 62.2 percent were females, compared to 37.8 percent for males. A similar predominance character- ized all of the evaluated sites. This may reflect, in part, the finding re- ported by Saari (1981) that sanction severity is related to offense serious- ness among males, but not among females. Female delinquents, in other words, may receive less attention for the *nature* of their illegal acts than for the very existence of those acts.

Lest the reader consider that these gender differences are not very striking, it is well to recall that most gender comparisons in delinquency research yield ratios anywhere from 2 to 1 up to 6 or 7 to 1, male to female. Especially in the case of official delinquency statistics, but also in self-report data on delinquency, juvenile offending is a predominantly male pursuit. Thus the greater equality in status offense rates speaks strongly to gender-based behavioral differences, or detection and pro- cessing differences, or both (Murray and Rubin, 1983: 24).

AGE

Of interest in the age distribution of status offenders referred to the program is the fact that the most frequent category is found in the 15- and 16-year-old age groups (see Table 3.3). Those under 12 years of age constituted a strikingly smaller proportion. Older youth represented ap- proximately 10 percent of total new referrals.

The age distribution suggests that status offenders tend to be concen- trated among youth during the middle and later stages of the adolescent career. It also suggests the need for caution regarding the assumption sometimes made asserting a general pattern of progression from status offenses among the younger group to later criminal offenses. However, the higher frequency of females among status offenders coupled with the pos-

TABLE 3.3   New and Return Referrals, All Sites, by Age

	Under 12		12-14		15-16		17 and Over		Total	
	N	%	N	%	N	%	N	%	N	%
New referrals	1,122	7.0	6,201	38.7	7,175	44.8	1,534	9.6	16,032	100.1
Returns	122	3.5	1,416	41.1	1,639	47.5	272	7.9	3,449	100.0
Total cases	1,244	6.4	7,617	39.1	8,814	45.2	1,806	9.3	19,481	100.0
% return cases	9.8		18.6		18.6		15.1		17.7	

TABLE 3.4   New and Return Referrals, Each Site, by Age

Program Site	Under 12 N	Under 12 %	12-14 N	12-14 %	15-16 N	15-16 %	17 and Over N	17 and Over %	Total N	Total %
Pima County, AZ										
New referrals	322	9.0	1,283	35.7	1,433	39.9	552	15.4	3,590	100.0
Returns	43	3.1	541	39.5	625	45.6	161	11.8	1,370	100.0
Total cases	365	7.4	1,824	36.8	2,058	41.5	713	14.4	4,960	100.0
% return cases		11.8		29.7		30.4		22.6		27.6
Alameda County, CA										
New referrals	179	6.1	1,132	38.8	1,247	42.7	361	12.4	2,919	100.0
Returns	15	2.5	256	42.8	279	46.7	48	8.0	598	100.0
Total cases	194	5.5	1,388	39.5	1,526	43.4	409	11.6	3,517	100.0
% return cases		7.7		18.4		18.3		11.7		17.0
Connecticut										
New referrals	13	3.1	201	48.7	199	48.2	—	—	413	100.0
Returns	2	4.2	23	47.9	23	47.9	—	—	48	100.0
Total cases	15	3.2	224	48.6	222	48.2	—	—	461	100.0
% return cases		13.3		10.3		10.4				10.4
Delaware										
New referrals	57	3.6	415	26.5	745	47.6	347	22.2	1,564	99.9
Returns	8	5.1	45	28.5	82	51.9	23	14.6	158	100.0
Total cases	65	3.8	460	26.7	827	48.0	370	21.5	1,722	100.1
% return cases		12.3		9.8		9.9		6.2		9.2
Illinois										
New referrals	102	3.9	1,022	39.2	1,421	54.4	65	2.5	2,610	100.0
Returns	36	4.8	311	41.9	381	51.3	15	2.0	743	100.0
Total cases	138	4.1	1,333	39.8	1,802	53.7	80	2.4	3,353	100.0
% return cases		26.1		23.3		21.1		18.8		22.2
South Carolina										
New referrals	395	11.9	1,495	45.2	1,361	41.2	56	1.7	3,307	100.0
Returns	13	8.0	90	55.2	59	36.2	1	.6	163	100.0
Total cases	408	11.8	1,585	45.7	1,420	40.9	57	1.6	3,470	100.0
% return cases		3.2		5.7		4.2		1.8		4.7
Clark County, WA										
New referrals	16	2.3	308	44.7	308	44.7	57	8.3	689	100.0
Returns	2	1.5	47	35.9	76	58.0	6	4.6	131	100.0
Total cases	18	2.2	355	43.3	384	46.8	63	7.7	820	100.0
% return cases		11.1		13.2		19.8		9.5		16.0
Spokane County, WA										
New referrals	38	4.0	345	36.7	461	49.0	96	10.2	940	99.9
Returns	3	1.3	103	43.3	114	47.9	18	7.6	238	100.1
Total cases	41	3.5	448	38.0	575	48.8	114	9.7	1,178	100.0
% return cases		7.3		23.0		19.8		15.8		20.2

sibility that they may come to official attention only as they become older can well affect the age distribution when the two genders are pooled.

Approximately 18 percent of all cases (new and return referrals) were re-referrals. For the most part, return cases exhibit substantially the same age distribution as do initial referrals. Note, however, as seen in Table 3.4, that the proportion of return referrals ranged from a low of 4.7 percent of all cases in the South Carolina program to a high of 27.6 percent in the Pima County program,[1] with a mean percentage of 17.7. Such extreme dispersion is a likely reflection of wide differences in policy among programs with respect to their use of resources, and to differences in jurisdictional policy on returning repeat offenders to treatment programs. Continued return referrals may well represent a protective, delinquency-tolerant approach concerned less with deterrence and recidivism than with avoidance of stigmatization and promotion of children's rights (status offenses being "noncriminal" in nature).

ETHNICITY

Not unexpectedly, the population served by the national status offender program was predominantly white. As shown in Table 3.5, for all program sites white youth constituted 67.2 percent of all individuals (new referrals) who received program services, and 66.3 percent of all cases (new and return referrals). Blacks constituted the next largest group, with corresponding percentages of 21.4 and 21.5. The Hispanic category, consisting principally of Mexican-American and Puerto Rican youth, constituted slightly less than 10 percent of the total, followed by about 3 percent for a residual "Other" group, made up mainly of Native American and Asian youth.

The data in Table 3.6 indicate the wide variation among sites in the proportion of the two major minority groups served, corresponding as expected to their proportion in the total population of these sites. The proportion Black ranged from a high of 40.7 percent of the Illinois program population (accounted for principally by the Cook County site) to a

TABLE 3.5   New and Return Referrals, All Sites, by Ethnicity

	White		Black		Hispanic		Other		Total	
	N	%	N	%	N	%	N	%	N	%
New referrals	10,801	67.2	3,435	21.4	1,356	8.4	483	3.0	16,075	100.0
Returns	2,152	62.3	769	22.3	450	13.0	83	2.4	3,454	100.0
Total cases	12,953	66.3	4,204	21.5	1,806	9.2	566	2.9	19,529	100.0
% return cases	16.6		18.3		24.9		14.7		17.7	

TABLE 3.6   New and Return Referrals, Each Site, by Ethnicity

Program Site	White N	%	Black N	%	Hispanic N	%	Other N	%	Total N	%
Pima County, AZ										
New referrals	2,167	60.3	325	9.0	859	23.9	243	6.8	3,594	100.0
Returns	878	64.0	92	6.7	348	25.4	54	3.9	1,372	100.0
Total cases	3,045	61.3	417	8.4	1,207	24.3	297	6.0	4,966	100.0
% return cases	28.8		22.1		28.8		18.2		27.6	
Alameda County, CA										
New referrals	1,843	62.8	660	22.5	290	9.9	140	4.8	2,933	100.0
Returns	362	60.4	165	27.5	58	9.7	14	2.3	599	99.9
Total cases	2,205	62.4	825	23.4	348	9.8	154	4.4	3,532	100.0
% return cases	16.4		20.0		16.7		9.1		17.0	
Connecticut										
New referrals	304	73.3	76	18.3	30	7.2	5	1.2	415	100.0
Returns	35	72.9	9	18.8	4	8.3	—	—	48	100.0
Total cases	339	73.2	85	18.4	34	7.3	5	1.1	463	100.0
% return cases	10.3		10.6		11.8		0.0		10.4	
Delaware										
New referrals	1,202	76.6	337	21.5	22	1.4	8	.5	1,569	100.0
Returns	96	61.1	60	38.2	1	.6	—	—	157	99.9
Total cases	1,298	75.2	397	23.0	23	1.3	8	.5	1,726	100.0
% return cases	7.4		15.1		4.3		0.0		9.1	
Illinois										
New referrals	1,364	52.1	1,066	40.7	153	5.8	37	1.4	2,620	100.0
Returns	319	42.8	380	50.9	39	5.2	8	1.1	746	100.0
Total cases	1,683	50.0	1,446	43.0	192	5.7	45	1.3	3,366	100.0
% return cases	19.0		26.3		20.3		17.8		22.2	
South Carolina										
New referrals	2,361	71.2	948	28.6	—	—	5	.2	3,314	100.0
Returns	108	66.3	55	33.7	—	—	—	—	163	100.0
Total cases	2,469	71.0	1,003	28.8	—	—	5	.1	3,477	99.9
% return cases	4.4		5.5		—		0.0		4.7	
Clark County, WA										
New referrals	679	98.4	3	.4	1	.1	7	1.0	690	99.9
Returns	129	98.5	—	—	—	—	2	1.5	131	100.0
Total cases	808	98.4	3	.4	1	.1	9	1.1	821	100.0
% return cases	16.0		0.0		0.0		22.2		16.0	
Spokane County, WA										
New referrals	881	93.7	20	2.1	1	.1	38	4.0	940	99.9
Returns	225	94.5	8	3.4	0	—	5	2.1	238	100.0
Total cases	1,106	93.9	28	2.4	1	—	43	3.7	1,178	100.0
% return cases	20.3		28.6		0.0		11.6		20.2	

low of 0.4 percent in the Clark County program. Black youth constituted approximately one-fifth of the program populations in Alameda County, Connecticut, Delaware, and South Carolina. The Hispanic group, with a mean percentage of 17.4, varied from approximately one-quarter (23.9 percent) in Pima County to none in three of the evaluated sites. Hispanics were slightly less than 10 percent in Alameda County and Connecticut and only 5.8 percent in Illinois. Again, it was principally in the Pima County and Alameda County programs that the smaller numbers of Native American and Asian youth received status offender services.

The highest proportions of return referrals occurred in the minority ethnic groups (Table 3.6). With a mean return referral rate of 17.7 percent overall, for whites it was 16.6, for Blacks 18.3, for Hispanics 24.9, and for the Other category 14.7. As previously noted, the elevated return rate in Pima County, accounted for in part as an effect of its Mobile Diversion Unit operation and in part as a reflection of the high proportion of Hispanics, principally Mexican-American, in the county as well as in the program population, may be reflected in the high average return rate for all evaluated sites.

OFFENSE PATTERNS

The kinds of status offenses that occasioned referral to the program included runaway, incorrigibility/ungovernability, truancy, curfew violation, possession of alcohol, and a variety of other acts defined as offenses in some but not other jurisdictions. Because over four-fifths of all offenses recorded on initial referral to programs to all sites (84.7 percent) consisted of runaway, incorrigibility, and truancy, the remaining types of offenses are grouped for purposes of this presentation in an "Other" category (Table 3.7). In the many instances in which multiple status offenses were recorded, the most "serious" in the list was counted. On the assumption that the seriousness of a status offense could reasonably be determined by the level of parental concern and of justice agency time and effort it evoked, runaway was designated as most serious, followed

TABLE 3.7   New and Return Referrals, All Sites, by Offense

	Runaway		Incorrigible		Truant		Other		Total	
	N	%	N	%	N	%	N	%	N	%
New referrals	6,131	38.2	5,736	35.7	1,743	10.9	2,450	15.3	16,060	100.1
Returns	1,769	51.3	1,123	32.6	160	4.6	397	11.5	3,449	100.0
Total cases	7,900	40.5	6,859	35.2	1,903	9.8	2,847	14.6	19,509	100.1
% return cases	22.4		16.4		8.4		13.9		17.7	

TABLE 3.8   New and Return Referrals, Each Site, by Offense

Program Site	Runaway N	Runaway %	Incorrigible N	Incorrigible %	Truant N	Truant %	Other N	Other %	Total N	Total %
Pima County, AZ										
New referrals	1,090	30.5	935	26.2	392	11.0	1,157	32.4	3,574	100.1
Returns	613	44.8	399	29.2	84	6.1	272	19.9	1,368	100.0
Total cases	1,703	34.5	1,334	27.0	476	9.6	1,429	28.9	4,942	100.0
% return cases	36.0		29.9		17.6		19.0		27.7	
Alameda County, CA										
New referrals	1,136	38.6	1,028	35.0	284	9.7	492	16.7	2,940	100.0
Returns	307	51.3	227	37.9	13	2.2	52	8.7	599	100.1
Total cases	1,443	40.8	1,255	35.5	297	8.4	544	15.4	3,539	100.1
% return cases	21.3		18.1		4.4		9.6		16.9	
Connecticut										
New referrals	330	79.7	79	19.1	4	1.0	1	.2	414	100.0
Returns	40	83.3	8	16.7	—	—	—	—	48	100.0
Total cases	370	80.1	87	18.8	4	.9	1	.2	462	100.0
% return cases	10.8		9.2		0.0		0.0		10.4	
Delaware										
New referrals	335	21.4	520	33.2	207	13.2	505*	32.2	1,567	100.0
Returns	30	19.0	88	55.7	17	10.8	23	14.6	158	100.1
Total cases	365	21.2	608	35.2	224	13.0	528	30.6	1,725	100.0
% return cases	8.2		14.5		7.6		4.4		9.2	
Illinois										
New referrals	1,856	70.9	692	26.5	23	.9	44	1.7	2,615	100.0
Returns	530	71.2	188	25.3	4	.5	22	3.0	744	100.0
Total cases	2,386	71.0	880	26.2	27	.8	66	2.0	3,359	100.0
% return cases	22.2		21.4		14.8		33.3		22.1	
South Carolina										
New referrals	485	14.6	2,019	60.9	713	21.5	97	2.9	3,314	99.9
Returns	23	14.1	107	65.6	25	15.3	8	4.9	163	99.9
Total cases	508	14.6	2,126	16.1	738	21.2	105	3.0	3,477	99.9
% return cases	4.5		5.0		3.4		7.6		4.7	
Clark County, WA										
New referrals	420	60.5	165	23.8	65	9.4	44	6.3	694	100.0
Returns	85	64.9	30	22.9	9	6.9	7	5.3	131	100.0
Total cases	505	61.2	195	23.6	74	9.0	51	6.2	825	100.0
% return cases	16.8		15.4		12.2		13.7		15.9	
Spokane County, WA										
New referrals	479	50.8	298	31.6	55	5.8	110	11.7	942	99.9
Returns	141	59.2	76	31.9	8	3.4	13	5.5	238	100.0
Total cases	620	52.5	374	31.7	63	5.3	123	10.4	1,180	99.9
% return cases	22.7		20.3		12.7		10.6		20.2	

*491 (97.2 percent of Other; 31.3 percent of Total) = minor in possession of alcohol.

by incorrigibility, truancy, curfew violation, possession of alcohol, and the residual set designated "Other." No claim is made that any of the program clients enumerated in one of the three major categories had restricted his or her status offenses to that type. Classification was created primarily to bring into view some of the underlying heterogeneity of the program population with respect to type of status offenses.

Not surprisingly, the highest proportion of return referrals fell into the runaway category. With a mean return referral rate of 17.7 percent for all offense categories, runaways showed a rate of 22.4 percent. Runaways, we have reason to believe, may in fact constitute a somewhat unique group among offenders, a point that will receive some empirical support in our later analyses (see Chapter 9). Our colleague Margaret Little (1981) has concluded from her research that runaways and police "are in a situation of unshared meanings." Whereas runaways judge their own acts in terms of their own competence and the appropriateness of their parents' role performance, police respond principally as a function of their interpretation of their own work context, both legal and organizational. The court's reliance on *parens patriae* and agency assumptions about treatment may both be in error in the case of many runaways, yielding higher recidivism.

Much of the variation in offense distribution across sites may be accounted for largely by the random patterning of combinations of offenses, with program clients classified only under the rubric of the one most serious in the set (Table 3.8). In addition, court and police policies varied with respect to the kinds of offenses regarded as most needing program services, as did the intake policies of the programs themselves. Thus, Connecticut, Illinois, and Clark County programs recorded extraordinarily high proportions of runaways (79.7, 70.9, and 60.5 percent, respectively), while in Delaware and South Carolina these were unusually low (21.4 and 14.6 percent). There were, of course, reciprocally low or high proportions of incorrigibles in each instance. High rates in the Other category occurred in the Pima County and Delaware programs. In the case of the 1157 Pima County youth whose referral offenses fell in the Other category, 58.9 percent were made up of the jurisdiction-specific "health and morals" offenses, with another 25.7 percent of alcohol possession violations. In the case of the 505 referrals in Delaware for Other offenses, 97.2 percent were for alcohol possession.

There was little variation in the distribution of return referrals among sites. The highest rates of return occurred in the runaway category, with two exceptions. In the Illinois program (heavily weighted by the Cook County site) the return percentage for runaways was approximately the same as for incorrigibles, and in the Delaware program the return rate for incorrigibility was almost twice that for runaways (14.5 versus 8.2 percent).

TABLE 3.9 New and Return Referrals, All Sites, by Source of Referral

	Police		Parent Guardian		Court		Self		School		Other*		Total	
	N	%	N	%	N	%	N	%	N	%	N	%	N	%
New referrals	7,073	45.5	2,325	15.0	2,007	12.9	909	5.8	1,884	12.1	1,352	8.7	15,550	100.0
Returns	1,786	52.5	543	16.0	359	10.6	211	6.2	182	5.4	318	9.4	3,399	100.0
Total cases	8,859	46.8	2,868	15.1	2,366	12.5	1,120	5.9	2,066	10.9	1,670	8.8	18,949	100.0
% return cases		20.2		18.9		15.2		18.8		8.8		19.0		17.9

+ Includes probation, parole, institution, and other.

SOURCE OF REFERRAL

For all cases dealt with by the program, both initial and re-referral, by far the largest portion (46.8 percent) came from police agencies (Table 3.9). In descending order, cases were referred by parents and guardians (15.1 percent), courts (12.5 percent), schools (10.9 percent), and "Other" (8.8 percent). An additional 5.9 percent were self-referrals. With respect to return cases, approximately equal proportions came from police, parents and guardians, self, and "other" (20.2, 18.9, 18.8, and 19.0 percent, respectively). Court returns were not far behind with 15.2 percent, but schools, with 8.8 percent, appeared to be least active in returning youth to the program.

Police as the source of referral for all cases ranged from a high of 84.3 percent in Connecticut to a low of 7.1 in South Carolina (Table 3.10). Excluding two extreme cases, the mean percentage of police-initiated referrals was 53.0. Alameda, Illinois, and Clark County, Washington, were above the mean, with Spokane County, Washington, Delaware, and Pima County below. With respect to the two extreme cases, the Connecticut program was so structured as to eliminate all but the police as the referral source. Only the "detainable" cases were, by design, eligible for program services. The South Carolina program, by contrast, defined as program eligibles a heterogeneous population of youth referred to the regional Youth Service Bureaus maintained by the State Department of Youth Services. It will be noted that over 42 percent of the cases in that program were referred by courts. Since many of these cases are likely to have been police initiated, the low police referral rate is probably misleading.

CUSTOMARY HOUSEHOLD OF PROGRAM CLIENTS

Because problems of incorrigibility and runaway constitute the two principal offenses that bring status offenders into the juvenile justice system, it was deemed useful to obtain data on the family situation of program clients. Data that were both accessible to the national evaluation and reasonably uniform across sites were necessarily restricted to variables of family composition. In order to avoid the distorting effect of such temporary living situations as foster or group homes, the information concerned the composition of the *customary* household rather than of the household lived in immediately prior to program entry. Households were classified as nuclear (natural father and mother living together), reconstituted (households with two parents reconstituted by remarriage of one or both parents, or similarly constituted household whether or not based on marriage), single parent, relative and extended family, and a residual category of "Other." The latter included foster homes and independent living in a variety of forms.

TABLE 3.10 New and Return Referrals, Each Site, by Source of Referral

Program Site	Police N	Police %	Parent Guardian N	Parent Guardian %	Court N	Court %	Self N	Self %	School N	School %	Other* N	Other* %	Total N	Total %
Pima County, AZ														
New referrals	1,364	38.1	716	20.0	171	4.8	403	11.3	431	12.0	496	13.9	3,581	100.1
Returns	644	47.0	311	22.7	75	5.5	110	8.0	93	6.8	137	10.0	1,370	100.0
Total cases	2,008	40.6	1,027	20.7	246	5.0	513	10.4	524	10.6	633	12.8	4,951	100.1
% return cases		32.1		30.3		30.5		21.4		17.7		21.6		27.7
Alameda County, CA														
New referrals	1,650	56.3	233	7.9	4	.1	146	5.0	437	14.9	461	15.7	2,931	99.9
Returns	378	63.7	34	5.7	—	—	37	6.2	37	6.2	107	18.0	593	99.8
Total cases	2,028	57.5	267	7.6	4	.1	183	5.2	474	13.5	568	16.1	3,524	100.0
% return cases		18.6		12.7		—		20.2		7.8		18.8		16.8
Connecticut														
New referrals	354	86.1	4	1.0	4	1.0	3	.7	2	.5	44	10.7	411	100.0
Returns	33	68.8	—	—	—	—	—	—	—	—	15	31.1	48	100.0
Total cases	387	84.3	4	.9	4	.9	3	.7	2	.4	59	12.9	459	100.1
% return cases		8.5		0.0		0.0		0.0		0.0		25.4		10.5
Delaware**														
New referrals	597	41.5	620	43.1	17	1.2	1	.1	160	11.1	43	3.0	1,438	100.0
Returns	33	23.2	84	59.2	3	2.1	—	—	13	9.2	9	6.3	142	100.0
Total cases	630	39.9	704	44.6	20	1.3	1	.1	173	10.9	52	3.3	1,580	100.1
% return cases		5.2		11.9		15.0		0.0		7.5		17.3		9.0

	N	%	N	%	N	%	N	%	N	%	N	%	Total	%
Illinois														
New referrals	2,012	77.7	70	2.7	233	9.0	15	.6	5	.2	255	9.8	2,590	100.0
Returns	549	74.1	25	3.4	110	14.8	10	1.3	1	.1	46	6.2	741	99.9
Total cases	2,561	76.9	95	2.9	343	10.3	25	.8	6	.2	301	9.0	3,331	100.1
% return cases	21.4		26.3		32.1		40.0		16.7		15.3		22.2	
South Carolina														
New referrals	214	7.2	493	16.6	1,260	42.5	241	8.1	741	25.0	15	.5	2,964	99.9
Returns	6	4.4	38	27.9	55	40.4	16	11.8	20	14.7	1	.7	136	99.9
Total cases	220	7.1	531	17.1	1,315	42.4	257	8.3	761	24.5	16	.5	3,100	99.9
% return cases	2.7		7.2		4.2		6.2		2.6		6.3		4.4	
Clark County, WA														
New referrals	370	53.3	181	26.1	2	.3	81	11.7	44	6.3	16	2.3	694	100.0
Returns	69	52.7	36	27.5	—	—	15	11.5	9	6.9	2	1.5	131	100.1
Total cases	439	53.2	217	26.3	2	.2	96	11.6	53	6.4	18	2.2	825	99.9
% return cases	15.7		16.6		0.0		15.6		17.0		11.1		15.9	
Spokane County, WA														
New referrals	512	54.4	8	.9	316	33.6	19	2.0	64	6.8	22	2.3	941	100.0
Returns	74	31.1	15	6.3	116	48.7	23	9.7	9	3.8	1	.4	238	100.0
Total cases	586	49.7	23	2.0	432	36.6	42	3.6	73	6.2	23	2.0	1,179	100.1
% return cases	12.6		65.2		26.9		54.8		12.3		4.3		20.2	

*Includes probation, parole, institution, youth agency, and other.

**The distribution refers to the source initiating the case. However, all referrals to the program were made by the court or the status offender intake unit of the court.

TABLE 3.11 New and Return Referrals, All Sites, by Customary Household

	Nuclear		Reconstituted		Single Parent		Relatives / Extended Family		Other		Total	
	N	%	N	%	N	%	N	%	N	%	N	%
New referrals	5,084	35.1	2,656	18.3	4,840	33.4	739	5.1	1,165	8.0	14,484	99.9
Returns	923	36.4	589	23.2	834	32.9	104	4.1	89	3.5	2,539	100.0
Total cases	6,007	35.3	3,245	19.1	5,674	33.3	843	5.0	1,254	7.4	17,023	100.1
% return cases	15.4		18.2		14.7		12.3		7.1		14.9	

As seen in Table 3.11, clients came in approximately equal proportions from nuclear (35.3 percent) and single-parent households (33.3 percent), with the next largest category consisting of reconstituted families (19.1 percent). While the proportion of cases from reconstituted families was a little over half that of either nuclear or single-parent households, the proportion of return cases was greater (18.2 percent versus 15.4 and 14.7 percent, respectively).

There was relatively little variation across sites in the proportion of clients from nuclear households (Table 3.12). It was the highest in Pima County, with 40.6 percent, and lowest in Spokane, with 30.4 percent. There was also relatively little variation across sites that characterized each of the other household types. However, sites varied widely in the proportion of total cases represented by re-referral to their programs. In the Spokane, Illinois, and Pima County programs the percentage of return cases was 20.1, 22.0, and 24.3, respectively, while it was 2.8, 6.1, and 3.9, respectively, in the Alameda County, Delaware, and South Carolina programs. In the remaining two, Connecticut and Clark County, the return percentages were 10.1 and 16.0. Extreme differences in return cases are likely to reflect policy differences in client eligibility requirements and in the emphasis placed on extending services to the maximum number of individuals.

The proportion of return cases for clients from reconstituted households was significantly higher in the Pima County and Illinois programs than in the other sites. These programs also showed the highest proportion of return cases from single-parent households. Both these differences probably reflect the high proportion of minority group clients in their program populations, although in these sites the return percentages were approximately the same for youths from nuclear households.

SUMMARY

A profile of the "typical" program client in the national status offender program may be drawn with respect to gender, age, offense, source of referral and household composition, despite variation across program sites. The program client was likely to be a white 15- or 16-year-old youth, slightly more often female, from a nuclear or reconstituted family, dealt with by the juvenile justice system as either an incorrigible or runaway who was referred to the program by the police. During the two-year program period the youth had approximately one chance in six of being returned for additional services.

The highest proportions of female clients were found in the Connecticut, Illinois, Clark County, and Spokane programs, with lowest proportions in Delaware and South Carolina. The age distribution was substantially similar across all sites. The Alameda County, Illinois, Delaware, and

TABLE 3.12 New and Return Referrals, Each Site, by Type of Customary Household

Program Sites	Nuclear		Reconstituted		Single Parent		Relatives / Extended Family		Other		Total	
	N	%	N	%	N	%	N	%	N	%	N	%
Pima County, AZ												
New referrals	1,460	41.1	643	18.1	1,090	30.7	161	4.5	202	5.6	3,556	100.0
Returns	447	39.1	262	22.9	346	30.2	45	3.9	44	3.8	1,144	99.9
Total cases	1,907	40.6	905	19.3	1,436	30.6	206	4.4	246	5.2	4,700	100.1
% return cases	23.4		29.0		24.1		21.8		17.9		24.3	
Alameda County, CA												
New referrals	964	33.0	534	18.3	1,111	38.0	125	4.3	187	6.4	2,921	100.0
Returns	33	39.3	16	19.0	26	30.9	4	4.8	5	6.0	84	100.0
Total cases	997	33.2	550	18.3	1,137	37.8	129	4.3	192	6.4	3,005	100.0
% return cases	3.3		2.9		2.3		3.1		2.6		2.8	
Connecticut												
New referrals	138	33.8	78	19.1	119	29.2	20	4.9	53	13.0	408	100.0
Returns	10	21.7	16	34.8	17	37.0	2	4.3	1	2.2	46	100.0
Total cases	148	32.6	94	20.7	136	30.0	22	4.8	54	11.9	454	100.0
% return cases	6.8		17.0		12.5		9.1		1.9		10.1	
Delaware												
New referrals	359	35.0	108	10.5	243	23.7	39	3.8	277	27.0	1,026	100.0
Returns	24	35.8	7	10.4	30	44.8	1	1.5	5	7.5	67	100.0
Total cases	383	35.0	115	10.5	273	25.0	40	3.7	282	25.8	1,093	100.0
% return cases	6.3		6.1		11.0		2.5		1.8		6.1	

Illinois												
New referrals	854	32.7	463	17.7	892	34.2	155	5.9	246	9.4	2,610	99.9
Returns	252	34.3	160	21.8	269	36.6	35	4.8	19	2.5	735	100.0
Total cases	1,106	33.1	623	18.6	1,161	34.7	190	5.7	265	7.9	3,345	100.0
% return cases	22.8		25.7		23.2		18.4		7.2		22.0	
South Carolina												
New referrals	760	32.6	386	16.5	916	39.3	173	7.4	98	4.2	2,333	100.0
Returns	30	31.6	13	13.7	42	44.2	9	9.5	1	1.0	95	100.0
Total cases	790	32.5	399	16.4	958	39.5	182	7.5	99	4.1	2,428	100.0
% return cases	3.8		3.3		4.4		4.9		1.0		3.9	
Clark County, WA												
New referrals	267	38.8	191	27.8	189	27.5	21	3.1	20	2.9	688	100.1
Returns	50	38.2	38	29.0	38	29.0	0	0.0	5	3.8	131	100.0
Total cases	317	38.7	229	28.0	227	27.7	21	2.6	25	3.0	819	100.0
% return cases	15.8		16.6		16.7		0.0		20.0		16.0	
Spokane County, WA												
New referrals	282	29.9	253	26.9	280	29.7	45	4.8	82	8.7	942	100.0
Returns	77	32.5	77	32.5	66	27.8	8	3.4	9	3.8	237	100.0
Total cases	359	30.4	330	28.0	346	29.3	53	4.5	91	7.7	1,179	99.9
% return cases	21.4		23.3		19.1		15.1		9.9		20.1	

South Carolina programs served a very large number of Black clients, while substantial numbers of Hispanics received services in the Pima County program. Runaways represented the presenting offense in relatively high proportions in the Connecticut, Illinois, and Clark County programs, while incorrigibility predominated in the South Carolina program. Police agencies were the major source of referral in the Connecticut and Illinois programs. Parents and guardians as the source of referral were prominent in the South Carolina, Delaware, and Clark County programs; courts were prominent in the South Carolina and Spokane programs. Schools as the referral source stood out only in South Carolina. Type of customary household showed little variation across evaluated sites, with the exception of Illinois and South Carolina, where a relatively large proportion of clients came from single-parent families.

REPRESENTATIVENESS OF
THE EVALUATED SAMPLE

The evaluation study was designed to obtain both client and program data at two levels of comprehensiveness. First, for *all* clients who entered the program a set of data was obtained that was restricted to the demographic items of age, gender, ethnicity, and size of community, and to school status, family structure, offense at referrals, and initial service assignment.

The anticipated number of referrals at each site was based by program personnel on past police and court data to the extent that these were available and accessible. These were counts variously of individuals or cases of status offenses or offenders recorded by police, courts, and detention centers. However derived, all estimates pointed to the likelihood that the number of project clients would be very large. It was thus apparent that in order to obtain and analyze the large body of additional data needed to assess the effect of the program on client conduct, a reduced subset of the total client population would have to be sampled.

For this sampled subset an expanded number of information items were required. These included, in addition to family socioeconomic status, the type and number of treatment service or services provided, the offense history of the client prior and subsequent to entry into the program, and responses to a self-report offense and social adjustment interview instrument. In two of the eight sites, Connecticut and Clark County, the number of clients was sufficiently small to obviate the need for sampling.

Sample Selection

The sampling design was an approximation to systematic quota sampling from monthly intake of program clients. The main effort with respect to representativeness was to reproduce in the sample so far as possible a sufficient distribution of the status offense types (such as runaway, truant) in the program population. Because it was desirable to identify and contact sampled subjects for the initial interview immediately after they were scheduled to become program clients, the possibility of using a probabilistic procedure was precluded, as, for example, by sampling subjects from a frame composed of all clients constituting the monthly program intake at the end of any one month. The solution was to employ a "forecasting" technique, in which a probabilistic procedure was approximated by adjusting monthly sampling fractions of offense types in advance of each month. The adjustments were to be made on the basis of earlier, cumulatively "smoothed" flows in given offense categories. The obvious risk in this procedure was misestimation of the correct sampling fraction in the early months of the evaluation period. Since no knowledge-based assumptions could be made with respect to the distribution of offense types in a status offender population, the only reasonable procedure appeared to be the use of a design giving each type an opportunity to be selected into the sample.

The total sample size needed for the types of analyses planned required site evaluators to select the first 12 in each of five offense categories entering their programs in each month. The categories in descending order of judged seriousness in the status offender population were, as before, runaway, ungovernable /incorrigible, truancy, curfew violation, minor in possession of alcohol, and a residual category of "Other." Constrained by the need to identify sampled program clients for early interview, the forecasting method posed difficult problems requiring at many of the sites extensive and, as will be seen later, distorting adjustments.

The absence of probability-based selection means that the population of inference must be restricted to those clients served by the national status offender program who were defined as "evaluation eligible" on evidence that they were referred to the program for having committed one or more of the designated status offenses. Generalization of findings to the wider population of all status offenders must be done cautiously. The degree to which the clientele of the national program is representative of the total U.S. population of status offenders cannot, of course, be known.

The sampling procedure posed two subsidiary problems. First, where youth were referred to the program on the basis of multiple status offense charges, the problem arose of selecting one of these charges as the appropriate categorization. The approach adopted, as noted above, was to classify the client according to the most serious status offense on which the referral was based, utilizing the order of seriousness indicated above. It was assumed that this offense would be the one most likely to determine the kind of treatment prescribed for the client. Some readers may wish to question this working assumption.

Second, and more critically, although the effort was made to select into the sample equal numbers in each of the five offense categories (twelve per category in each month of program intake), for various reasons these quotas could not always be met. Some categories consistently produced fewer than twelve cases per month, either because the site did not generate these numbers or because the policy of the jurisdiction was to take no official action with respect to certain types of status offenses (such as curfew violation or minor in possession of alcohol). It became apparent early that it would not be feasible to implement the intended sampling procedure in a number of instances. The fallback position was then adopted to assure an adequate sample size at each site irrespective of its distribution on offense type. At the very least, this would provide sufficient numbers in each of the many client-service-offense categories required by the analysis. There was in any case no possibility of estimating a priori the category proportions of the total program population together with their likely variances on measures of outcome variables. Were this possible, it would, of course, have been desirable to sample disproportionately among offense categories for analysis purposes. Hence, site evaluators were requested, to the extent feasible, to meet the total monthly quotas required by the national evaluation design.

"EVALUATION-ELIGIBLE" PROGRAM POPULATION

Clients referred to the eight programs numbered 16,103. Of these, 8,563, or 53.2 percent, were, for a variety of reasons, defined as eligible for inclusion in the population from which the evaluated sample was drawn. [2] The reasons for exclusion were varied. In two cases (Arizona and South Carolina), as programs came into operation and their availability became known in their communities, clients who were troubled youth in need of counseling or were cases of neglect and abuse with no specific status offenses of the five types indicated were referred to and admitted to the programs. In another program (Illinois), only five of its counties were included as evaluation sites. In still another (South Carolina), a similarly limited number of sites became the focus of evaluation interest, to the exclusion of the rest of the state. Excluded as well in all sites were clients who entered the program prior to the initiation of the evaluation study and subsequent to a termination date set by the end of funding. [3] At the request of OJJ, a basic record consisting only of demographic information, source and reason for referral, and service assignment was compiled on all clients entering the program, without regard to evaluation-eligibility status. These clients were included in the total program population count of 16,103 recorded at the eight evaluated sites. As stated, approximately half of this number (8,563) formed the frame from which an evaluated sample of 4,010 clients was drawn.

Given the nonprobabilistic procedure used in drawing the sample, its representativeness of the evaluation-eligible population is open to question. The question is addressed by examining the comparative distribution of characteristics in the nonevaluated eligible population and in the evaluated sample. As noted, offense type was the only characteristic for which an effort was made initially to reproduce in the sample approximately the same proportionate distribution as existed in the population eligible for evaluation.

Three questions arise. First, how closely does the distribution of the offense types in the sample aggregated over the eight sites resemble that in the nonevaluated eligible population? Second, if the comparative distributions with respect to offense type in the two groups are similar, is the comparative distribution for the two groups similar for gender, age, ethnicity, and source of referral? And third, to what extent did specific program sites vary in sample bias on each of the client characteristics?

Offense Type

Aggregated over the eight sites, the distribution of instant[4] status offenses for the evaluated sample is remarkably similar to the distribution of instant offenses in the nonevaluated eligible sample (Table 3.13), varying by less than 2 percent in each category. Similarity of the two samples in their pattern of distribution across offense types was most evident in Illinois, and least so in Spokane County. Connecticut and Clark County, with almost total population inclusion in the samples, were of course even more stable in this respect than any other site.

TABLE 3.13   Comparison of Instant Offense Distributions for Evaluated and Nonevaluated Eligible Samples, All Sites

Sample	Runaway		Incorrigible		Truant		Other*		Total	
	N	%	N	%	N	%	N	%	N	%
Nonevaluated	1,704	38.4	1,490	33.6	423	9.5	822	18.5	4,439	100.0
Evaluated	1,600	39.9	1,301	32.5	432	10.8	673	16.8	4,006	100.0
Total	3,304	39.1	2,791	33.0	855	10.1	1,495	17.7	8,445	99.9

*Includes curfew, MIP, and other.

TABLE 3.14   Comparison of Age Distributions for Evaluated and Nonevaluated Eligible Samples, All Sites

Sample	Under 12		12-14		15-16		17-18		Total	
	N	%	N	%	N	%	N	%	N	%
Nonevaluated	337	7.6	1,731	39.1	1,876	42.4	479	10.8	4,423	99.9
Evaluated	175	4.4	1,497	37.4	1,880	47.0	449	11.2	4,001	100.0
Total	512	6.1	3,228	38.3	3,756	44.6	928	11.0	8,424	100.0

Age

Here, again, when aggregated over all sites, the age distribution of the evaluated sample appears to be very similar (Table 3.14), the largest difference being less than 5 percent. Age distribution by site disclosed best representativeness in Delaware, South Carolina, and Pima County.

Gender

Aggregated for the eight sites, the evaluated sample reproduces reasonably closely the male /female distribution in the nonevaluated group (Table 3.15). This was most true for Delaware, Illinois, and South Carolina, and less so for Pima, Alameda, and Spokane counties (always excluding the special cases of Connecticut and Clark County).

Ethnicity

Again, for the eight sites together, the distributions of ethnicity in the two samples are reasonably comparable (Table 3.16). The evaluated samples were particularly representative in Pima County, Delaware, South Carolina, and Spokane County.

Referral Source

The pattern of distribution with respect to referral source for the evaluated sample was substantially similar to that for the nonevaluated eligibles when aggregated across the eight sites (Table 3.17), and especially in Delaware, Illinois, and South Carolina. Pima and Spokane counties yielded some substantial differences.

TABLE 3.15   Comparison of Gender Distributions for Evaluated and
                       Nonevaluated Eligible Samples, All Sites

Sample	Female		Male		Total	
	N	%	N	%	N	%
Nonevaluated	2,474	55.6	1,974	44.4	4,448	100.0
Evaluated	2,142	53.4	1,867	46.6	4,009	100.0
Total	4,616	54.6	3,841	45.4	8,457	100.0

TABLE 3.16   Comparison of Ethnic Distributions for Evaluated and
                       Nonevaluated Eligible Samples, All Sites

Sample	White		Black		Hispanic		Other		Total	
	N	%	N	%	N	%	N	%	N	%
Nonevaluated	2,693	60.6	946	21.3	587	13.2	221	5.0	4,447	100.1
Evaluated	2,676	66.8	897	22.4	320	8.0	111	2.8	4,004	100.0
Total	5,369	63.5	1,843	21.8	907	10.7	332	3.9	8,451	99.9

TABLE 3.17 Comparison of Distributions of Source of Referral for Evaluated and Nonevaluated Eligible Samples, All Sites

Sample	Police		Parent/Guardian		Court		Self		School		Other*		Total	
	N	%	N	%	N	%	N	%	N	%	N	%	N	%
Nonevaluated	2,139	48.2	606	13.7	207	4.7	294	6.6	596	13.4	595	13.4	4,437	100.0
Evaluated	2,111	53.0	706	17.7	430	10.8	101	2.5	371	9.3	263	6.6	3,982	99.9
Total	4,250	50.5	1,312	15.6	637	7.6	395	4.7	967	11.5	858	10.2	8,419	100.1

*Includes probation, parole, institution, and other.

TABLE 3.18   Comparison of Distributions of Source of Referral for Evaluated
and Nonevaluated Eligible Samples Using Justice/Nonjustice
Dichotomy, All Sites

Sample	Justice		Nonjustice		Total	
	N	%	N	%	N	%
Nonevaluated	2,435	54.9	2,002	45.1	4,437	100.0
Evaluated	2,583	64.9	1,399	35.1	3,982	100.0
Total	5,018	59.6	3,401	40.4	8,419	100.0

Referral Source: Justice and nonjustice

In order to gain a clearer view of the relative prominence of juvenile justice agencies as the source of referrals to the program, referral sources were collapsed to two categories. As seen in Table 3.18, when the data are aggregated across the eight sites, the distribution for justice and nonjustice sources of referral differ by 10 percent. A larger than desired difference was observable principally in Pima and Spokane counties.

SUMMARY

The estimates of evaluated sample representativeness suggest that, overall, the evaluated sample did not differ substantially from the nonevaluated eligibles in the distribution of most client and offense characteristics (again excepting Connecticut and Clark County, where virtually all evaluation-eligible clients were included in the evaluation sample). However, this varied substantially at specific sites.

With respect to offense type, age, gender, and ethnicity, the aggregated percentages in the evaluated sample substantially mirror those in the nonevaluated eligible group. Referral source also yields similar patterns, although a full 10 percent difference emerges when the justice / nonjustice dichotomy is employed. Given the disruptions in sampling plans, this pattern of overall similarity is encouraging and means that the analyses to be reported in later chapters can be generalized with reasonable confidence to the entire evaluation-eligible population.

With respect to individual sites, it may be noted that successful quota filling by the site evaluators was most evident in Illinois, Delaware, and South Carolina. There is no clear pattern of a consistently unrepresentative sample in any state, and of course the Connecticut and Clark County samples are representative by virtue of including most of their eligible populations.

NOTES

1. To be noted in connection with the high proportion of return cases in Pima County, evident in all of the data presented in this chapter, is the fact that this may reflect the operations of its Mobile Diversion Unit (MDU; see Chapter 5). The MDU operated at the neighborhood level, responding continuously to calls for assistance from the police and residents. Repeat referrals to the program escalated as a function of the high level of MDU responsiveness and a program intake procedure that recorded a repeat referral on multiple MDU contacts with the same youth.

2. This is the maximum number of individual clients in the evaluation-eligible population. It is based on gender data, for which there were virtually no missing values. Variations in the number of missing values for other client characteristics account for differences in the totals for each.

3. The final date for intake into the evaluated sample was set to allow for at least a six-month follow-up and to include a sufficient number in the sample from each site. Extensions were allowed in some sites to accomplish this and to provide data to the national evaluators in time for processing.

4. "Instant" is the terminology used for the offense that led to client inclusion in the program.

chapter **4**

Offense Patterns of Status Offenders

with Frank R. Hellum and John Peterson

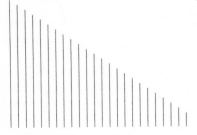

$\mathbf{A}$*s we noted earlier, two kinds* of arguments have been advanced in support of the status offender deinstitutionalization movement. The first has been based on legal and ethical doctrines. It asserts that there can be no justification for subjecting those who commit noncriminal acts to the same deprivation of liberty as is imposed on youth guilty of criminal violations. Quite apart from the effect that incarceration in detention facilities or correctional institutions may

This chapter is adapted, by permission of the publisher, from a chapter appearing in CRITICAL ISSUES IN JUVENILE DELINQUENCY, edited by David Shichor and Delos H. Kelly (Lexington, Mass.: Lexington Books, D.C. Heath and Company, Copyright 1980, D.C. Heath and Company).

have on noncriminal youth—that is, whether such treatment deters or stimulates future misbehavior—the secure confinement of status offenders is judged to be both unwarranted and morally repugnant.[1]

A second set of arguments marshaled in support of the movement rests on the perspective of labeling theory (Lemert, 1951; Becker, 1963; Schur, 1971). Proponents of this view have asserted that deviant identity becomes a fixed element of the person's self-concept primarily as a consequence of being dealt with as a deviant by the agents of the official control institutions. The meaning of an act and therefore its significance for the person's self-concept is defined by the response to the act on the part of those who wield societal authority. Status offenders who are arrested and must appear before the court in the same manner as youthful criminal offenders, are on this reckoning subtly pressed to see themselves as delinquents, however minor, transitory, or fortuitous their status offenses might have been. In many cases, such pressures may induce an adaptive response in which the young person seeks the companionship and social support of those similarly stigmatized. This outcome is seen as more likely if status offenders are held in detention facilities and committed to correctional institutions, where they are thrown into close association with youth held for criminal offenses. However unintended, the result, the argument runs, is to encourage the development of delinquent careers. Youth whose initial deviance may have been confined to the status offenses now expand their misbehavior to include the more serious offenses by virtue of exposure to institutional treatment.

Data generated in the course of the DSO project presented an opportunity to examine the evidence for two central propositions that constitute the empirical rationale for the status offender deinstitutionalization movement generally and for the DSO program specifically. The first of these asserts that there exists an identifiable population of young offenders who confine their misbehavior to status offenses, who endanger themselves rather than the community, and who require a quite different treatment approach than that accorded the young criminal offender. The second proposition asserts that there occurs a progression from status to criminal offenses, resulting in part from the labeling process to which status offenders are exposed and in part from their exposure to young criminal offenders in detention and correctional facilities.

Prior research has severely challenged both these propositions, that there exists a status offending "specialization" and a general progression from status offenses to delinquent offenses. An extensive review of this research (Klein, 1983) has covered 33 reports of analyses of approximately 60 independent samples of juveniles. In only 4 of these instances did the analyses reveal a pattern of offense specialization among juveniles (such as status offenders, thieves, or violent offenders). The overwhelming number of reports indicated quite the opposite, a "versatile" pattern of offending or a "general delinquency" factor suggesting that most offending youngsters involve themselves in a substantial *range* of illegal acts. Although somewhat counterintuitive to many, this very common research finding needs to be acknowledged by criminologists and justice practitioners alike.

Interestingly, the literature review found that the pattern of versatility holds up across all forms of statistical analysis (for example, simple correlations, factor analyses, and the analysis of conditional probabilities), across all levels of sample seriousness (for example, nonarrested, arrested, court, and correctional samples), and for both official (arrest and court records) and self-report forms of delinquency measurement. These findings have been interpreted as supporting a versatile or "cafeteria-style" view of juvenile offense patterns in which "today's status offender is tomorrow's burglar and vice versa" (Klein, 1979). There are, however, a few studies involving status offenders as a potentially separate subgroup, and we review these briefly here.

Clarke (1975) reported major differences among types of juvenile offenders in the Philadelphia birth cohort data (Wolfgang et al., 1972). Among the 3475 males who acquired a police juvenile record, 23.4 percent (n = 812) first appeared as status offenders. Comparisons with those who were *first* arrested for a criminal offense reveal the following: (1) criminal offenders recidivated at over twice the rate of status offenders (61 percent versus 30 percent having at least two offenses); and (2) 21 percent of the initial criminal violators become "chronic" offenders (at least five offenses), in contrast to only 10 percent of the status offenders. The less serious nature of delinquency involvement among status offenders was apparent in additional measures reported by Clarke, and identical patterns were found among white and nonwhite males analyzed separately.

The contradiction between the findings reported by Clarke and the conclusions of the other studies may be explained by a number of factors. Beyond the common focus on offense patterning, these studies varied considerably in terms of the selection of research issues, the choice of research design, and even the definition of major terms. For instance, possession of alcohol by a minor may have been counted as either a status or criminal offense; some studies examined birth cohorts as compared to cross-sectional data; and an interest in repeated violation of a specific statute (such as burglary) is a separate issue from that of concentration within broader categories of offense behavior or of movement toward nonrecidivism. Since such variations might have led to varying conclusions, we will take a closer look at several of the more pivotal studies for evidence bearing upon the specific issue raised in this research: Are there youth who confine their offense behavior to status violations?

Some of the earliest cited findings (Klein, 1971) were gathered in evaluations of programs directed at gang delinquency in five major cities. In at least one site, Los Angeles, an attempt was made to determine the correlations between specific, officially recorded violations among individuals in five male gangs. The finding of "no systematic ordering of offenses" (Klein, 1971: 125) supported the conclusion of versatility in offense behavior. While gang members in that study had on occasion been charged with status offenses, the population was not representative of juvenile offenders, nor was an analysis reported of patterns or progressions involving the broader categories of status and criminal violations.

The previously discussed findings offered by Clarke (1975) are of limited value in ascertaining patterned offense behavior. A major limitation is the absence of females, who represent a substantial portion of the status offender population. For the male birth cohort, the data do show that initial status offenders are the least seriously delinquent group and that 70 percent appeared only for a single status violation. However, there is no indication of the extent to which criminal offenders subsequently appeared for status violations, nor is it possible to determine the types of violations for which status offenders recidivate. The latter issue is of importance because it bears upon our second proposition, namely, that status offenders become involved in a progression toward more serious violations. In recomputing some of the reported information it is possible to suggest at least the direction in which status offenders progress.

An additional measure of seriousness examined in the study was the average number of "index" offenses attributable to the initial offender groups. These offenses consist of more serious violations involving injury, theft, or property damage. This classification was also used to divide the initial criminal violators into two groups—index and nonindex offenders. In the total population, the index offense average for the three *initial* groups consisted of the following: status, .354; nonindex, .727; index, 2.053. If a progression toward more serious violations was evident in the data, then one would expect that the disparity between average number of index offenses would be substantially reduced for those in the initial groups who committed further law violations. In other words, the recidivists would appear to be much more similar in this respect than the initial offender groups. Recomputation of the average number of index offenses beyond the first offense for the recidivists in the initial groups yielded the following expected reduction in differences: status, 1.191; nonindex, 1.219; index, 1.686. When examining only recidivism there are a number of reasons for this reduced disparity among the groups; the first index offense of the initial index offenders is automatically excluded, and the smaller number of repeat offenders in the initial status offenders group affects the average figure considerably. Nonetheless, it does appear that when initial status offenders are involved in further violations, the seriousness of the behavior approaches that of the initial criminal offenders. In sum, the Philadelphia cohort data are at least suggestive of both a specialized status offender population and of some progression toward more serious violations.

Thomas (1976) examined offense patterns among 2092 youths appearing in the juvenile court records of two cities during the years 1970 through 1974. From the analysis he concluded that the data provided "little or no support for those who have contended that status offenders are a distinctly different group of juveniles" (Thomas, 1976: 454). Notwithstanding the nuances of the term "distinctly different," the conclusion may be unwarranted, since the data contained in the published report of the study support an alternative interpretation. The data suggest that in the earlier stages of their offense careers status offenders *are* readily distinguishable from criminal violators, but with *further* involvement their offense behavior progresses toward more serious violations.

In examining differences among types of offenders, Thomas divided the population according to their most serious charge at initial appearance in court records and obtained the following three groups: felony (n = 467), misdemeanor (n = 1053), and status (n = 572). Comparisons were then made of the offenses charged for as many as three reappearances. For the first reappearance, Thomas (1976: 445-446) noted that initial status offenders did not differ in the expected direction toward fewer repeated violations. Status offenders were reported as having the *highest* rates of recidivism (status, 38 percent; misdemeanor, 22 percent; felony, 31 percent). However, inspection of the data reveals that this finding was entirely a function of the initial status offenders' being more likely than any other group to have reappeared for a status offense. If first reappearance rates had been reported for criminal offenses only, the ordering of initial offender groups would have changed considerably (status, 20 percent; misdemeanor, 17 percent; felony, 28 percent). A major difference among the groups was that the initial status offenders, constituting approximately 27 percent of the total population, accounted for 63 percent of all status violations recorded at first reappearance. Similar figures can be obtained for the distribution of offenses at the second and third reappearances as well. In other words, contrary to Thomas's conclusion, the data indicate that status offenders differ from criminal offenders in that their subsequent offenses more often involve repeated status violations.

With regard to progression in offense careers, Thomas (1976: 449) states that "evidence in support of the hypothesis that court appearances encourage movement toward more serious delinquency is difficult to find in any of the tables present in this analysis." It should be noted, however, that there are alternative methods of analysis that might have uncovered supporting evidence. One possibility would be simply to examine the relationship between types of initial and subsequent offenses to determine if there was a shift toward more serious violations at each level of increasing court involvement.

The necessary data can be abstracted from the published report (Thomas, 1976: 445-446) and are shown in Table 4.1. The analysis shows that at first reappearance there is a moderate relationship between initial offense type and the type of offense at reappearance (gamma =

45; p < .01). This is consistent with the previous observation of differences among groups. At the point of first reappearance those who committed a second offense showed the highest percentage of involvement for the same type of violation as was initially charged: For returning felony offenders (n = 147), 46 percent reappeared as felony violators; among the misdemeanor recidivists (n = 227), 55 percent committed a misdemeanor; and for the reappearing initial status offenders (n = 217), 46 percent returned for a status violation. If progression is suggested by the data, then it would be expected that the relationship between initial and subsequent offenses would decline with increasing reappearances in court records (that is, knowledge of the initial offense would not predict the type of later offense because the groups had become more similar in their law violating behavior). The test of this relationship at later reappearances shows evidence of progression toward more serious violations. At second reappearance the relationship is reduced considerably as the initial status offenders show a greater proclivity for criminal violations, but the differences between the groups still approach statistical significance (gamma = .29, p < .02). By the third reappearance the measure of association remains stable, but the group differences are not statistically significant (gamma = .30; p < .10). In other words, the differences that

TABLE 4.1   Subsequent Offenses of Status and Delinquent Offenders (from Thomas, 1976)

	Type of Offense at Initial Appearance					
	Status		Misdemeanor		Felony	
	N	%	N	%	N	%
Type of Offense at First Reappearance[a]						
Felony	38	18	59	26	67	46
Misdemeanor	79	36	125	55	63	43
Status	100	46	43	19	17	12
Totals	217	100	227	100	147	100
Type of Offense at Second Reappearance[b]						
Felony	22	20	42	40	26	37
Misdemeanor	50	46	44	42	34	49
Status	36	33	18	17	10	14
Totals	108	99	104	99	70	100
Type of Offense at Third Reappearance[c]						
Felony	14	27	22	46	17	41
Misdemeanor	20	38	21	44	20	49
Status	18	35	5	10	4	10
Totals	52	100	48	100	41	100

a. Gamma = .45, p < .01.
b. Gamma = .29, p < .02.
c. Gamma = .30, p < .10.

were observed in their early offense careers appear to diminish with further juvenile court involvement as the recidivists among the initial offender groups become more heavily involved in criminal violations.

As a final comment on the Thomas study, an explanation should be attempted as to why a reanalysis of reported data could lead to conclusions that vary from those of the original author. An important clue can be found in the title of the Thomas study—"Are Status Offenders *Really So Different?*" (italics added). This question seems to imply a standard of absolute difference in comparing juvenile offenders. According to this standard, Thomas's conclusions are absolutely correct. Even in their early offense careers *some* status offenders reappear for felony violations, and *some* criminal violators return for status offenses. It is also possible to maintain that there is an absence of *pronounced* homogeneity in offense careers (Thomas, 1976: 447), that juvenile offenders are not *bound* to a single type of delinquency involvement (p. 448), and that the type of initial charge is an *imperfect* predictor of subsequent offense (p. 453). However, the present review of the Thomas data has focused on relative differences. According to this standard, status offenders do appear to be somewhat different from criminal violators, although the difference becomes relatively less pronounced with increased involvement in the juvenile justice system.

A more recent analysis appears in Erickson (1979) and employs both self-reported and officially recorded delinquency in several populations of juvenile offenders. The data that are comparable to the studies reviewed here are drawn from the official records of a birth cohort including both males and females, and include all violations for 2843 juveniles in the years prior to their eighteenth birthdays. The analysis of official offenses is quite dissimilar to the tracking of initial offender groups as undertaken by both Clarke and Thomas, and there are very few parallel findings that can be abstracted from the published data. Also, Erickson's data are largely reported as percentages of the total population; therefore, the following must be viewed as approximated figures.

Erickson (1979: 21) reported that 50 percent of the cohort first appeared in court records as status offenders. This represents an obvious disparity with the 23.4 percent figure in Clarke's data and the 27.4 percent from the Thomas study. Since none of these studies states the specific violations included in the classification of status offense, it is difficult to determine if the difference is a matter of definition or represents some other source of variation.

Erickson also indicated that criminal violators were *less likely* than status offenders to reappear for a second offense. In the total population, 38 percent were reported as one-time offenders for either a felony or misdemeanor violation. Since the total population was evenly divided between status and criminal offenders, this means that 76 percent of the initial criminal offenders were nonrecidivists. For initial status offenders only 40 percent were reported as having never returned for a second offense. In other words, the data showed almost a complete reversal of the Clarke findings that 39 percent of the criminal offenders were nonrecidivists, compared to 70 percent of the status violators. Comparable figures from the Thomas study showed that 75 percent of the combined criminal offender groups never returned for a second offense, and that nonrecidivist status offenders accounted for 62 percent of the initial group (with the difference being attributed to repeated status offenses in the status offender group).

Erickson's analysis was primarily aimed at demonstrating the rarity with which juveniles are concentrated in the category of "pure status offenders" and that with increasing involvement in court processing the offense careers of juveniles assume an "erratic-random" pattern. Until the data are subjected to further analysis, it is impossible to determine if a progression toward more serious violations by status offenders is present in Erickson's data. The only difference noted by Erickson that would seem to favor specialized treatment of status offenders is found in his category of static careers. Here it was found that 15 percent of the total population having multiple-offense careers persisted in the commission of a single type of offense. Within this category 11 percent of the total population committed only status violations, with the number of offenses varying from as few as 2 to as many as 27 in a single offense career. Relative to the 50 percent of the total population who first appeared for a status offense, this means that approximately two-thirds (62 percent) either did not return for a second time or reappeared only for status violation.

Thus recent research offers evidence of the existence of a fairly large group of initial juvenile offenders who tend to restrict their violations to the status offenses, of whom a small subset recidivate as "pure" status offenders. While some progression from status to delinquent offenses is apparent in the Thomas data, those who appeared initially as delinquents (that is, misdemeanor or felony offenders) were significantly more prominent in the same subsequent offense categories than were those who appeared initially for status offenses. Similarly, status offenders on initial appearance showed much higher proportions of status than of delinquent offenses in their subsequent appearances. Status offenders may not be distinctly different from delinquent offenders, as Thomas asserts, but they are distinguished by a tendency to reappear in police and court records as status offenders in significantly higher proportions than are youth who commit misdemeanor and felony offenses. Finally, Erickson's data provide clear evidence that a very small proportion of all juvenile offenders fall into the "pure" status offender group, and underscore the prominence of versatility in juvenile offense patterns. [2]

However, these findings may not be entirely relevant to the need for special programs to deal with the status offense problem. The opportunity and incentive to commit status offenses is generally available to all youth, including those with records of serious and persistent delinquency, minor and intermittent delinquency, and no delinquency. Of all youth who at any juncture in their careers are arrested or cited for a status offense, it should be possible in principle to differentiate this population in terms of somewhat typical juvenile career patterns, each of which encompasses some degree of offense versatility. These may include, at a minimum, the "heavies" who are predominantly serious delinquent offenders, a category of "lightweights" made up of misdemeanants, and a group of predominantly conforming youth, whose misbehavior may occasionally come to the attention of the juvenile authorities. Each of these groups is in one sense made up of "status offenders," but the meaning of the status offense differs for the members of each group, for the community, and for the juvenile justice system. For the "heavies" a status offense is likely to be a largely incidental event. For those given to minor and intermittent delinquent acts, for the possibly very small group that restricts itself to multiple status offenses, and for those who gain admission to a population recorded as having committed a status offense by an occasional outburst of rebellion against adult authority, the act may well be symptomatic of a set of problems unique to this group. Clearly, then, the question of the potential usefulness of special programs of any kind, including a program for the deinstitutionalization of status offenders, will rest largely on the relative size of the second and third of the three groups identified.

These considerations suggest that in examining the evidence in support of the status-to-delinquency offense progression assumption, it is essential to focus on the latter two groups, should it turn out that they are in fact discriminable. The hazard of escalation from status to delinquent offenses involves these groups principally. Youth whose records may include status offenses but whose delinquency is of the more serious variety raise other concerns. An opportunity to examine these issues empirically is provided by the data collected for the DSO project.

THE DATA:
THE PREPROGRAM POPULATION

During the two-year period of federal funding of the national program, over 16,000 juveniles charged with status offenses were served by the eight programs. Demographic, socioeconomic, and family data were obtained on all juveniles referred to the program. In addition, treatment and both self-report and official offense data were collected on some 4,000 program clients constituting the evaluated sample. With the exception of self-report offense and treatment data, similar information was obtained on a comparable control group of status offenders dealt with in each program jurisdiction during the year prior to the establishment of the program. The preprogram comparison group consisted of approximately 3,000 individuals. Evidence for the existence of a discriminable population of status offenders, and of progression from status to criminal offenses, was examined with reference only to the preprogram group, for which the special deinstitutionalization program was not yet available, and who therefore were more likely to be exposed to the threat and /or the experience of secure detention and commitment to correctional institutions.

The preprogram population in each site consisted of a sample of juveniles from the preprogram year who became eligible for selection into the sample upon their first status offense for that year. This first status offense, for the period and not for the individual career, was defined as the "instant" status offense. The sample was selected so far as possible to match the program clientele at each site with respect to sociodemographic and offense characteristics. Court files were searched for the record of all offenses prior and subsequent to the "instant" offense, as well as the record of "charges" in police files that were available and accessible in all but one site. The record of subsequent offenses was compiled for two periods, yielding a six-month follow-up for approximately 75 percent of the evaluated sample, and a smaller twelve-month follow-up cohort, consisting of approximately 37 percent of the sample. The research cohort was classified by four offense categories with respect to both prior and subsequent offenses: no offenses, status offenses only, mixed status and criminal (both misdemeanor and felony) offenses, and criminal offenses only. Those with prior records of mixed or criminal offenses will be referred to here as "delinquents" in order to distinguish them from the "pure" status offenders.

THE STATUS OFFENDER POPULATION

Two questions are addressed in examining the evidence for the existence of a population constituted predominantly by status offenders. First, is there a segment of the juvenile offender group that confines its infractions wholly to status offenses, and, if so, what is its relative size? Second, do the age, gender, and ethnic characteristics of this segment differ from those of a population whose records contain some proportions of delinquent offenses as well?

As seen in Table 4.2, those with no offenses of either kind recorded prior to their initial appearance in police and court files for a status offense constituted half (51.9 percent) of a population dealt with as status offenders at a given point in time. When the additional 11.2 percent of those whose prior offenses were only of the status variety is added, almost two-thirds

(63.1 percent) of the population dealt with as status offenders had no official record of a prior delinquent—that is, criminal—act.[3]

Two cautions must be observed in the interpretation of this finding.
First, it is based solely on official records. Self-report delinquency studies
have provided ample evidence of the large number of delinquent acts
that result in neither apprehension nor court action. On the other hand, it
has also been noted that as concerns the more serious offenses against
property and persons, the discrepancy between self-report and officially
recorded offenses is substantially reduced (Empey, 1978: 164). Further,
we noted earlier in this chapter that the evidence for versatility versus
specialization seems unaffected by use of self-report or official measures.
Hence the sole use of officially recorded offense data in assessing the
distribution of offense patterns among those dealt with as status offenders is warranted when, as in the present study, interest centers on the shift
from status to the more serious forms of delinquency. It is entirely likely
that the offense record is incomplete with respect principally to the minor
and occasional offenses commonly viewed by control agents as unde-
serving of their time, attention, and effort.

The second caution regarding the offense pattern of the preprogram
sample concerns the effort to match it to the program clientele. The latter
group was selected into the program on the basis of referral by police,
courts, schools, and others for a status offense. Criteria employed in determining eligibility for program services varied widely from site to site. In
some instances eligibility criteria excluded the more persistent offenders,
such as those with more than two prior status offenses, or those already
on probation for a previous status offense. To the extent, then, that the
match between preprogram and program subjects was successful, the
preprogram group may well have been biased toward the selection of
individuals less likely to include the "mixed" and criminal offense only category.

These cautions notwithstanding, the proportion represented by those
whose only prior offenses were of the status variety can suffer a material
corrective reduction and still constitute a very large proportion of all

TABLE 4.2   Prior Offense Pattern of Preprogram Population, by Age

Offense Type	Under 13		13-14		15-16		Over 16		Total		Offense Type
	N	%	N	%	N	%	N	%	N	%	%
No offense	173	11.1	510	32.7	738	47.3	139	8.9	1,560	100.0	51.9
Status only	19	5.7	122	36.3	178	53.0	17	5.1	336	100.0	11.2
Delinquent only	42	7.3	185	32.0	283	49.0	68	11.8	578	100.0	19.2
Mixed	30	5.6	171	32.1	295	55.5	36	6.8	532	100.0	17.7
Total	264	8.8	988	32.9	1,494	49.7	260	8.6	3,006	100.0	100.0

NOTE: $\chi^2 = 42.06$; df = 9; p < .001.

those dealt with by police and courts as status offenders. In brief, there does appear to be an identifiable group in the juvenile offender population whose infractions are largely restricted to status offenses. Most of these, however, are *one-time* offenders. [4]

Age and Gender Characteristics

Juveniles cited for status offenses among the preprogram group fell principally in the 13- to 16-year-old age groups (Table 4.2) with half (49.7 percent) consisting of 15- and 16-year-olds. About one-third (32.9 percent) were 13 and 14 years old, and a residual 17.4 percent were equally distributed between those under 13 and over 16. With respect to age distribution, the question of interest is whether age level is related to differences in the proportion with prior delinquent offenses, a relationship that may have a bearing on an assumed progression from status to delinquent offenses. The percentage of those with no prior offenses, or with status offenses only, declines steadily from 72.7 percent in the group under 13 years of age to 60.0 percent in the group over 16 (Table 4.3). However, when the "no prior offense" category is excluded from the sample, it becomes evident that there is virtually no relationship between age and prior delinquent offenses (Table 4.4). [5] Even for those under 13 years of age, over three-quarters had records of prior delinquent offenses. The proportion with such prior records remains remarkably stable through age 16.

TABLE 4.3   Major Type of Prior Offense Pattern, by Age

Offense Type	Under 13 N	%	13-14 N	%	15-16 N	%	Over 16 N	%	Total N	%
No offense and status only	192	72.7	632	63.9	916	61.3	156	60.0	1,896	63.1
Delinquent and mixed	72	27.3	356	36.1	578	38.7	104	40.0	1,110	36.9
Total	264	100.0	988	100.0	1,494	100.0	260	100.0	3,006	100.0

NOTE: $\chi^2 = 13.95$; df = 3; p < .01.

TABLE 4.4   Prior Offense Pattern of Preprogram Population, by Age, with "No Offense Priors" Excluded

Offense Type	Under 13 N	%	13-14 N	%	15-16 N	%	Over 16 N	%	Total N
Status only	19	20.9	122	25.5	178	23.5	17	14.0	336
Delinquent only and mixed	72	79.1	356	74.5	578	76.5	104	86.0	1,110
Total	91	100.0	478	100.0	756	100.0	121	100.0	1,446

NOTE: $\chi^2 = 7.46$; df = 3; p < .05.

TABLE 4.5 Prior Offense Pattern of Preprogram Population, by Age and Gender

Offense Type	Under 13 Males N	%	Females N	%	13-14 Males N	%	Females N	%	15-16 Males N	%	Females N	%	Over 16 Males N	%	Females N	%	Total Males N	%	Females N	%	Offense Type Males %	Females %
No offense	93	13.7	80	9.1	198	29.2	310	35.3	308	45.5	429	48.8	78	11.5	60	6.8	677	100.0	879	100.0	44.4	59.6
Status only	10	12.0	9	3.6	27	32.5	95	37.5	39	47.0	139	54.9	7	8.4	10	4.0	83	100.0	253	100.0	5.4	17.1
Delinquent only	30	6.8	12	8.6	130	29.6	55	39.6	218	49.7	65	46.8	61	13.9	7	5.0	439	100.0	139	100.0	28.8	9.4
Mixed	21	6.4	9	4.4	97	29.8	73	35.6	180	55.2	115	56.1	28	8.6	8	3.9	326	100.0	205	100.0	21.4	13.9
Total	154	10.1	110	7.5	452	29.6	533	36.1	745	48.9	748	50.7	174	11.4	85	5.8	1,525	100.0	1,476	100.0	100.0	100.0

NOTE: For males, $\chi^2 = 28.09$; df = 9; p < .001. For females, $\chi^2 = 19.64$; df = 9; p < .02.

TABLE 4.6 Major Type of Prior Offense Pattern, by Age and Gender

Offense Type	Under 13 Males N	%	Females N	%	13-14 Males N	%	Females N	%	15-16 Males N	%	Females N	%	Over 16 Males N	%	Females N	%	Total Males N	%	Females N	%
No offense and status only	103	66.9	89	80.9	225	49.8	405	76.0	347	46.6	568	75.9	85	48.9	70	82.4	760	49.8	1,132	76.7
Delinquent and mixed	51	33.1	21	19.1	227	50.2	128	24.0	398	53.4	180	24.1	89	51.1	15	17.6	765	50.1	344	23.3
Total	154	100.0	110	100.0	452	100.0	533	100.0	745	100.0	748	100.0	174	100.0	85	100.0	1,525	99.9	1,476	100.0

NOTE: For males, $\chi^2 = 21.17$; df = 3; p < .001. For females, $\chi^2 = 3.00$; df = 3; n.s.

The data on gender distribution confirms the prevailing impression that among officially recorded status offenders females constitute a far larger proportion than among delinquent offenders (Table 4.5). Approximately half of the total preprogram population (49.2 percent) are females, representing a 1:1 ratio. This is in striking contrast to the 4:1 ratio of males to females in the general delinquent population (Gottfredson et al., 1977: 487). Further, the data shown in Table 4.5 disclose a perceptible difference between male and female status offenders in the age distribution across the four patterns of prior offense. Although there is a relationship between age and pattern of prior offense for both genders, it has a higher level of probability for males than for females (p < .001 versus p < .02). This is seen even more clearly when the four prior offense patterns are collapsed to two: no offenses-status offenses only, and delinquent-mixed (Table 4.6). Here, percentages are calculated for each age group. For females, the probability level of the relationship becomes nonsignificant, while for males it retains its definitive character (p < .001). These findings may be interpreted to mean that at every age level females in higher proportions are found in the no offense-status offense only prior offense category. Among males, on the other hand, the proportion in this category declines with increasing age. Put another way, three-quarters to four-fifths of the females across the entire span of juvenile age may be found in the no offense-status offense only prior offense category, while the proportion of males in this category declines from about two-thirds in the youngest group to somewhat less than one-half in the older group.

Ethnic Characteristics

The ethnic breakdown of the preprogram population indicates that in all patterns of prior offense white youth had the highest ratios, followed by Blacks, Hispanics, and a residual "other" group, respectively (Table 4.7). Since no data were obtained on the distribution of white and minority populations in the program jurisdictions, it cannot be determined which of these groups were disproportionately represented in the preprogram status offender sample. The Hispanic group in the sample included principally Mexican-American youth in program jurisdictions located in the West and Southwest regions of the United States, and Puerto Rican youth in the Midwest and East. The residual "other" category was drawn from Native American and Asian groups at all sites.

With the exception of the last group, whose numbers were too small to yield a stable measure, the two major minority groups show relatively smaller proportions than white youth in the no offense and status offense only categories, and larger proportions in the delinquent only and mixed categories.

The relationship of ethnicity to prior offense pattern is more clearly seen in Table 4.8, particularly with respect to the comparative distribution of the prior offense pattern for the Black and Hispanic groups. The former showed a higher proportion in the no offenses-status offenses only category, the latter in the delinquent only-mixed category.

Main and Interaction Effects of Age, Gender, and Ethnicity

The differential effects of age, gender, and ethnicity on the probability of a prior pattern of delinquent offenses in a population of status offenders requires further assessment. A regression model was developed to measure the main and interaction effects on the likelihood of a pattern of criminal offenses (delinquent only plus criminal /status) prior to the "instant" offense.

The three variables were operationalized in the following manner:

(1) Program site was treated as a set of seven effect-coded dichotomous variables and entered into the equation prior to age, gender, and ethnicity.
(2) Age, from 7 through 18, was used as a straightforward interval-level variable.
(3) Gender was treated as a dummy variable, coded 1 for males and 0 for females.

TABLE 4.7   Prior Offense Pattern of Preprogram Population, by Ethnicity

Offense Type	White N	White %	Black N	Black %	Hispanic N	Hispanic %	Other N	Other %	Total N	Total %	Offense Type %
No offense	1,115	71.4	326	20.9	79	5.1	41	2.6	1,561	100.0	51.9
Status only	213	63.4	95	28.3	21	6.3	7	2.1	336	100.0	11.2
Delinquent only	333	57.6	169	29.2	61	10.6	15	2.6	578	100.0	19.2
Mixed	300	56.4	164	30.8	61	11.5	7	1.3	532	100.0	17.7
Total	1,961	65.2	754	25.1	222	7.4	70	2.3	3,007	100.0	100.0

NOTE: $\chi^2 = 79.28$; df = 9; p < .001.

TABLE 4.8   Major Type of Prior Offense Pattern, by Ethnicity

Offense Type	White N	White %	Black N	Black %	Hispanic N	Hispanic %	Other N	Other %	Total N	Total %
No offense and status only	1,328	67.7	421	55.8	100	45.0	48	68.6	1,897	63.1
Delinquent and mixed	633	32.3	333	44.2	122	55.0	22	31.4	1,110	36.9
Total	1,961	100.0	754	100.0	222	100.0	70	100.0	3,007	100.0

NOTE: $\chi^2 = 67.13$; df = 3; p < .001.

(4) Ethnicity was operationalized as a set of three dummy variables, reflecting a four-category classification, as follows: Hispanic = 1 if client was Hispanic, 0 otherwise; Black = 1 if client was Black, 0 otherwise; Other Ethnic = 1 if client was not Black, white, or Hispanic, 0 otherwise; and white clients constituted the omitted category implied by the set of three dummy variables.[6]

Variables were entered into the regression in four stages as follows:

(1) Seven site effect codes.
(2) Additive versions of the client variables, namely, age, gender, and ethnicity.
(3) Interaction terms, successively added to the base model established at stage 2. These included (a) multiplicative terms reflecting interaction between age and ethnic categories; (b) interaction of age and gender; and (c) interaction of gender and ethnic categories.
(4) Based on the results of stage 3, a final regression equation was developed that included stage 2 variables plus the age-gender interaction term *and* the gender-ethnicity interaction terms.

Site location proved to be a substantial determinant of delinquent priors. The additive effects of site on the likelihood of a delinquent offense pattern prior to the "instant" status offense was found to explain approximately half of the variation in delinquent priors accounted for jointly by client characteristics and site.[7] This suggests that, independent of age, gender, and ethnicity, the probability that the status offender will fall into the delinquent prior offense category is substantially affected by the jurisdictions in which he or she resides. Such a finding certainly suggests caution in drawing generalizations from similar research carried out in single jurisdictions. Most studies cited earlier in this chapter are single-jurisdiction studies.

When the effects of age, gender, and ethnicity on the likelihood of a pattern of prior delinquent offenses were included, explained variance was increased to 19.5 percent (Table 4.9). More detailed information regarding the determinants of prior offense pattern is provided by an examination of interaction effects. The interaction of age and gender by itself has a significant effect on the probability of a pattern of prior delinquency. The age-ethnicity interaction was not found to be significant when added to the basic equation for additive effects alone. However, when the gender-ethnicity interaction is included in the basic equation, the explained variation for prior delinquent offense is significantly increased. These statistical tests indicated that while the age-ethnicity interaction has no significant effect in relation to prior delinquent offense pattern, both the age-gender and the gender-ethnicity interactions do.

While the effects of age, gender, and ethnicity on the likelihood of a prior delinquent pattern are significant in an additive model, their effects were found to fall below an acceptable level of significance (p = .05) when the interactions among these variables were included in the equation. On the other hand, interaction between age and gender is a significant determinant, as is the set of terms capturing gender-ethnicity interaction. Of the latter set, only the variable reflecting whether or not the youth is a Hispanic male is individually significant, indicating that Hispanic males are more likely to show a pattern of prior delinquency than would be predicted by gender or ethnicity as separate variables. The age-gender interaction coefficient suggests that the likelihood of a pattern of prior delinquent offenses increases at a higher rate for males than for females with an increase in age. Further, among the set of gender-ethnicity interaction coefficients, the only one that is individually significant is that for Hispanic males, indicating that they are more likely to show a pattern of prior delinquency than would be predicted by either gender or ethnicity alone.

Thus, as seen in the additive model displayed in Table 4.9, the variables of age, gender, and ethnicity were positively and significantly related to the probability that a status offender in the preprogram sample would have a record of prior delinquent offenses. The main effects of the variables, along with information as to jurisdiction, accounted for 19.5 percent of the variation in the incidence of a prior delinquent offense pattern. While quite modest, the .4 percent increment in explained variation due to the addition of age-gender and ethnicity-gender interaction terms is statistically significant, owing to the large sample size. Individually significant interaction

TABLE 4.9   Regression Coefficients of Prior Delinquent Patterns on Age, Gender, Ethnicity, and Two-Way Interactions[a] (N = 2993)

Variables	Additive Model		Interaction Model	
	B	Beta	B	Beta
Male	.252	.261*	−.145	−.150
Age	.001	.037**	−.004	−.013
Black	.061	.054***	.035	.032
Hispanic	.097	.052***	.012	.006
Other ethnic	.083	−.026	.010	.003
Age × gender	—	—	.026	.398***
Other ethnic × gender	—	—	−.171	−.039
Hispanic × gender	—	—	.145	.061***
Black × gender	—	—	.052	.035
(Constant)	.309		.262	
	$R^2 = .195$		$R^2 = .199$	

a. Site effect codes entered as controls, but not presented.
*p < .001.
**p < .01.
***p < .05.

terms suggest that being an older male or a Hispanic male raises the probability of a prior delinquent career beyond what might be predicted on the basis of age, gender, and ethnicity considered separately.

Progression from Status to Delinquent Offenses

While the data revealed an identifiable subgroup of juvenile offenders whose only recorded offenses prior to their identification were of the status variety, the question remains whether they tend over time to commit with increasing frequency the "delinquent" offenses, that is, misdemeanors and felonies.

To assess this question, the officially recorded offenses were examined subsequent to as well as prior to the "instant" status offense. As stated earlier, the "instant" offense was defined as the first occurrence of a recorded status offense during the preprogram year. The preprogram sample was classified by four types of prior offense: no offenses, status offenses only, delinquent (misdemeanor and felony) offenses only, and mixed status and delinquent offenses. The sample was then cross-classified by the same offense categories subsequent to the "instant" offense, utilizing six-month and twelve-month follow-up periods. Since the "instant" offense could occur at any point during the preprogram year, it was necessary to eliminate from the follow-up cohorts those members of the sample who, by virtue of the date of their "instant," were not at risk for six months in one case and for twelve months in the other. Consequently, each of the follow-up cohorts represents a reduced subset of the preprogram sample, larger for the six-month cohort, smaller for those having a twelve-month risk period.

As seen in Table 4.10, six months after their first recorded status offense, most of the group in this follow-up cohort (68.7 percent) had no record of a subsequent offense. Of those with no prior offenses, a substantial 83.1 percent remained free of subsequent offenses of any kind. Very small proportions of those with no prior offenses turned up as having committed status offenses (8.3 percent), and even fewer in the delinquency only (6.1 percent) and the mixed (2.6 percent) categories. The "no prior offense" subset in the twelve-month follow-up cohort exhibited substantially the same absence of subsequent offenses, with 75.9 percent remaining free of recorded offenses of any kind (Table 4.11). It may thus be noted at the outset that there exists a very large group of youth of which, on a first citation for a status offense, from three-quarters to four-fifths are unlikely to commit further offenses of any kind during the following year. *This finding raises the question whether the official intervention in a status offense case is warranted for the protection of either the person or the community, and supports the contention of those urging a "do nothing" approach in dealing with status offenders.* At the same time, however, it cannot be determined from these data whether nonappearance for a recorded subsequent offense may be attributed to the deterrent effect of official intervention, to increased knowledge of how to avoid arrest, or to intensified informal pressures from family members for conforming behavior, among other possibilities.

The issue of progression from status to delinquent offenses is best examined by excluding the large group for which no offenses were recorded either prior or subsequent to the "instant" offense. This procedure yields a 2 × 2 table in which the prior status only and delinquent/mixed categories are cross-classified by the same categories at six- and twelve-month follow-up. The sample may now be regarded as "purified" by the exclusion not only of those who had no prior offenses, but of those as well who had no subsequent offenses. The "status offense only" priors are now constituted by individuals for whom two or more status offenses were recorded (at least one of which occurred prior to the "instant"), and they may be viewed more appropriately as a "pure" status

TABLE 4.10   Subsequent Offense Pattern of Preprogram Sample at Six-Month Follow-up

| | Prior Offenses | | | | | | | | |
| Subsequent Offenses | No Offense | | Status Only | | Delinquent Only | | Mixed | | Total | |
	N	%	N	%	N	%	N	%	N	%
No offense	1,302	83.1	191	56.7	335	57.8	245	46.0	2,073	68.7
Status only	130	8.3	80	23.7	66	11.4	89	16.7	365	12.1
Delinquent only	95	6.1	29	8.6	126	21.7	117	22.0	367	12.2
Mixed	40	2.6	37	11.0	53	9.1	82	15.4	212	7.0
Total	1,567	100.1	337	100.0	580	100.1	533	100.1	3,017	100.0

NOTE: χ^2 = 416.4; df = 9; p < .001.

TABLE 4.11   Subsequent Offense Pattern of Preprogram Sample at Twelve-Month Follow-up

| | Prior Offenses | | | | | | | | |
| Subsequent Offenses | No Offense | | Status Only | | Delinquent Only | | Mixed | | Total | |
	N	%	N	%	N	%	N	%	N	%
No offense	555	75.9	85	45.2	130	46.1	99	35.6	869	58.8
Status only	76	10.4	53	28.2	30	10.6	57	20.5	216	14.6
Delinquent only	63	8.6	18	9.6	75	26.6	63	22.7	219	14.8
Mixed	37	5.1	32	17.0	47	16.7	59	21.2	175	11.8
Total	731	100.0	188	100.0	282	100.0	278	100.0	1,479	100.0

NOTE: χ^2 = 237.2; df = 9; p < .001.

offender group. Further, since those in the mixed category are known to have committed both delinquent and status offenses, their merging with those recorded as "delinquent only" creates a category of youth known to have committed delinquent offenses.

Almost half of those with "status only" prior offenses at both the six- and twelve-month follow-up had records of delinquent offenses (45.2 and 48.5 percent, respectively; Tables 4.12 and 4.13). But notable in the same data is the distinction that persistently emerges between two groups in the preprogram sample: those whose offenses tend to remain predominantly in the status offense category, and those given principally to delinquent offenses. Approximately 70 percent of those with delinquent priors had only delinquent subsequent offenses, and approximately 50 percent of those with only status offense priors had only status offense subsequents. These seem to represent two discernibly different groups with respect to offense pattern. A third group emerges, clearly apparent only when the "no offense" individuals in either their prior or subsequent of-

TABLE 4.12   Subsequent Offense Pattern of Preprogram Sample at
Six-Month Follow-up, with "No Offense Priors and
Subsequents" Excluded

	Prior Offenses					
	Status		*Delinquent Only*			
Subsequent	*Only*		*and Mixed*		*Total*	
Offenses	N	%	N	%	N	%
Status only	80	54.8	155	29.1	235	34.7
Delinquent only						
and mixed	66	45.2	377	70.9	443	65.3
Total	146	100.0	532	100.0	678	100.0

NOTE: $\chi^2 = 33.3$; df = 1; p < .001.

TABLE 4.13   Subsequent Offense Pattern of Preprogram Sample at
Twelve-Month Follow-up, with "No Offense Priors and
Subsequents" Excluded

	Prior Offenses					
	Status		*Delinquent Only*			
Subsequent	*Only*		*and Mixed*		*Total*	
Offenses	N	%	N	%	N	%
Status only	53	51.5	87	26.3	140	32.3
Delinquent only						
and mixed	50	48.5	244	73.7	294	67.7
Total	103	100.0	331	100.0	434	100.0

NOTE: $\chi^2 = 34.3$; df = 1; p < .001.

fenses are excluded from the follow-up cohorts, constituted by a subset of status offenders of whom a substantial proportion show subsequent records of delinquency. In the six-month cohort, of the 146 juveniles with prior status offenses only, 45.2 percent had subsequent records of delinquent acts. The corresponding percentage among the 103 juveniles with prior status offenses only in the twelve-month follow-up cohort was 48.5 percent.

These findings offer some support for the progression thesis, but only with respect to a limited segment of a status offender population. However, the evidence is subject to an important qualification. In light of the probable differential treatment of female status offenders—namely, their higher vulnerability to recording as delinquent offenders on the basis of probation violation—it is entirely possible that a very high proportion of the recorded subsequent delinquent offenses of prior status offenders may be ascribed to female probation violators.[8] Hence the impression of progression from status to delinquent offenses suggested by the data of this study may be misleading. In addition, there is evidence for "regression" from delinquent to status offenses as well as for "progression" from status to delinquent offenses. The data shown in Tables 4.10 and 4.11 indicate that at six-month follow-up 19.6 percent of those with "status only" priors were recorded as having subsequent records of delinquency ("delinquency only" plus "mixed"). The corresponding percentage of twelve-month follow-up was 26.6. However, of those with "delinquent only" priors, 11.4 and 10.6 percent had "status only" subsequents at six- and twelve-month follow-up, respectively. This suggests, of course, the substantial degree of offense versatility exhibited by most juvenile offenders, repeatedly noted in prior research as summarized earlier in this chapter.

DISCUSSION

Two major assumptions inform the current movement to deinstitutionalize status offenders by reducing and ultimately eliminating the power of police and courts to deal with them as they do with youth who commit criminal offenses. Supporters of the movement contend, first, that status offenders constitute a distinctive and identifiable category of juvenile offenders, largely free of involvement in criminal acts. It follows from this that the use of secure detention and commitment to correctional institutions has neither legal nor ethical justification. A second assumption holds that, by virtue of being accorded standard police and court treatment, status offenders tend increasingly to commit more serious criminal offenses. Hence, the removal of status offenders from the jurisdiction of the juvenile justice system is expected over time to prevent delinquency.

Our data presented an opportunity to test the support for the empirically more accessible of these assumptions. The analysis yielded, first, the unanticipated finding that, in any population identified by a citation for a status offense, by far the largest proportion is likely to be youngsters for whom there exists *no official record* of a prior offense of any kind. They fall principally between the ages of 13 and 16, with approximately equal proportions of males and females. With reference to ethnicity, the Black and Hispanic minority groups were found to have higher proportions of their prior offenses in the delinquent category than were whites. The group free of official records of offense prior to an arrest or citation for a status offense tend not to reappear either as status or as delinquent offenders subsequently. It is likely that on the whole this group undergoes minimal penetration into the juvenile justice system and represents those customarily diverted by the police.

A second finding, less unexpected, was that, of those with offense records prior to a status offense arrest, about 1 in 10 consist of youth who have committed only status offenses. Of this group, about one-quarter continue to confine their infractions to the status offenses, another quarter show a subsequent record of delinquent offenses, and approximately half remain free of recorded offenses.

In general, it appears that a population identified by an arrest or appearance before the juvenile court for a status offense contains two quite distinguishable groups. About two-thirds consist of a majority of youth virtually free of recorded prior offenses and a minority showing records of prior status offenses only. The prior records of the remaining one-third of this population designate either solely delinquent offenses or mixed delinquent and status offenses. That the distinction between the no offense-status offense only group and the delinquent only-mixed group remains relatively stable is attested to by the subsequent offenses of the two groups. The latter group remains disproportionately in the delinquency-mixed categories; the former in those of no offense-status offenses only.

Findings on gender differences indicate that males at every age level are very much more likely than females to acquire records of nonstatus offenses. Fully half of the male members of the sample had delinquent (that is, nonstatus) recorded offenses, compared to less than one-fourth of the females.

Examination of the relative predictive utility of jurisdiction, age, gender, and ethnicity revealed jurisdiction to be an important determinant of the probability that a youth cited for a status offense would have a record of a prior delinquent offense. Certain combinations of age, gender, and ethnicity were found to increase this probability. Thus the likelihood of a prior record of delinquent offenses increased with increasing age at a higher rate for males than for females. When this interaction is combined further with ethnicity, it was found that older Hispanic males had the highest probability of recorded prior delinquency.

On the basis of the data available for this analysis, the evidence for progression from status to delinquent offenses remains debatable. If the population under consideration is made up of youth cited for a status offense within a given time period, irrespective of the number of prior status offenses, the overwhelming majority within a twelve-month follow-up are found either to have no subsequent offenses or to confine their subsequents to the status offenses. On the other hand, if the population of concern is composed of youth with two or more prior status offenses, there is virtually equal probability that their subsequent offenses will be either of the delinquent or of the status variety. In other words, youth marginally involved in status offense behavior are in little danger of moving into the more serious forms of delinquency. However, those for whom status offense behavior has become chronic appear to be as likely subsequently to commit misdemeanor and criminal offenses as they are to confine themselves to the status offenses.

But there remains strong and consistent evidence for the existence of three relatively separable groups, each distinguishable on the basis of the predominant character of offenses. The first consists of status offenders with little tendency to commit the more serious delinquent offenses; the second includes juveniles whose records show a predominance of delinquent offenses. Finally, as a finding of some importance, the data revealed the third and largest group to consist of juveniles without records of either a status or a delinquent offense both prior and subsequent to the single incident that defined their membership in a status offender population.

Thus only one of the basic assumptions of fact on which the status offender deinstitutionalization movement rests is provisionally supported by the evidence of the present study. While its boundaries cannot be sharply drawn, there does appear to be a distinguishable subgroup of misbehaving youth whose infractions are confined principally to the status offenses. It does not appear that they tend to commit the more serious delinquent offenses in increasing numbers or with increasing frequency. They thus constitute an identifiable subgroup whose problem behavior may be sufficiently differentiated from that represented by acts in violation of the criminal law to warrant distinctive forms of response and treatment. There is little support for the notion that they tend in substantial proportions to become serious delinquents. What evidence there is in support of that assumption has reference only to that relatively small segment of a status offending population consisting of chronic status offenders. They are as likely in time to engage in serious delinquent offenses as they are to remain status offenders.

Finally, nothing in the data of this study can throw light on the third basic assumption of the status offender deinstitutionalization movement asserting that traditional juvenile court processing increases the likelihood of progression from status to delinquent offenses. However, the evidence does indicate that contained within any population of juvenile offenders defined by a citation for a status offense are substantial numbers of delinquent offenders. Whether the use of secure confinement in the treatment of this group reduces their recidivism or increases community protection is a separate issue. But with respect to the group of status offenders who show little inclination to engage in the more serious forms of delinquency, no form of secure confinement would appear to be warranted on either preventive or ethical grounds.

NOTES

1. Surveys conducted during the decade 1965-1974 in a variety of jurisdictions have found that half of all juveniles arrested for a status offense were placed in secure detention for periods ranging from several days to several months (LEAA, 1975: 1-3). One-third of all juveniles in correctional institutions (training schools, group homes, halfway houses) were committed as adjudicated status offenders (LEAA, 1974).

2. We should note here a contrary review by Murray and Rubin (1982), which concludes that there is greater specialization than we find in our own review or will report in succeeding pages.

3. The data on prior offense and gender are presented by age as a summary indication that age distribution does not differ materially between those whose prior offenses do and do not include a substantial proportion of delinquent offenses.

4. Attention is directed to the fact that the records were entered in a search for instant status offenses. The number of those who were primarily status offenders in terms of their prior records constitutes 63 percent of the total as defined by our entry criteria. The same number of status offenders would constitute a far smaller proportion of the total arrested and adjudicated juvenile population. A project on delinquent or mixed offenders, using an analogous record-entry procedure, would have yielded large numbers of predominantly delinquent or predominantly mixed offenders. A not unreasonable alternative in estimating the proportion of status offenders in the preprogram population is to exclude the 1560 individuals with no recorded offenses prior to the "instant" on grounds that they are essentially nonoffenders. With their exclusion, the n = 1446, of which 336, or 23.2 percent, have substantial prior records of offenses only (see Table 4.2). As will be seen, however, this proportion is further reduced when offenses subsequent to the "instant" at six- and twelve-month follow-up are taken into account.

5. The exclusion of the "no prior offense" category is warranted for present purposes since a large proportion in the category are likely to be one-time offenders. Thus 43.2 and 37.5 percent, respectively, had no record of a subsequent offense of any kind at six- and twelve-month follow-up.

6. The dependent variable of "delinquent priors" was operationalized as a dummy variable, with 1 = record of a delinquency prior to the "instant" offense, 0 = no such record. Anticipating the objection that the use of dummy variables in regression equations violates the necessary assumption of homoscedasticity, it should be stated that in this instance the dichotomy is not badly skewed. In the 2993 cases in the regression, the proportion in 1 was 37 percent; in 0, 63 percent.

7. This was ascertained in a special analysis of the independent effects of site location. Site terms were entered after the client variables, permitting assessment of their contribution to explained variance due solely to their addition.

8. Most jurisdictions treat violation of probation as a delinquent offense. Females were found to constitute approximately half of the preprogram sample. Since female status offenders are more likely than males to receive probation on a first offense because of concern over alleged sexual misconduct, they may be more likely to acquire a higher risk of probation violation, and therefore be recorded for a delinquent offense.

PART II

PROGRAM
MODELS

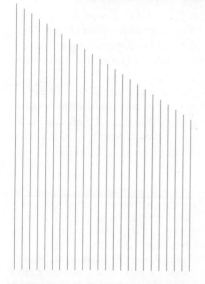

INTRODUCTION:
PROGRAM MODELS FOR
DEINSTITUTIONALIZATION

Of the twelve programs funded by OJJ in its deinstitutionalization initiative, eight were included in the national evaluation study. Sharing a set of

general objectives, the eight programs were designed to prevent the placement of status offenders in detention facilities and correctional institutions
by providing alternative community-based facilities, and to register progress in reducing the number of status offenders currently incarcerated in
correctional institutions. Common to these "community-based programs"
as well was a rather generally defined body of treatment practices.

Robert Coates (1981) has provided perhaps the most cogent analysis
yet of what constitutes the "community-basedness" of a program. It is
important in a multiple-sited program such as DSO to describe the variations that exist on this theme. As Coates (1981: 88) notes, "It is one thing
to have a view of what is bad about an institution-based system; it is quite
another to think systematically about the qualities that we would like to
see in a community-based system that replaces it." Several publications
provide reviews of presumably appropriate program models and conceptual dimensions applying to them; see in particular Rutherford and
Bengur (1976) and Young and Pappenfort (1977). These reports also
contain materials pertinent to the humaneness rationale and to the dangers of net widening. Spergel (1975) provides dramatic examples of
community-based agencies ranging from politically sophisticated youth
gangs to federally funded community action programs.

While it might seem that eight programs initiated to deal with status
offenders would at the very least share some etiological assumptions
upon which to base their treatment programs, this was not really the case,
as our descriptive materials will illustrate. This seeming paradox was
noted in a national overview provided by Smith et al. (1980: 155):

> Officials of treatment, control, and welfare organizations deal in models (or
> stereotypes) that imply specific etiologies and standardized methods of treat-
> ment. It is significant that, while many institutions exist for the purpose of pro-
> cessing delinquents, there are no established institutional structures for "de-
> linquency prevention," and certainly no dominant standardized procedure for
> dealing with the problems of noncriminal misbehavior. In that definitional vac-
> uum, conflict over programs takes place on the issue of whether the status
> offender is to be treated as a nuisance, a victim, or a potential criminal.

The programs reviewed here shared little beyond general features.
Each was distinctive both in regard to the institutional and community
setting in which it functioned and in the specific variant of treatment approach adopted. As such, each program may be seen as prototypical for
all jurisdictions in which the same contextual conditions exist and the
same treatment approaches are employed. Accordingly, these programs
may be regarded for analytic purposes as individual models open to assessment with respect to their advantages and weaknesses. Further, so
far as each program was engaged in an enterprise of institutional change,

and in an effort to introduce and gain acceptance for novel procedures in the treatment of status offenders, each encountered obstacles in the course of program implementation that are likely to be typical of comparable community and institutional settings. Success and failure in coping with such difficulties, the victories, defeats, and accommodations the program experienced, can illuminate further the virtues and shortcomings of each program model.

Narrative descriptions of each of the eight programs were included in the National Evaluation report submitted to NIJJDP and are available from that agency. These descriptions were based on our data collection forms and on recorded interviews with key participants in the programs. These included program directors and their staffs; court personnel, including judges and probation workers; the police; the leaders as well as the line staff of youth agencies that provided community-based services; site evaluators; and in some instances officials of juvenile justice planning agencies. The aim of the narrative presentations was to provide a concrete and detailed account of the community and institutional forces that shaped the program, including the latent and open conflicts that arose, at times resolved at the cost of subverting, and at other times in ways entirely favorable to, the implementation of program objectives. It was inevitable in this type of situation that a "Rashomon" problem would arise, in which the same events and problems are diversely perceived, described, and interpreted. In these circumstances, as in all historiography and ethnology, the "objective truth" becomes elusive. However, every effort was made to achieve factual accuracy and, so far as possible, to reflect faithfully the various perspectives of the informants in order to produce a balanced portrayal.

For purposes of the present volume, to bring to the reader some feeling for the programs to which our evaluative data refer, we present an overview of differences among programs with reference to their fundamental features. Here, only gross typifications will be employed, under two very broad headings of "receptive" and "conflicted and resistive" sites, enabling the reader to discern the contextual and programmatic elements that constitute the program models. [1]

PROGRAM DESIGN FEATURES

Figures II.1 and II.2 provide a general overview of two categories of program characteristics. *Contextual factors* (Figure II.1) differentiate programs in terms of the community and justice system conditions within which programs functioned. Although at several of the sites (Alameda County, California; Pima County, Arizona; Clark County, Washington) juvenile justice agencies were the grant recipients, there was considerable

FIGURE II.1 Program Characteristics: Selected Contextual Factors

Program Site	Statutory Restriction on Detention and Incarceration			Community Tolerance			Justice Control of Program			Availability of Residential Facilities		
	Absent	Partly Restricted	Fully Restricted	High	Medium	Low	High	Medium	Low	High	Medium	Low
Alameda County, CA		X			X		X			X		
Pima County, AZ		X		X				X			X	
Connecticut	X					X	X			X		
Delaware	X					X	X				X	
Illinois		X				X		X			X	
South Carolina	X					X		X				X
Spokane County, WA		X			X				X		X	
Clark County, WA		X			X		X					X

Program Sites	Organizational Design[a]			Eligibility for Program Services		Primary Program Strategy			System Penetration During Referral				Program Control of Client[c]		
	Formalistic	Mixed	Personalistic	Status Offenses Only—"Mixed" Cases Excluded	Instant Status Offense as Sole Qualification	Family Crisis Counseling	Youth Advocacy	Eclectic	Justice Agency Referral Required YES	NO	System Penetration HIGH	LOW	HIGH	MEDIUM	LOW
Alameda County, CA	X				X	X			X			X			X
Pima County, AZ	X				X		X		X			X			X
Connecticut	X			X				X	X			X			X
Delaware	X			X				X	X			X		X	
Illinois[b]	X			X			X		X			X			
South Carolina	X			X				X	X			X			X
Spokane County, WA			X		X	X				X		X	X		
Clark County, WA			X	X		X				X		X	X		

FIGURE II.2   Program Characteristics: Selected Operational Factors

a. In the formalistic design, referrals of clients for service are typically routed through a central coordinating agency. Direct and unmediated referrals from one to another agency in the service network is represented in the personalistic organizational design.

b. No attempt was made to obtain information on program control of client.

c. Data are based on program facility responses to a list of possible rule violations and the severity of sanctions imposed. Those placed in group home facilities were present for too brief a period to permit implementation of sanctions for rule violation. Overall, the DSO programs exercised relatively low control over clients because of the short-term nature of services provided. Data were not collected from foster home facilities.

variation in the degree of control exercised by each of these agencies over program operations. "Justice control" as used in this context indicates the extent to which the justice system *exercised* its control over the program.

Operational (Figure II.2) factors differentiate programs in terms of their basic design and operations. The characterization of programs with reference to their features was based on a variety of information sources, including program directors, site evaluators, and service providers. Where appropriate and feasible, classifications were based on available data, as in the use of school district disciplinary records for the assessment of community tolerance, and the use of survey data provided by site evaluators to determine levels of residential bed space, and by service providers with reference to the degree of client control exercised by program facilities.

At the most general level, each program may be characterized with reference to an ideal-typical set of contextual and operational features envisioned as optimal by the deinstitutionalization initiative. Thus, with respect to the community and juvenile justice system setting of any program, progress in deinstitutionalization would be maximally feasible in jurisdictions (1) highly tolerant of status offending youth, (2) with detention and /or commitment to correctional institutions either prohibited by statute or discouraged by administrative practice; (3) having adequate bed space in nonsecure residential facilities as alternatives to detention, and (4) in which the program was conducted by a community-based youth-serving agency outside the control of the juvenile justice system. [2]

Further, as suggested by guideline specifications, an ideal-typical deinstitutionalization program would include the following as critical program elements:

(a) reasonably nonrestrictive eligibility criteria for admission to program services;
(b) maximum mutual access to and communication among program personnel throughout the youth service network of the jurisdiction;
(c) reduction of "system penetration" by diversion of status offense cases to the program at the police or court intake level;
(d) provision of treatment facilities that avoids the stigmatization of program clients by reducing the level of behavioral control exercised; and
(e) an eclectic treatment strategy based on both a crisis intervention and a youth advocacy model.

There was, of course, no expectation that any of the programs would or could provide all of the elements of this prescription. However, it does provide a standard against which differences in the character of the several programs may be assessed. Figures II.1-II.3 present a summary description of the programs in relation to the conditions initially assumed to favor the implementation of program aims.

Figure II. 1 presents a summary account of selected success in achieving heterogeneity in program contexts. Relevant conditions are defined by the legal, community attitude, community resource availability, and the local justice system involvement in the management of the deinstitutionalization effort. Sites varied with respect to statutory provisions in their juvenile codes for the degree to which detention and other forms of secure confinement in status offender cases were prescribed or prohibited. Sites operating under codes that prohibited such confinement were less restricted in the development of their programs.

As measured by the single indicator of rates of school expulsion and suspension, communities varied in the climate of opinion in which justice and youth services agencies felt free to pursue program aims. They differed also in the extent to which there was already in place a network of facilities for the residential care of those status offenders for whom return to their own homes was precluded.

Finally, whether the program grant recipient was an agency of the juvenile justice system (typically a juvenile court), a public welfare agency, or a coalition of private youth-serving agencies could potentially have important consequences for client perceptions of the stigmatizing effect of program services.

Figure II.2 similarly summarizes the major dimensions along which site programs differed in concrete content. Networks of community-based service agencies were of two main types, with a third possibility in which the two were combined. The formalistic organizational design was one in which all referrals to the program were to a central agency for evaluation with respect to eligibility for program services and for judgment regarding the type of service needed by program-eligible clients. Referrals were then made to volunteer or contracted service agencies with the requirement for accountable recording and reporting to the central DSO agency. There was little or no interaction and communication among the personnel of the service agencies with respect to problems of individual clients. In contrast, the personalistic organizational design, regardless of the source of initial referral to the DSO program, encouraged active communication among the personnel of service agencies, such that clients were referred freely from one to another in the search for services deemed appropriate in each case.[3]

Eligibility for program services differed in relation to the legal status of the status offender. Some site programs accepted only those youth whose set of charged instant offenses did not include either violations of the criminal codes and /or were not currently on probation for a prior offense of any kind. In other sites, programs accepted any youth whose instant offense or set of instant offenses included status violations.

Three broad types of primary program strategy were identified. The major treatment approach at virtually all sites was the provision of crisis

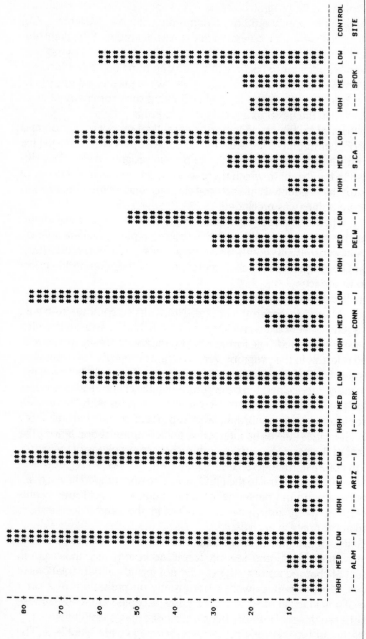

Figure II.3 Percentage of Service Provider Agencies at Each Site, by Level of Control Imposed on Client Behavior[a]

a. Level of control was estimated from service providers' judgments of the severity of sanction (from "termination from program" to "no action taken") imposed by the agency for either occasional or frequent infraction of one or more of eleven typical agency rules. The Illinois program was excluded from the site list because of the very brief period during which clients were under the supervision of DSO staff.

counseling, which most frequently included members of the client's family. In a second type of program strategy, several sites emphasized a youth advocacy approach. This consisted variously of efforts to mediate conflicts between the youth and the family, the court, or the school, and efforts to provide help in remedying educational deficits and obtaining employment. A third program strategy avoided a special emphasis on either of the first two, and attempted to combine both in an eclectic approach.

The extent to which status offenders penetrated the juvenile justice system in various site programs also varied. The main distinction was whether justice agency referral was a requirement for program services eligibility, and, as a summary dichotomous judgment, whether the penetration of the juvenile justice system by the clientele of the site program was high or low.

Finally, Figure II.3 presents information that was obtained regarding the extent to which programs attempted to maintain control over the behavior of their clients. Rutherford and Bengur (1976: 19-20) have identified five general forms of achieving control: achievement systems, threat of incarceration, peer pressure, program regimentation, and surveillance. For DSO, we determined to concentrate on negative sanctioning approaches to client control.

Implicit in the labeling theory assumptions of the DSO program was the aim of avoiding the stigma attached to formal justice processing. Commonly seen as the specifically stigmatizing impact of formal processing is the use of punitive threat as the means of controlling delinquent behavior. However, this effect is also highly likely when community-based nonjustice agencies to which status offenders are referred exercise restrictive control over the behavior of their clients. This is particularly the case if referral has been initiated by the police or the court, with the clear implication that continued misbehavior can result in remand of the youth to the control of the court. An important feature of the program, therefore, varying among sites, was the scope of control over client behavior exerted by community-based agencies. This was systematically assessed through a survey questionnaire completed by all service providers with the exception of foster homes. Agencies were requested to specify the type and frequency of sanctions imposed for various forms of client violations of agency rules. Estimated from these returns was the percentage distribution at all sites of high, medium, and low sanction severity and frequency imposed for rule violation.

Elements of the classification scheme reviewed here will be referred to selectively in the course of the program descriptions that follow. This is designed to bring to the reader's attention the rationale of evaluation concerns with contextual conditions created by legal and community factors and with program characteristics as these have affected the specific site programs under discussion.

When the Office of Juvenile Justice publicized its readiness to provide funding support to state and local jurisdictions to help them reduce the use of secure confinement in status offense cases, it received over 1000 program proposals. As in all instances of an offer of federal funding support, the objectives that the funds were to serve were clearly and elaborately specified. However, it was by no means the case that all those responding to the offer were fully and without qualification committed to the goal of deinstitutionalizing status offenders.

This was true enough for those already attuned to the deinstitutionalization movement, some of whom had achieved some progress in reducing the use of detention for status offenders. These saw in the OJJ offer an opportunity to build the community-based facilities called for in the federal program for dealing with the status offender problem outside the juvenile justice system.

However, many of the program proposals were submitted in the interest of obtaining supplemental support to meet a felt need to enlarge a fiscally constrained and therefore limited range of services available for dealing with status offenders. Although it had been made abundantly clear in the program solicitation materials issued by OJJ, the requirement that federal funds be used primarily to develop private sector, community-based treatment facilities was in effect regarded as an objective for whose realization they could only pledge their best efforts. There were a number of reasons for such qualified although acceptable commitment. In some instances, program proponents were not entirely persuaded that the use of secure confinement for status offenders invariably had the negative consequences alleged. Program proposals initiated by organizations outside the juvenile justice system were in other instances regarded by judicial or probation personnel as challenging both their competence and legal authority to deal constructively with status offender problems. And in those instances in which the juvenile court itself solicited OJJ funding support, there occurred widespread foot dragging by probation personnel who by virtue of their intake duties function as the doorkeepers of the juvenile justice system.

Given the variety of motives and interests surrounding decisions to apply for status offender deinstitutionalization grants, it becomes useful to classify the jurisdictional sites in which DSO programs were established as falling into three types. There were, first, the receptive sites. These were marked by their readiness to implement program objectives as indicated by their having already progressed toward the goal of status offender deinstitutionalization prior to the submission of their program proposals. Programs in three such sites are described in Chapter 5.

A second group of four sites exhibited some degree of resistance to the goal of deinstitutionalization, despite its pro forma acceptance. Among these, two subtypes may be distinguished on the basis of degree of resistiveness. There were the conflicted sites, characterized by frank and open opposition between elements of the juvenile justice system and youth service agencies, whether private or public. But most resistive among the jurisdictions with a qualified commitment to deinstitutionalization were the sites marked by persisting but usually unstated disagreement with the aims of the program by enforcement agencies and by probation personnel, exerting a pervasively obstructive effect on program progress. Resistive and conflicted sites will be described in Chapter 6.

NOTES

1. Other research on these programs, emphasizing their organizational and networking properties, can be found in Miller (1980), Miller, Lincoln, and Olson (1981), Gordon (1980), and Miller, Gordon, and Heck (1981).

2. Aside from the control issue, Rutherford and Bengur (1976) have cited other advantages of private over public locus of programs, most of the advantages having to do with programmatic and staff flexibility.

3. The dangers of "label spread" inherent in this process are addressed within our data set by Gordon (1980). As we note elsewhere, the dangers were confirmed.

chapter 5

Receptive Sites

with Elaine M. Corry

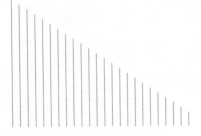

PIMA COUNTY

In undertaking to implement the DSO program, a number of sites enjoyed the considerable advantage of an existing commitment to the desirability of status offender deinstitutionalization. Nowhere had the commitment gone forward more vigorously than in Pima County. For several years before receiving its OJJ grant, the Pima County Juvenile Court, under the leadership of its presiding judge, had all but eliminated the use of detention in status offense cases.

Further, during the year preceding the DSO grant, the court had established its neighborhood-based Mobile Diversion Unit (MDU), staffed by probation officers, to deal with status offense cases without recourse to formal court processing. The unit received police referrals, responded to requests from parents for assistance in these cases, provided counseling services to families, and referred cases to social agencies for needed services. This was a drastic shift in policy from a prior heavy use of detention in these cases, and it did not go unchallenged. Enforcement agencies in the jurisdiction as well as some court personnel opposed the change. The opposition soon became sufficiently well organized politically to induce the Arizona Supreme Court to suspend the juvenile court judge pending an investigation of charges that he was "soft" on "juvenile thugs and hoodlums." In response to his suspension, community support for the judge and the new policy was mobilized and the suspension was rescinded.

Thus vindicated, the court moved quickly to consolidate and expand the program. It enlarged the MDU, established a number of shelter-care facilities for runaways, procured the services of a state-funded family counseling program, launched a program to train school personnel in dealing with problems of truancy and classroom incorrigibility, and encouraged and funded a variety of agencies and organizations to conduct youth development programs.

Despite the virtual termination of detention for status offenders and the introduction of alternative community-based services, the court as well as OJJ justified the program grant to Pima County on grounds that the effort to deinstitutionalize status offenders was in only its early stage of development. There was still a long way to go before Pima County could be regarded as committed officially to the value of deinstitutionalization. Given the continuing conflict in this southern Arizona community between the "hard liners" and the "progressives," this was indeed the case.

Program Design and Development

Heartened by its success in overcoming initial opposition, and now braced with added funds, the juvenile court moved with enthusiasm to expand community services for status offenders. Here the court faced a crucial policy crossroad. One option was to allocate its grant funds to the "main-line" social agencies of the community to enable them to expand services to the now-diverted status offenders. The county's established youth-serving agencies reasonably expected to play a central role in the development of the program. Their support, willingly granted, had been solicited by the court early in the preparation of the successful project proposal submitted to OJJ.

A second option was to make only the most marginal use of the facilities of these agencies, emphasizing instead the encouragement and support of neighborhood-based "grass-roots" youth agencies and school-centered outreach programs. In selecting this option, court personnel moved decisively to link the deinstitutionalization program to a general delinquency-prevention objective. They were convinced, first, that the youth problems underlying status offense behavior were continuous with those involved in all delinquent behavior, and, second, that the established youth agencies were unlikely to succeed in reaching the large pool of "hard to reach" unserved youth.

To implement this policy, the court funded 19 community agencies and organizations to which status offense cases were to be referred. In line with the court's general prevention objectives, the single largest category (7 agencies) consisted of neighborhood- and school-based outreach programs, with 5 newly established shelter-care agencies following closely. Among the remaining 7 were (a) a truancy-prevention program in the major school district of the county, located in the city of Tucson; (b) an expansion of the crisis intervention services provided by the court's already developed Mobile Diversion Unit; (c) a counseling service operating in school locations; (d) a program for female high school students to improve their social and occupational skills; and (e) an advocacy program for young women focusing on the entire range of their problems.

Thus the main feature of the Pima County program design was its coupling of expanded detention-alternative facilities with a bold move into the uncharted waters of prevention programming and youth advocacy. The former capitalized on marginally established shelter-care agencies, using grant funds to increase their resources. The seven outreach programs included one located in the Black community, one in the American Indian community, one in an isolated Mexican-American neighborhood, and one in the county's rural hinterland. The organizations funded to conduct these programs were directed and staffed by residents of the respective neighborhoods or by persons well established in their helping roles and trusted by the residents. With few exceptions the programs operated as multiservice centers responding to the needs of youth and their families. The remaining three programs used a variety of devices to attract the young to their program services: enriched educational services in one case, training in the use and care of motorbikes in a second, and a crisis intervention program to supplement the work of the court's Mobile Diversion Unit in a third.

Briefly, then, the intervention strategy of the Pima County program model combined crisis intervention with a unique pattern of youth advocacy.

Institutional and Community Contexts

The institutional and community contexts into which the program was introduced variously favored or limited the achievement of its aims. The campaign to discredit the juvenile court judge, who had earlier ended the detention of status offenders, and the success of his defense testified to the divided views in this community about appropriate treatment. The level of community tolerance for status offense behavior during the year preceding the DSO program was consequently largely dependent on the views of those in a position to control the disposition of status offense cases. The enforcement agencies of the county, reflecting an important segment of public opinion, regarded the use of detention as a salutary reinforcement of adult authority and an effective deterrent experience. However, the police agencies were unable to influence court policy in this matter. Before and during program operations, status offenders continued to be arrested and delivered to the court's detention center, maintained as an unlocked facility, from which arrested status offenders were free to leave or to use the counseling services of a probation officer. Few left.

A second institution with "hands-on" control of status offense cases was the county's school system. The evaluation study used their suspension and expulsion records of the year prior to DSO program inception as a measure of community tolerance. On this measure, the Pima County community was found to be the most tolerant of status offense behavior among the eight evaluated program sites. However, this judgment rests on observation and measurement of the action of only one major public agency for the control and training of the young. That their policies may not have been an accurate reflection of majority community opinion is suggested by the conflict that had erupted with the initial move to reform court policy.

Other elements of community context that imposed constraints on the Pima County program model may be noted briefly. Neither prior to nor during the first program year was there statutory prohibition on the use of detention or long-term incarceration of status offenders. There was thus no legislative support for their exclusion by the Pima County court. Since the court was the project grantee, the program was totally under its control. This created the danger that all program operations might have been overlaid with the coercive authority that clings to judicial power. In effect, however, the court had voluntarily reduced its direct control of status offense cases and created a set of community-based programs of both a general preventive and a direct service character. Thus, although the court had total control of the program through its selection of contracted youth-serving agencies, it used its power to reduce to a minimum the effect of court authority.

Program Operations and Their Problems

The specific features of DSO programs in very large part reflected the prevailing community and institutional constraints within which they operated. In part, however, they also reflected the project director's ideas of how, within the constraints, to implement the general objectives of status offender deinstitutionalization. These included notions regarding organizational structure, client eligibility for program services, strategies of treatment, the role of juvenile justice agencies in the DSO effort, and the level of control to be imposed on the behavior of clients during their participation in the program.

Organizational structure. The court assigned to a small group of probation officers the task of selecting for funding program proposals solicited
from social agencies and neighborhood organizations in the county.
These then constituted the network of youth-serving agencies to which
status offense cases were referred as they were brought to the attention of
the court by the police, the schools, and the court's own neighborhood-
based Mobile Diversion Unit. The organizations and agencies making up
the network were carefully selected to support the court's policy of pursuing DSO objectives through a strategy of primary prevention.

Convinced that the status offender problem was no more than symptomatic of family and neighborhood conditions underlying the more general problem of juvenile delinquency, the court funded a variety of newly
developed neighborhood organizations. The leadership of these organizations was largely inexperienced in dealing with problems of fiscal management. More important, because their programs were intended to be
responsive to the entire range of problems among the families and youth
of their local areas, they had little interest in confining their attention to
managing and recording the case treatment of status offenders among
those that were referred to them. There was consequently little prospect
that formal procedures would be observed through which the progress of
status offense cases were to be monitored and recorded. This was not
true, of course, of the small number of community agencies contracted to
provide standard shelter-care facilities; these tended to be entirely ortho-
dox in their case management and recording practices.

Thus in its formal structure the Pima County program was designed to
identify, refer, and treat status offenders in a manner that would permit
the monitoring and recording of the process. Its policy thrust, however,
impelled the court to invest a major share of its program resources in
newly developed grass-roots types of neighborhood organizations devoted to general prevention objectives. The disjunction between policy
and program structure remained an unremitting source of strain throughout the life of the program.

Client eligibility. The sole criterion for formal referral to program services was the commission of a status offense, without regard to the record
of prior offenses. Intake policy thus accorded with the prevention and
advocacy interests of the court. A large proportion of the Pima County
program population may consequently have consisted of youth who
would have been *ineligible* for status offender services in the programs of
other sites. In other sites they may have been classified as "neglect and
dependency" cases, as being "essentially" delinquents (that is, criminal
offenders), or as unlikely to come to the attention of the authorities at all.
The Pima County eligibility criteria may thus have had the double effect
of reducing needed controls on delinquent offenders who happened to

commit a status offense on the one hand and, on the other, of imposing services in cases where the need was dubious.

Primary program strategy. A substantial investment of resources was made in the general prevention programs of neighborhood grass-roots organizations. So far as these provided remedial education and recreation services, the treatment in individual cases is best characterized as youth advocacy. An advocacy approach describes as well the work of the Mobile Diversion Unit. Status offenders who were referred to this program or who otherwise came to its attention were routed to various agency services. Only in the relatively small number of cases dealt with in the shelter-care programs developed with program funds were individual and family counseling emphasized. On the whole, therefore, the program strategy employed in the Pima County program may be described as a combination of delinquency prevention and youth advocacy.

System penetration and client control. The avoidance of formal processing by juvenile justice agencies was perhaps most fully realized in the Pima County program, despite its location within the administrative structure of the juvenile court. Although the court's Mobile Diversion Unit was heavily involved in dealing with status offenders at the neighborhood level, the continued eligibility of clients for program services was not contingent on their avoidance of further delinquent or status offenses. Both system penetration and program control of clients were thus reduced to the vanishing point in the Pima County program.

Summary

The DSO program in the Pima County site was undertaken in the face of opposition from politically powerful groups in the jurisdiction, and later from many of the established social agencies. The program had the character of a crusade mounted by the juvenile court under the charismatic leadership of a presiding judge who was determined to end the excessive use of detention and institutionalization in that jurisdiction. Since this objective had been substantially accomplished in advance of the DSO grant, the juvenile court as program sponsor undertook to consolidate its deinstitutionalization policy largely by supporting the development of youth advocacy and delinquency-prevention activities among neighborhood groups in high-delinquency areas.

ALAMEDA COUNTY

California has occupied a prominent place in the national imagination as a frontier for the exploration of new directions in cultural and institutional change. The state has been a seedbed of cultural innovation, new social and political movements, and bold efforts to reform traditional practices in many institutional areas. Not least has been its front-runner role in efforts to improve the system of juvenile justice. California was the first to establish a Youth Authority several decades ago, and more recently developed a major subvention program to encourage counties to reduce commitments to the Youth Authority's training schools for delinquents. The effect of such continuing legislative receptivity to innovation and experimentation in juvenile justice has been to induce in a number of metropolitan county jurisdictions an alertness to the possibilities of constructive reform. Alameda County, with its major industrial city of Oakland, was one of these.

Sensitive to the progressive thrust of the national status offender deinstitutionalization movement, leaders of the juvenile justice community had induced the state legislature to give serious and favorable consideration to ending the detention of status offenders. In anticipation of impending statutory change, the Alameda County Probation Department reassessed its practices with respect to the treatment of status offenders, and decided to reduce its use of detention.

Institutional and Community Contexts

As a result, the Probation Department developed during several years prior to the establishment of the DSO program a separate unit with the tasks of dealing with cases of status offense and of initiating a positive and constructive procedure of family crisis counseling and placement of status offenders in foster homes whenever necessary. The forthright and early move to change status offender treatment policy was facilitated by an already existing statewide commitment to deal tolerantly with juvenile incorrigibility in the schools. To guard against tendencies to cope with the problem by expelling and suspending students, all school districts had been required by statute to submit such cases for disposition to local school attendance review boards. As indicated by relatively reduced rates of expulsions and suspensions, Alameda County offered a moderate level of tolerance for status offense behavior. The jurisdiction was also well supplied with foster homes and other out-of-home placement facilities, providing a readily available alternative to the use of detention.

Further, the county's juvenile justice system provided a singularly favorable setting for the advent of the DSO program. The separate group of probation officers that had been established to handle all status offense cases, the Family Crisis Intervention Unit (FCIU), was committed to the goal of ending all court intervention in these cases by substituting direct referrals of police arrests to community-based agencies. To foster this objective, the group had enlisted the willing cooperation of the county's Criminal Justice Planning Board.

Program Design

The problem confronting the leadership of the status offender deinstitutionalization movement in Alameda County closely paralleled that faced by the leaders of the movement in Pima County. Progress in both cases had already been made in reducing the use of detention by the time OJJ's status offender initiative made its appearance. Both regarded the prospect of federal funding as an opportunity to carry the movement forward by creating a system of community-based services for status offenders outside the juvenile justice system. But where the leadership in Pima County resided in the judge of the juvenile court, in Alameda County it came from supervisory personnel in the probation department who had developed its Family Crisis Intervention Unit with strong support from the county's Criminal Justice Planning Board. In fact, this latter agency had formulated the program proposal, designating the probation department as the grantee.

The program proposed to achieve five objectives: (1) an increase in the number of community-based resources; (2) a rise in the level of competence in conducting family crisis intervention among staff of community-based agencies; (3) inducement for police agencies to refer status offense cases directly to community agencies or the FCIU rather than to Juvenile Hall detention; (4) coordination of the work of police officers, the FCIU, community agencies, and schools in the treatment of status offense cases; and (5) as the ultimate objective, the total elimination of detention for status offenders.

Program Implementation Problems

Of these objectives, only two were completely achieved, with a third only partially accomplished. With the use of program funds the foster home facilities of the county were expanded through the expedient of supplementing the per diem county payment for the service, and two short-term specialized "crisis receiving homes" were established, one at the north end and one at the south end of the county. These latter functioned as model alternatives to detention; some police agencies were willing to transport arrested status offenders to them instead of to Juvenile Hall. They did this, however, only on explicit prior approval of their commanding officer in each case and on notification of the probation department.

The model crisis receiving home located in the heavily urbanized north end of the county did, however, face an unexpected displacement problem. In their efforts to deal with a persistent problem of prostitution among teenage girls in a ghetto area, the police had found it convenient to reduce the girls' presence on the street by treating the most recalcitrant of them as status offenders. They were repeatedly picked up and delivered to the crisis receiving home. Mingling there with runaways and assorted other status offenders, they had several days to rest and recuperate from the demands of the profession.

While the development of the crisis receiving homes was on the whole a striking achievement, the objective of enlisting the full collaboration of the police was not realized. Police agencies had earlier accepted and approved the already established practice of the probation department's FCIU in eliminating the use of detention in all but a minority of status offense cases. However, with the advent of the federally funded status offender program, the police were now confronted with the problem of moving beyond this stage in the deinstitutionalization process to the direct referral of custody cases to private sector youth service agencies. The main components of the county's youth service network were the youth service centers (YSCs), most of which favored an advocacy approach in dealing with youth problems. Except for a few of the county's police agencies that were accustomed to working with their YSCs in connection with pre-existing diversion programs, most viewed as proper and desirable the routing of status offender custody cases to the FCIU in the probation department, the competence and judgment of which they had come to trust. In short, the police, for the most part, did not bypass the probation department and refer the status offense cases directly to community-based agencies.

The situation of police attitudes and cooperation was stated in the following way by a supervisory FCIU staff member:

> [The police expressed] a high level of criticism and a prediction of failure. On the diversion aspect [the police wanted to know] how can you expect the YSCs to do the work that Probation has been doing? The police are really concerned, and they still are. Some of our biggest [police] supporters still want to have Probation in it. . . . Police can accept the lack of Juvenile Hall better than they can diversion to other agencies for providing the service. . . . They're really worried about not having Probation to rely on for services. . . . They want to know that Probation will always be there. The direction of the status offender program now is to see if we can't eliminate Probation as the service provider.

The most important of the program objectives, basic to the achievement of the rest, was to upgrade the professional competence of YSC and probation department staff members in conducting family crisis intervention. That is, the prospect that effective services for status offenders would be available in community-based agencies was regarded as dependent on the ability of their staffs to master the technique of family crisis intervention. Professionally well trained themselves, and having elaborated a theory of family crisis intervention as the method of choice in dealing with status offense problems, program leaders viewed as central the training of YSC staff located in various regions of the county. But because of the commitment of the program leadership to an exclusive doctrine of treatment, the training program for all practical purposes failed to materialize. Even among professionally trained probation workers, the supervisors of the probation department's FCIU who led the program represented something of an intellectual elite in their political and social sophistication, their capacity for conceptualization, their orientation to the importance of ideas, and their articulateness. As is common, however, the weakness of those possessed of these virtues is a tendency toward exclusiveness, a touch of arrogance in dealing with those less competent in ways they value, and a sharply reduced ability to communicate effectively.

Thus handicapped, the leadership neglected to draw fully into the program planning phase crucial collaborators for the implementation of the DSO program. As mentioned, some of the police agencies retained strong reservations regarding the aim of diverting status offenders from the probation department. More important, there was also failure to bring into the planning process the leaders of the county's youth service centers, the principal community-based resource depended upon to provide treatment services. Most of the YSCs were in any case little disposed to forgo their own commitment to a youth advocacy approach in dealing with all youth problems in favor of adopting, in status offense cases, an exclusive family crisis intervention approach. Failure to gain the agreement of the main service provider network during the planning phase to adopt family crisis intervention as the primary means of serving the needs of status offenders resulted in the failure of the training program. Attendance of YSC staff members at training sessions was sparse, and those who did come attended irregularly.

There was, however, one notable success in winning the full conversion of a youth service center to the doctrine of family crisis intervention. This was achieved in the case of a youth service center established and developed by the DSO program leaders in a Black neighborhood of Oakland. Although initially viewed by residents as an alien intrusion, the center was able within a few months—under the direction of a sensitive, sophisticated, and skilled white social worker—to gain their acceptance and support, and to provide in a growing number of cases professionally competent family services. It was clear, however, that this one instance of success in procuring a YSC totally attuned to the Alameda County intervention strategy rested on its creation *de novo* by the DSO program leaders.

As a final implementation problem, the leaders of the DSO program failed to win the unqualified support of the administrators of the probation department and some members of its staff. Administrators were on the whole satisfied with the record of reduced detention achieved by the work of the FCIU, and questioned the value of transferring its function to noncourt agencies in the community. And some members of the line probation staff regarded this aim as threatening a loss of an important department function, with a consequent reduction of work load and loss of budget support.

Summary

As a site highly receptive to the aims of the status offender deinstitutionalization movement, Alameda County had recorded substantial progress in reducing the use of detention in such cases prior to the establishment of its DSO program. The program was designed to move beyond detention reduction, with the use of the probation department as the alternative service provider, to the creation of a community-based youth service network as the service provider. The achievement of this aim was, however, limited by the parochialism of an elite leadership wedded to a doctrinaire view of the status offender problem. As members of the probation department staff, they were well situated to influence department policy. They were successful there in developing a family crisis intervention program at a high level of professional competence. Their effort, through the DSO program, to move the locus of the program to the county's youth service centers was strongly supported by the politically sophisticated administrators of the county's Criminal Justice Planning Board. However, these advantages were offset by failure in the program planning phase to accommodate the divergent views of the status offender problem held by crucial elements of a youth service network, including in part court personnel and police agencies. In particular, success in efforts to "train" community-based agency workers in the use of family crisis intervention met with sharply limited success. The accomplishments of the program were confined to an expansion of the jurisdiction's foster home resources, the development of two well-run "crisis receiving homes" somewhat reluctantly used by some police agencies as a temporary alternative to the use of the detention center, and the establishment of a professionally staffed neighborhood center in one of Oakland's high-delinquency neighborhoods.

SPOKANE COUNTY

As the third of the three sites receptive to the message of the status offender deinstitutionalization movement, Spokane County launched a

DSO program distinctive for the exemplary way it mobilized community support. Favoring this development was the fact that the program took shape in a community with a strong concern for youth welfare, a coherent organizational structure committed to giving effective expression to that concern, and a reasonably full complement of youth-serving facilities. Several years prior to program inception, the Spokane Area Youth Committee (SAYC) was established by resolution of the Spokane City Council and the governing commission of Spokane County. The goals of the SAYC were to act as a policymaking body concerned with the needs of youth, and to coordinate the activities of both public and private youth-serving agencies in responding to those needs.

Unlike most coordinating efforts, which frequently perish in the hot sun of agency autonomy, the SAYC undertaking possessed a number of unique features. Its membership embraced the leadership of the entire spectrum of local organizations charged with the control, care, and education of the young. In addition to administrators of the juvenile court and of the police agencies of the county, its charter mandated the inclusion of the heads of the major private social agencies, the superintendent of its largest school district, a representative of the County Commission, the Spokane County Sheriff, the Spokane City Chief of Police, the sitting judge of the Spokane County Juvenile Court, and the Spokane regional director of the State Department of Social and Health Services. The members of the SAYC thus personally constituted the set of community influentials. Each had the power to determine policy for the agency represented.

As reflected in school disciplinary action, this display of initiative by the power brokers of Spokane County was the more notable in the face of little evidence of a high level of community tolerance for juvenile misbehavior. Moreover, there apparently existed little in the way of a tradition of providing placement facilities for troubled youth as an alternative to detention and institutional treatment. There was a distinct shortage of bed space in foster homes and group homes for this purpose. Above all, statutory provisions concerning status offense cases contained no prohibition of either pre- or postadjudication use of secure confinement.

However, as Spokane County undertook to reform its treatment of status offenders, very tentative similar moves were being made at the state level. Shortly after the program started in 1976, the juvenile code was altered to provide for a 30-day maximum commitment of incorrigibles to a diagnostic and treatment facility, a provision that was not to come into effect, however, until 1979. Even so, this change in the statute was silent about the use of detention in status offense cases. When, finally, in 1978 the state legislature moved decisively to alter the treatment of status offenders, it divested the juvenile court of jurisdiction in these cases, transferring legal authority to the state's major welfare agency, the Department of Social and Health Services. Thus, as in a number of other

program sites, legislative action for the deinstitutionalization of status offenders was proceeding simultaneously with the establishment of the federal status offender program. The case was somewhat different in this
jurisdiction because it was several years prior to the imposition of statutory restriction on the use of secure confinement for status offenders that
the Spokane County Juvenile Court had already taken the initiative in
ending their detention. The court had come to this view because of its
concern that status offenders were taking an excessively large share of its
resources. As one observer stated, "Status offenders had been a problem
because [the court] spent so much more time with them than with the
delinquent population."

A somewhat complex organizational structure was created to carry out
the DSO program. As the coordinating body, SAYC was regarded as an
inappropriate operational group. SAYC consequently developed Youth
Alternatives (YA) as a new organization with the mandate to receive referrals of status offenders from the police and the court, provide a family
crisis intervention service, evaluate client needs, and refer the case to an
established social agency appropriate to the presenting problem. Youth
Alternatives was established as a private agency, with a board consisting
of lower-level administrators of the same agencies whose executives
composed the SAYC board. With some misgivings, a well-placed and
respected juvenile court functionary was selected as the YA program director and was directed to recruit its staff, organize its board of directors,
and establish its operating procedures. The concern over the selection of
a program director identified with the court was that the shadow of the
court, with its formal procedures and devotion to the protection of the
community, would be cast over the enterprise. This turned out not to be
the case, as the program director brought with him an already established
court commitment to avoid so far as possible the use of detention and
correctional institutions in status offense cases. Despite the full involvement of the court in the Spokane County DSO program, at no time was
the program perceived as dominated by the court.

Program Design

With the court determined to divert all status offense cases not only
from detention but from court processing as well, YA became the specialized agency in Spokane County for dealing with status offenders. Since
the police are the main source of referral of status offense cases, particular effort was devoted to cultivating close collaboration with them. Police
at both the command level and the line level of the Spokane Police Department were involved in the planning of the program. Because there
was a sharp awareness that, as a YA worker put it, "there have always
been strong feelings [of hostility] between cops and social workers," a

number of methods were used to deal with the problem. During the early period of program operations, YA workers were invited to attend police roll call sessions to explain the purposes and procedures of the program. An important part of the training of newly recruited YA staff included riding in squad cars on routine police patrols. YA staff came ultimately to see many of the police as professionals "who were probably more in contact with more people more of the time than anyone else in town." In turn, the police on their part came to appreciate the 24-hour, on-call availability of YA workers to respond to their calls to take over in status offense arrest cases, relieving them of an unwelcome social work function. Particularly appreciated by the police was the YA practice of providing a follow-up report on the outcome of each case referred, including the agency, if any, to which the client was sent, whether a family conflict situation was resolved, and the like. This procedure was decisive in cementing the communication link between YA staff and the police.

Effective as these procedures were in inducing police cooperation, they were made possible basically by the solid support for the program by the top echelon of the Spokane Police Department. As one line officer interpreted the posture of the police chief, "[The officers] will do it this way [cooperate with the YA program] or maybe a little time off will teach them a little better." But quite apart from such official pressure, some police officers were sufficiently persuaded of the value of the program to volunteer their free time to assist the YA staff.

As one of the principal movers in the development of the Spokane DSO program, the juvenile court's role was essentially to refer to YA all status offense cases that some police officers insisted on bringing to court intake despite directives from their superiors. In addition, the court was instrumental in defining the size of the DSO client population by determining who would be eligible for program services. Initially, the court decided that all status offenders on probation for a prior delinquent offense would be ineligible, but that probationers with a prior status offense would be referred to YA. By law, the court could take jurisdiction in the latter cases since probation violators were defined as dependent and neglected. The decision rule was later altered to refer to YA all status offending delinquents on probation for minor offenses unless the remaining period of probation was greater than six months. By the end of the program period the eligibility rule finally included all delinquent probationers without respect to the length of the remaining probation period. Such cases were closed and dismissed prior to referral to YA.

Program Content

At the center of the YA treatment approach was the use of family crisis intervention as the initial step in dealing with the status offense problem.

While the program was designed to refer cases to community-based youth service agencies for counseling or other forms of help, there was a strong conviction that most status offenses reflected chronic parent-child conflict brought to crisis. The prevailing view of the cause of family conflict, strongly held by court personnel, was failure of the control agencies to hold parents accountable for the care and welfare of their children. Crisis intervention in the YA program was consequently designed to defuse the immediate conflict and to arrange for the reentry of the client into the family. An incidental but important effect of this approach was to reduce drastically the need for short-term out-of-home placement resources.

Essentially, the YA staff was organized to respond to police referrals of status offenders on a 24-hour basis, to provide a crisis intervention and diagnostic service, to return the offender to his or her home if possible, and, where further services were indicated, to refer the case to an appropriate youth service agency in the community.

Program Implementation Problems

Few and minor problems arose in the execution of the program design. A small number of police officers, concerned with the legality of diverting status offenders from court intake, persisted in bringing them to court. As mentioned, the court promptly referred these cases directly to YA without further processing. A somewhat more troublesome problem arose around the issue of YA referrals to the private sector social agencies of the community. There remained among some a concern about YA as a competitive threat for "holding on" to clients beyond the initial crisis intervention. One agency executive asserted, for example, that YA expanded the crisis intervention procedure to include counseling. This was faulted on grounds that for therapeutic purposes the two types of service should be provided by different persons in different agency settings. YA staff members denied the charge, pointing out that the average time devoted to each case was restricted to slightly more than one day.

Nonetheless, there remained a problem built into the program design that somewhat limited the use of community-based agencies in serving the needs of status offenders. Based on the view of the status offense problem as an eruption of family conflict into crisis, YA found relatively little need in a large number of cases to do more than defuse the family conflict and return the child home. Their records show that crisis intervention was the sole service provided in half of their cases. Another 25 percent were referred for longer-term counseling, with the final one-fourth of cases receiving a variety of services other than longer-term counseling. However, the fact that brief crisis intervention seemed all that was required for so large a proportion of program clients does not necessarily mean that no further intervention was needed. This may also mean that the program served a large number of clients for whom even brief crisis intervention may have been superfluous. Indeed, Spokane shared with many of the other programs an inability to avoid a net-widening effect, in which many youth who would otherwise have been spared exposure to "treatment" were brought to YA as clients. In its zeal to cooperate with the program, the county's major police agency, the Spokane City Police Department, discovered an unintended further purpose that the program could serve. With the YA's 24-hour availability for receiving status offender cases, the police came to appreciate the convenience of avoiding the troublesome tasks of either attempting to make a "field adjustment" and returning the youth home or transporting the offender to the court's detention facility together with the required documentation.

Summary

The DSO program in Spokane County was a striking case of community receptivity to status offender deinstitutionalization based entirely on a commitment to its value by the decision makers responsible for the control and socialization of the youth population. Spokane County differed in this respect from the two other receptive sites, where program support was founded either solely on the initiative of the juvenile court in the face of substantial official and community opposition, or on growing legislative endorsement for status offender deinstitutionalization. Prior to the development of the DSO program, Spokane County had fostered a climate of community support by creating a general youth welfare organization with a constituency of opinion leaders, who then accorded first priority to the status offender problem. This body developed Youth Alternatives as a specialized community-based organization designated to deal with all status offenders detained by the police or brought to the court. Around-the-clock program services consisted principally of family crisis intervention and case diagnosis, with some referral to private sector youth service agencies. By the end of the two years of federal funding, Youth Alternatives was regarded by the court, the enforcement agencies, and, with some qualification, the private social agencies of Spokane County as having provided a viable and useful tool in coping with the status offense problem.

chapter **6**

Conflicted and Resistive Sites

with Elaine M. Corry

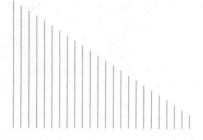

T*he reluctance to grasp the nettle* of status offender deinstitutionalization on the part of five of the eight sites in which DSO programs were evaluated differed in degree and character. The statewide programs in Illinois and Connecticut were caught up in chronic conflict over program efforts to remove status offender cases from the exclusive control of the court. This, after all, was what the DSO program was intended to accomplish. In two additional statewide programs, Delaware and South Carolina, there was from the beginning no prospect that conflict over this issue would arise, but for quite special reasons. Little inclination existed there to question either the legitimacy or the appropriateness of the court's total control over both serious and minor juvenile misbehavior. Although there are medium-sized cities in both states, their populations are predominantly small town and rural, with political and social attitudes rooted in traditional values. Among these values is an intolerance of youthful deviant behavior and a view of formal legal control as continuous with the informal controls exercised by parents, schools, and neighbors. That minor and noncriminal juvenile infractions might be more constructively dealt with separately from the invocation of legal machinery was, consequently, an alien notion. Those in the forefront of efforts to reform the juvenile justice system in such settings, if only in the treatment of status offenders, were constrained to accommodate the pervasive view that the system was not in need of reform, and had to confine themselves to tentative and cautious moves.

A fifth site in the conflicted and resistive category, operating with very limited federal funds, is omitted from this set of program descriptions. By design, the DSO program in Clark County, Washington, avoided conflict over program control in two ways. First, its principal feature was merely the addition of two persons to the probation department staff of the court. They were assigned the tasks of receiving and investigating all status offender cases brought to the court by enforcement agencies and providing individual and family counseling in the cases they could handle with their highly limited personnel and time resources. Second, since the court had made itself the locus of the program, virtually no effort was made to bring together into a network of youth service agencies a set of local organizations that might serve the needs of status offenders. Cases requiring out-of-home placement were referred to the statewide agency that provided foster home services. The single additional program element that qualified as community centered was a group family counseling service for parents of status offenders conducted on a voluntary basis by a neighborhood church.

ILLINOIS

The DSO program in Illinois took shape during a period following the passage of legislation to divert noncriminal young offenders from the standard processing accorded delinquent youth. The state's Minors in Need of Supervision statute prescribed referral of the so-called MINS cases to the statewide Department of Children and Family Services (DCFS) for treatment. While foreclosing the commitment of MINS cases to institutions for delinquent offenders, the statute did not prohibit the use of detention, and it was soon found that juvenile courts throughout the state were using their discretion in this respect to detain large numbers of status offenders.

Failure of the pre-DSO effort in Illinois to induce its courts to reduce the preadjudication detention of status offenders foreshadowed the problem that was to confront its DSO program throughout the two years of its existence. Those who were determined to foster the status offender deinstitutionalization movement in Illinois, including principally the private youth-serving agencies and the state's criminal justice planning body, were consequently faced with a situation of limited opportunity. The recalcitrance of the courts to reduce the use of detention in the interest of implementing the MINS statute was read as a signal that, even in the "progressive" jurisdiction of metropolitan Cook County, there would be little prospect that the court would willingly share its control of status offender cases with community-based youth service agencies. Thus, while the proponents of the deinstitutionalization movement in Illinois were constrained to accommodate the power of the courts, the DSO program remained encumbered with the tension of conflict between the two.

Organizational Design

While crucial in determining its basic character, this was not the only conflicting interest engaged in the development of the Illinois DSO program. Four distinct issues arose, some of which provoked spirited controversy in the planning of the program. The Office of Juvenile Justice had declared an interest in funding a number of statewide programs. In part, because of the earlier legislative initiative in establishing its MINS statute, Illinois was regarded as a candidate site. However, the feasibility of going statewide was sharply questioned in some quarters because of the size of the state and its political, economic, and social diversity. Location of the program in either the single large urban area of metropolitan Chicago or in a limited set of its more rural counties appeared to be more manageable. The proponents of statewide coverage prevailed.

This decision dictated the resolution of a second issue. It concerned the question of whether the organization to be designated as the agency to conduct the operations of the DSO program should be drawn from the public or the private sector. A number of large and well-established agencies in the youth field entered the lists to become the DSO grant recipients, but most eager to take on the task were the Youth Service Bureaus. These had expanded during preceding years with substantial funding by the Illinois Law Enforcement Commission (ILEC), and were conducting diversion programs in many localities. However, since it was hoped that the DSO program was to be established in all regions of the state, there was need for a statewide, centrally administered agency equipped to provide services to youth. The organization that most fully met these requirements was the Illinois Department of Children and Family Services. The agency had, in addition, access to the supplemental public funds for program support that were certain to be needed. To a chorus of criticism from the proponents of grass-roots resident involvement in youth work, ILEC selected DCFS as the DSO grant recipient.

Suffering from what it felt to be inadequate funding for its established program, and burdened with a formidable work load, DCFS accepted the assignment with markedly restrained enthusiasm. Instead of expanding its existing staff with DSO federal funds to meet its added undertaking, it created the Illinois Status Offender Services (ISOS) as a separate unit under its general supervision. As ISOS faced the task of devising the concrete procedures required to implement DSO program objectives, a third issue emerged. ISOS undertook to identify, select, and contract with youth service agencies in the several counties in which it succeeded in establishing active and viable program operations. The issue concerned whether to contract with the old-line, well-established youth agencies or to seek out as service providers the smaller and newly created agencies that had emerged in response to the expansion of the human service "industry," but were neighborhood based and staffed by paraprofessional workers with close ties to local residents. The outcome was a split decision. The program in Cook County, the jurisdiction of overshadowing concern because of the size of its population and its prominence in the state's juvenile offender problem, opted for the use of small, neighborhood-based agencies. In the downstate regions, the ISOS staff itself, recruited from among professionally trained social workers, conducted the DSO program.

The other major issue, and the one that imparted to the Illinois DSO program design its distinctive character, concerned the distribution of program emphasis between the two main DSO program objectives. These were, on the one hand, the development of community-based treatment facilities for status offenders and, on the other, the reduction of their preadjudication detention. Given the climate of judicial opinion in Illinois, the outcome was hardly in doubt. The use of community-based youth services for status offenders entailed to some degree the sharing of the court's control of these cases with noncourt agencies. Courts in Illinois had already shown in their response to the MINS statute their opposition to any move to reduce their discretion in the disposition of status offense cases. The strategy consequently adopted by ISOS was to avoid engaging this issue head on by restricting the program to no more than the reduction of the use of detention prior to case adjudication.

Program Content

Operating in 11 of the 18 DCFS regions of the state, ISOS launched its Alternatives to Detention program with an OJJ grant of $1.5 million. As its name suggests, the program undertook no more than to provide an alternative to the placement of status offenders in detention centers pending a court hearing. The program population thus consisted of status offenders for whom a petition for a court hearing was initiated, typically by the police. In effect, the youth was to be maintained briefly in the community while technically in detention status prior to a court hearing for the disposition of the case. The period of "community detention" under the control and supervision of the Alternatives worker varied among court jurisdictions. In Cook County, the period was restricted to 10 court days.

The interception operation of the Alternatives program required that agreements be established not only with each court, but with local enforcement agencies as well. Agreements with police were entered into in which all arrested status offenders on whom a court petition was filed would be referred to an Alternatives worker for temporary detention. This type of agreement was most fully carried out in Cook County, and may be treated as prototypical of those the program tried to establish in the downstate regions, but with somewhat less success.

On the basis of an agreement with the major enforcement agency of the county, the Chicago Police Department, officers taking a status offender into custody called on a "hotline" to a central switchboard maintained by ISOS. The message was then relayed to the ISOS worker covering the police district concerned. An Alternatives staff member attached to a contracted agency was required to appear at the police station—within an hour on the average—to take charge of the youth. In the meantime, the police officer prepared a request for a petition, to be reviewed the following day by the intake unit of the juvenile court. In the absence of this procedure, the youth would have been placed in the court's detention center pending the screening intake on the next court day. The Alternatives worker now had the task of assuring the appearance of the youth at the court hearing if that turned out to be the decision of the intake screening unit.

The Alternatives worker typically returned the youth to his or her home under the worker's supervision. If the home situation made this impossible, the worker had available temporary foster care facilities provided by the contracted agency. When the police-initiated petition was reviewed by the intake screening unit, the Alternatives worker furnished whatever information he or she had acquired on the case, but participated in the discussion of the case only at the invitation of the probation officer heading the screening unit. If the decision was to grant the petition for a court hearing, the worker was permitted to retain supervision of the case for the 10-court-day maximum period. In effect, then, the Alternatives to Detention program placed a detained status offender under the very temporary supervision of a community-based youth service agency, whose workers functioned as one variety of "youth advocates."

This was the pattern of operation in Cook County. There, the chief judge of the juvenile court had issued an order prohibiting the routine placement of status offenders in the court's detention center prior to a formal court hearing. The effect of the order was virtually to force police officers to refer cases to the Alternatives program. The situation was quite different, however, in the downstate regions of DCFS. Many judges

refused to issue a similar blanket order banning pre-adjudication detention, although in some jurisdictions agreements were obtained permitting
the program to serve those youth judges felt might be benefited. Typically, status offenders were brought into detention centers on petition,
their cases were reviewed by probation officers, and a selection was
made of those that appeared to be appropriate for the Alternatives program. Those regarded as "hard-core" cases remained in detention until
their court hearings.

Program Implementation Problems

As noted earlier, the decision to use the DCFS as the grant recipient
evoked vigorous objection from those sectors of the youth service community convinced that only small-scale, neighborhood-based agencies
enjoying the support and participation of residents were equipped to exercise effective control over the behavior of delinquent youth. But while
the proponents of the grass-roots approach lost that battle, in Cook
County at lest they won the war. DCFS had in effect distanced itself from
the DSO program by creating ISOS as the operating agency, and giving it
the power to determine program policy. Without significant opposition,
ISOS from the beginning adopted the policy of seeking out and contracting with neighborhood-based organizations prepared to staff the Alternatives to Detention program in their local police districts with youth advocacy workers. These were mostly paraprofessionals ranging from
street-wise young men to students enrolled in community colleges, all of
whom possessed as their important qualification a knowledge of neighborhood residents and their problems.

As might be expected, creating an organizational structure of this design was a slow and arduous process. Both police officials and probation
department personnel were initially unhappy with the prospect of diverting youth taken into custody to Alternatives workers whose credentials
for assuming their responsibilities were regarded as dubious. Further,
many of the contracted agencies were relatively newly organized and had
little background of experience in recruiting, organizing, and supervising
a youth service staff. For example, it took virtually the entire first year of
the two-year program before the Alternatives workers achieved an average one-hour response time to pick up a status offender in police custody. These and other difficulties were eventually overcome, but, as was
true of the DSO program at all the other sites, program implementation
suffered from OJJ's failure to provide the lead time needed to overcome
initial problems.

More specifically, problems in achieving program objectives arose in
relations with both the police and the court. As to the former, once the
misgivings of police officials regarding the qualifications of Alternatives
workers were put to rest, and problems of response time to police calls

were resolved, police at the line level cooperated with the program only too well. The police came in time to appreciate the service afforded them by the program in quickly taking status offenders off their hands, relieving them of the task of transporting the youth to the detention center. But in time, also, the police relieved themselves of the burden of deciding whether to file a petition for a court hearing in the many marginal cases that, in the absence of the readily available services of the Alternatives program, might well have resulted in a warning, a reprimand, and a "station adjustment." These practices had the effect of net widening, that is, of increasing without need the exposure to court processing of many more minor offenders than would otherwise have occurred. On the other side of the picture as well, according to Alternatives workers, was an increase in the number of delinquent offenders, many of whom are also additionally chargeable as status offenders, who were referred to the program when police felt "the kid needed a break." But it was the net-widening effect that persisted as a serious and unmanageable problem for the program.

While persistent, troublesome, and never altogether resolved, problems with the court were of a quite different order. These arose not at the judicial level, the source of the court order compelling police cooperation, but in relations with its probation department. This was the more surprising since the reach of deinstitutionalization undertaken by ISOS, restricted to a very brief period of preadjudication "community detention," would hardly seem to invade the jurisdictional domain of the department. The program was intentionally designed to achieve the most modest of objectives in order to create the least possible disturbance to the operations of the court and of its probation department. The most that could be hoped for, consequently, was that probation department personnel would be persuaded that the use of community-based youth advocate agencies to prevent the preadjudication detention of status offenders was a constructive and fruitful innovation.

They were not so persuaded. They found many reasons to oppose the program, some justified and others openly self-serving. Most justified was the complaint that the program needlessly imposed an added burden on the department by increasing the number of alleged status offenders they were required to process through court intake. In addition, department personnel occasionally experienced difficulty at the end of the ten-day period in locating youth that the Alternatives workers may have placed in foster homes, frequently in the far reaches of the county. But their main reason for opposing the Alternatives program was a refusal to acknowledge any shortcoming of probation department procedures in dealing responsibly and competently with status offenders. The only deficiency they were prepared to admit was attributed to a shortage of funds to enable them to purchase the services for status offenders that the court could not itself provide. As the head of the department put it:

There is no question in our minds that the court could do a better job [than Alternatives workers] of providing alternatives to detention. . . . But we don't have the money in our staff to implement such a program. Philosophically, I don't think any of us in the court are opposed to the idea of nonsecure detention. . . . But I still think that the court needs that bottom line control, because it's never been proved to me that another agency outside the court is able to provide it adequately.

Finally, as a source of conflict during the early stage of the program, probation officers found objectionable the efforts of Alternatives workers, whom they regarded as lacking their own level of professional training, to function as advocates of the welfare interests of youth under their temporary control. But most telling in their critical response to the Alternatives program was the tendency to ignore its essential feature, namely, the elimination of preadjudication detention.

Summary

The conflicts that attended the development of the DSO program in the Illinois site are traceable in the first instance to judicial reluctance to transfer any part of court discretion in dealing with status offense cases. It was thus unlikely from the outset that the leaders of the status offender deinstitutionalization movement in Illinois could undertake any more than the most minimal alteration in established court practices. While this situation defined the fundamental character of the DSO enterprise in the Illinois site, those who were determined to push the reform were sharply divided in their views of how best to exploit their reduced opportunity. The decision to mount a statewide program, favored by OJJ, was challenged by those who preferred to concentrate program resources in a limited number of jurisdictions in order to demonstrate the program's delinquency reduction value. Those who favored locating administrative control of the program in the private sector youth service agencies were unhappy with the decision to use a statewide public agency for this purpose. The decision to use as service providers in the major metropolitan jurisdiction of Cook County a set of small, neighborhood-based organizations and agencies staffed by "indigenous" paraprofessionals was sharply and persistently questioned in many quarters.

As ultimately organized, the DSO program was conducted by the quasi-autonomous Illinois Status Offender Services, created and administered by the state's Division of Children and Family Services. ISOS undertook only to take charge of status offenders on whom police had entered a petition, and to provide helpful supervision pending the court hearing. Concentration of program resources on "community detention" precluded by design efforts to develop a network of community-based youth services for adjudicated status offenders as an alternative to other forms of standard court dispositions. In Cook County, ISOS engaged the services of neighborhood-based agencies to implement the program; in downstate regions the function was performed by an ISOS-recruited staff of professionally trained workers.

CONNECTICUT

The second of the two conflicted sites, Connecticut, launched its DSO program into waters mined by a type of opposition that was entirely specific to the actors engaged in the enterprise. The opposition was not to its manifest objectives, but to the auspices under which they were to be achieved and to the burden of providing information useful for evaluation, which, uniquely in Connecticut, the program was designed to produce. The underlying conflict that characterized the Illinois site was a relatively straightforward matter of judicial disagreement with the asserted pragmatic and ethical superiority of using noncourt agencies to treat status offenders. The judiciary in Connecticut accepted the DSO tenet, but remained convinced throughout the life of the project that the placement of adjudicated status offenders in community-based agencies and their control should remain in the hands of the court.

The absence of strong judicial support was not the only obstacle the program faced. Connecticut statutes made no distinction between status offenders and youth who committed criminal offenses. Both types of offenders were subject to secure confinement, although there was some reduction in the use of long-term institutional confinement for delinquent youth generally during several years preceding the DSO program, a possible indication of growing sensitivity to the national deinstitutionalization movement. As measured by school suspensions and expulsions, there was little tolerance in this state for minor juvenile misbehavior; Connecticut was among the highest on this measure among the eight evaluated sites. Paradoxically, however, the state was well supplied with out-of-home placement facilities for youthful offenders, suggesting, as turned out to be the case, an ongoing development of youth services under private agency auspices.

Organization of the Program

The Connecticut program was developed by the state's Council on Human Services (CHS) with the participation, support, and sponsorship of Connecticut's criminal justice planning agency, the Criminal Justice Commission (CJC). The program grant was awarded to the CJC, which in turn subgranted the funds for administration to the CHS. Action to develop contracts with private sector youth services agencies had hardly gotten under way when a newly elected state administration abolished the CHS in an economy move. The Justice Commission then transferred the grant to the state's Department of Children and Youth Services (DCYS).

The program was designed in close collaboration with the OJJ-funded site evaluators at the University of Connecticut. Under their leadership and urging, DCYS made two basic program design decisions. The first was to select as the appropriate target population only those status offenders for whom there was virtual certainty that they would otherwise have been placed in detention prior to a court hearing. This was seen as a crucial cautionary move to keep the program focus on the reduction of secure confinement (deinstitutionalization), and to prevent its transformation into a "diversion" program serving a mixed bag including status offenders who would in any case never have seen the inside of a detention center. As a result, eligibility for program services was rigidly restricted to hard-core recidivistic status offenders. At the insistence of the court, excluded as well from program services were cases with mixed status and criminal charges, status offenders with prior criminal charges still pending, and those on probation for a prior status offense. Furthermore, to ensure that only those clients who were actually "at risk of detention" would be referred to program services, that phrase was operationally defined as actual placement, however temporary, in one of the state's four detention centers.

The second crucial decision was to build into the program a number of elements of experimental design. Treatment approaches in dealing with the problems of status offenders were to differ in each of the state's three judicial districts with a view to testing the comparative efficacy of each. In one district, a court-based minimum intervention program was to be established; in a second, there was to be a community-based minimum intervention program; and in the third, a community-based maximum intervention program was planned. Status offenders at risk of detention who elected to participate in the program were then to be randomly assigned to standard court treatment and to the program model established for the judicial district in which they resided, with all charges dropped. Although this design was supported by DCYS and endorsed by the OJJ *evaluation* monitor, it encountered strong objection from the OJJ *program* monitor on grounds that status offenders randomly sorted into the normal court processing alternative would be denied program benefits. The proposed experimental procedure was consequently modified to exclude randomized assignment of program eligible clients. The sole element of the design that survived was assignment of status offenders to the program type placed in their judicial district.

In sum, the Connecticut program plan called for (a) restriction of program services to cases of "pure" status offense in which the charged youth was neither on probation for a prior status offense nor had criminal charges pending, and was "otherwise detainable" as evidenced by the fact of actual detention; (b) referral to program services only with the signed consent of client and parents; and (c) provision solely of the specific type of treatment intervention assigned to the judicial district in which the client resided, variously furnished by probation workers or by community-based youth services agencies.

Program Implementation Problems

As in all the others, the DSO program in the Connecticut site had to deal on the one side with the court and on the other with the community agencies engaged to provide services to status offenders. In this site, problems in DCYS relations with the court arose, basically, from the court's strong reservations about both the need for and the value of the DSO program, despite its pro forma agreement to extend cooperation. The court took the position that its procedures in dealing with status offenders were altogether adequate for the protection of both the youth and the community, and that its own judgment regarding appropriate case disposition was soundly grounded in experience. This view of its competence in deciding cases was described by a member of the DCYS staff:

> The court believed that they were doing a fairly good job, and that all they needed was money to place the kid when they made a decision to do so. So if they felt that a particular status offender belonged in [the state's secure facility], they felt they had good reason for that. There was a whole host of other things the kid might have done, although [the court] might not have been able to prove it. The only thing that was provable might have been a status offense. But they really honestly believed that when they sent a status offender to [the secure facility] there were very good reasons for it. So they strongly believed in what they were doing.

Beyond this, with respect to the need for reducing recourse to the court in status offense cases, the court was inclined to view the substantial expansion of the state's Youth Service Bureau (YSB) network as the primary resource for this purpose. The fact was that with substantial LEAA funding over a period of years the YSB network had expanded since 1970 to cover a total of 54 local communities in the state, serving approximately 80 percent of the state's youth population.

Given the court's posture on the program, it was perhaps inevitable that its probation personnel would take a similarly oppositional stand. As a leading DSO staff member put it:

> You have it from your top level [of the court] saying, "We don't like your research, we don't like your program, we don't think this is the way you handle

status offenders." In all honesty, you can't expect probation officers to fight that system.

And, as elaborated by another DSO staff member:

> The court very strongly believes that detention is a preferable place for kids in some situations where, for example, a sexually acting out girl who threatens to run away from home is safe in detention because the staff in detention [centers] know how to handle 13-year-old promiscuous girls. . . . There are a great many [voluntary] agencies in [the judicial district] that have worked with clients before they came into the court system. There is a philosophy often expressed by probation officers and court personnel . . . that the court can handle cases where voluntary agencies fail. The need for the court is because of the failure of voluntary agencies. [They say that] kids who have been involved in voluntary programs have bombed out, that voluntary agencies can't help kids, and that they need to lock them up in a secure place in order to deal with them effectively.

Its lack of enthusiasm for the objectives of the DSO program notwithstanding, it would be inaccurate to conclude that the court opposed the deinstitutionalization of status offenders. It appeared to be the court's view that in the Connecticut situation, with its well-developed network of community-based youth service agencies engaged in preventive programming, the status offenders who were referred to the court were principally those for whom prior intervention efforts had failed. Even with these, the court felt it made every reasonable effort to obtain suitable remediation services. In brief, the court saw itself as using detention and institutionalization in status offender cases only as a last resort. Moreover, in the traditional manner the court defined as an essential aspect of its responsibility the need to take into account the entire pattern of behavior of the juvenile charged with a current status offense. Thus the Connecticut juvenile court regarded itself as already engaged in what may be termed a program of "maximum feasible deinstitutionalization."

The task of enlisting the services of community-based agencies presented the second of the two major program implementation problems. Most consequential was the objection the agencies raised to the provision that only those status offenders placed in detention would be eligible for referral to program services. Handicapping program implementation as well was its experimental feature requiring contracted service agencies in each judicial district to restrict their treatment procedures to the type prescribed for that district.

The requirement of detention prior to referral for program services was regarded by the state's major youth service agencies as altogether unacceptable, resulting in the end in their refusal to participate. This provision in particular alienated the network of Youth Service Bureaus, considered to be most desirable as potential service providers. A key DSO staff member described the response of the state's major social agencies in these words:

> I thought it would be just great if the private agencies could come together and plan a joint response, with each one providing the expertise that they had [in order to implement the maximum intervention model]. They did a whole planning process. But they screamed bloody murder when the program planners said the kids had to go to detention. . . . They screamed bloody murder [about the need for 24 hour, 7 days a week availability to effect quick removal of status offenders from detention centers], although I think they could have worked that out. And, they weren't hungry [for the funding]. This is a United Way group of agencies that makes its own way plus.

Another staffer nonetheless defended the rationale of restricting DSO services to detained status offenders:

> [There was a serious problem] in getting . . . really top-flight bidders on the contracts [for services to status offenders]. Our dream was that the United Way and the Youth Service Bureaus would just jump at this. The main reason was that the large social agencies in [one of the state's three judicial districts] was opposed to the child being brought to detention. They wanted the child to come directly from the police. Those of us who planned the project with the federal monitor agreed that if we let the children be referred from the police, the police would flood the project, and we really wouldn't get the status offender that was earmarked for detention We'd be getting all kinds of kids.

Program personnel were of course acutely aware of the difficulties the detention requirement created for program implementation. In addition to losing the support of the most qualified service providers, the requirement tended to limit program eligibles to the most chronic status offense cases and to reduce the numbers available for the comparative test of treatment procedures. The policy of limiting program eligibles to those placed in detention was nonetheless defended as representing an honest implementation of the purpose of the national status offender program. In this view, its purpose was to test and demonstrate the feasibility of *deinstitutionalizing* status offenders. Indeed, it was seen by program planners as perhaps the only genuine attempt to do so, compared to the way in which funded status offender programs at other sites were conducted. Thus, according to one staffer:

> [Our program] was probably the only one [of those funded] that was a true deinstitutionalization rather than a diversion project, because we were in fact focused on kids institutionalized, that is, detained. Again, the greatest anxiety [in organizing the program] was our insistence that the only way a kid could

qualify for this program was if you brought him to the detention center. That's the strongest point in the program competitively across the country, and it's the weakest point in terms of program acceptability in Connecticut. . . . All of the [status offender] programs except ours were doing police diversion and pre-police diversion. Ours was the only funded program focused solely on deinstitutionalization. . . . How do you justify [the use of money] for deinstitutionalization of kids who in fact would never go to an institution? We took the tougher course, and we took a hell of a lot of heat for it. We incurred the resentment of most of the community programs in Connecticut, and Connecticut has a lot of community programs.

The effort at experimental variation of treatment approaches created its own set of problems. Service agencies raised two objections. First, service providers in each of the judicial districts would have preferred to be assigned the maximum intervention model, as this corresponded to their normal mode of treatment. Two of the districts were assigned the minimum intervention model, one court based, the other community based. The districts that were denied the maximum intervention model felt, as one observer put it, "that they had been done a dirty turn." Although an attempt was made initially to deal rationally with this issue by allocating the maximum model to the district with the fullest complement of service agencies, for reasons that were unclear the court reallocated the models before the program got under way, with the maximum model assigned to a district with less than desirable capacity to carry it out.

Ideological objections to the experimental feature of the program were raised as well. The program was viewed by some of the service agencies as an opportunity to explore and develop creative ideas in reaching and treating status offenders. The opportunity was frustrated, they felt, by the need to restrict treatment to the specified intervention models in order to obtain the data needed for the comparative test of intervention approaches.

Summary

The DSO effort in Connecticut was unique in taking seriously and literally the federal program mandate to focus on the task of deinstitutionalizing status offenders. This it did by restricting its target population to those who were placed in detention pending adjudication, thus avoiding the tendency, evident in the DSO programs at many other sites, to devote program resources to status offenders unlikely in very many cases to be detained. The distinction between the deinstitutionalization of status offenders as the reduction in their secure confinement and their diversion as the reduction in resort to official processing at all levels of the juvenile justice system is clear in concept. But in practice the distinction is readily lost, with a consequent diffusion of program resources and effort devoted to large numbers of youth for whom neither detention nor institutionalization is likely to be in store.

The Connecticut experience thus offers an opportunity to examine the problems associated with a "pure" status offender deinstitutionalization program. The "conflicted" character of the Connecticut DSO program derived largely from its assiduous focus on detained status offenders. Tensions in relation to the court surfaced over the issue of supplanting the judgment of program personnel for court decisions regarding appropriate case disposition. The court's reluctant agreement to permit program staff to refer to community agencies those status offenders who agreed to participate in the program preempted its own judgment in the matter. This procedure cut across the court's own already developed practice of utilizing the state's placement facilities, Youth Service Bureaus, and other community-based youth service agencies for both preadjudicated as well as adjudicated juvenile offenders. In fact, the insistence of the DSO program to serve only detained status offenders induced the court to place in detention larger numbers than might otherwise have been the case. This resulted in the somewhat anomalous finding of an increase in detention between the preprogram and the program periods, as shown in the data in Chapter 10. The court, in other words, saw itself as engaged in a DSO program of its own.

The insistence of the Connecticut DSO program on strict adherence to a detention reduction objective created a quite different type of conflict with the state's youth service agencies. These agencies displayed a naive, and perhaps understandable, inability to recognize as valid a distinction between deinstitutionalization and diversion. Informed during the program planning stage that only detained status offenders were to be referred for service, the major "main-line" agencies rejected the opportunity to participate.

The subsidiary conflict centering on the effort to design evaluability into the program by systematically varying the treatment approaches in serving the needs of status offenders, while unique to Connecticut, was not altogether absent from DSO programs in other sites. Elsewhere, however, such conflict was precluded by the refusal of DSO program personnel to accord the same high priority to evaluation aims.

The Connecticut experience, finally, raises the question of the feasibility of maintaining a program of status offender deinstitutionalization as distinctive from the more generic diversion programs. The preventive, "treatment," doctrine of youth service agencies, whose participation in the deinstitutionalization effort is crucial, is likely to remain an inescapable obstacle. Moreover, as was evident in Illinois, as well as in the Connecticut case, courts in many jurisdictions are likely to regard themselves as altogether competent to conduct their own DSO-type programs and to decide by their own lights which among status offenders should and should not be subjected to preadjudication detention.

As noted earlier, the distinction between the Illinois and Connecticut pair of conflicted sites and the two resistive sites to be described below is a matter of degree. In none of these four sites was there the preexisting commitment found in the receptive sites to the value of avoiding the secure confinement of status offenders, limiting their contact with the agents of juvenile justice, and engaging the services of community-based agencies to deflect them from careers of delinquency. The conflicted sites "bought into" only part of this package of objectives. They endorsed the aims of judicious reduction in the use of secure confinement and the fuller use of community-based agencies, but they retained a strong conviction that the control of the deinstitutionalization effort should be centered in the court. On the other hand, in Delaware and South Carolina, the two resistive sites, support for all three of these basic objectives ranged from minimal to nonexistent. These sites are characterized as resistive in the specific sense that the DSO doctrine was regarded as a strange and alien intrusion upon their traditional conduct of juvenile justice.

Why, then, did they submit applications for federal funds to launch a DSO program? In all jurisdictions there may be found those attuned to "progressive" efforts at juvenile justice reform. Located principally in the professional human service community, and not without some standing in the juvenile justice system, they were predictably eager to participate in the federal DSO program. On their part, those wanting in enthusiasm for DSO aims could see in the infusion of federal funds an opportunity to supplement their budgets, even if at the cost of undertaking an uncongenial innovation.

DELAWARE

The Delaware program exemplifies the adaptation of the DSO reform that characterized the two resistive sites. A small border state consisting of three counties, Delaware shares a southern regional culture rooted in a rural and small-town economy in spite of the presence in its northernmost county of the thriving industrial metropolis of Wilmington. In regions of this kind, social control generally, particularly the control of juvenile behavior, is traditionally informal, relying for its effect on the face-to-face mutual surveillance indigenous to the small community. Formal agencies of justice in such settings tend to be viewed as an organized extension of the efforts of parents, schools, and neighbors to check and correct the deviant conduct of the young. With respect to juvenile misconduct, the use of the criminal sanction thus tends to be seen not as different in kind from the failed efforts at informal control, but as their amplification through the use of coercive restraint. Delaware, for example, was among the most intolerant of status offenders among the DSO program sites as measured by rates of school suspensions and expulsions and, as will be seen, exercised total control of its DSO program. Delaware's juvenile code imposed no statutory restriction on the use of secure confinement for status offenders. The state had relatively sparse resources for out-of-home placements and status offenders serviced by its DSO program underwent deep penetration into its juvenile justice system. Given these background factors, the feature of DSO doctrine aimed at the diversion of status offenders from court processing in the interest of stigma reduction was spontaneously regarded as its least urgent requirement.

Program Design and Organization

An OJJ grant of slightly under $1 million to Delaware, supplemented by state funds, was initially administered by the state's Division of Services to Children and Youth, a unit of the Department of Health and Social Services, under the guidance of an advisory council appointed by the governor. Reorganization of the state's health and social service functions at the end of the first program year eliminated this division, and program administration was shifted to the Governor's Commission on Criminal Justice.

The Delaware program was designed to provide a set of community-based services as an alternative to the detention and institutionalization of status offenders. However, without question or controversy the selection for program services of youth brought to court on status offense charges was solidly lodged in the hands of the court. Program funds were used to staff a court intake unit assigned solely to deal with status offense cases. Such units were established in the family court branches in each of the state's three counties. The special court intake units identified cases on the court docket entered on status offense charges, obtained a dismissal of the charges in those cases deemed suitable for program services, made a determination of the presenting problem, provided crisis counseling, and returned the youth home if possible, arranging in the meantime for referral to needed services, including placement outside the home if indicated.

A second and unique component of the program was a legal advocacy service, contracted to a private agency, the Community Legal Aid Society, Inc. (CLASI). In addition to providing legal counsel at court hearings in status offense cases that went to adjudication, CLASI's main task was to conduct a continuing review of cases institutionalized at the state's two training schools. They identified those committed for status offenses, reviewed their case histories, and in selected cases initiated proceedings to return the person home or to placement facilities. CLASI undertook in addition to provide counseling and psychological services for some of the status offenders whose releases were obtained.

A third element of program structure was still another status offender unit located in the state's Division of Social Services. It developed placement facilities, assigned youth to appropriate placements, and maintained general supervision of these cases. The unit was staffed by six social workers, two in Newcastle County, one each in the two lower counties, and an additional worker to serve both. Their support came from program funds.

Diagnostic and case evaluation services were contracted to three counseling centers, one in each county. The centers provided individual counseling and, if needed, medical diagnosis for cases referred to them by the status offender court intake unit and the comparable unit in the Division of Social Services. The centers also furnished family counseling when it was considered appropriate.

Finally, residential services were provided in the form of shelter care and long-term group foster care. An eight-bed shelter facility was operated in Wilmington, supplemented by foster homes. In the two lower counties shelter care was provided exclusively by foster homes. An effort to establish an eight-bed shelter facility in the two southern counties was successfully opposed by the community selected for its location.

The program design thus included the standard complement of counseling and diagnostic services. The single unusual feature of the Delaware program was its provision of a legal advocacy service. Of the seven DSO programs reviewed here, Delaware may seem unlikely as the only site to be concerned with the legal rights of status offenders. However, this service was established as a major program focus for two reasons. First, unlike those at other sites where most of the effort was directed to the diversion of status offenders from preadjudication detention, the Delaware DSO program took seriously the mandate of the program to remove status offenders from long-term institutions. Second, again in contrast to many other sites, in Delaware long-term institutions for delinquents included a high proportion committed for status offenses.

Program Content

As noted, all cases appearing on the court calendar were routinely examined by the status offender court intake unit, which had also been given court authority to remove all status offense cases found still in detention. Except in cases of repeated runaway, chronic incorrigibility, mental disturbance, or occasional parent referrals, the unit terminated the adjudication process and initiated services. According to one estimate, approximately 90 percent of cases determined by the unit to involve primarily status offenses were returned to their homes. The balance were held for a court hearing if the status offender unit determined that there was a need for out-of-home placement or institutionalization. A court order was then required to transfer custody to the Department of Social Services under the care of its status offender unit.

For most cases, however, the status offender court intake unit initiated services by arranging for crisis counseling while developing an assessment of the underlying individual or family problem. The intake unit's service procedures took up to 30 days to complete, during which time counseling might be provided intermittently or contact with the youth maintained by telephone. Apparently, much if not most of the services made available to status offenders were provided by the court's special intake unit, although in theory it was to furnish only crisis counseling and case assessment. The court was thus fully and centrally involved in the Delaware DSO program, offering a sharp contrast with DSO programs at sites that encouraged the direct referral of status offender cases from the police to DSO program staff established outside the direct control of the court.

Program Implementation Issues

Indicative of the pervasive reluctance with which the DSO program was approached in this site was the crisis encountered in getting it organized. Initially, the program was slated to be developed and supervised by the Delaware Department of Health and Social Services (DHSS). However, the leaders of this agency expressed strong reservations about the usefulness of the DSO program, finding particularly onerous the task of establishing the additional shelter homes planned by the program. But behind the irritation with this unwanted burden lay their own view of the appropriate way to deal with status offenders. Their position, as one informant put it, was that "kids of this age really have to be handled with an iron fist." An administrative reorganization intervened to rescue DHSS from the task and a six-month search was required to locate another state agency willing to take responsibility for the program. Finally, in the interest of salvaging the federal grant, the governor's office itself took over the program, assigning its supervision to the Commission on Criminal Justice.

Relations with the police, crucial where attempts were made to obtain direct referrals of arrested status offenders to program staff, offered no problems in Delaware. Because only those status offenders who were charged and brought to court intake were eligible for program services, police agencies were not solicited to alter their procedures. It is nonetheless important to note that, although they were excluded from participation, they held decidedly negative views of the program. For example, a leading police official offered the prediction, somewhat gratuitously, that any legislative effort to reduce police authority to arrest youth for status offenses would be countered by shifting the supporting charge to a variety of criminal offenses. To the extent that the police were aware of the program, they were resentful of many of its features, expressing the general conviction that any reduction of punitive action in juvenile cases hampered the deterrent effectiveness of police work. And, referring to another side of police work frequently mentioned by police at this and other sites, another police official questioned the need for the DSO program. He pointed out that it was customary procedure for police to divert "deserving" juvenile cases from detention and adjudication and to make what effort they could to obtain help for them.

Relations with the court were not without their problems, either, although these were more troublesome in the two rural counties and in dealings with the lower-level magistrates' courts. On noncourt days the latter were empowered to decide whether to release arrested juvenile offenders to their homes or to place them in detention pending the next family court day. These courts exhibited a decided preference for detention. Program leaders' efforts to persuade magistrates to reduce their use of detention were fruitless, and only intensified their native antagonism to the program. Most of the state's family court judges were skeptical of the value of the program on grounds that they were better equipped by their experience with young offenders and knowledge of the needs of the community than were social workers to deal with the problems of status offenders. But despite their reservations, they saw the program as an opportunity to increase the funds needed by the court to expand the services available to cope with the status offender problem. It was principally on grounds of this promise that judges agreed to set up the special status offender intake units in their courts.

As matters turned out, the promise was late in realization, undermining the sole grounds of judicial support for the program. Delays were encountered first in the early six-month hiatus in settling on a state agency in which to lodge administrative control of the program, and later in the time taken to establish contracts with service providers. Judges were consequently quick to fault the program for failure to provide in a timely way the one value that had persuaded them to accept it. Other objections were also raised. Judges were critical of the use of unlocked facilities in cases of female runaways. Some judges resented the tendency of intake workers to ignore criminal charges in mixed status-delinquent offense cases in order to avoid adjudication. One judge, for example, while agreeing that status offenders may not belong in court, insisted that many are not "just status offenders." Other judges were antagonistic to the intrusion of the legal advocacy service provided by the program, finding it difficult to accept in principle the notion that juvenile offenders had legal rights. However, despite such criticisms, the work of the special status offender intake units in the courts became a fixed feature of court procedure, and was regarded by program leaders as having achieved very real progress. They were convinced that as the program progressed, fewer status offense charges reached the adjudication stage, and that, while the numbers detained by the magistrates' courts did not decrease, there occurred a substantial reduction in time spent in detention.

Beyond these difficulties in relations with the courts lay further problems in carrying out program service plans. In addition to the crisis intervention services furnished by the court intake units, Delaware attempted to remedy an acute shortage of shelter home space and to provide long-term counseling service. Of these, the effort to expand shelter home bed space turned out to be unfeasible. Instead, having funded a special unit of the Department of Social Services to obtain out-of-home placements for status offenders, the program shifted to the admittedly less desirable use of foster homes for this purpose. The main problem here was that foster homes were in short supply on the base of Delaware's small population. Added was the fact that foster parents expressed a preference for young children rather than the angry and often emotionally upset teenagers who were typical of status offenders. Nonetheless, the use of this public agency was widely regarded as one of the most successful aspects of the program.

As for the crucial status offender intake units in the family court, the main problem that arose was uncertainty over the scope of services they were designed to provide, and the often protracted time between intake and the provision of further services when indicated. In metropolitan Newcastle County, initial crisis counseling was followed by intermittent follow-up counseling pending a determination of the services that might be needed from a contracted diagnostic evaluation agency. The period from intake to service decision often took as long as 30 days, during which the intake unit may have been heavily involved in efforts to deal with the problem of the youth and family. Further, clients referred to community agencies who failed to appear were not followed up and the cases tended to be dropped. In the two rural lower counties, there was substantially less investment on the part of intake units in providing service beyond crisis intervention. Even more pronounced than in Newcastle County was their tendency to return most status offenders to their homes. Only those who were repeatedly returned to the court by the police were referred to contracted counseling agencies.

Summary

Launched in a jurisdiction that regarded status offenses as no less serious than delinquent offenses, the Delaware DSO program was conducted essentially as an operation of the family court. Under the administrative control of the state's Commission on Criminal Justice, the program established and funded status offender intake units in the courts of the state's three counties to divert status offenders from detention and adjudication. The intake units furnished crisis counseling, assessed needs in each case, referred to community agencies those requiring additional services, and removed from detention status offenders held by the local magistrates' courts. The program funded a legal aid agency to monitor violations of the legal rights of status offenders whose cases went to adjudication and reviewed the cases of institutionalized status offenders with a view to their release to the community. Also funded was another special unit in the Department of Social Services to provide foster home placements of status offenders whose return to home was inadvisable. For particularly complex cases, diagnostic and long-term counseling services were contracted to private agencies and organizations.

The program design was not without its problems. The court had reluctantly accepted the program on the prospect that it would expand the treatment resources for status offenders beyond those the court could provide. For some judges, the long delay in making the program operational, and for others the practice of the intake units of disregarding criminal charges in mixed status offense-delinquent offense cases, undermined the court's support of the program. The intake units tended to enlarge their gatekeeping, detention reduction, and referral functions by providing extended counseling services that, in theory, were to be removed from the court to community-based agencies. And while the state was desperately lacking in short-term shelter homes as a substitute for detention, the program was unable to develop them. Finally, there was failure to reduce significantly the net use of detention in Delaware because of program failure to overcome the obstinate insistence of the magistrates' courts on placing arrested status offenders in detention centers.

Despite these difficulties, at the end of the two-year period of federal funding the leaders of the Delaware DSO program could point to signs of progress in overcoming Delaware's generally reluctant acceptance of the DSO mission. The state legislature had been persuaded to give serious consideration to altering the juvenile code to restrict the use of secure confinement in status offense cases. Perhaps more to the point, both the courts and the Department of Social Services, as a result of their participation in the program, had decided to include in their future budgets a request for funds to continue the work of the special status offender units within the structure of their own program.

SOUTH CAROLINA

As one of the more politically and socially conservative states, South Carolina had remained relatively untouched by movements, long predating the advent of the DSO program, that pressed continuously for the improvement of juvenile justice virtually since the establishment of juvenile courts. In this state, by statute as well as by administrative practice, both noncriminal and criminal juvenile offenders were defined and dealt with as a single undifferentiated class, with a heavy use of institutional confinement. As in all predominantly rural regions, the juvenile courts of the state tended to be seen and saw themselves not as the custodians of juveniles whose control had eluded all earlier effort, but as formally organized institutional extensions of the normal control efforts of the family and neighborhood.

This was the situation until the early 1970s, when the *Christian Science Monitor* published an exposé of abuses in the treatment of juvenile offenders, including harsh conditions of incarceration, then existing in South Carolina as well as a number of other states. Stung into action, the state legislature established an agency to oversee the practices of juvenile institutions, and vested it with authority to release committed offenders. The Juvenile Placement Bureau was directed to review the cases of all juveniles in correctional institutions at three-month intervals.

Encouraged by the break in custom, those who had been urging reforms in juvenile justice pressed forward. Within the next several years, the Department of Corrections, with jurisdiction over the state's juvenile institutions, was renamed the Department of Youth Services (DYS) and was given the added function of developing a statewide delinquency prevention program. DYS promptly undertook to develop a network of locally based and funded Youth Service Bureaus (YSBs) as its principal delinquency prevention tool. But within a short time the agency discovered that local communities had neither the interest nor the resources to support their YSBs. DYS then succeeded in obtaining state funds for the employment of personnel to staff and operate the YSBs located only in the more populous counties.

During the period when the Youth Service Bureau structure was under development, it became evident that federal funds might become available to develop programs for the deinstitutionalization of status offenders. The Division of Youth Services submitted a program proposal designed both to remove status offenders currently confined in long-term institutions and to divert them from detention. With the state-supported Youth Service Bureau network already in place, the YSB staff was to serve both functions.

The South Carolina program thus took shape against a background of a belated effort to pull abreast of current developments in juvenile justice. But having established the Juvenile Placement Bureau to monitor the incarceration of juvenile offenders, the Youth Service Bureau network to serve troubled youth generally, and a Reception and Evaluation (R&E) Center for postadjudication detention, South Carolina preserved in other respects its traditional modes of response to juvenile offense. The courts continued to make liberal use of locked facilities by remanding adjudicated status and delinquent offenders to the R&E Center, where final case dispositions were made on the basis of case study. Offenders were held there for varying lengths of time, in some instances for more than a month. Nor was there any alteration in tolerance for status offenders: Rates of school suspensions and expulsions remained very high during the two-year period preceding the DSO program. The single upbeat note was the development of community-centered placement facilities through a volunteer foster home program established throughout the state.

Program Design

In the light of public and judicial conservatism regarding the treatment of status offenders, it would have been reasonable to introduce the federally supported status offender program on a modest scale. However, the proposal submitted and funded undertook to mount a statewide program on the base of the YSB structure that the Division of Youth Services had only recently established. With status offender program funds supplementing its state support, the YSB division underwent an explosive expansion within a single year, arousing the concern of the judicial community and other agencies of state government. As one program leader put it:

> We expanded this division from about a $400,000 program to a $2 million program in a year's time. I think that scared a lot of people because, basically, the state was going to have to pick up those kinds of funds.
>
> Despite the fact that there's been some significant attitude changes about keeping status offenders out [of locked facilities], some of the initial reactions we've had from the judges of being concerned about the whole issue helped contribute to the problem of continued funding. Although they might have supported the concept [of deinstitutionalization], it was like they wanted more time to do it their way without having something shoved down their throat. Of course, we tried to present [the program] in such a way that it wasn't going to be shoved down their throat.

Overlaid as it was on the existing Youth Service Bureau network, the South Carolina DSO program was shaped on the warp of its structure and activities. The YSB quite understandably provided services to troubled youth, whatever the character of the problem and the source of referral. Accordingly, intake policy encouraged referrals from nonjustice as well as from justice sources. This meant that the program accepted as eligible for services whoever may have been regarded as "in danger of becoming status offenders." The effect of this policy on the DSO program was to broaden the eligibility criteria for program services. For example, of the total number of clients who entered the program during its two-year existence, over half consisted of school and parent referrals, and few had been in any trouble with the law.

While program managers were not unaware of the net-widening effect of the policy, they insisted that its benefits could only be positive. As one administrator said, "After all, the bottom line is helping kids. And, as long as we don't go out and bring them in, and they do need services, they are eligible for program service." As a further justification of the "open" intake policy, program leaders pointed out that status offenders often fit poorly into traditional categories of problem youth, remain a neglected population treated by default as delinquents, and thus tend to be pushed into correctional institutions.

An additional feature of the South Carolina situation that pushed its DSO program into diverting status offenders from the "front end" of the juvenile justice system was the heavy use made in this state of its R&E diagnostic facility in detaining status offenders. Prohibited by law from referring adjudicated juvenile offenders directly to nonjustice agencies, the courts were obliged to remand them to the R&E Center for diagnostic workup and ultimate case disposition. Program administrators consequently saw early intervention in problem cases from nonjustice sources as interrupting a highly predictable process that would first bring the offender into court, with a high proportion sent to R&E detention. It was in this sense that program leaders equated diversion with deinstitutionalization. They claimed, for example, that in one Youth Service Bureau region referrals to the R&E Center were cut in half by the program in one county, and by about 80 percent in another. In the absence of the program, it was claimed, some three-quarters of all status offense cases would have gone to court adjudication. Of these, approximately half would have been remanded to detention in the R&E Center.

In addition to reducing detention by diverting status offenders from an initial court appearance, the South Carolina DSO program undertook to remove within a five- to ten-day period status offenders remanded by the court to the R&E Center. The release procedure required notification of the Youth Service Bureau in the offender's region of residence of his reception at the center. A staff member then visited the court from which the youth was committed in order to ascertain that the commitment was for a status offense. Once verified, the worker developed a placement plan, which was then presented to the agency that had sole authority to release juvenile offenders. Those who were removed were no longer at risk of commitment to long-term correctional institutions, at least as a result of the current episode, although there was no certainty that this would have been the R&E disposition.

It was in light of this effort to shorten the period of detention, and in particular to prevent the commitment of status offenders to long-term institutions, that program administrators justified their claim that they were in fact deinstitutionalizing status offenders. However, as one program worker commented, "Kids were DSO'd, no question about that. . . .

But it's impossible to tell whether a kid would have gone to an institution if he hadn't been DSO'd."

While the bulk of referrals to the program consisted of miscellaneous cases of problem youth generated by the ongoing YSB operation, referrals for program services also came from the courts. Other than having developed the Youth Service Bureau network, the Division of Youth Services was retained as the major state agency to which the court at its option could refer youth charged with delinquent or status offenses prior to their adjudication. In fact, before the DSO program made its appearance, the court in one of the larger urban centers of the state had collaborated with the DYS in conducting a pretrial intervention program for criminal youth. In that program, adjudication proceedings were suspended and an opportunity given to the local YSB to provide remedial services. With the DSO program in place, the DYS now urged the courts to refer all status offense cases to the YSBs, excluding only those with criminal charges pending and those on probation for a prior criminal or status offense. There were thus two "filters" for case intake, one finely screened by the court, and one virtually unscreened by community sources of referral.

Program Content

DSO program services included residential placement, counseling with use of a crisis intervention model, educational services, and referral to community-based recreational and mental health services as needed. Some of the latter services were obtained by contract with private practice psychologists. However, most of the referrals for contracted services were made to recreational agencies, with the bulk of services furnished by the program being provided directly by YSB staff. One regional supervisor estimated that four-fifths of all services received by DSO clients were provided by YSB staff.

Program funds were used to establish 1 shelter and 3 group homes, each with a capacity of 20 residents, to supplement existing residential facilities. The latter consisted of two categories: a statewide network of over 100 volunteer foster homes, and locally based residential care facilities. The volunteer foster home organization was active in removing youth from jail detention, reportedly effecting some 200 such removals during 1978. The second category of locally based residential care institutions housed large populations, some of which were used primarily as orphanages. The Youth Service Bureaus used such institutions as shelter-care facilities for status offenders when no alternative was available, with their staff assuming responsibility for providing needed services. Unfortunately, in many cases these placements occurred outside the youth's community of residence as the result of a not uncommon practice among some judges of ridding their communities of their "bad apples."

Both the design and the content of the South Carolina DSO program came under sustained criticism by the state's planning agency for criminal justice, despite the fact that it had initially approved the program proposal. First, the program was faulted for failing to place major emphasis on strengthening community resources for the treatment of status offenders, rather than on expanding and stabilizing the state-supported network of YSBs as the primary source of youth services. Program administrators conceded that this would indeed have been desirable had there been a willingness on the part of local agencies to devote greater resources to the status offender problem.

Second, there was objection to the use of the YSBs, since these were an arm of the Division of Youth Services, the state's juvenile correctional agency. The point was made that such auspices carried with them the stigma of treatment by a delinquency control agency. Program personnel asserted that the YSBs were seen by clients not as part of the state's correctional apparatus, but as an element of its structure of social services.

Third, the use of a large portion of program funds to divert youths defined as "in danger of becoming status offenders" was assailed for neglecting the task of removing status offenders already committed to long-term institutions. Critics argued that a genuine policy of deinstitutionalization required a major investment of funds in finding community placements for the hard-to-place status offenders. The contention was that status offenders committed to such institutions were principally those for whom placement facilities in their home communities were inadequate or nonexistent.

Thus, the main features of the South Carolina DSO program included (a) the use of a preexisting state-supported network of Youth Service Bureaus as the principal resource for providing services to status offenders; (b) emphasis on minimizing the insertion of "troubled youth" into the juvenile justice system by diverting them from court processing, coupled with an effort to obtain the early release of adjudicated status offenders committed to the state's Reception and Evaluation Center; (c) provision of residential placement services in three small group homes, in volunteer foster homes, and in large "orphanage"-type institutions; and (d) limited use of contracted counseling services to supplement those furnished by YSB staff. Program funds were used primarily to expand and strengthen the state-supported network of Youth Service Bureaus.

Program Implementation Problems

Since the South Carolina program was conducted by the state's juvenile corrections agency, the Division of Youth Services, relations with the court essentially required cooperation between two arms of the justice system. Unlike other program sites where courts were requested to refer status offense cases to private sector youth agencies, in South Carolina the request was to refer cases to another public agency within the same system. Nonetheless, virtually all of the problems in program-court relations typical in other sites surfaced here as well.

A principal problem was the fact that the program was not centered in the court, an arrangement that would have obviated the need to share their control in status offense cases. Court concern with this matter was expressed most vigorously in connection with program efforts to obtain the early release of status offenders remanded to the R&E Center. To many judges this activity seemed an unwarranted rejection of the court's judgment in committing the youth. One program administrator commented: "We had a problem in trying to convince the judges that status offenders should be returned to their communities. They put a kid in [the R&E Center], and we get them out. . . . The judges call us the revolving door because some of them reappear in court."

In some counties, judges agreed not to institutionalize status offenders only if DYS agreed in turn to their adjudication in order to place them on probation. Cases could then be referred to a YSB for service. The arrangement enabled courts to feel that they still maintained control over the case, and, as one program worker mused, "at least it kept the kids out of institutions."

Competition over case control was not the only source of difficulty with courts, particularly in the smaller counties. There, in addition, the program was hampered by the court's concern with maintaining an adequate caseload. Said one YSB worker, "It got to be a turf problem. They feared that if they didn't have status offenders, what would they have in a small community?"

Thus, while the courts were one important source of referral to the program, court personnel tended to view the program variously as an intrusion on their authority and competence, as a source of acceptable help in dealing with status offenders, as an unwarranted subversion of the deterrent effect of incarceration, or, in the smaller counties, as a threat to their jobs. Despite the range of response, the net impression remained that program administrators managed their relations with the courts well enough to open a view to the possible values of deinstitutionalization in status offense cases.

There were few problems in relations with service providers, but only because with minor exceptions services to status offenders were provided directly by the Youth Service Bureaus. They were virtually the only source of service in the smaller counties. Although there existed youth service agencies in the large population counties, they were not prepared to add status offenders to their already burdened caseloads. A small proportion of all services were contracted out on an ad hoc basis to private practice psychologists, youth and family counselors, group homes, physicians, and recreation agencies. By far the largest category of contracted services was to recreational agencies. The single serious problem that arose with respect to YSB services was work overload. There was a failure to anticipate the complexities often encountered in status offender cases, and workers were assigned caseloads based on DYS experience with delinquent probationers. In describing the problem, one YSB worker sounded a note of despair:

> I wonder what keeps me going, and I really don't know. These status offender kids are very difficult to deal with. The Department of Youth Services looks at staff compared to the number of kids you have, not the number of man-hours spent with certain kids, so it's overwhelming.

There were no problems in relations with police agencies for the simple reason that in this site the DSO program did not attempt to engage the police as a source of referral. It was in fact an indication of community attitudes about the status offender problem that the police generally ignored this type of offense. In cases of status offense in which a complaint was lodged, they preferred to handle the case independently. As one Youth Service Bureau regional supervisor put it:

> Police just don't want to deal with ungovernables or truants. They honestly don't care about keeping them overnight [for further processing]. Unless someone else has brought a formal charge against the juvenile, they just won't keep them. They feel that is something the court should take care of. The police have simply not been a major factor in the program.

Implementation problems thus centered predominantly on program-court relations. Relations with private sector service providers and with police agencies were nonproblematic. In the former case almost all status offender services were provided directly by program personnel; in the latter case police remained almost entirely uninvolved with the program. Where they existed, difficulties with the court concerned primarily uneasiness or downright objection to the program practice of returning to the community status offenders the court had remanded to the state's R&E Center.

Summary

Introduced into a site reluctant to accept the doctrine that status offenders should be treated differently from delinquent offenders, the DSO program in South Carolina was grafted onto an earlier reform of its juvenile justice system. An effort to moderate the harsh conditions under which all juvenile offenders had been traditionally incarcerated was extended to include the development of a Youth Service Bureau network charged with the task of dealing with troubled youth at the local level as a delinquency prevention measure. Supported by state funds and administered by its juvenile corrections agency, the Division of Youth Services, the Youth Service Bureau was selected to operate the South Carolina DSO program with a $2 million OJJ grant. Since it was the YSB mission to serve the needs of all varieties of troubled youth, it designed the DSO program to be similarly responsive, defining eligibility for program services as "in danger of becoming a status offender."

However, in addition to devoting DSO funds to expand and strengthen the customary YSB services, in many cases diverting status offenders from a preadjudication court hearing, substantial effort was devoted to the early termination and return to the community of adjudicated status offenders remanded to the state's major detention center. Although this was a generally successful operation, the courts accorded this type of intervention only qualified support, since it had the effect in many instances of countermanding the decision of the court to subject the offender to an experience of incarceration.

Virtually all DSO program services were furnished by the YSB staff. These included crisis intervention counseling and out-of-home placement in volunteer foster homes and in large locally based institutions used as temporary shelter homes. Less frequently used were contracted services furnished by private agencies, principally to provide recreational services.

Because the South Carolina DSO program was virtually indistinguishable from the normal operations of the state's Youth Service Bureaus, there were those in the state who questioned program success in advancing the status offender deinstitutionalization mission. Approximately half the referrals to the DSO program were of the type "in danger of becoming status offenders." Of the half consisting of postadjudicated status offenders the program was able only to limit their stay in detention.

Program leaders pointed out, however, that substantial progress was made in overcoming a pervasive lack of awareness among both juvenile justice personnel and youth service agencies that the noncriminal juvenile offender represented a separate and special problem. For example, in what may have been an overstatement, one Youth Service Bureau staff member claimed that in 1976, the year prior to the start of the program, there were no more than three judges in the state "who knew what a status offender was." By the end of the funding period, he asserted, the status offender concept and the arguments favoring the treatment of status offenders in the community were familiar to almost all judges. Thus, whatever else the program did or did not accomplish, it may well have had visible impact as an educational enterprise.

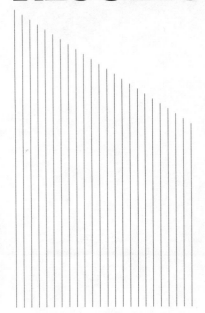

PART **III**

RESULTS

chapter 7

Client Recidivism and Program Components

A Multilevel Analysis

with Carl L. Heck

Our interest in this chapter is in disentangling the contribution of program variables to client recidivism. By classifying these variables according to distinguishable program components, we may be able to identify those more amenable to change in future program efforts. Saari (1981: 34) has noted with respect to juvenile programs generally that "variables such as race, gender, and state are critical in predicting differential use of community vs. institutional placements, not crime rate or effectiveness."

Despite differences in the detail of their implementation, the programs at the eight evaluated sites exhibited some common basic content and procedures. Each operated within a political, administrative, and organizational context provided by the court and police jurisdictions in which it was set. Each program found or developed facilities to provide a set of services to a population of clients referred for status offenses. Accordingly, four major determinants potentially affecting client recidivism may be identified: *site, client characteristics, type of service furnished,* and the *character of the facility* furnishing the service.

Site, as well as each of the other recidivism outcome determinants, was treated as a composite indicator created by multiple variables. There really is no other way to treat Pima County, or the State of Connecticut, as a variable. For instance, Saari (1981) describes the variable "state" as including the dimensions of socioeconomic heterogeneity, level of interest group activity, correctional agency autonomy, and administrative ideology and leadership in the correctional agencies. Included in her first factor are racial balance, income inequality, percentage poor and undereducated, and political culture of the state. *Site,* then, whether it refers to a whole state or to a segment thereof, is clearly a gross proxy for a host of unmeasured variables.

For convenience, our four sets of variables, or variable domains, are here referred to as "levels," although no suggestion of heirarchical order is intended. However, the variable domain levels did appear to be differentially open to manipulation by program personnel. With existing statutory provisions about the use of secure confinement in status offense cases, and established administrative procedures in their implementation, site appears to be a "given" and least open to manipulation. Also largely fixed are client characteristics, although program intake policy varied on client eligibility across sites. Some programs were more restrictive than others in limiting intake to "detainable" status offenders. By way of contrast, both the type of service provided and the service facilities selected, or available, to provide the service seemed to offer maximum opportunity for choice and discretion in intervening to reduce the likelihood of subsequent offense behavior. For the sake of implementing successful programs, then, one would hope to find in our analysis that type of service, and type of facility, the levels more open to program manipulation, would be the levels most directly related to client change.

The effects of *site, client characteristics, services* provided and *facility* characteristics, treated as levels of program input on the dependent variable of subsequent offense behavior, will be examined here. The dependent variable is made up of all delinquent and status offenses entered into court and police records during the six-month period following the date of the client's entry into the program. The impact of these program dimensions on client offense behavior is assessed through the use of regression analysis, a procedure that offers an efficient means of examining the extent to which each of the four program levels accounted for offense behavior outcome, above and beyond the influence of the other three.

Two of the eight sites have been excluded from the analysis. Data on facility characteristics in the Connecticut program were not sufficient for inclusion. While facility data were available from the Illinois program, it was also excluded because most of its program clients were served directly by part-time personnel hired by contracted agencies to act as youth advocates during a short-term home detention period. Clients were not directly exposed to the usual services provided by those agencies. The remaining six sites were Pima County (Arizona), Alameda County (California), South Carolina, Delaware, and Clark and Spokane counties (Washington).

PROGRAM LEVELS AND
THEIR CONSTITUTIVE VARIABLES

An effort was made to obtain so far as possible a data set sufficiently comprehensive to serve a variety of purposes. These purposes included not only the empirical search for relationships between a wide range of program input variables and client responses, but the purpose as well of providing a data base of potential use in the future development of testable hypotheses. Despite the volume of data acquired, neither purpose was altogether satisfactorily accomplished. The opportunity to obtain some of the data at a requisite level of detail was foreclosed largely by the refusal of program personnel at the various sites to invest the time and effort needed to record the requested data systematically. In lesser part the failure was due to a lack of direct control over the field data recording operation. As a consequence, while a large volume of data was generated, some of the variables desired for a number of analytic purposes are not available. However, the range of information at hand is sufficiently broad to provide a choice of variables that can function as surrogates for information forgone.

Variables selected to represent various levels were those that might reasonably function as determinants of variation in subsequent client offenses. Their selection was based on etiological assumptions implicit in the national status offender program and on the research findings in the juvenile delinquency literature. Variable selection was a problem principally in connection with the *client* and *facility* levels of the program. *Site* information was contained in five effect-coded nominal variables, with the sixth treated as the omitted category. The *service*-level variables were established as a set of eight categories of treatment modalities. In an auxiliary analysis, clients whose variables had missing data at *client* and *facility* levels were included by assigning to them the means on those variables, and then creating dummy variables to indicate the presence or absence of a value on the variable. This was done in order to include an expanded number of clients in the regression equation.[1]

Site. Treated as a set of effect-coded nominal dummy variables, site is conceived of as consisting of a number of unmeasured dimensions. Included principally are (a) the extent to which statutory provisions prohibit or permit secure confinement in status offense cases; (b) the operational policies and practices followed by police and courts in the implementation of statutory prescription; and (c) the level of community tolerance for status offense behavior. These varied by virtue of the *selection* of sites for the DSO program due to their placement on these dimensions.

Client-level variables. Client characteristics selected for construction of the *client* program level were drawn from data recorded in Forms 1-A, 1-B, 1, 3, and 5-A, 5-B, and 5-C. (These and all other data collection forms used in DSO are available from OJJ in the volume *National Evaluation Design for the Deinstitutionalization of Status Offenders Program.*) The selection was based on the commitment in the national status offender program to the assumptions of labeling theory (LEAA, 1975). The central proposition of labeling theory holds that juvenile offense behavior varies as a function of the frequency with which the youthful offender is processed by juvenile justice agencies (Becker, 1963; Schur, 1973). It follows that any feature of client experience or background that increases the likelihood of such processing is interpretable as contributing to the labeling effect. Thus, in addition to the specific most serious status offense for which the client was referred to the program, variables were selected that may be reasonably related to variation in exposure to juvenile justice processing, and for which there is research evidence of their relationship to variation in subsequent offense behavior. Included were the following:

(a) *prior offenses:* the number of prior delinquent and status offenses, multiple status offenses, and multiple nonstatus offenses (Wolfgang et al., 1972; Glueck and Glueck, 1940; Mannheim and Wilkins, 1955)

(b) *family socioeconomic status:* father's and mother's occupational status[2] (Shaw and McKay, 1969; Empey, 1978)[3]

(c) *family intactness:* dummy variable, nuclear family versus all other family constellations[4] (Monahan, 1957; Nye, 1958; Barker, 1940)[5]

(d) *attachment to school and family:* school adjustment scale; school attendance status; client's perception of time spent with family (Elliott, 1966; Polk and Halferty, 1966; Polk and Schafer, 1972; Empey and Lubeck, 1971; Hirschi, 1969)

(e) *age:* interval variable, age of client (8-18) at instant offense (Sellin, 1958; Mannheim and Wilkins, 1955)[6]

(f) *gender:* dummy variable, male and female[7]

(g) *ethnicity:* dummy variable, minority and nonminority; minority group category consisted of Black, Mexican-American, Puerto Rican, other Hispanic, Native American, and Asian or Asiatic Pacific[8]

Service-level variables. Eight types of service, each treated as a dummy variable, represented this program component. They were (1) diversion /evaluation, consisting of case evaluation followed by brief client-oriented crisis intervention; (2) temporary shelter home placement; (3) longer-term group home placement; (4) long-term client counseling; (5) referral to a multiple-service center, such as YMCA or similar broad-spectrum youth service agency; (6) "outreach intervention," consisting of neighborhood-centered problem-resolution services; (7) "multiple-impact therapy"; and (8) a residual category of miscellaneous, low-frequency "other" services.[9] It was unfortunately necessary to omit from the regression equation foster home placement as a service type in one analysis because problems of confidentiality made it difficult to obtain full data on facility characteristics, including experience and training of foster parents, number of own and foster children, household regimen, and the like. However, this variable was included in the auxiliary analysis referred to above, in which missing data values were allocated.

Facility-level variables. Nineteen variables were employed to measure facility characteristics, drawn from the Survey of Program Facilities and the Organizational Survey instruments. They were selected on the basis of current ideology and practice in the delinquency prevention field, labeling theory, and program assumptions about the utility of community-based treatment in the reduction of status offense behavior. These considerations suggested four dimensions of facility characteristics as likely determinants of variation in client recidivism: professional level of the facility staff; diversity of services; focus of intervention strategy employed; and the extent to which program staff engaged local community resources in serving program clients. These are described more fully below:

(a) *professional level of facility staff:* percentage of staff professionally trained, preprofessional, paraprofessional, and volunteer.[10]
(b) *diversity of services:* number of types of services offered by facility[11]
(c) *intervention strategy:*[12] use of coerciveness (frequency of imposition of sanction for violating conditions of acceptance into program, that is, average frequency of sanction imposition); strategy of intervention (judicious use of sanction, focus on psychological adjustment, focus on improving client relations with family and peer group, focus on changing societal institutions concerned with the training and control of youth, such as school, police, court); ideology respecting cause of delinquency (responsibility for behavior resides in person, psychological maladjustment, pathology lies in immediate social milieu, behavioral deviance traceable to malfunctioning societal institutions)

   (d) *engagement of community resources:* level of staff activity to generate
       support for the program, frequency of staff contact with community orga-
       nizations and agencies in behalf of improving services to clients, staff per-
       ception of cooperation elicited from community organizations.

   The final set of variables tested for the relevance to recidivism of program assumptions about the importance of engaging the services of community-based agencies and organizations as an alternative to processing
by juvenile justice agencies. In this as well as in other deinstitutionalization programs, the intensive use of community-based agencies is prescribed as the primary means of reducing the labeling effect and therefore subsequent offense behavior (Coates et al., 1978).

   The dependent variable: subsequent offenses. This variable consisted
of the number of offenses, both status and nonstatus, for a six-month
period subsequent to program entry. Because of excessive skewness, this
measure of recidivism was transformed to the base 2 logarithm of subsequent offenses ($+ 1$) to improve the shape of the distribution.

ANALYTIC PROCEDURES

   The initial order of entry of the four program levels into the regression
equation was based on the distinction made between those variables assumed to be more and those assumed to be less subject to manipulation
by program personnel. Least manipulable were site and client characteristics, which were entered in that order. On the assumption that program
personnel took account of client characteristics in making referrals for
services, both the service type and the facility to provide the services
offered some choice.
   These differences among levels suggested an order of priority in their
entry into the regression equation, moving from those less open to program manipulation to those relatively more open. Thus the effect of client
characteristics could be examined controlling for site, the effect of treatment services could be examined controlling for client characteristics,
and so forth. This reasoning suggested the following additive model for
the initial regression equation, according priority to site and client characteristics in explaining variation in the dependent variable of client offenses subsequent to program entry:

$$\text{subsequent offenses} = \text{site} + \text{client characteristics} +$$
$$\text{service type} + \text{facility} + E$$

This initial model provided a means of assessing whether or not each of
the levels did indeed have an effect on subsequent offenses.

However, assumptions regarding the manipulability of program components may well be qualified by the limited scope of choice that was available at program sites with respect to the selection of clients, services, and facilities. Each program was constrained by financial resources and by the number and kinds of youth service agencies available in the jurisdiction. In the light of these constraints, a second model was used that assumed no differences in the discretionary control of the program levels and thus addressed only the issue of the differential impact of the levels. In this model, the order in which each of the program levels was entered into the regression equation was systematically varied to enter each level last. The purpose of this strategy was to determine the size of the *additional* increment to explained variance in client recidivism accounted for by each program level, above and beyond the contribution of the remaining three. The rationale of the procedure was that the level providing the largest additional increment to explained variation when entered last into the equation is the level that contributes most to the R^2 measure. The rank of each level with respect to its effect on client recidivism could thus be ascertained.

DATA LIMITATIONS

The difficulties and complexities of obtaining an extensive body of data on a large program population dispersed across eight sites created a substantial problem of missing data. The largest data gap occurred in the facility-level variables (see Figure 7.1), although there was data loss at the client levels as well. As mentioned, two sites had to be dropped from the multilevel analysis. The analysis thus covers six of the eight program sites, with findings descriptively applicable only to the programs in those sites. Within

Source	Number
(a) evaluation-eligible cases at 8 sites	3,481*
(b) loss due to omission of Illinois and Connecticut and nonreturn of Facilities and Organizational Survey instruments, all sites	1,355
(c) loss due to omission of data items, partially completed survey instruments, remaining six sites	146
(d) additional loss due to missing client data	70
(e) total missing cases (b + c + d)	1,571
(f) cases included in analysis (a − e)	1,910

FIGURE 7.1   Distribution of Missing Data Items

*The difference between the total N for the program-preprogram six-month client recidivism analysis (3,714) and the N for the multilevel recidivism analysis (3,481) is accounted for by the exclusion in the latter analysis of those clients who had no Series 1 service assignment (233). This group consisted of clients whose problems were presumably dealt with by DSO program personnel without formal referral to a treatment facility, or by referral to a facility outside the network of DSO facilities.

these sites as well, clients were deleted from the analysis if there was no return of the Survey of Program Facilities or the Organizational Survey instruments. There was substantially less data loss at the client level.[13] Neither the site nor service level was affected by failure to record data items, because a radically simplified categorical scheme was provided.

A second problem of reduced numbers for this analysis resulted from the fact that clients could receive services in more than one facility. Of the 3481 program clients entering the program at the six sites who received services in one or more facilities, 1555 (approximately 45 percent) were referred for service in a second facility, and 532 (about 15 percent) were served in three or more facilities. Each entry or reentry of a client into the program marked the beginning of what was defined as a new service pattern. Each referral within a service pattern by program personnel to a facility was defined as a "series." Thus the Series 1 clients were those referred to at least one facility, the Series 2 clients to at least two facilities, and the Series 3 clients to three facilities.

However, an increase in the number of facility referrals increased the volume of missing data from the client and service levels as well as from the facility level, resulting in a particularly sharp reduction in Series 2 and Series 3 client numbers available for the analysis. The number of cases for Series 2 was 462, and for Series 3, 105.

The scope and distribution of missing data presented a dilemma. The analysis could focus on the Series 1 clients, who represented the largest number and thus provided the most stable estimates of the effect of program levels on client recidivism. However, this would sacrifice information on the importance of the additional services and the additional exposure to treatment represented by the reduced numbers in the Series 2 and Series 3 categories. On the other hand, the sharply reduced numbers in the latter groups would yield highly unstable estimates. The choice was made to omit the analysis of the Series 2 and Series 3 data in this presentation, focusing the multilevel analysis on the Series 1 data. Supporting this decision was the fact that of the total number of referrals to the program, almost two-thirds (62.5 percent) represented client referrals to a single facility only.

As noted earlier, an effort was made to remedy the missing data problem in the Series 1 group. In an auxiliary analysis, clients with missing data on variables at the *client* and *facility* levels were included by assigning to them the means on those variables (Cohen and Cohen, 1975). With the use of this allocation method, the number of clients in the auxiliary analysis was increased by 583, or about 30 percent.

FINDINGS

The question addressed in the multilevel analysis was the relative importance of various program elements as determinants of client recidivism. In addition to other values sought, the national status offender program hoped to demonstrate as one of its effects a reduction in the offense behavior of status offenders, and the findings on this issue will be presented in the next chapter. However, the issue of concern here is the extent to which variation in recidivism (regardless of whether it increases or decreases) is related to distinguishable program components as defined in the present analysis.

The issue has direct policy relevance. Program effort may be variously distributed among the several potential avenues to achieving recidivism reduction. Is it more important to invest effort in changing the juvenile code and administrative procedures to reduce the use of secure confinement than to provide the types of treatment procedures specific to the problems of status offenders? What is the relative effect on status offender recidivism of a judicious selection of youth for referral to community-based treatment agencies as compared to the experience, ideology, and treatment orientation of the youth-serving facilities that provide the service? In the Massachusetts Experiment, Coates (1981) reports that "what a youngster brought into the program" made the greatest difference. This included personal characteristics and community environment.

The issue was examined in a regression analysis utilizing both the Series 1 data and the Series 1 data with missing values allocated. The first step was to test the significance of the overall regression equation each time a new level was added, until all levels were in the equation. The F values for the equation after each new level was added are displayed in Table 7.1. With each new level added, the equation remained significant beyond chance at .05, establishing the utility of the model.

Next to be assessed was the significance of the increment of each program level to explained variance in client recidivism (R^2) at each successive step of entry into the regression equation (Table 7.2). The contribution at each level was found to be significant with use of Series 1 data. With the data base expanded by the allocation procedure, *site, client,* and *facility* had significant F values, but the value for *service* drops just below the test level of significance.

Although the test displayed in Table 7.2 shows the significance of the increment to explained variance in client recidivism at each level, this does not address a further important question. Not disclosed is the program level that provides the largest *additional* increment to the R^2 measure with all of the other levels controlled for in the regression equation. The procedure required for this test is to enter each program level last in a series of regression equations. The last entered level that produces the largest additional increment to the R^2 measure is interpreted as the one that contributes most to explained variance.

Displayed in Table 7.3 is the rank order of importance of program levels as determinants of client recidivism, with use of both the Series 1 data and the Series 1 data with missing data allocated. Top rank is held by the *client* level, followed by *site* and *facility*. *Service* fails to add significantly to explained variance in client recidivism when controls are instituted for the other three program levels.

This test of the relative importance of program levels as determinants of client recidivism controlled for the number of variables in each level.

TABLE 7.1   Significance Test Results for Equation with Addition of Each
             New Program Level, Subsequent Offenses Regressed on
             Program Levels

Step	Program Level in Equation	Series 1			Series 1, Missing Data Allocated		
		DF^a	CV^b	F	DF^a	CV^b	F
1	site only	5 / 1,904	2.21	9.68*	5 / 2,407	2.21	14.78*
2	site and client	38 / 1,871	1.00	6.95*	38 / 2,454	1.00	9.38*
3	site, client, and service	45 / 1,864	1.00	6.22*	46 / 2,446	1.00	8.05*
4	site, client, service, and facility	63 / 1,846	1.00	4.99*	69 / 2,423	1.00	5.98*

a. Degrees of freedom: upper number associated with numerator; lower number with denominator in F ratio.
b. Critical value: minimum F value at .05 level.
*p < .05.

TABLE 7.2   Incremental Increases to Explained Variance in Client Recidivism,
             by Program Level Steps

Step	Program Level	Series 1				Series 1, Missing Data Allocated			
		DF^a	CV^b	R^2	F	DF^a	CV^b	R^2	F
1	site	5 / 1,904	2.21	.025	9.68*	5 / 2,487	2.21	.029	14.78*
2	client	33 / 1,871	1.00	.124	6.40*	33 / 2,454	1.00	.127	8.34*
3	service	7 / 1,864	2.01	.131	2.10*	8 / 2,446	1.94	.131	1.63
4	facility	18 / 1,846	1.63	.146	1.80*	23 / 2,423	1.54	.145	1.72*

a. Degrees of freedom: upper number associated with numerator; lower number with denominator.
b. Minimum F value for p < .05.
*p < .05.

This number varied substantially among levels. Estimates of R^2 increments were adjusted or standardized in these tests by dividing the raw R^2 increments by the degrees of freedom based on the number of variables constituting each program level.

The number of variables in each program level was constrained by the character of the program component that each level represented. For example, *site* level could be constituted by no more than six variables, since only six program sites were appropriate for use in the analysis. Similarly, the number of variables constituting the *service* level was restricted to the eight categories of treatment services. On the other hand, both the *client* and the *facility* levels were constructed from a large number of variables. As noted earlier, these were selected from a wider set of obtained data items, the relevance of which for delinquent behavior was suggested by research-based knowledge.

In the light of such extreme variation in the number of variables in each program level, adjustment of the R^2 increment measure by the degrees of freedom may well have introduced a distorting statistical artifact. The use of standardization by adjusting for the number of variables in each level carries the potentially misleading implication that each of the variables in each level has, on the average, equivalent impact on recidivism. Although the variables that were entered into the regression equation were, a priori, "reasonable," particularly in the *client* and *facility* levels, their selection could not be based on rigorous theoretical grounds with reference specifically to status offense behavior. Knowledge of the determinants of status offense behavior was simply too sparse to permit other than a "grounded theory" approach to the analytic problem (Glaser and Strauss, 1967). It was in any case reasonable to examine the degree to which the rank order to the contribution of each program level may have been affected by the constraints imposed by differences in the number of variables in each level.

This was tested by examining the rank order of levels, with the R^2 measures unadjusted for degrees of freedom. As seen in Table 7.4, *client*

TABLE 7.3   Rank Order of Added R^2 Increment, Each Level Entered Last

Rank by R^2 Difference	Series 1		Series 1, Missing Data Allocated	
	Level	R^2 Increment	Level	R^2 Increment
1	client	.00279*	client	.00275*
2	site	.00151*	site	.00081*
3	facility	.00083*	facility	.00061*
4	service	.00040	service	.00021*

*p < .05.

level retains a leading position in its contribution to explained variance, but *site* now ranks third. Second in rank order is taken by *facility,* which was third in the standardized version of the same test.

Evident in both the adjusted and the unadjusted versions of the test is that the characteristics of program clients provides the largest contribution to the R^2 measure when all other features of the program are statistically controlled. The *facility* and *site* levels of the program follow in rank order of their contribution, depending on which of the two tests is used. Most striking in the unadjusted test is the emergence of facility—that is, the orientation, ideology, and experience of service providers—as an important determinant of client recidivism, second only to *client* level.

This multilevel analysis has been concerned only with the relationship of program levels to the subsequent offenses of clients. As noted earlier, each level was composed of sets of variables. A final point of interest is the identification of the specific variables in each set that exhibited a significant F value at each step of level entry into the regression equation. As displayed in Figure 7.2, based on the Series 1 data with missing values allocated, each column is labeled with the new level that was entered into the equation for that step. Thus step 1 included only the site-level variables; step 2, site with the added client-level variables; step 3, site plus client, with service level added; and step 4, the first three with the facility-level variables added. Program levels are arranged by rows as well, so that it is possible to follow a row level across the figure to note the significance status of variables as new levels were added. Both the significance of its F value and whether the variable was found to be positively or inversely related to subsequent offenses are indicated.

When *site* variables at step 1 were entered into the equation, four of the six sites showed significant relationships to subsequent offenses, two positive (+) and two inverse (−). With the entry of *client* variables at step 2, only Delaware (+) and South Carolina (−) remain significantly related to subsequent offenses. At this point the significant client variables

TABLE 7.4   Rank Order of Added R^2 Increment, Unadjusted, Each Level
             Entered Last

Rank by R^2 Difference	Series 1			Series 1, Missing Data Allocated		
	Level	R^2 Increment	F Values (Unadjusted)	Level	R^2 Increment	F Values (Unadjusted)
1	client	.09206*	6.40*	Client	.09086*	8.34*
2	facility	.01499*	1.80*	Facility	.01397*	1.72*
3	site	.00407*	9.68*	Site	.00757*	14.78*
4	service	.00280	2.10*	Service	.00168	1.63

*$p < .05$.

	Step 1 Site	Step 2 + Client	Step 3 + Service	Step 4 + Facility
Site	Alameda County***(+) Delaware****(+) South Carolina****(−) Clark County**(−)	Delaware**(+) South Carolina****(−)	Delaware***(+) South Carolina**(−)	Spokane County**(+)
Client		all prior offenses****(+) prior status offenses only**(+) gender**(+) age**(−) minor in possession of alcohol***(−) other status offenses**(−)	all prior offenses****(+) prior status offenses only**(+) gender**(+) age**(−) minor in possession of alcohol***(−)	all prior offenses****(+) gender**(+) age***(−) minor in possession of alcohol***(−) father's occupation**(−)
Service			diversion-evaluation***(+) outreach intervention**(+)	
Facility				institutions cause delinquency**(−) cooperative community agencies***(−)

FIGURE 7.2 Significant Variables at Each Step of Entry into Regression Equation

**p < .05.
***p < .01.
****p < .001.

emerge: all prior offenses (+), gender (+), age (−), the instant offense of minor in possession of alcohol as the most serious of the instant status offenses (−), and other instant offenses as the most serious among the instant offenses (−). With *service* variables entered at step 3, the same two sites remain significant, as do the client variables referred to, with the single exception of other instant status offenses as the most serious. With the addition, finally, of *facility* variables at the fourth step, the site variables that emerged at previous steps disappear, to be replaced by Spokane County alone (+). Again, the significant client variables identified at steps 2 and 3 remain significant, with prestige level of father's occupation now emerging as a significant client variable (−). In addition, two facility variables were found to be significant: staff belief that institutional malfunction is the cause of delinquent behavior (−), and staff perception of success in obtaining cooperation from community agencies and organizations in serving clients (−).[14]

DISCUSSION

In assessing the findings of this chapter, the reader is again reminded that the intention here was to determine the importance of each of four major program elements for client recidivism. The question of concern was the comparative effect on recidivism of each of these components. How important was the *site* in which deinstitutionalization programs were launched, varied as they were with respect to their statutory and administrative provisions for dealing with status offenders and differing in their tolerance for minor forms of juvenile misbehavior? What was the effect of the kinds of *youth service facilities* that served the needs of program clients? What was the importance of the kinds of *services* these facilities provided, and the kinds of *clients* who were referred to the program? More explicitly, the technical question to which an answer was sought was which, if any, of these program factors "explained" the variation in client recidivism, that is, "made a difference" one way or the other with respect to recidivism and, of those that did, whether the influence was favorable or unfavorable.

Of the four program components, *client* characteristics emerged as the major factor affecting variation in recidivism. The client variables that were significantly related to *reduced* recidivism were age (older clients recidivated less); minor in possession of alcohol as the instant, or referral, offense (inversely related to recidivism); and father's occupation (the higher the father's occupational status, the less likely the client's recidivism). The client variables that were significantly related to *increased* recidivism were number of prior offenses (the larger the number the more likely the recidivism) and gender (females were more recidivistic than males). With reference to the last, account should be taken of the likelihood that females are more often placed on supervised probation and are therefore at greater risk of re-referral.

Least important as a factor affecting variation in recidivism for better or worse was type of *service* furnished. There may have been a number of reasons for this. First, the major type of service provided was short-term crisis counseling. Given the often involved and complex character of the problem represented by status offense behavior, intervention of this kind may be incapable of effecting significant change. Second, those eligible for program services included a very large proportion of first-time offenders, many of whom in the absence of program intervention were unlikely to become repeaters in any case. Third, the predominance of counseling among the types of services provided requires for its effective implementation a level of skill and experience that may have been absent in the treatment staffs employed at some of the program sites.

When considered by itself, site appeared to have a substantial relationship to variation in recidivism. This is to say that the program in some sites seemed to be successful and in others unsuccessful in reducing recidivism. However, when account is taken of differences among them in the kinds of services provided (that is, when these program components were statistically controlled), the effect of site on recidivism was insignificant. Perhaps it is common in most jurisdictions to give major weight to features such as offense history, family capacity to provide supervision, age, and gender. This would result in high uniformity in the treatment of the majority of status offense cases. While this explanation is admittedly speculative, it would account for the failure of program site differences in policy and practice to show an effect on variation in recidivism.

Youth services facilities as a program component showed only a marginal and tenuous relationship to recidivism. Of the 19 variables constituting this component, only two exhibited a relationship to recidivism, with all variables in the other three program components statistically controlled. These two, found to be inversely related to recidivism, were cooperation among the staffs of the local network of community-based services, and staff attribution of the cause of delinquency to deficiencies in the major control and educational institutions for youth. The latter suggests the possible importance, other things being equal, of an emphasis on an advocacy approach in any of its various forms.

These findings should be viewed with caution; we indicated earlier that there were substantial problems in operationalizing these variables. The findings are nonetheless of sufficient potential importance for effective intervention to warrant further research.

The policy-relevant purpose in undertaking the analysis presented in this chapter was to identify the relative contribution of each of four program components to changes in offense behavior and, in those that did so contribute, the specific features of each component that appeared to be more effective. The underlying assumption was that each program component was potentially important in achieving that aim of the deinstitutionalization effort. Its failure to do so raises the following question: What was its specific shortcoming and, in the interest of guiding future program effort of this kind, how may the deficiency be remedied?

The review that follows is based on this chapter's findings as presented in Figure 7.2. There, the variables in each program component accounting for variation in client recidivism, either favorably or unfavorably, are indicated. Observations concerning those features of program operation that were manifestly important for recidivism, either for good or ill, as well as those that appeared to be irrelevant (that is, were unrelated to variation in recidivism) are drawn from findings in other chapters of this volume.

Site

Sites differed widely with respect to prevailing statutory provisions and other conditions likely to affect the implementation of program objectives. Prior to the introduction of the program, in some sites an effort was already under way to divert status offenders from detention and to reduce the use of long-term institutionalization. At other sites, it had long been customary in these cases to make full use of detention facilities and to commit status offenders to locked institutions. However, neither of these features of site context appeared to have a clearly independent effect on recidivism. In both types of sites, an initial appearance of impact vanished when account was taken of the effects of other program components. The neutrality of site characteristics for recidivism levels suggests that in sites both receptive and resistive to deinstitutionalization, there may have been failure to achieve full program implementation for entirely different reasons. In the receptive sites, there is some evidence that while diversion activity was given additional support resources, police and court practices established during the preprogram period continued largely unchanged. Any gain in affecting status offender recidivism in these sites would have had to come from two related sources: targeting program effort more sharply on the subset of status offenders more likely to recidivate and, in sites where this was the case, relaxing client eligibility requirements to accept such categories of ineligibles as those currently on probation for prior status or delinquent offenses.

On the other hand, in many of the resistive sites, program implementation weakness tended to center on failure to focus the effort to divert status offense cases from formal processing at the "front end" of the juvenile justice system, that is, at the police or court intake level. In a number of sites of this type, diversion from the system was either temporary or placed at the "deep end," in the form of procuring releases of status offenders already institutionalized or preventing their commitment.

Program Services

The failure of program services to affect status offender recidivism may be ascribed principally to extraordinary narrowness in the range of services actually furnished. The main service given the overwhelming majority of program clients was brief crisis counseling. Program guidelines requiring implementation explicitly prescribed the use of *varied* types of services in relation to the character of the client problem, in which crisis counseling figured as only a first step. The restriction to counseling of this type was likely to be most effective with clients least likely to recidivate. That brief counseling emerged as the dominant service modality despite explicit guidelines to the contrary speaks strongly to widespread practitioner preference for this form of service. Future programs must be wary of this dominant bias toward a modality with undemonstrated value.

Service Facilities

This program component also exhibited no perceptible independent effect on recidivism. Variation in recidivism was apparently unaffected by such facility characteristics as level of staff professionalism, the use of volunteers or paraprofessionals, the diversity of services offered (where this was in fact the case), or the use of coercive authority in treating status offenders. However, there was suggestive but inconclusive evidence that two features of youth service facilities may have been related to reduced recidivism; staff attribution of the cause of delinquency to institutional malfunction, and staff perception of high levels of cooperation from community-based youth service agencies. This finding requires validation through further research and, if validated, would suggest as important for delinquency control a youth advocacy posture on the part of treatment personnel and a need to engage more fully the interest and resources of youth-serving institutions and agencies in the delinquency control effort.

Client Characteristics

This program component was by far the most important determinant of variation in recidivism. Whatever success delinquency reduction programs might anticipate thus hangs largely on the selection of their clientele. The data presented in this chapter suggest that programs serving a clientele constituted predominantly of older male status offenders with few or no prior offenses can expect a favorable outcome in recidivism. The outcome can be expected to be unfavorable if the served population has a high proportion of females, younger males, and, in any of these categories, those with multiple prior offenses. Thus, to be *meaningful,* program success in reducing recidivism among status offenders cannot be claimed unless clients are of the latter type. It would appear, then, that the most critical aspect of program policy in efforts to reduce recidivism involves client selection. Status offense behavior is probably the most widespread form of juvenile misconduct, most of it of an occasional or transitory nature. Programs seeking an appropriate clientele are consequently under strong temptation to cast a wide net and to provide services to youth whose need for them may be questionable. Evidence from other sections of this report suggests that this is precisely what happened at several of the program sites. The policy implication would seem to be clear: The service eligibility criteria of deinstitutionalization programs should be designed to focus on those who are most likely in the future to require institutionalization either as persistent status offenders or as serious delinquent offenders. Since this requirement goes contrary to "natural" client selection preferences, extra effort and control must be accorded in maintaining the appropriate client selection criteria, so that "success" cannot be claimed where it would have occurred in any case.

NOTES

1. In this procedure, the mean value of a variable is first assigned to those cases that have missing data on the variable; one then creates a new dummy variable coded 1 if the client lacked data, and 0 if the client data were present (Cohen and Cohen, 1975).

2. Occupational status was based on the National Opinion Research Center (1975) occupational prestige scale.

3. The widely assumed inverse relationship of family socioeconomic status to delinquency has been called into question by self-report delinquency studies. However, the offense data in this analysis are based on police and court records. The class status-delinquency relationship with respect to officially recorded offenses as distinguished from self-reported offense behavior has been repeatedly confirmed in ecological studies and is supported by Wolfgang et al. (1972; see also Shannon, 1963). As Empey (1978: 155-157) has observed, the social conditions surrounding disadvantaged youth increase the likelihood of intervention by police and courts, and consequently creation of an official record. This may be even more the case with respect to the status offenses.

4. Other constellations included one-parent family, reconstituted family (previously divorced mother or father), institutional home, and a category of "other" made up of miscellaneous low-frequency living arrangements.

5. But see Toby (1957a) and Hodgkiss (1933) for evidence that the broken home has more serious impact on preadolescents and on females than on male delinquents. The fact that approximately half the program population was female further warrants the inclusion of family intactness variables.

6. The studies cited found age of first offense and recidivism to be inversely related: The younger the age at first offense the greater the likelihood of a second offense and the shorter the time span between first and second offense. Moreover, implied in labeling theory is the notion that the younger and presumably more impressionable the person when exposed to formal processing by the juvenile justice system, the greater the probability of the labeling effect.

7. Studies of the gender distribution of populations in juvenile institutions and detention centers have found those committed for status offenses to be disproportionately female (Pappenfort, 1970; California Youth Authority, 1974). Further, females have been found more susceptible to incarceration for status than for criminal offenses. Lerman (1974) found that of total admissions to the New Jersey Training School for Girls in 1972, 57 percent were for status offenses. Of 169 girls 10-16 years of age in juvenile institutions in June 1974 in South Carolina, 62 percent were confined for status offenses. The corresponding proportion for the 437 institutionalized boys in that state during the same month was 8.4 percent (South Carolina Department of Youth Services, 1975).

8. Minority group status as a determinant of delinquency is known primarily with respect to Blacks. However, to the extent that minority group status is associated with depressed socioeconomic status, the observations respecting the relationship of the latter to delinquency will apply to the former (see Empey, 1978: 155-159). But it is likely that the association of class status and delinquency is more prominent during the earlier stages of juvenile justice processing. Thornberry (1973) found that lower-class youth are not convicted of charged offenses at higher rates than are higher-status youth.

9. See Chapters 5 and 6 for site variations in the implementation of these program types.

10. The importance of trained social workers in delinquency control remains controversial (Rutherford and Bengur, 1976). The argument has been made that a professionally trained staff is important for success in community-based corrections programs, as well as in the more standard forms of agency practice (Fox, 1977: 226; Levine, 1977: 146; Nejelski, 1976: 403). However, the importance of such training in the treatment of deviant youth, particularly in urban areas of high delinquency rates, has been questioned, and has given rise to a movement extolling the replacement of trained social workers with "indigenous" workers (Kobrin, 1959). The use of paraprofessionals and volunteers in corrections work has since been generally accepted as supplementing if not replacing professionals despite the competitive tension between the two (Marris and Rein, 1973; Joint Commission on Correctional Manpower and Training, 1970).

11. Facilities varied with respect to the range of services offered. Some emphasized the value of a particular form of treatment in dealing with status offender problems, such as group therapy, family or individual counseling, or youth advocacy. Others were less wedded to a particular theory of effective treatment and attempted to provide the type of treatment thought useful in the individual case. It was of interest to examine empirically the bearing of the two types of emphasis on the subsequent offense behavior of program clients.

12. Programs at each site had the identical objective of reducing the use of secure confinement in status offense cases, but sites differed in the ways they attempted to implement it. Variables were selected to measure, first, the differential impact of a deterrent strategy on subsequent offense behavior, consonant with labeling theory, as contrasted with varieties of treatment that sought to avoid the labeling effect. Among the latter, treatment approaches appeared to fall into the three rather standard categories that characterize current treatment ideology, and that correspond to three types of theory in the explanation of deviant behavior (Cohen, 1966: 41-47). These place the locus of the problem in the psychological makeup of the individual, in the person's relationships with the "significant others" of his or her primary groups, or in the features of the wider institutional order that provide or deny opportunities for development as a conforming person.

13. In some sites, clients were referred for services to non-DSO facilities where local evaluators found it impossible to obtain family data. In one site, where only DSO facilities were used, restrictions were placed on the recording of family data when, in the judgment of program personnel, this would interfere with treatment.

14. The findings on the two facility variables require qualifying comment. They would seem to indicate that reduced recidivism is a function of staff linkage to community-based services and of staff attention to malfunction in youth-serving institutions as the source of youth problems. However, community linkage was operationalized in part by scaled staff perception of cooperation elicited from community agencies. Unknown is whether these perceptions reflected a generally positive and enthusiastic approach to program clients as well as to community agencies, in which case the reduced client recidivism may be accounted for independently of cooperation elicited from community agencies. As to the causal attribution variable, its inverse relationship to subsequent client offenses showed up principally in the Organizational Survey returns in which precisely these questionnaire items were typically not completed. These returns were assigned the mean scale values of those who did complete the item. The fact of consistent nonresponse to this causal attribution item in the face of willingness to respond to other causal attribution items may be accounted for speculatively in a variety of ways, none of which can be ascertained. Further, the fact that only 2 of 19 relationships were statistically significant raises the obvious problem of random variable appearance. Cross-validation is required before making much of these relationships.

chapter 8

Recidivism Among Program and Comparison Youth

with John Peterson

In *this and the following chapters,*
we come to what many will consider the heart of the matter, namely, the
attempt to answer the question "Did it work?" Of course, we must face
the usual problems of defining what is meant by "it" and what is meant by
"work." The "it" refers to those programs, described in Chapters 5 and 6,
that were designed to bring about deinstitutionalization and provide alternatives for temporary and long-term incarceration.

But even if the program descriptions provide the answers to what "it" was, we are hardly on solid ground yet to describe how "it" worked, for two reasons. First, the entire DSO effort was not designed in such a way as to provide definitive answers to whether or not it worked. Second, there are numerous ways to define "work," only some of which were incorporated in the national evaluation. Thus, depending on one's choice among the appropriate effectiveness measures, it is possible to conclude that (a) effectiveness was not appropriately measured, or (b) the program succeeded in providing useful service, or (c) the program did substantially achieve its deinstitutionalization aims, or (d) the program failed and may even have been more harmful than helpful to its thousands of youthful clients.

Before considering these possible outcome statements further, we must first be clear about the comment above that the entire DSO effort was not designed so as to provide definitive evaluation results. The comment is based upon a number of realities:

(a) Several of the eight sites selected for the program had already initiated deinstitutionalization, thus making it difficult to attribute to the DSO program whatever subsequent declines in institutionalized populations may have occurred.

(b) The staff of OJJDP gave very low priority to field experimentation, with the result that random assignment of youths to various experimental and control conditions was not undertaken.

(c) The eight sites varied widely in their system data capacities and data banks, erring generally on the side of inadequacy. Thus attempts to demonstrate DSO-related changes in client flows was very difficult.

(d) Program operations in a number of sites made it impossible to obtain client interviews close in time to client intake, thus preventing the use of social adjustment measures to assess changes from preintervention to postintervention periods (some "first wave" interviews took place weeks, even months, after intake, in some instances after intervention had been completed).

(e) Finally, client eligibility criteria varied so widely, and generally were so ill defined, that the DSO program intervened in the lives of many youngsters who, in the absence of the program, may not normally have been detained or institutionalized. To assess the effects of a deinstitutionalization program on clients for whom it may not have been appropriate would seem to test the outer limits of evaluation fantasies. We do not assess the effectiveness of parole on nonadjudicated adults, nor of detoxification programs on nonaddicts or teetotalers. Why assess the effects of deinstitutionalization for minor offenders for whom institutionalization was in any event highly unlikely?[1]

Now we can return for a brief comment on the several possible outcome statements posited earlier. For instance, the limitations of the research just listed certainly support the first possible conclusion, that effectiveness was not appropriately measured. Under the circumstances described, that conclusion might be inevitable. Further, the national evaluation chose not to measure some things that others might consider important. Choices were made in the light of limited resources and intractable logistical problems. Among matters excluded were cost-effectiveness,[2] social adjustment of clients and their families, changes in community delinquency patterns, and changes in the behavior and opinions of various segments of the community such as political leaders, education and welfare workers, and criminal justice officials.[3] If one values *these* particular criteria highly, one could also conclude that the program's effectiveness has not been appropriately assessed.

By way of contrast, the eight program descriptions can just as easily be used to claim program success. While some qualifications are noted from site to site, it seems eminently clear that many services were implemented for many thousands of youths deemed in need of such services. Given the federal carrot, eight highly diverse county and state mechanisms were successfully engaged, and service delivery systems of substantially greater scope than those that had existed previously did emerge. If such matters are taken as legitimate outcome goals, then DSO has every right to proclaim itself a successful venture.

The third possibility, that the program achieved substantial success in achieving a reduction in institutionalized populations, can be reasonably entertained *so long as one does not require proof of causal connections.* As materials reported in Chapter 10 indicate, the period of the DSO program over all eight sites saw a reduction in numbers of youth detained of about 25 percent, and a reduction in numbers of youth institutionalized of about 50 percent. Neither figure reaches the original requirement of the federal legislation, but both are substantial and in the desired direction. However, the details of the analysis suggest that, rather than a function of program effort, this reduction possibly represented further progress in deinstitutionalization that was already under way in several of the sites before the program was initiated.

Finally, then, we come to the fourth possible outcome statement, that the program failed and may even have been more harmful than helpful. The available data that might be pertinent to testing such a conclusion are of four kinds.

First, there is the issue of reducing the numbers of youth incarcerated. It is assumed by most critics, and made explicit in the federal legislation, that deinstitutionalization is humane. Thus we achieve humaneness in proportion to the number of status offenders who are released from or diverted from incarceration. The figures cited above suggest that the program achieved some increment of advance in the humaneness with which status offenders were treated.

Second, we can determine the degree to which status offender flows in the juvenile justice system have changed, in what fashion, and whether the system has adjusted to these flows in a consonant fashion. A report by Carter (1981), summarizing the system rates changes during the DSO program, provides inconclusive evidence at best. Carter was severely handicapped by the inadequacies of the available data bases, but at the very least this much can be said: The impact of the DSO program on offender flows in the eight juvenile justice systems was not of sufficient magnitude to be revealed by the data available from those systems.

Third, we can ask whether the appropriate youngsters were served by the program. As revealed by the separate local evaluations as well as the overall national analysis, it is clear that among the clients engaged by the DSO program there were very substantial numbers who were *not* properly the clientele of the program (see Chapter 4). These were youngsters whose offenses and careers would *not* have justified their detention normally, nor the level of service to which they were exposed. The analysis of the offense patterns of program clients indicated that the largest single group of program clients had no officially recorded offenses either prior to or subsequent to the "instant" offenses that occasioned their referrals to the program. Their inclusion in the program may well be a classic example of "net widening" wherein the justice system, inadvertently or otherwise, has actually increased the level of client penetration into its mechanisms. The potential for harm through stigmatization and improper associations is obvious, and it is precisely what the DSO program was designed to prevent, not to promote.

Finally, we come to the question of recidivism, the rate at which program clients acquired police records for status or other offenses following program intervention. We have looked at this outcome measure in three different ways. In the preceding chapter, we assessed the degree to which recidivism rates could be attributed to (a) different sites, (b) different kinds of clients, (c) different kinds of programs and program facilities, and (d) different specific services offered within each site. In the following chapter, we will describe analysis of the effectiveness of specific types of service applied to specific types of clients, or "what works for whom." In this chapter, we will compare the recidivism rates of program clients with the rates of youths selected from court records during a preprogram period. As can be seen, this last approach, the program/preprogram comparison, comes closest to asking the question "Did it work?" as a positive means of delinquency reduction, while the other two approaches are more concerned with understanding policy-related connections between what went into the DSO program and what resulted.

THE PROGRAM /PREPROGRAM COMPARISON

Ideally, assessment of recidivism as an impact measure would employ comparisons between experimental and control groups to which clients had been randomly assigned. However, random or matched assignment was not actively encouraged in the OJJDP program solicitation and was actively discouraged by OJJDP staff during site visits to potential program grantees. Thus a genuine experimental design was not achieved in any of the eight sites.[4]

Of various possible substitute comparisons considered, the national and local evaluators settled on the use of a preprogram group in each site as the most feasible approach. There were several reasons for this choice. First, the availability of court records made possible the selection of known, detainable status offenders. Second, these same records could provide at least minimal data on the prior records and demographic characteristics of the comparison group. Third, gathering data from record sources alone meant that this part of the research process would not interfere with, and therefore not encounter resistance from, the program staffs in the eight sites and in OJJDP.

Each local evaluator, in consultation with the national evaluators, selected a preprogram period consisting of the full year prior to program start-up.[5] There were three criteria for selection of preprogram cohorts: Cases were drawn in which the instant offense was one of the five selected for the program population; they were drawn from a preprogram month corresponding to the program month, and only if they had not been selected into the sample for a prior preprogram month; and they excluded cases not eligible for some form of detention.[6]

The recidivism criterion selected for the comparisons to be reported here is total counts of charges in all officially reported police incidents. To have employed a deeper-penetration criterion such as court appearance would not have yielded a sufficient amount of variation for the analysis.[7] While the rearrest criterion certainly has its drawbacks because it reflects an unknown combination of youth behavior and adult reaction, no more feasible criterion seemed possible. Self-report data, for instance, was a logical impossibility for the preprogram cohort.

Recidivism data were collected by the local evaluator in each site from police and court records and delivered to the national evaluation staff. (Only records of arrests were actually used in this analysis.) After checks for missing information were completed, data cleaning and file construction were undertaken by the national staff and variables were constructed for number of subsequent offenses at six months and at twelve months following the date of program entry of each client for the program group,[8] and following the date of the instant offense for the preprogram group. Relationships among the six- and twelve-month scores, and among scores based on court records alone and police and court records combined, yield intercorrelations ranging from $+.80$ to $+.98$. The analysis to be reported here will include the six-month period for all sites, and a twelve-month period for six sites. Connecticut and Clark County were excluded from the twelve-month scores because, for various reasons, a follow-up period of this length was not available.

PROGRAM AND PREPROGRAM COMPARISON VARIABLES

The variables on which the two cohorts could be compared were limited to those rather routinely available in police files. Among these, consultations among local and national evaluators led to the selection of the following variables.

Dependent Variables

The dependent variables consisted of the number of subsequent offenses at six months (eight sites) and twelve months (six sites).[9] Because the distribution was heavily skewed, it was transformed to the base 2 logarithm of number of charges (plus 1). This improved the shape of the distribution but could not overcome skewness due specifically to the large number of clients with no recidivism charges.

Independent Variables

Site

The sites were effect coded, using Spokane as the omitted category and seven effect-coded nominal variables.

Offense History

There were three characterizations of each client's prior record:

(1) the log transformed number of recorded prior offenses;
(2) the number of prior status offenses, similarly transformed; and
(3) status offense purity, dummy coded by scoring 0 if there was no prior record or if the prior record included nonstatus offenses, and scored 1 if the prior record consisted of status offenses only.

Instant Offense

Instant status offenses were specifically defined and were classified in several ways:[10]

(1) Preprogram and program youth were coded for six possible types of instant offense. For program clients, the instant offense is defined as a status offense that resulted in a referral to the program. For preprogram youth, the instant offense is a status offense that occurred within the monthly time frame specified for the preprogram year that resulted in a police or court record. As already noted, the six offense types were runaway, ungovernable, truant, curfew violation, minor in possession of alcohol, and other. In a large number of cases multiple instant status offenses were recorded,

indicating the likelihood that the defiant and rebellious behavior represented by this type of infraction could frequently be expressed simultaneously in a number of ways. A youth could run away from home because of his ungovernability, in turn leading to such other status offenses as curfew violation and others. Where multiple charges or "allegations" exist, which or how many of these the police or court might single out for recording as a basis for action was deemed likely to be in large part arbitrary. The decision was therefore made to collapse multiple instant status offenses on some reasonable basis to only one of those recorded. This was done by imposing the assumption that the six status offenses can be ordered according to a loss of parent or guardian control over the youth's behavior. On this basis a hierarchy of seriousness was constructed in the order of runaway, ungovernable, truant, curfew, possession of alcohol, and other. In all cases of multiple instant status offenses, the single most serious was coded.

(2) Six dummy variables were used for the status offense categories, except in sites where some categories remained unfilled. In the multiple regression analysis for the aggregate eight-site six-month subsequent offense follow-up, only three or fewer were used, since runaway, ungovernable, and truant were individually significant. In this analysis, clients who were curfew violators, minors in possession of alcohol, or "other" fell into the residual category for the regression. The dummies are thus exclusive: a client is coded 1 on only one instant status offense.

(3) Separately from the specific instant status offense to which multiple instants were collapsed, information was retained to distinguish those with a single instant offense from those with multiple instant status offenses. The former were dummy coded 0, the latter 1.

Demographic Characteristics

Four dummy-coded variables were employed to describe the personal status of clients:[11]

(1) gender, scored 1 if female, 0 male;
(2) ethnicity, scored 1 for Anglo, 0 for any other;
(3) age, scored as an interval variable in years at the time of the referral or instant offense (the range was from 7 to 18); and
(4) customary household, describing whether it was with the nuclear family, scored 1; nonnuclear scored 0.[12]

Time Variables

In order to control for any interaction effects associated with date of program referral and date of instant offense of preprogram cases, or associated with date of the initiation of data collection (researchers, too, show activity trends over time), variables were included to equate the cohorts and investigate possible time confounding. Also, seasonal effects were effect coded for entry into the equations since a preliminary regression had indicated lower recidivism rates for summer referrals.

Comparability

The variables above were to be used in regression equations in the program/preprogram comparisons of recidivism. Obviously, it is useful to compare the two cohorts on the relevant variables first to ascertain their overall comparability. The number of cases available for these analyses is quite substantial, although reduced somewhat by data problems. Of a total of 7109 cases combined, 147 were "crossovers," appearing in both cohorts. Eliminating these from the program cohort yielded 3017 preprogram and 3945 program cases. In preparation for the regression analysis, missing data cases were also deleted, yielding final cohorts of 2959 (preprogram) and 3714 (program), for a total of 6673. This refers to the numbers available for the six-month recidivism analysis. The twelve-month analysis, primarily due to the loss of Connecticut and Clark County, was based on a somewhat smaller number of cases.

Table 8.1 presents, for each site separately and for all sites combined, the means or proportions (as appropriate) for each of the comparison variables in the preprogram and program cohorts. Also indicated are two-tailed probability levels based upon t tests using pooled or separate variance as necessary.

Looking first at the last column of Table 8.1, it can be seen that the two cohorts differed significantly on the majority of the comparison variables. The size and direction of these differences is consistent but not very substantial, except in the case of prior offenses. Since prior record has uniformly appeared as a major predictor of recidivism—often as *the* major predictor—this difference is of major importance. Thus the absence of control groups is costly, and the current analysis must attempt to control on prior record (as well as the other differentiating variables) while undertaking comparisons of recidivism rates. But after-the-fact statistical controls do not equate with random assignment controls.

For those less accustomed to interpreting data such as those displayed in Table 8.1, we can offer the following with respect to the differences at the national level. The program groups had significantly fewer prior offenses, including fewer status offenses, and they did not have delinquent charges included in the instant offense. Thus, in terms of offense history, they constituted a less serious group of offenders, confirming earlier comments about "net widening" in the DSO program and adding this program to a growing list of instances documenting the phenomenon of net widening in juvenile treatment programs.[13]

Program clients did not differ significantly on age or ethnicity, but were more likely to be female. With respect to household composition, they were significantly *more* likely to come from intact parental situations—homes with two parents, whether natural or step. This, again, suggests a client selection process favoring less serious cases than those in the pre-program cohort, although the difference is not a large one.

The expectation from these indications of a less serious program clientele are clear and very important to keep in mind: Less serious cases, other things being equal, should yield lower recidivism rates. Thus, in our comparative analysis, if the program/preprogram comparison yields lower recidivism rates for the program group, we will be hard put to credit this to the program, even with the inclusion of the control variables in the regression equation. If the analysis yields differences in rates that are either equivocal or unfavorable toward the program group, then the implication will be that the program may have contributed to a higher level of recidivism than probably would have occurred without the program.[14]

Since the analysis will look at the results in each site, it is appropriate to look down each column in Table 8.1 to observe the intersite differences. For instance, the Alameda comparison reveals almost no difference between the two cohorts; Alameda might thus stand as a critical case for the recidivism analysis.[15] By way of contrast, Pima County differs on virtually all the comparisons; recidivism comparisons in that site must be viewed with the greatest degree of skepticism.

Clark County is somewhat different from the others in that it shows major reversals in direction; it has more prior offenses and more nonintact family situations among its program clients. On the other hand, the preprogram group was such a nonserious group to begin with that no other result might have been possible.

In terms of the general seriousness of the cases selected in each site, other contrasts also emerge. For instance, Illinois clearly involved the most serious prior offense patterns. One must wonder, especially in the case of South Carolina, with .16 mean score for prior offenses,[16] whether the "D" in DSO had any real meaning at all.

RECIDIVISM

Six-Month Recidivism

The procedure for establishing the nature of recidivism rate differences between the two cohorts was to enter in a regression equation each of the variables listed earlier in this chapter. These variables fell under the categories of site, offense history, instant offense, demographic characteristics, time variables, and recidivism measures. With all these variables included, and with the inclusion of the site by program interactions, a highly significant multiple r of .39 is achieved, explaining 16 percent of

TABLE 8.1 Comparisons on Input Variables Between Preprogram and Program Cohorts: Six-Month Cohorts

Variable	Pima	Alameda	Connecticut	Delaware	Illinois	South Carolina	Clark	Spokane	National
Mean prior offense score[a,c]									
preprogram	1.09	.88	.76	.95	2.12	.31	.09	.90	.96
program	.68	.87	.54	.78	1.42	.14	.34	.44	.75
t	6.64	.24	1.97	2.68	10.03	4.32	-5.29	5.28	7.65
p	<.01	ns	<.05	<.01	<.01	<.01	<.01	<.01	<.01
Mean prior status offense score[a]									
preprogram	.47	.31	.48	.30	1.36	.08	.04	.53	.46
program	.24	.33	.32	.27	.94	.04	.15	.18	.36
t	5.43	-.31	1.91	.88	7.05	1.64	-3.38	5.22	5.05
p	<.01	ns	<.10	ns	<.01	<.10	<.01	<.01	<.01
Proportion pure prior status offenders									
preprogram	.10	.09	.22	.07	.25	.03	.04	.17	.11
program	.07	.07	.12	.09	.29	.03	.12	.07	.12
t	1.99	.87	2.36	-1.35	-1.44	.22	-2.92	3.15	-.84
p	<.05	ns	<.05	ns	ns	ns	<.01	<.01	ns
Proportion mixed instant offenses									
preprogram	.16	.04	.01	.05	.07	.01	.00	.06	.06
program	.03	.05	.03	.02	.02	.01	.00	.05	.03
t	7.26	-1.06	-1.45	2.90	3.66	-.56	—	.18	5.75
p	<.01	ns	ns	<.01	<.01	ns	ns	ns	<.01
Proportion females									
preprogram	.34	.52	.69	.43	.54	.51	.59	.59	.49
program	.43	.43	.71	.47	.63	.51	.57	.66	.53
t	-3.31	2.51	.42	-1.45	-3.17	-.14	.43	-1.79	-3.33
p	<.01	<.05	ns	ns	<.01	ns	ns	<.10	<.01
Proportion white									
preprogram	.66	.64	.72	.68	.35	.62	1.00	.92	.65

program	.60	.67	.70	.76	.35	.76	.97	.94	.67
t	2.12	-1.00	.29	-3.04	-.13	-4.55	2.60	-.74	-1.49
p	<.05	ns	ns	<.01	ns	<.01	<.01	ns	ns
Mean age									
preprogram	14.33	15.16	14.08	15.17	14.51	13.85	14.60	14.65	14.59
program	14.70	14.74	14.06	15.07	14.50	13.98	14.50	14.72	14.62
t	-4.13	3.46	.12	1.13	.08	-1.05	.62	-.50	-.96
p	<.01	<.01	ns	ns	ns	ns	ns	ns	ns
Proportion nuclear customary household									
preprogram	.38	.31	.25	.43	.30	.37	.52	.35	.37
program	.48	.34	.37	.47	.31	.32	.40	.32	.39
t	-3.50	-.42	-2.19	-1.39	.37	1.63	2.34	.69	-1.89
p	<.01	ns	<.05	ns	ns	ns	<.05	ns	<.10
Proportion reconstituted customary household									
preprogram	.12	.16	.22	.18	.12	.10	.14	.37	.16
program	.16	.18	.23	.15	.17	.18	.22	.29	.19
t	-1.80	-.38	-.27	1.33	-2.90	-3.59	-2.15	2.72	-3.59
p	<.10	ns	ns	ns	<.01	<.01	<.05	<.01	<.01
Proportion intact customary household[b]									
preprogram	.50	.47	.46	.61	.42	.47	.66	.72	.52
program	.63	.52	.60	.62	.49	.50	.62	.61	.58
t	-4.80	-.68	-2.25	-.41	-2.35	-.93	.69	2.54	-4.47
p	<.01	ns	<.05	ns	<.05	ns	ns	<.05	<.01
N									
preprogram	506	440	167	557	437	452	228	172	2,959
program	766	302	145	723	734	393	173	478	3,714

a. Logarithmic functions.
b. Intact household is a summary measure meaning *either* nuclear or reconstituted.
c. Mean prior offense scores (untransformed) were, for preprogram cohort: Pima, 2.07; Alameda, 1.46; Connecticut, 1.30; Delaware, 1.92; Illinois, 4.72; South Carolina, .52; Clark, .09; Spokane, 1.52; National, 1.88. For the program cohort the scores were: Pima, 1.09; Alameda, 1.53; Connecticut, .99; Delaware, 1.41; Illinois, 2.79; South Carolina, .16; Spokane, .62; Clark, .39; National, 1.33.

the total variance in recidivism. The largest single contribution, as might be expected, is the number of prior offenses.

If one reviews the overall regression equation without seeking intersite variation, it appears that program participation had no significant effect.[17] That is, six-month recidivism rates did not differ between preprogram and program cohorts once the comparison variables were controlled statistically. *At this most gross level of analysis, DSO failed to reduce rates of recidivism* in comparison with expectations derived from the preprogram group. However, this statement fails to be sensitive to the intersite variations in program, which are of course very substantial. Thus the regression was rerun with site by program interactions included. These interaction terms, which boost the overall multiple r only slightly, to .40, are included to capture information on differences between sites in the effects of program participation.

The result of this new analysis is to produce a significant and negative F value for the site by program interaction, significant beyond the .001 level of probability. *Overall, the analysis shows a moderately deleterious impact—higher recidivism rates at six months—attributable to program participation.* The exception to this conclusion is Pima County, which shows a significant *positive* effect (beta coefficient −.09, F = 39.03) The other sites show no significant departure from the overall negative main effect.

Whatever qualifications may be put on these findings,[18] they raise serious questions regarding program impact on the recidivism of its clients. Even though the differences we have found are not large, they are in a direction opposite to the expected program effect of reduced recidivism, except in the single case of Pima County. Pima County, it will be recalled, stood out in our analysis of comparison variables as the most "suspect" of all because its preprogram cohort differed so markedly from its program cohort. Further, these findings of deleterious impact stand in face of the expectation, in view of the nonserious nature of the overall program cohort, that recidivism should be less in this cohort even without the introduction of the DSO program.

However, before allowing this conclusion to stand as final, we will test complications that might have arisen from two sources, the *very* low prior offense mean and variance in Clark County and the aforementioned preprogram problem in Pima County.

The problem with Clark County data, and less so with South Carolina as well, is that the necessarily low variance in the offense data might have attenuated the overall national effect. Therefore the entire regression analysis was repeated using seven rather than eight sites, with Clark County excluded. The results were almost identical to the earlier findings except for the emergence of instant offense truancy as a predictor of recidivism and a very slight reduction of variance explained from .16 to .15.

The Pima County problem needs some elaboration. It was noted earlier that the program group in Pima County was more divergent from the preprogram group than was the case in any other site. The selection of the *period* of the preprogram cohort might have been the reason for this. As noted earlier, there were in fact *two* such periods and two cohorts selected in Pima County. The year immediately prior to the program was selected, as it was in all other sites, in order to reduce extraneous intervening factors related to time. However, the main ingredient of the Pima County program was the Mobile Diversion Unit (see Chapter 5). As in most other sites selected for the DSO program, Pima County was already moving in the direction of status offender deinstitutionalization. Specifically, the Mobile Diversion Unit was in place and functioning during the year immediately preceding the program.

Because of this program continuity, it was felt advisable to select a second preprogram cohort, representing a period *two* years prior to the program, when the Mobile Diversion Unit was not yet functioning. It was in fact this "pre-preprogram" cohort that was reflected in Table 8.1 and in the regression analyses reported above.

The use of this cohort was not incorrect; it was merely a choice between two nonsatisfactory alternatives, between a group more distant in time but "program pure" and a group more close in time but "contaminated" by possible anticipatory program effects. Perhaps the major problem with having employed the more distant time period is that Pima County was the only one of the eight sites with such a preprogram period. Thus it could be that this site's production of a beneficial program, as contrasted with the other seven, is an artifact of period selection.[19] The case can also be made that the immediately preceding year—with Mobile Diversion—is the appropriate year because it was in existence without the federal DSO carrot; that is, the DSO program was merely a veneer over an already functioning structure.

With these thoughts in mind, we undertook a regression analysis of the Pima County program and immediate preprogram groups. The result, employing the same control variables as before, was that there was *no* significant difference in recidivism between the two cohorts. The use of the same time period in Pima County as was used in other sites had the effect of washing away the one case of beneficial impact. DSO seems not to have added any impact of value on recidivism over and above what was apparently already taking place in the absence of DSO.

Twelve-Month Recidivism

The advantages of assessing recidivism over a longer time period are several. Any delayed program effects, either positive or negative, have a greater opportunity to appear. Program effects that take place toward the end of the treatment period or that are cumulative in effect have a greater opportunity to appear. Independent reactions, positive and negative, to initial recidivism offenses can be demonstrated more clearly. Delayed effects, dependent upon interactions with maturation or community changes likewise have more opportunity to become evident. Finally, from a statistical viewpoint, more time means more offenses committed and greater variance within which to discern differential impact.

However, the character of the DSO program damaged the twelve-month analysis to an unfortunate extent. Two sites, Connecticut and Clark County, had foreshortened data collection periods. In the case of Connecticut, this was due to a very considerable delay in program start-up. In Clark County the shorter follow-up period resulted from the failure of an initial effort to obtain a comparison group by the random assignment of clients to the program and to normal court processing. An attempt was then made to substitute a preprogram comparison group for the now unusable control group. However, the effort was undertaken too close to the end of funded activity to permit more than a six-month follow-up. Thus the twelve-month recidivism analysis has been carried out on the data from the remaining six sites, excluding Connecticut and Clark County.

In this analysis, we are dealing with far smaller numbers in each of the six sites because the period between program completion and the last date on which data could be collected was variably less than twelve months. Thus many clients simply did not have sufficient time "at risk" to be included here. The new numbers are shown at the bottom of Table 8.2, which is the twelve-month counterpart to Table 8.1, comparing the two cohorts on input variables.

Not much need be said about the data displayed in Table 8.2. The general pattern is similar, as would be expected, to that of Table 8.1, which was based on the larger full six-month cohorts. Row differences remain substantially the same except that the finding of significantly more females in the program cohort does not hold true for the twelve-month comparison.

Reading down the columns, it appears that Pima County remains the site with the greatest number of differences, but the effect is now smaller. Alameda remains a case of few differences, but it is now Delaware that has the fewest. Overall, there has been a reduction of 29 percent, from Table 8.1 to Table 8.2, in the number of differences reaching the .05 level of significance. This general trend toward reduction of differences, while not very pronounced, should reduce slightly the difficulty in uncovering "true" recidivism differences between the two cohorts.

Since the reader is familiar with the pattern of the six-month regression analysis, we can report the results of the twelve-month regression more briefly. The variables employed in the equation account for a slightly greater amount of the total variance. With a multiple r of .46, an R^2 of .21 is obtained. This is an additional .05 over the variance explained in the six-month analysis. Once again, the equation without the site by program interactions reveals no significant program impact. However, the site by program interactions are highly significant ($F = 10.18$, $p < .01$), suggesting that the program, in light of an apparently heavy inflow of relatively minor offenders, may have increased client recidivism. As was the case earlier, Pima County emerges with a statistically significant countertrend (beneficial) based upon the pre-preprogram cohort. If the preprogram cohort exposed to Mobile Diversion were employed, this program effect would presumably be substantially reduced. Unfortunately, these twelve-month data were not collected in Pima County and this cannot be clearly demonstrated.

Overall, then, the twelve-month recidivism analysis confirms the six-month analysis; on the criterion of rearrest, the DSO program does not emerge as a success. It has apparently contributed to a somewhat higher rate of recidivism among a cohort of youngsters, many but certainly not all of whom were probably not appropriate clients for a deinstitutionalization program. Whether such a result would have occurred in sites that had not yet instituted significant movement toward deinstitutionalization is an unanswerable question: We are reluctant to generalize from the one pattern to the other. [20]

SITE-BY-SITE COMMENT

All of the preceding material constitutes one part of the "national" analysis. But in truth, there has been debate since the first day of research planning for the DSO program over whether or not a "national" analysis was appropriate or even possible. This debate, involving the national evaluation staff, the local evaluators, the NIJJDP staff, and the advisory committee to the national staff, consisted of a friendly yet intense discussion concerning the process of aggregating data over eight rather disparate sites.

The basic question in these discussions was the feasibility of disentangling the contextual effects of *site*, as a categorical variable, from the effects of client characteristics and the effects of program and service variables. Further, even if one could disentangle these effects, might there not be additional unmeasured characteristics associated with site, as a variable, which would confound any aggregated analysis?

No final resolution to the question achieved consensus; indeed, the debate mirrored what are currently unresolved positions in evaluation research generally. Our approach in this report has been to "surround" the question with several analytic approaches, accepting the premise that what we have are not eight *replications* of a DSO program, but eight *variations*. Further, we explicitly accept the probability of contextual and selective biases associated with the site variable. That is, we acknowledge that different sites will reflect differences in client selection and process-

TABLE 8.2 Comparisons on Input Variables Between Preprogram and Program Cohorts: Twelve-Month Cohorts

Variable	Pima	Alameda	Delaware	Illinois	South Carolina	Spokane	National
Mean prior offense score[a,c]							
preprogram	1.10	.87	.88	2.09	.34	.90	1.00
program	.61	.93	.79	1.54	.13	.46	.76
t	5.53	-.57	.96	5.34	4.03	4.78	6.04
p	<.01	ns	ns	<.01	<.01	<.01	<.01
Mean prior status offense score[a]							
preprogram	.54	.35	.33	1.41	.07	.53	.51
program	.20	.36	.35	1.00	.04	.18	.37
t	5.52	-.19	-.37	4.65	1.20	5.01	5.06
p	<.01	ns	ns	<.01	ns	<.01	<.01
Proportion pure prior status offenders							
preprogram	.15	.11	.07	.27	.04	.17	.13
program	.06	.09	.12	.32	.02	.06	.12
t	3.14	.90	-1.78	-1.18	.95	3.43	.88
p	<.01	ns	<.10	ns	ns	<.01	ns
Proportion mixed instant offenses							
preprogram	.16	.04	.04	.07	.00	.06	.06
program	.03	.05	.02	.02	.02	.05	.03
t	4.74	-.36	1.16	2.77	-1.26	.35	3.48
p	<.01	ns	ns	<.01	ns	ns	<.01
Proportion females							
preprogram	.39	.54	.43	.59	.51	.59	.51
program	.42	.37	.50	.59	.48	.66	.51
t	-.64	3.40	-1.61	.07	.72	-1.41	.22
p	ns	<.01	ns	ns	ns	ns	ns
Proportion white							
preprogram	.57	.65	.67	.34	.64	.92	.62

program	.55	.63	.74	.33	.78	.93	.64
t	.49	.31	-1.59	.34	-3.32	-.24	-1.01
p	ns	ns	ns	ns	<.01	ns	ns
Mean age							
preprogram	14.10	15.11	15.33	14.49	13.99	14.65	14.62
program	14.67	14.74	15.07	14.44	13.95	14.70	14.61
t	-4.32	2.16	1.83	.34	.22	-.34	.14
p	<.01	<.05	<.10	ns	ns	ns	ns
Proportion nuclear customary household							
preprogram	.32	.31	.44	.29	.37	.35	.35
program	.44	.41[b]	.46	.30	.31	.33	.38
t	-1.30	-.99	-.44	-.08	1.42	.44	-1.52
p	ns	ns	ns	ns	ns	ns	ns
Proportion reconstituted customary household							
preprogram	.12	.16[b]	.18	.08	.09	.37	.16
program	.16	.14	.12	.18	.18	.30	.19
t	-1.18	.32	1.69	-3.45	-2.64	1.61	-2.15
p	ns	ns	<.10	<.01	<.01	ns	<.05
Proportion intact customary household							
preprogram	.44	.47[b]	.61	.37	.47	.72	.50
program	.60	.55	.58	.47	.49	.63	.56
t	-3.90	-.68	.78	-2.32	-.47	2.04	-3.09
p	<.01	ns	ns	<.05	ns	<.05	<.01
N							
preprogram	214	283	261	228	286	172	1,444
program	449	152	252	320	193	316	1,682

a. Logarithmic functions.
b. Alameda preprogram group had 130 cases with missing family data.
c. Mean prior offense scores transformed.

ing, differences in program development and style, and differences in specific services offered.

This premise, and the acknowledgment of such differences, is implicit in the preceding chapters and in the earlier pages of this chapter. We have attempted, both descriptively and analytically, to provide *both* a national overview and a sensitization to differences associated with the eight sites. The additional reports by Carter (1981) and Miller (1980) also mirror the concern for site differences and give less attention to the need for cross-site aggregation. Finally, the analyses reported in Chapters 7 and 9 help to triangulate on this issue of the level of analysis.

As a complement to the preceding aggregate-level analysis, we present below some thumbnail sketches of the six- and twelve-month analyses *within* each of the eight sites.

The aim of the intrasite analyses was to replicate as closely as possible the structure of the regression analysis reported above on the aggregated data. However, certain site idiosyncrasies made this impracticable. There were, in different combinations, empty or near-empty categories of instant status offense, yearly quarter of referral, and ethnicity. This meant that in different sites, the possible combinations of dummy or effect-coded dichotomous variables would vary and that, for the instant status offense variables, the "omitted category" implied by the intrasite regressions would vary as well.

Pima County

Using the pre-preprogram cohort, we find that overall program impact is positive and statistically significant at six months, as noted earlier. Instant offenses of runaway and ungovernability are significantly related to increased recidivism, while nuclear customary household is significantly related to reduced recidivism. As we are accustomed to finding, number of prior offenses is the single best predictor of recidivism.

At twelve months, the proportion of variance explained almost doubles, from .14 at six months to .24. This and other increased coefficients are probably due, at least in part, to the greater variation available in twelve-month recidivism scores. For instance, at twelve months, both mixed instant offense and gender now have significant F values. The program effect remains significantly positive at twelve months.

However, when the preprogram cohort is used, the one more analogous to the seven other preprogram cohorts but with an ongoing Mobile Diversion Unit, the picture is quite different. At six months, there is *no* program effect whatsoever, and only prior record and instant offense of runaway are significantly related to recidivism. As noted earlier, no twelve-month data were collected on this preprogram cohort.

Alameda County

The proportion of total variance explained is .14 at six months and .16 at twelve months. In both analyses, program effect appears deleterious, but it is not statistically significant. Prior record predicts to increased recidivism in both analyses. Ungovernability does so in the six-month analysis, but fails to reach significance at twelve months. The same is true of a pure status offense prior record. Mixed instant offense emerges as a significant predictor at twelve months but not at six. Remembering our earlier suggestion that the Alameda program /preprogram comparisons perhaps best typified the aggregated national picture, the small number of significant effects and their inconsistency over time in this site may serve as a bellwether of disappointing relationships between program inputs and results.

Connecticut

The state of Connecticut proved a difficult site in many ways, and necessary compromises may have worked against a satisfactory evaluation. Resistance to the DSO program on the part of the court, police, and service provider agencies was far greater here than elsewhere. The most properly restrictive client definition emerged here (that is, the closest to the concept of a "detainable" client). Access to police records was generally not obtainable by the local evaluator, and access to court records was only partially achieved after much negotiation and bad feeling on all sides.

Total variance explained was .12 at six months. There was no twelve-month analysis. The program effect at six months was deleterious, although not at a statistically significant level. Mixed instant offense, gender, and age predict to recidivism, as does runaway instant offense but, surprisingly, prior record does not. This latter may be a function of the record access problem noted above.

Delaware

Variance explained in this site was .13 at six months and .16 at twelve. The program effect was deleterious but nonsignificant at both points in time. At six months, several instant offenses and gender, along with prior record, are the significant predictors. At twelve months, instant offenses generally fail to retain significance, while age and nuclear family are added to gender and prior record as significant predictors. Thus personal or demographic characteristics emerge as primary while offense type and program involvement predict less effectively. This type of finding emerged more generally in analyses reported in Chapter 7. At twelve months, it may be recalled from the earlier aggregated analysis, Delaware emerged with Alameda as typical of the overall national picture.

Illinois

While Illinois was spoken of as a state program, the evaluation took place only in Cook County (Chicago) and several downstate counties. Due to the inequality of population densities, the findings most generally reflect the situation in Cook County. For instance, Illinois had by far the most serious offenders in its program, to judge from their prior records, and the largest proportion of offenders from nonintact homes. In this sense, DSO might have had its most critical test in this site. On the other hand, the Illinois program was the narrowest in conception and consequently cannot provide a very comprehensive test.

Total variance explained is .11 for six months, increasing to .18 for twelve months. The program effect is in the deleterious direction but not significant. Prior record, gender, age, and ethnicity are the significant predictors in both the six- and twelve-month cohorts. Instant offense type, limited essentially to runaway and ungovernability, was not related to recidivism. As in Delaware, demographic characteristics are the predominant predictors.

South Carolina

South Carolina had the most nonserious program clientele of any of the sites. Most had no prior records and no juvenile justice contact in connection with the instant "offense" (the quotation marks are necessary; the "offense" is a service worker's description, not an official charge). One would worry in such a situation about the creation of a criminal record via unjustified client selection and stigmatization. And indeed, at six months, although not at twelve, the deleterious program effect almost reaches statistical significance at the .05 level.

With the least serious offenders and the youngest offenders of all sites, one might also expect recidivism to show more randomness and less responsiveness to patterned variable relationships. Again, the expectation is fulfilled; proportion of variance explained with our variables is only .08 at six months (rivaled only by Clark County) and .11 at twelve. In both the six- and twelve-month cohorts, only prior record (as usual) and mixed instant offense emerge as significant predictors of recidivism. The question may be raised whether the South Carolina clientele was altogether appropriate for a *deinstitutionalization* program. They were "swallowed up" in the service track of a far larger Youth Service Bureau program, in which a variety of youth problems, many not necessarily related to delinquency, were served in the DSO program. Thus it may be small wonder that South Carolina provides so little of value to our analysis. Yet its near-significant deleterious program effect should stand as a warning against "treating" those not yet targetable as appropriate clients.

Clark County

As with Connecticut, we have only a six-month analysis for this site. As with South Carolina, we can explain only 8 percent of the variance and, following the South Carolina pattern, we have a deleterious program effect, but in this case one that well exceeds statistical significance. This may be due to the low variation in recidivism in the preprogram as compared to the program cohort, such that recidivism effects could only be manifested in the program group. This was the reason, earlier, for running a seven-site regression that, as it turned out, yielded the same results as the full regression.

Still, the Clark County results show the same pattern as those for South Carolina, with exaggeration. Not only are there no significant predictors other than program involvement, but even prior record fails to relate to recidivism. The lesson of these two sites would seem to be two-fold: (1) with inappropriate clientele (net widening) the usual delinquency-related variables are inoperative, and (2) the danger of creating recidivism may be significantly increased. *There may be no greater criticism than this for programs that aim to treat "predelinquents." Early intervention receives no support from the DSO evaluation.*

Spokane

Here, total variance explained was again low—.11 in both time periods. The program effect, while in the beneficial direction, was very insignificant. At six months, the significant predictors were prior record, age, and time period variables. At twelve months, the same pattern emerges except that gender replaces age. Again, the intrasite analysis shows more randomness than hints for successful programming.

SUMMARY AND CONCLUSIONS

Among the several ways in which the effect of the DSO program may be assessed, this chapter examines its impact on the offense behavior of program clients. Their offenses recorded in police and court records for six and twelve months subsequent to program entry were compared to the recidivism of a cohort of officially recorded status offenders during the year preceding the start of the program at each of the eight sites included in the evaluation study. For reasons beyond the control of the study, the comparability of the two groups was reduced by the occurrence of larger proportions in the preprogram cohort of individuals with prior criminal and status offenses, that is, the kind of youngsters more likely to be the targets of a deinstitutionalization program. Other differences between program and preprogram cohorts existed but they were insubstantial on the average over the eight sites. The range of comparability was defined by the Alameda County program at one extreme, in which there were virtually no differences between the two cohorts, and the Pima County program, in which the cohorts differed substantially in offense history as well as in the demographic and family variables.

To obtain post hoc statistical control in view of the approximate comparability of the two groups, a multiple regression procedure was employed in data analysis. The following findings emerged:

(1) With the comparison variables controlled statistically, recidivism rates aggregated over the eight sites did not differ between the program and the preprogram cohorts at six-month follow-up.

(2) However, when site as a variable was taken into account, with the site-program interaction term included in the regression equation, the program cohort overall exhibited statistically significant higher recidivism rates at six-month follow-up than did the preprogram cohort. Clients in the Pima County program were the single exception: Their recidivism rates were lower, with the difference statistically significant.

(3) The exception to this finding, the Pima County program, may be accounted for by the fact that, in contrast to other sites, the preprogram cohort was drawn from a period predating the general movement to deinstitutionalize status offenders. To a greater or lesser extent, in all other sites status offender deinstitutionalization was under way during the year prior to program start-up.

(4) With minor exceptions, the twelve-month recidivism analysis yielded findings identical to those of the six-month analysis.

(5) Recidivism analysis of the data disaggregated by site revealed that in only two sites were the offense scores for the program clients lower than for the preprogram cohorts: Pima County and Spokane. In the former the difference, as already noted, was statistically significant; in Spokane it was not. In the other six sites, offense scores for the program clients were higher than for the preprogram comparison groups, although only in Clark County did the difference reach statistical significance.

It should be at once apparent that the findings from the aggregated and the disaggregated data differ with respect to the level of statistical significance attached to the higher recidivism scores of program clients. In the latter case the difference usually falls short of an acceptable level of probability. However, the major trend is in a direction that suggests the probable validity of the finding based on the aggregated data, namely, that program clients tended to be slightly more recidivistic than their comparison cohorts. This is all the more unexpected in view of the more substantial offense histories of the comparison cohorts.

The findings of the comparative recidivism analysis may be interpreted in diverse ways. First, they provide some support for the view that furnishing a program of noncourt services for minor juvenile offenders, many of whom might not have come to official attention, may have the effect of increasing their visibility and entangling them unnecessarily in the sanctioning machinery of juvenile justice. Offense rates may reflect official action as much as they do actual offense behavior. Paradoxically, this is precisely the effect that a deinstitutionalization strategy seeks to avoid.

Second, the strikingly deviant case of the Pima County program, where the comparison group constituted more appropriately a sample drawn from a pre-deinstitutionalization era,[21] suggests on the other hand that the avoidance of secure confinement of status offense cases does in fact reduce recidivism. However, this interpretation should be entertained with caution. The eligibility criteria for entry into the Pima County program were among the most liberal of all, possibly exceeding those of the South Carolina program.

Finally, in view of the difficulties encountered in obtaining entirely adequate data, and of the small and frequently nonsignificant differences in recidivism scores between the program and comparison groups in five of the eight programs, the findings may also be interpreted reasonably as indicating "no difference." In that case, the question of a beneficent effect of the program may be reversed to challenge the preventive utility of secure confinement in status offender cases. Briefly, if status offenders who are not detained and institutionalized exhibit approximately the same rate of recidivism as those who are subjected to confinement, why lock them up? The preprogram comparison group was not provided an expanded set of services, but their recidivism rates did not differ materially from those of the program clients who received such services.

The diversity of possible interpretations of the recidivism analysis seems to foreclose the kind of definitive recommendation that evaluation studies are expected to provide. However, a balanced view suggests the following: Pending the development of intervention programs in status offense cases that are demonstarably more effective than those of the prevailing type, there is no gain in recidivism reduction associated with either secure confinement or referral to programs of remediation.

NOTES

1. A separate study of juvenile court processing in Cook County, Illinois (Reed et al., 1981) revealed that status offense (MINS) complaints stemmed more from the parents than from the community. Weisbrod (1981) confirms this trend in a study of the New York family court.

2. A cost study was conducted, but it was restricted to a comparison of costs of community versus institutional treatment in a limited number of sites with contrasting program strategies (see Peat, Marwick, Mitchell & Co., 1981).

3. However, see the report by Gardiner (1981) on value positions of these community members.

4. An exception occurred in one site in which the local evaluator convinced program personnel to implement a randomized assignment design. With this accomplished, and because resources were limited, the evaluator was able to eliminate "wave one" interviews on the assumption that experimental and control groups would have yielded similar scores. However, the local evaluator left the monitoring of randomization in the hands of local program personnel, who, as is often the case, failed properly to maintain the assignment system. As a result, the experimental and control groups differed greatly on significant personal background variables (especially gender) and a proper comparison was negated. And of course there was no way to retrieve the omitted "wave one" interviews.

5. In addition to a preprogram sample drawn from the first year, the Pima County, Arizona, program also drew a "pre-preprogram" sample from the second year prior to program start-up. The analysis of program /preprogram differences in recidivism scores focused principally on the pre-preprogram cohort. There were several reasons for this. During the first preprogram year, the court had begun to implement an extensive program of diverting status offenders from detention and providing many services similar to those in the subsequent DSO program. This was Pima County's "Mobile Diversion Unit." In an effort to avoid stigmatization, status offense cases were handled informally by neighborhood-based units, and it was difficult to recover adequate records of client characteristics. Since these difficulties did not exist with respect to the pre-preprogram cohort, which in any case represented a more appropriate comparison, the six- and twelve-month follow-up data presented here are for this group in Pima County.

6. The procedure is illustrated by the following exerpt from the evaluation guidelines:

> For each month of the preprogram period (i.e., the 1975-76 month corresponding to the evaluation month), it will be necessary to identify the total population of status offenders from juvenile court intake records. (Depending upon local procedures, some sites may also require a search of police records for initial identification.) The monthly cohort should then be randomly subsampled to gain equal representation of five status offense categories: runaway, ungovernable, curfew, truancy, and minor in possession of alcohol. Each of these randomly selected subsamples should contain 12 members and the total sample of the monthly cohort should contain 60. If there are 12 or less in the monthly flow of any category, then all cases are to be selected into the subsample. If there are more than 12 in the monthly flow of any category, then the random selection procedure will select out the necessary 12 cases. This same procedure should be repeated each month, except that all subjects selected in a previous month are to be excluded from a later monthly sample. (Also, transient runaways and other status offenders who are returned to a jurisdiction outside of the DSO program area should be excluded from the sample.)

> The instant offense for the comparison group is defined as the first status offense *recorded* for a subject during the preprogram month under consideration. Two additional rules apply to the determination of the instant offense. First, if the subject's instant offense consists of multiple charges, all of which are status offenses, then assign the subject to the most serious category. The order of most to least serious is as follows: runaway, ungovernable, truancy, curfew, and minor in possession of alcohol. For example, a subject charged with runaway and curfew would be eligible for selection in the runaway subsample. A second rule regarding the instant status offense is that if a subject's instant offense consists of multiple charges, one of which is a delinquent offense, then the subject should be excluded from selection into a sample; that is, the subject's instant offense should be a "pure status offense."

7. However, court data only were used in the case of the Connecticut program, since police report data were not made available to the site evaluator.

8. Throughout these analysis chapters, "program group" and "program cohort" refer to the *evaluation sample*. The sample consisted of only those clients whose offenses on referral to the program were one or more of the five status offenses listed above.

9. The fact that the same measure is used in all sites should not be taken to mean that the arrest data in each site are comparable. Van Dusen (1981) has noted post-deinstitutionalization arrest patterns to differ between a group of Northern California and Southern California counties, one expressing "protectionism" and the other expressing police frustrations.

10. Of 6962 cases in the two cohorts, only 17 had missing data on instant offenses. These have been omitted from the analyses.

11. Missing data caused deletion of some cases, as follows: gender, 7; ethnicity 17; age, 22; customary household and current residence (combined), 410.

12. The validity of t tests of customary residence as a determinant of subsequent offenses with use of the eight-site aggregate data is undermined by missing data from the Alameda County site, where there were substantial differences in Ns for these and for other variables.

13. Some of the more prominent cases of this pervasive phenomenon are noted in Blomberg (1980), Coates et al. (1978), Klein (1979), Lerman (1975), and Saari and Vinter (1976). With DSO, a good example is provided by Pima County, which "reflects a concern of many critics of diversion that once a referral is made, the recipient agency will virtually always attempt to provide a service whether it is necessary or not" (Rojek, 1978: 6).

14. This judgment is, of course, qualified by the fact that the control group (offense matched preprogram sample) was not generated by a random assignment design.

15. An unfortunate mix-up in research procedures in Alameda County forced the local evaluator there to reconstitute the evaluation sample. The reconstituted sample was derived by an ex post facto matching procedure that presumably is the basis for the absence of differences between the two Alameda cohorts. This is, for evaluation purposes, a fortuitous if serendipitous situation.

16. This is the actual, untransformed score.

17. Tables are available from the authors on request.

18. An important caution to be observed in interpreting this finding is that to the extent the program succeeded in reducing the use of detention, its clients were likely to have enjoyed more "street time" than was available to the preprogram group, with increased opportunity to commit delinquent acts. The program may thus have reduced the incapacitation effect of detention on program clients.

19. However, this one case of beneficial effect based on the use of an earlier preprogram group suggests that the use of a preprogram group drawn from the year prior to program start may have obscured a similar effect at other sites. If so, the effect would be attributable to the general movement to deinstitutionalize status offenders rather than to the program itself. In varying degrees most sites had also been reducing the use of detention in delinquent as well as status offender cases. It is possible that the positive effect seen in Pima County would have been reproduced at other sites if the preprogram comparison groups there had also been drawn from an earlier period.

20. This reluctance should not, however, be taken as endorsement of DSO programs elsewhere. For example, in California, the state planning agency used LEAA funds to support a "how-to" volume *based on the assumption of DSO success* in the absence of any adequate demonstration (see Lloyd, 1980). The two projects used to buttress the assumption were seriously flawed. In one case (Baron and Feeney, 1976; cited in Lloyd, 1980), case restrictions and absence of an appropriate no-treatment control group seriously limit confidence in external validity. In the other (Wimmell, 1973; cited in Lloyd, 1980) no inde-

pendent evaluation was undertaken. Further, Lloyd cites but fails to note negative conclusions from the California studies of the California Youth Authority (Johns and Bottcher, 1980) and of Teilmann and Klein (1979). There are far too many instances in our field of dedicated practitioners who are undeterred by contrary data.

21. The reader may raise the question of why the comparison groups were not drawn at all sites from a period more remote from the initiation of the program. The reason for this was the naive assumption of the evaluation research design that all deinstitutionalization programs would be funded in jurisdictions in which the detention and institutionalization of status offenders was still in full flower.

chapter 9

What Works for Whom

The Uses of Deinstitutionalization

by Katherine Teilmann
Van Dusen
and John Peterson

T*he purposes of this chapter are* to compare the relative effectiveness of the various types of services offered to clients in the eight sites and to determine whether certain types of services are more effective for certain types of clients. The first section of this chapter describes the services offered and their variation across sites. The second section describes the methods of sampling and data collection. The third section analyzes the "biases" involved in assigning clients

Authors' Note: This chapter, taken from the final report of the DSO project, has been edited minimally from the original version by Van Dusen and Peterson.

to services, thereby indicating potential confounding variables in the relation between service type and recidivism. The remainder of the chapter presents results of the analyses.

SERVICES

In this chapter, the focus is on the services delivered to DSO clients. It is important, therefore, to describe them and how they differed in the various DSO program sites. For example, a service defined as "crisis intervention" by one site may not be so termed by another site, and this fact must be taken into account when interpreting analyses that inspect the effectiveness of crisis intervention for reducing recidivism.

If one is to compare the relative effectiveness of many services, some means must be devised to categorize the services along meaningful dimensions. Dimensions along which services could be categorized must surely be infinite (the degree to which they control behavior, what assumptions are implicit about client problems, therapeutic style, and so on). In DSO, most possible classifications were precluded for lack of information on what services were furnished to specific clients. It was not possible to obtain data on service delivery beyond the most general classification of the type of services usually offered by the agency to whom the client was referred. Given this constraint, the national evaluation team set out to devise categories that would have meaning to practitioners, although we recognized that most abstractions beyond the individual client would be unsatisfactory to many practitioners. Eight categories (including "other") were ultimately used to classify services received. In the analysis in this chapter, however, there are usually only six categories, because the three residential services were often collapsed to one category (that is, "residential"). For readers particularly interested in service modalities, descriptions of these categories and how they varied across sites are presented below.

Category 1: Diversion, Diagnostic, and Evaluation Screening

This category refers to a unit that (a) made decisions about clients determining which, if any, of various treatment intervention strategies and programs the client would receive and (b) was considered a specific DSO program service that provided a referral for additional service, such as Mobile Diversion Unit, Diagnostic and Evaluation Center, or "emergency" crisis intervention. The last refers to an intervention strategy that attempted to resolve crises during single meetings, with a capacity to refer clients to additional service(s). This can be contrasted with "extended" crisis intervention, where the strategy included a capacity for continued contacts and possible referral to additional service(s). Extended crisis intervention would be coded as outreach (category 6) or counseling, (category 7), depending upon the nature of the service and the client's situation. Following are descriptions of the programs in each site that fit this general description.

Pima County. The Mobile Diversion Unit consisted of five to six radio-equipped cars in the field, operating 24 hours a day, staffed by probation officers. Units picked up clients from police, courts, schools, and so on, attempted to return clients to parents' homes, and resolved crises. Clients were referred to additional services if required.

Alameda County. This site utilized 24-hour specialized family crisis intervention unit. Attempts were made to deal with the family while in a crisis situation, and then to return the client home as soon as possible. Some agencies were staffed by probation officers and others by private practitioners.

Connecticut. Status offenders were removed from detention and given one-time-only crisis counseling. The program was run and staffed by the Department of Child and Family Services (a public welfare agency).

Delaware. This was a unit run by the family court that took clients from detention facilities and provided advanced diagnostic screening for referral to service agencies.

Illinois. This program was staffed by youth advocates hired for the specific purpose of intervening at police or court intake and returning clients to their homes or to temporary shelter care while awaiting court hearings.

South Carolina. The Department of Youth Services staff (the state's juvenile correctional agency) did crisis counseling, testing, and youth advocacy. Referrals came from courts, schools, parents, and self-referrals.

Clark County. Crisis family counseling was provided on a 24-hour basis by court staff hired for this function. Clients came only from court intake.

Spokane County. This was a specialized family crisis intervention unit operating 24 hours per day. It was run by Youth Alternatives, a private agency with trained counselors. Counseling was short term and oriented to the immediate crisis. Concerted efforts were made to return clients to their homes as soon as possible, resolve the family conflict, and then, when necessary, to refer clients to agencies for services designed to meet their special needs.

Residential Treatment

Category 2: Shelter Care

This service refers to temporary residential facilities where placement is 30 days or less. Examples included emergency housing and care for runaways, homes for children awaiting some official action that would lead to another placement, and a temporary community-based residential program for acting-out clients. There *may* be crisis or short-term intervention services, such as counseling, provided on a routine basis within this facility. In such cases, these were not coded as separate or additional services.

Category 3: Group Home

This category refers to residential facilities where placement was for 31 days or more. There might be services routinely provided at the facility, such as counseling, recreation, job placement or training, and youth advocacy. In such cases, these services were not coded as separate or additional services.

Category 4: Foster Home

This would be a residential placement in a single family home with the adult male and /or female serving as parent surrogate. In some instances, where foster parents have been trained, there were special services provided that were not coded as separate or additional services. A report by Handler and Zatz (1982:9), unlike the DSO experience, found foster care to be "looming large as an alternative out-of-home placement for status offenders."

Following are descriptions of the programs in each site that were coded into the categories described above (2,3, and 4).

Pima County. Temporary shelter care only was used; no group homes. These facilities were privately run.

Alameda County. Two crisis receiving homes were funded under the DSO program. Police were able to refer to them directly if parents were unavailable. Length of stay averaged less than two or three days. Short-term foster homes were used as well if crisis homes were overloaded.

Connecticut. Only privately run emergency shelter care was used to any significant degree in Connecticut.

Delaware. Privately run emergency shelter care was the major mode of residential care used in Delaware.

Illinois. Temporary shelter in private foster homes, or shelter or group homes was provided where needed until the child's court date (within ten court days).

South Carolina. Foster home placement consisted of volunteer families provided by the Alston Wilkes Society. The families agreed to take, without pay, one or two clients per year for a period of from one day to one week. Other residential placements consisted of large group homes and orphanage-type institutions.

Clark County. The DSO program contracted with the public welfare agency (DSHS) for foster, shelter, and group homes, usually for short-term care.

Spokane County. Privately run emergency shelter-care and group homes were used in this site.

Category 5: Multiple Service Centers

This service type refers to nonresidential agencies and organizations such as the YMCA, youth service bureaus, and neighborhood drop-in centers where the focus of services was on recreation, handicrafts, character building, employment referrals, advocacy, tutoring, and so on, rather than solely on psychological counseling or crisis intervention. Also, such services are generally designed for the general youth population, rather than for a special problem group. If these services were provided in a shelter or group home setting as part of their routine programming, then MSC (category 5) was not coded separately. Following are site-specific descriptions of the uses of this code.

Pima County. Several programs in this site fell into this category: The YMCA minibike program, arts, grooming, theater, recreation, and advocacy programs, as well as a unique Young Women's Center, which provided a variety of services including counseling for pregnancy, health care, abortion, GED (general education diploma), and advocacy.

Alameda County. Programs in this site conformed quite well to the general description above. The programs did have an advocacy "flavor" to them, however.

Delaware and Illinois. These programs provided no services that would fall into this category as part of their regular options. A few clients were referred to outside services.

South Carolina, Clark County, and Spokane. Programs in these three sites did not vary in any unique way from the general description above.

Category 6: Outreach Intervention

Programs of this category varied a great deal across sites. They would probably be best thought of as another "other" category, as they really are quite disparate. The category was meant to include short-term, intensive, nonresidential intervention that responds to situational requirements and is designed to effect change in a variety of the clients' physical, social, and emotional circumstances. It is an outreach strategy in that the service is provided outside the agency office, such as in the home, on the street, or in other similar locations. Below are site-specific descriptions of programs coded into this category.

Pima County. Programs coded into the outreach category in Arizona were varied and might appropriately be called multiple service center programs except that they were not formally organized in the way a YMCA, boys' club or girls' club, or the like are. The programs were usually in rural or suburban areas, catered to a general population, but responded to referrals resulting from trouble as well. They provided such services as counseling, advocacy, recreation, employment, and suicide counseling.

No outreach was systematically offered in the Alameda, Connecticut, or Delaware sites.

Illinois. In this site, outreach involved general supervision by youth advocates for the period during which the client was in home detention or in temporary shelter. A primary function of the advocates was to ensure the youth's appearance in court.

South Carolina. In this site, programs were coded as outreach that focused on youth advocacy, opportunity enhancement, and some counseling. The programs were run by the Youth Service Bureaus (part of the Department of Youth Services).

Clark County. Here outreach was coded where specialized services were contracted for. Such services included alcoholism programs, economic opportunity programs, legal aid, Campfire Girls, and so on.

Spokane County. No outreach was offered in this site.

Category 7: Counseling Only

In general, these programs were nonresidential ones in which the sole or primary service was individual or group psychological counseling or therapy, including work with the DSO client's family. While the service duration was variable, it was offered at a specific location and on a scheduled basis. The actual service provided could be on a purchase-of-service arrangement or a DSO-funded program. Typically, this took place in a community center. However, if counseling was included in services provided by or at any of the other program service types on a routine basis, those service types were coded.

Pima County. Few DSO clients were referred to programs that were oriented exclusively to counseling. The one major program of this type took its clientele from a general youth population through active recruitment, so most were not recorded in police files as status offenders. The program was DSO funded and run by private agencies.

Alameda County. Clients categorized in this manner were referred to probation-run family crisis intervention units and private youth service centers focusing on extended family counseling.

Connecticut. The DSO program in this state was divided into three districts. The intention was for the districts to vary in the intensity of intervention. However, they ended up looking very much alike. Individual and family counseling were part of each program. Referrals almost always came from court for youth placed in detention centers for status offenses. The counseling services were provided by private agencies.

Delaware. Individual and family counseling was provided by contracted private agencies.

Illinois.[1] Few cases were referred to counseling agencies. Where they were used, it was for minimal counseling while awaiting court hearings.

South Carolina. Individual, family, and group counseling was provided by Youth Service Bureaus (part of the Department of Corrections) and contract service agencies.

Clark County. The majority of the counseling referrals were to a court-based extended family counseling program.

Spokane County. Referrals coded into this category were cases judged to need more than was offered in the crisis intervention program provided by Youth Alternatives. Youth Alternatives made a concerted effort to obtain specialized services to meet the needs of the individual. In this site, it appeared that status offenses frequently resulted from drug-related problems. Therefore, clients with these kinds of problems were referred to agencies specializing in drug problems.

Category 8: Other

Programs that could not be classified under the first seven categories were coded 8. Programs coded in this category are described by site below.

Pima County. The following services were coded under "other": Youth Service Bureaus, reading clinic, employment agency, legal services.

Alameda County. No programs were classified as "other," although a few clients were sent to outside agencies that could not be otherwise classified.

Connecticut. Non-DSO-funded long-term residential support services were coded into this category.

Delaware. The following services were coded under "other": legal services provided to clients upon request by Community Legal Aid Society (CLASI) and contracted by DSO, detention, and non-DSO services.

Illinois. This category was not used for DSO clients.

South Carolina. The following services were coded under "other": psychological testing services contracted for by Youth Service Bureaus, R&E Center testing and observations (clients could be held for up to 45 days), and detention—holding for disposition prior to court appearance.

Clark County. Protective custody (detention) was coded under "other."

Spokane County. Big Brothers, Boy/Girl Scouts, employment and education programs were coded under "other."

As would be expected, services were distributed differently across sites. The majority of clients (51 percent) received only one service, while 97 percent received no more than three services. [2] Based on this distribution, only three services were coded per client. Further, the analysis reported in this chapter deals only with original referrals. It was possible for a youth to terminate (successfully or unsuccessfully) one referral and later be re-referred to the DSO program. Services offered under such second referrals were not considered in this analysis. About 19 percent of all first referrals were followed by a second referral.

Table 9.1 shows the distribution of types of services by site. Unfortunately, not all sites offered all services, so most comparisons can be made only on a limited number of sites. It should be noted that Table 9.1 indicates the number of clients who received each type of service regardless of what other services may or may not have been given to the youth. [3] In other words, youth who received two services will appear in the table twice. Those who received three services will appear three times. Combinations of services will be addressed later.

Some combinations of services were quite common and should be dealt with as units rather than just separately. Table 9.2 shows the common combinations of two services and forms the basis for selection of certain combinations to be tested in the analysis.

TABLE 9.1 Services Received, by Site

Service*	Pima County (N = 800)		Alameda County (N = 326)		Connecticut (N = 143)		Delaware (N = 380)		Illinois (N = 750)		South Carolina (N = 361)		Clark County (N = 156)		Spokane County (N = 470)	
Diversion/Evaluation	549	68.6	136	41.7	41	28.7	104	27.4	740	98.7	25	6.9	140	89.7	468	99.6
Shelter	87	10.0	104	31.9	39	27.3	62	16.3	13	1.7	12	3.3	22	14.1	29	6.2
Group home	0	0.0	1	0.3	4	2.8	10	2.6	29	3.9	45	12.5	2	1.3	26	5.5
Foster	2	0.8	17	5.2	2	1.4	26	6.8	314	41.9	3	0.8	1	0.6	0	0.0
Multicenter	225	28.1	31	9.5	3	2.1	4	1.1	0	0.0	26	7.2	0	0.0	74	15.7
Outreach	79	9.9	0	0.0	2	1.4	0	0.0	184	24.5	15	4.2	5	3.2	0	0.0
Counseling only	98	12.2	155	47.5	107	74.8	259	68.2	6	0.8	350	96.9	69	44.2	115	24.5
Other	76	9.5	5	1.5	23	16.1	113	29.7	2	0.3	68	18.8	12	7.7	44	9.4
Total services received	1,116		449		221		578		1,288		544		251		756	

*If more than one service received, client appears in the table under each service received.

223

TABLE 9.2 Common Combinations of Two Services, by Site

Combination	Pima County (N = 800)	Alameda County (N = 326)	Connecticut (N = 143)	Delaware (N = 380)	Illinois (N = 750)	South Carolina (N = 361)	Clark County (N = 156)	Spokane County (N = 470)
Diversion/shelter	56 / 7.0	78 / 23.9	13 / 9.1	22 / 5.8	12 / 1.6	— / —	18 / 11.5	28 / 6.0
Diversion/multiservice	99 / 12.4	—	—	—	—	—	—	73 / 15.5
Diversion/outreach	19 / 2.4	—	—	—	177 / 23.6	—	—	—
Diversion/counsel	53 / 6.6	11 / 3.4	— / —	53 / 13.9	— / —	21 / 5.8	57 / 36.5	113 / 24.0
Diversion/foster	—	10 / 3.1	—	14 / 3.7	310 / 41.3	—	— / —	— / —
Diversion/group	—	—	—	—	26 / 3.5	—	—	26 / 5.5
Diversion/other	16 / 2.0	—	17 / 11.9	38 / 10.0	—	—	—	44 / 9.4
Shelter/multiservice	13 / 1.6	— / —	— / —	—	—	—	— / —	— / —
Shelter/foster	—	15 / 4.6	— / —	—	—	—	— / —	— / —
Shelter/counsel	—	11 / 3.4	25 / 17.5	29 / 7.6	—	10 / 2.8	12 / 7.7	— / —

Shelter/other	—	—	—	16 4.2	—	—	—	—
Group/counsel	—	—	—	—	—	40 11.1	—	—
Group/other	—	—	—	—	—	18 5.0	—	—
Foster/outreach	—	—	—	—	99 13.2	—	—	—
Multiservice/outreach	22 2.8	—	—	—	—	—	—	—
Multiservice/counsel	15 1.9	—	—	—	—	25 6.9	—	—
Outreach/counsel	26 3.3	—	—	—	—	14 3.9	— —	—
Outreach/other	12 1.5	—	—	—	—	—	—	—
Counsel/other	—	—	—	39 10.3	—	64 17.7	—	—
Other combinations of two	36 4.5	20 6.1	38 26.6	39 10.3	28 3.7	38 10.5	32 20.5	43 9.1

NOTE: Percentages of the total number of cases are shown; therefore, percentages do not add to 100.0.

TABLE 9.3 Common Combinations of Three Services, by Site

Combination	Pima County	Alameda County	Connecticut	Delaware	Illinois	South Carolina	Clark County	Spokane County
Diversion/shelter/counseling	—	—	—	10 2.6	—	—	11 7.1	—
Diversion/counseling/other	—	—	—	11 2.9	—	—	—	—
Diversion/foster/outreach	—	—	—	—	96 12.8	—	—	—
Group/counseling/other	—	—	—	—	—	16 4.4	—	—
Other combinations of three	51 6.4	22 6.7	15 10.5	31 8.2	48 6.4	31 8.6	13 8.3	41 8.7

NOTE: Percentages of the total number of cases are shown; therefore, percentages do not add to 100.0.

226

There were even some combinations of three services that were common enough to note. Table 9.3 shows these distributions across sites.

Of course, not all variables will be used on all sites since no site offered all program types. In fact, not all combinations shown in Tables 9.2 and 9.3 actually appear in the analysis of even one site, since they had to meet certain criteria, not shown here, to be included in actual analyses. Specific criteria used are described later in this chapter.

SAMPLING

While sampling was discussed more thoroughly in Chapter 3, a very brief review will be presented here to refresh the reader's memory on salient issues. The initial sampling plan looked toward a sample stratified by offense type. Stratification was employed as a means to assure variation in client types, as it is known that status offenders are not evenly distributed among status offenses. For example, arrests of runaways are more common than arrests of minors in possession of alcohol. Quotas were set up for each of five offense types: (1) runaway, (2) ungovernable, (3) curfew, (4) truancy, and (5) minor in possession. It soon became clear, however, that quotas for the last three categories could not be filled. Several sites began taking all youths who entered the program and who had committed a definable status offense. Some even enlarged the original geographic areas constituting the evaluation sites. Tables 3.13-3.18 (Chapter 3) indicated the results of this sampling process. Since the difference between the evaluated and nonevaluated sample has been discussed in Chapter 3, the focus of this section will be on the differences in evaluated clients across sites.

There was a much higher proportion of girls in Connecticut, Illinois, Clark County, and Spokane County than in the other sites. Anglos predominated in all sites but Illinois. In Clark and Spokane counties, the samples were almost exclusively Anglo. Alameda County, Connecticut, Delaware, Illinois, and South Carolina had substantial proportions of Blacks in their samples, especially Illinois, where Blacks constituted the majority of the sample. Hispanics appeared in negligible numbers in all sites but Pima County, Arizona, and Alameda County. "Other" was noticeable only in Arizona, where it usually indicated Native Americans.

Age distributions varied little across sites. Pima County, Alameda, Delaware, and Spokane had noticeably older populations than the other sites, but the difference was not extreme. Connecticut and South Carolina showed the youngest samples in the groups.

With respect to distributions by offense type, several features stand out. First, only the runaway and incorrigible (sometimes referred to as ungovernable) categories were consistently large enough to allow comparisons

TABLE 9.4 Mean Prior Offenses, Transformed and Raw, by Site: Six-Month Cohort

	Pima County (N = 800)	Alameda County (N = 326)	Connecticut (N = 143)	Delaware (N = 380)	Illinois (N = 750)	South Carolina (N = 361)	Clark County (N = 156)	Spokane County (N = 470)
Mean prior offenses plus one, transformed to log 2	.71	.85	.57	.81	1.43	.15	.36	.44
Mean prior offenses, raw	1.15	1.48	1.04	1.35	2.81	.18	.41	.62

across all sites. Second, Pima County, Alameda County, and Delaware produced remarkably even distributions across offense types. Connecticut and Illinois were very heavily weighted with runaways, while South Carolina was quite disproportionate in the number of incorrigibles.

The differences among sites in the number of prior offenses exhibited by evaluated clients are quite large, as shown in Table 9.4. In this case the data are not in frequencies but in means. Shown in Table 9.4 are means of log 2 transformations of the number of prior offenses (plus 1) as well as the untransformed means.[4] It is clear that the samples in Illinois, Alameda, and Delaware included juveniles who had more prior involvement with the justice system than did clients in other sites. Particularly "soft" cases appear in South Carolina and Clark County. The middle-range figure (raw score of 1.04 and transformed score of .57) seen in Connecticut may be misleading since the figure reflects court referrals, not arrests at the law enforcement level. Typically there are fewer referrals to court than arrests since police dispose of cases in ways other than court referral. We should assume, then, that the Connecticut figure is an underestimate of justice system contact compared to the other sites.

Most of the variables under discussion here have been shown many times by delinquency research to be associated with recidivism, or, more generally, frequency of arrest. Four of the five will be shown later in this chapter to relate to recidivism in the manner expected according to prior studies: prior record, ethnicity, gender, and runaway. One, however, deviates in this data set from common expectations: Here, younger clients appear to be more rearrest prone compared to older ones. We will be able to proceed toward a better and more cautious interpretation of the data emerging from the analysis if we can characterize each site in terms of these high-risk variables, since they are commonly related to subsequent offenses and therefore to recidivism.

The sites with the most clients in high-risk categories are Illinois, Connecticut, and Alameda County. Illinois shows disproportionate numbers of boys, Blacks, runaways, and youth with longer prior records. Connecticut selected a sample with larger proportions of boys, Blacks, runaways, and young offenders compared to other sites. Alameda's sample includes many Blacks, Hispanics, and clients with many priors.

The sites with the most low-risk groups are Pima County, Clark County, and Spokane. Pima County evaluated a sample heavy only in one high-risk category: Hispanics. Similarly, Clark County and Spokane have high proportions of boys, but in all other respects show "easy" groups.

Delaware and South Carolina fall in the middle of the continuum, with two factors working against program success. The South Carolina evaluated group included somewhat higher proportions of Blacks and younger clients.

In summary, there is considerable variation in sample composition across sites, with some taking on an apparently more difficult clientele than others. One group that is traditionally considered more arrest prone, older youth, show the opposite tendency in this sample.

Six-Month / Twelve-Month Sample Differences

Naturally, a cutoff date for the end of data collection was necessary. As always, this results in a potentially longer follow-up period on the earlier referrals compared to the later referrals. As was the case in the analyses in Chapters 7 and 8, the decision was made that the shortest follow-up period would be six months and the longest twelve months. All referrals who came into the sample too late for a twelve-month follow-up to be possible were truncated to six months to provide comparability. Consequently, the entire sample can be analyzed using a six-month follow-up period and a subgroup (of early referrals) can be analyzed on the basis of a twelve-month follow-up. This implies two sets of analyses corresponding to the two follow-up periods. It is important, therefore, that any differences between the groups be pointed out and taken into account when interpreting results. Table 9.5 summarizes the differences found, but, as was implied in the previous chapter, these were very few.

Pima County is the site where the strongest differences appear. Here early referrals were a less serious group. There were fewer clients with priors, fewer runaways, and more "other" status offenses, but more minorities and fewer youths from nuclear families. Three sites admitted more males early in the program period: Alameda, Illinois, and South Carolina. The other differences are few and quite unsystematic.

Data

The data collected on evaluated clients have been described in the earlier chapters. However, for the current analysis we are able to add, for interviewed clients, several additional sets of data.

Occupation and education information of mother and father was gathered at the interview (and therefore not on all evaluated clients). The rest of the interview concerned (1) self-reported delinquency and (2) social adjustment information in the areas of school, family, church, and work.

Efforts were made to interview evaluated clients soon after program referral, six months after referral, and twelve months after referral. Many clients could not be interviewed the first time for three reasons: (1) refusals, (2) difficulties in locating clients to interview, and (3) priority of program service requirements. The sample was, of course, further reduced for similar reasons at the time of the second interview, and again at the third. In addition, some clients were referred late enough in the program period that there was no time to interview them a third time or to collect twelve-month arrest data before evaluation funding ceased. This, of course, further reduced the sample of clients. Consequently, the major focus of the analysis will be on the six-month follow-up group.

TABLE 9.5 Differences Between Twelve-Month Follow-Up Group and Entire Sample

	Pima County	Alameda County	Connecticut[a]	Delaware	Illinois	South Carolina	Clark County[a]	Spokane County
Sex	no difference	more males	NA	no difference	more males	more males	NA	no difference
Ethnicity	more minority	more minority	NA	no difference	no difference	no difference	NA	no difference
Age	no difference	no difference	NA	no difference	no difference	no difference	NA	no difference
Family	fewer nuclear	no difference	NA	no difference	no difference	no difference	NA	no difference
Priors	fewer priors	no difference	NA	more pure status[b]	more prior more pure status[b]	no difference	NA	no difference
Instant offense	fewer runaway more "other" more multiple status charges	no difference	NA	no difference	no difference	no difference	NA	more runaways fewer "other"

a. These sites had no twelve-month group.
b. Offenders were coded 1 if they had priors and all priors were status offenses; they were coded 0 otherwise. Thus interpretation should be considered carefully.

Preliminary Analyses

We are concerned in this chapter with two major issues: (1) the relative effectiveness of the service types described earlier in the chapter for reducing recidivism (after accounting for potentially confounding variables) and (2) the relative effectiveness of the service types for particular types of youth. By and large, the "types of youth" of interest will be represented by the same variables that are treated as confounding variables in the first analysis question. Before variables are put into any model, however, we will test (a) for their relations with the dependent variables and (b) for their relations with service types (that is, assignment biases).

The following variables were considered for inclusion in this analysis (some will be abbreviated for convenience, but will be described fully here):

Prior Offense Characteristics

L2PRIORS: Number of prior arrest charges (or probation referrals if no arrest was involved or measured), transformed to its base 2 log.

PRISTAT: Number of prior status offenses transformed to its base 2 log.

PURESTAT: Coded 1 if the client had prior to offenses and they were all status offenses; coded 0 otherwise.

Instant Offense Characteristics

MULTSTAT: Coded 1 if there was more than one status offense involved in the instant offense; coded 0 otherwise.

MIXED: Coded 1 if there were both status and delinquent offenses involved in the instant offense; coded 0 otherwise.

RUNAWAY: Coded 1 if there was a runaway charge in the instant offense; coded 0 otherwise.

UNGOVERNABLE: Coded 1 if there was a charge of ungovernable on the instant offense and no runaway was charged; coded 0 otherwise.

TRUANCY: Coded 1 if there was a charge of truancy on the instant offense and there was no runaway or ungovernable charged; coded 0 otherwise. The coding of these last three offenses implies a comparison with clients charged with minor in possession of alcohol and "other" offenses.

Client Descriptions

GENDER: Coded 1 if the client was male; coded 0 otherwise.

ANGLO: Coded 1 if the client was Anglo; coded 0 otherwise.

AGE: Measured in years of age.

Family Characteristics

NUCLEAR: Coded 1 if the client resided with natural or adoptive parents; coded 0 otherwise.

RECONSTRUCT: Coded 1 if the client resided in a reconstructed family (i.e., with one stepparent); coded 0 otherwise.

NUCRECON: Coded 1 if the client resided in either a nuclear or reconstructed family; coded 0 otherwise.

ONEPAR: Coded 1 if the client resided with one parent only; coded 0 otherwise.

DETENTION: Coded 1 if client resided in a detention center or correctional facility; coded 0 otherwise.

FATHEROCC: Father's occupation was coded using the NORC Occupational Prestige Scale.

MOTHEROCC: Mother's occupation was coded using the NORC Occupational Prestige Scale.

FATHERED: Father's education was measured in years of education.

MOTHERED: Mother's education was measured in years of education.

Social Adjustment Variables

SCHLSTAT: Coded 1 if client was a full-time student at time of referral; coded 0 otherwise.

SCHLADJ: This is an index of school adjustment consisting of the following items:
(a) Good grades are important to me.
(b) I care what the teacher thinks.
(c) Finishing high school is important to me.
(d) College is important to me.
(e) How much homework do you do?
(f) How high are your grades compared to other kids in your same school year?

FAMTIME: This is a question, coded ordinally, about how much time the client spends with family.

Finally, as was the case in Chapter 8, a set of variables was included to adjust for any spurious effects of the particular time a client was referred to the program. First, seasons were coded to take account of the types of clients that might be referred in the summer compared to in the winter, and so on. Second, another adjustment was made for the amount of time the program had been in operation (in months) at the time of each client's referral (the variable is called TIME). The season variable would not suffice for this since programs started at different times of the year.

All variables were tested for their relationships with the dependent variables. Variables that contributed to the variance explained in the dependent variable (statistically significant at the .05 level using F tests) across all sites or only in one site were retained. Those that did not pass this test were dropped from the analysis. The following variables, by this criterion, will be used throughout the analysis, using official recidivism as a dependent variable:

L2priors	GENDER	SUMMER
PURESTAT	ANGLO	WINTER
MULSTAT	AGE	SPRING
RUNAWAY	NUCLEAR	TIME
UNGOVERNABLE		

With the exception of the season and time variables, these will be the client characteristics used as controls while determining the relative effectiveness of service types. In the second phase of the analysis the same variables will be used as the "client types" when comparing the effectiveness of service types for particular client types.

ASSIGNMENT BIASES

Table 9.6 summarizes the assignment biases [5] observed in the various sites. The variable of gender made a difference in service assignment in four of the eight sites. In Pima County and Alameda, girls received more services than did boys. Boys were more likely to receive counseling only in Alameda and a multiservice center referral in Pima County. Girls were more likely than boys to be referred to diversion in Arizona, shelter in Alameda and Delaware, multiservice centers in Alameda, and group homes in Spokane.

In two sites (South Carolina and Spokane) Anglos got more services than non-Anglos. In Alameda the opposite was true. Few other regularities are seen although the effects of ethnicity on service assignments are observable in a variety of ways in six of the eight sites.

Age is an apparent factor in assignment in five sites, but with very little consistency in type.

One of the clearer patterns in Table 9.6 is seen in the nonnuclear family category. In four of the eight sites (Pima County, Alameda, Connecticut, and Delaware) clients from nonnuclear families are assigned to more services than are clients from nuclear families. In two of the sites (Alameda and Delaware), the nonnuclear family clients were more likely to receive shelter care than their nuclear counterparts. The only service more prevalent among nuclear family residents was counseling only (in Connecticut and Delaware).

Clients with few priors, as with clients from nuclear families, seemed prone solely to counseling only as a service assignment, this occurring in two sites (Alameda and Delaware). Clients with longer prior arrest records were, in two sites (Alameda and Connecticut), likely to receive more services, and in two others (Alameda and Spokane) were disproportionately assigned to shelter care.

Clients whose prior record consisted only of status offenses were, in

Alameda and Connecticut, likely to receive more services than those who had no prior record or mixed arrests. In the same sites they were more likely to receive diversion /evaluation assignments. In Alameda and Delaware they were more likely to be assigned residential services of various kinds. In interpreting these "biases" the reader should be reminded that the dichotomy coded here is between (a) those who had prior records that consisted only of status offenses and (b) those who either had no priors or whose priors contained criminal offenses—an unusual dichotomy.

Being arrested for runaway seems to have led clients to be assigned more services than other types of offenders. [6] This was the case in four sites: Pima County, Alameda, Delaware, and Spokane. In three sites (Pima County, Alameda, and Clark County) they were assigned to shelter-care services disproportionately, and in another three (Pima County, Connecticut, and Delaware) they were likely to be assigned to diversion / evaluation services. It is more difficult to see patterns in the assignment of ungovernables. Status offenders of other kinds (especially curfew) were often sent disproportionately to counseling only.

Few patterns are observable among those clients who had multiple status offense as their instant offense or who had only one instant charge. However, it should be noted that very few clients fell into the multiple status offense category, so statistically significant differences would be unlikely.

Overall, it is clear that assignments did not approximate randomness and the sources of bias must be controlled. Even after such controls, however, we shall have to refer back to Table 9.6 in interpreting future results since statistical controls are not perfect.

Offense Categories

One final preliminary analysis is desirable before proceeding to the impact analysis. The instant status offense is a central variable to the analysis. It would be prudent, then, to determine the ways in which this variable relates to other variables in the equations so that interpretations of effects apparently due to offense type will be carefully considered. Table 9.7 offers a summary of the relations between each offense type and all other variables to be used in predicting subsequent offenses (with the exception of service variables, which have already been analyzed).

Probably the most consistent pattern observable in Table 9.7 concerns the distribution of gender across offense categories. Ungovernables and "other" status offenses are much more likely to be male, while runaways are more likely than other types of offenders to be female. In four sites ungovernables are disproportionately male, while the same is true of other status offenses in seven sites. South Carolina is the major excep-

TABLE 9.6 Service Types in Which Client Type Is Overrepresented Compared to Other Service Types

	Pima County	Alameda County	Connecticut	Delaware	Illinois	South Carolina	Clark County	Spokane County
Sex								
male	multiservice	counseling only	none	none	none	none	none	other
female	more services diversion	more services shelter multiservice center (small)	none	shelter	none	none	none	group home
Ethnicity								
Anglo	diversion	counseling	none	none	group home (small)	more service other	none	more services
Non-Anglo	multiservice	more services	shelter	none	foster	none	none	none
Age								
older	more services diversion	diversion	none	none	none	none	none	none
younger	multiservice	counseling only	none	diversion	none	none	counseling only	multiservice
Family								
nuclear	none	none	counseling only	counseling only	none	none	none	none
nonnuclear	more services	more services shelter	more services diversion	more services diversion shelter other	none	none	none	none

Priors							
less	none	counseling only	none	counseling only	none	none	none
more	none	more services shelter	more services diversion	none	none	none	shelter
All status	none	more services diversion shelter foster	more services diversion	group home	none	none	none
Instant offense							
runaway	more services shelter diversion	more services shelter	diversion	more services diversion	none	shelter	more services
ungovernable	multiservice	none	counseling only	diversion counseling only	none	shelter	none
Other	none	counseling only	counseling only	none	none	more services counseling only	none
Multiple status offenses	multiservice	more services	none	none	none	insufficient cases	group home
One status offense	diversion	none	none	none	none	none	none

TABLE 9.7 Client Characteristics Disproportionately Represented in One or Two Instant Offense Categories[a]

	Pima County	Alameda County	Connecticut	Delaware	Illinois	S. Carolina	Clark County	Spokane County
Runaway	more pure status offenses more Anglos	more males	more priors more pure status offenses older	more female more Anglo	more pure status offenses	more priors more males more nuclear families	—	more priors
Ungovernables	more males more Anglos	—	more males	—	more males	more Blacks	—	more priors more males
Other status offenses	more priors more males older	more males	more males	more priors more males more Anglo older more nuclear	more males	—	more males	more males

a. Characteristics appear in categories where they are overrepresented.

tion, with more runaways than other categories being male. There is also some tendency for runaways to have more priors (three sites) and for the priors to be purely status offenses (three sites).

Differences in client characteristics with respect to the offense categories of ungovernable and other status offenses are on the whole unpatterned, although some differences in these characteristics are more pronounced than others. These were more diverse in Pima County and Delaware than in other sites, and should be noted carefully in the analysis based on the two sites.

In summary, the data reveal some patterns that are consistent and others that are virtually random. This suggests that the decisions of program personnel about the referral of status offenders to services may be based on widely varied judgments about client characteristics from site to site. Such inconsistency in approaches to treatment suggests at the very least the need for guidelines based on tested theory to maximize program effect in dealing with status offender.

ANALYSIS OF OFFICIAL ARREST DATA

The central data analysis will be concerned with the six-month follow-up with official arrest data (or court referrals in the case of Connecticut). Following the six-month analysis, the final models applied to this analysis will be applied to the twelve-month group. Finally, the six-month *self-report* data will be subjected to a separate analysis that takes advantage of the higher frequencies of self-report by taking offense dimensions into account.

The first set of analyses, those concerned with the six-month group, will be of two types. The first type seeks to find the most parsimonious model to describe what is important (predictively) in each site, and to describe the relationships observed. The second analysis of the six-month data will compare service types across sites regardless of their strengths or statistical significance in an effort to find *any* discernible patterns of effects across sites. These would presumably provide the most sound basis for treatment recommendations elsewhere in the United States.

Toward Parsimony

It should be stated at the outset that there are several limiting problems in the data set that make confident statements of impact difficult. First, as described earlier, the clients are quite diverse across sites. Second, services differed considerably across sites, even when they were given the same name. Third, there was no effort to randomize services, nor any possibility of matching. All controls must, therefore, be statistical—a method fraught with pitfalls. The first two difficulties make cross-site comparisons for national implications dangerous, and therefore must be approached very cautiously. However, a fourth difficulty could conceivably militate against discerning any effects of services and will require a liberal use of informed judgment. That is, distributions across services within sites are highly skewed, with most clients receiving some services and virtually none receiving others. This, together with "biased" service assignment, makes true effects difficult to identify and untangle. So a combination of caution and judgment must be employed in order to discern effects that may be there but not to be misled by artifacts of the data.

An expanded and more accurate description of the central six-month analysis is that it is an effort to find (1) what types of services generally work best for status offenders and (2) what types of services are most effective with particular types of status offenders. A test of such effects requires the use of a great many combinations of client types and services, and it would be impossible to accomplish this task in one predictive equation. Consequently, a serial approach was taken. Also, since each site differs by clientele and by services offered, the process was different for each site. It would require far too much space to describe the process of determining the most parsimonious model for each site; therefore, we will merely set out the general rules that were applied across sites.

Ignoring combinations of services for the moment, the following is a review of the 26 variables used in the initial regression equations for all sites (with the few exceptions where there were too few cases):

L2PRIORS	AGE	MULTSTAT	MULTISERVICE	COUNSELING
PURESTAT	NUCLEAR	SERVNUM	FOSTER	"OTHER"
FEMALE	RUNAWAY	DIVERSION	GROUP	RESIDENTIAL
ANGLO	UNGOVERN	SHELTER	OUTREACH	L2SUBS (Dep.)
AGE16UP	AGE13UP	TIME	SUMMER	WINTER
				SPRING

Combinations of services were considered as terms for the equation only if the cross-tabulation of the two variables involved in the combination yielded at least ten cases in each cell. Fewer than ten would create the danger of estimating effects that would be far too unstable.

The steps designated here were applied to each site in order to settle on a parsimonious model for predicting program success in terms of arrests subsequent to program intervention.

Creating a Base Model
Against Which
Interactions Were Tested

(1) Age and number of services (SERVNUM) were tested for linearity. Where the relation was linear, the continuous variable of AGE was put

into the base model. Where the relation was not linear, appropriate dummy variables were added to the model. These variables were: AGE16UP to account for differences in older offenders, and AGE13DN to account for particularly young offenders and their differences. SERVNUM related linearly.

(2) TIME, WINTER, SUMMER, and SPRING were tested for effects on subsequent offenses. Where they were statistically significant they were added to the base model.

(3) All other "client" variables were added: L2PRIORS, PURESTAT, MALE, ANGLO, NUCLEAR, RUNAWAY, UNGOVERN.

Testing Combinations and Interactions Against the Base Model

(4) All single services offered in the site were entered as a group into an equation with the base model. They were tested for significance [7] both as a group and individually. They were, however, kept in the equation as part of the base model while interactions concerning them were being tested, regardless of their statistical significance.

(5) All combinations in the site that met criteria for numbers described earlier were entered into an equation including the base model. The combinations were tested for significance as a group. Where the group was not significant, all were dropped from further consideration. Where the group was significant, individually significant variables from the group were entered into a final (or semifinal) model late in the process.

(6) When combinations proved significant, the additive or single services involved in the combinations were kept in the equation regardless of significance.

(7) Sets of client/service interactions were tested serially against the base model. The sets were defined by client variables. For instance, a set of terms would represent the assignment of runaways to all services. The purpose of this set of terms would be to test the relative effectiveness of the services for runaways. Another set making this test for ungovernables would be tested next, and so on, through all client variables. When a set of such interactions proved significant, its individual terms became eligible for the final model, together with its additive component parts.

(8) All terms that proved significant in preceding steps were included in a semifinal model. Where terms that were significant decreased to nonsignificance in this final equation, they were removed in a final equation. Some terms, however, remain in the final equation even though they are not significant. This occurs when another term that is significant is in the equation and is correlated with the nonsignificant term to such an extent that their unique effects cannot be separated from one another. In such cases, both terms are left in. This occurs often with SERVNUM

(number of services), which is often correlated highly with residential services or, in Clark County, with counseling services.

Pima County

No single service stood out from the others in effectiveness or deleteriousness. (See Table 9.8 throughout this entire analysis.) The only combination of services that explained a significant amount of variance in subsequent offenses was that of diversion/evaluation (sometimes called crisis intervention) in combination with "other" services. Unfortunately, there were only 16 cases receiving this combination of services, leaving

TABLE 9.8   Equations for Each Site: Six-Month Follow-Up

Variable	Regression Coefficient	Std Error	F	$p \leq$
Pima County ($R^2 = .14$; N = 800)				
L2PRIORS	.26	.03	88.20	.001
PURESTAT	.25	.10	6.26	.05
RUNAWAY	.13	.06	4.46	.05
MULTSTAT	−.12	.09	2.05	N.S.
SERVNUM	.09	.04	4.46	.05
DIVERSION	.09	.06	1.85	N.S.
OTHER	.13	.11	1.33	N.S.
DIVER/OTHER	−.54	.22	5.95	.05
Constant	.01			
Alameda County ($R^2 = .19$; N = 326)				
L2PRIORS	.25	.04	41.01	.001
MULTOFF	.52	.19	7.21	.01
SERVNUM	.20	.07	8.18	.01
COUNSELING	−.06	.09	.42	N.S.
MULTOFF/COUNSEL	−.60	.28	4.53	.05
Constant	.03			
Connecticut ($R^2 = .08$; N = 143)				
L2PRIORS	.03	.09	.13	N.S.
AGE	−.19	.07	7.25	.01
RUNAWAY	.42	.21	4.00	.05
MULTISTAT	−.08	.23	.13	N.S.
SERVNUM	.15	.10	2.12	N.S.
Constant	2.74			
Delaware ($R^2 = .19$; N = 380)				
L2PRIORS	.20	.04	24.47	.001
AGE	.16	.06	6.19	.05
AGE16UP	−.60	.15	16.57	.001
AGE13UN	.46	.18	6.44	.05
SPRING	−.21	.11	3.91	.05

TABLE 9.8   (Continued)

Variable	Regression Coefficient	Std Error	F	p≤
SUMMER	−.24	.09	6.56	.05
SERVNUM	.19	.06	12.42	.001
LONGTERM	−.49	.16	9.62	.01
COUNSELING	−.17	.09	3.50	N.S.
Constant	−1.78			
Illinois (R^2 = .13; N = 750				
L2PRIORS	.27	.03	92.59	.001
ANGLO	−.21	.07	9.45	.01
AGE	−.07	.02	10.05	.01
Constant	1.62			
South Carolina (R^2 = .15; N = 361)				
L2PRIORS	.22	.07	10.74	.01
MALE	−.12	.05	6.92	.01
RUNAWAY	−.11	.08	2.28	N.S.
SERVNUM	.12	.04	7.46	.01
COUNSELING	−.39	.14	7.60	.01
OTHER	−.14	.09	2.73	N.S.
RESIDEN	.14	.09	2.18	N.S.
PRIORS/RES	−.30	.12	5.74	.05
RUNAWAY/OTHER	.45	.15	9.37	.01
RUNAWAY/RES	−.50	.16	9.63	.01
Constant	.41			
Clark County (R^2 = .11; N = 156)				
AGE	.14	.06	5.74	.05
AGE16UP	−.34	.15	5.37	.05
AGE13UN	.40	.18	5.12	.05
NUCLEAR	−.19	.10	3.81	N.S.
SERVNUM	−.07	.08	.77	N.S.
COUNSELING	.27	.13	3.96	.05
Constant	−1.63			
Spokane County (R^2 = .12; N = 470)				
L2PRIORS	.17	.04	14.72	.001
MALE	.21	.07	8.78	.01
AGE	−.06	.02	8.27	.01
RUNAWAY	−.10	.08	1.34	N.S.
MULTSTAT	−.05	.11	.23	N.S.
TIME	−.03	.01	11.70	.001
SUMMER	−.19	.07	7.56	.01
SERVNUM	.06	.07	.69	N.S.
MULTISERVICE	−.30	.16	3.68	N.S.
COUNSELING	−.18	.13	2.12	N.S.
RUNAWAY/MULTISERV	.36	.18	3.91	.05
RUNAWAY/COUNSEL	.31	.15	4.23	.05
Constant	1.44			

us little confidence in the finding. In its favor, however, is the fact that analyses of assignment biases do not lead us to be suspicious of the clientele for this combination. In other words, the clients in diversion and "other" services were not significantly less serious than clients assigned to other services. If the effect is stable, it would be in an ameliorative direction; thus the content of "other" should be described. The distribution of services among those clients who were coded "other" as well as "diversion /evaluation" was divided among the majority who were referred to the Child Protection Services (presumably a residential placement) and a lesser number who were referred to health clinics but were "no shows."

There appeared to be no client types whose subsequent offenses were increased or decreased by one service more than another, that is, no client-service interactions were statistically significant.

Although there were no services or client-service combinations that were better than any others in terms of reduction in subsequent offenses (with the possible exception of diversion /other) it is worth noting the variables that were important in Pima County in predicting success or failure. First, the model explains 14 percent of the variance—a moderate amount in the context of this program. Prior record takes its traditional position as the most powerful predictor of subsequent offenses regardless of intervention. Beyond this expected result, PURESTAT (prior status offenses only) and RUNAWAY proved to predict subsequent offenses quite well. Thus in Arizona the feelings of many practitioners are confirmed that offenders who have only status offenses on their records are more difficult to change than many other offenders. Similarly, runaways are more predisposed to subsequent offending than are other types of status offenders. It may be worth noting, from a separate analysis, that "runaway" as an instant offense is correlated with pure status offense records $(r = .15)$

The remaining significant term in the equation is SERVNUM, indicating that SERVNUM (more services rendered) is associated with more subsequent offenses. An analysis of the assignment biases for this variable indicates a preponderance of runaways and clients from nonnuclear families in the condition of more services, leading us to expect more subsequents from clients in this group anyway. However, the other biases associated with number of services assigned are not associated with higher probabilities of arrest in Pima County (males and older clients). We cannot be sure, then, whether the assignment of more services leads to more trouble with the law or whether the types of offenders who are assigned more services are the types who would get into trouble regardless of services rendered. In either case, it is clear that assignment of more services does not overcome any predispositions toward recidivism.

Alameda County

Again, in Alameda single services did not predict one way or the other to subsequent offenses, at least as a group. It should be noted that residential services predicted subsequents early in the equation process but was completely usurped by SERVNUM, which is highly correlated (.81) with residential services. Likewise, combinations of services as a group did not predict level of subsequents. The groups of client-service interactions were not significant with one exception: multiple status offenders. Among multiple status offenders, counseling produced fewer subsequents than other services. However, there were few cases of multiple status offenders who received counseling only, and we are wary of emphasizing this finding.

The final equation for Alameda County predicted about 19 percent of the variance in subsequents—one of the larger proportions in this analysis. As usual, much of this proportion is accounted for by the length of clients' prior records regardless of what services they received. In addition to clients with prior records, clients with multiple charges on their instants proved to be more difficult to deal with than other clients (significantly so). Again, number of services given is solidly associated with subsequents, but this is to be expected since clients assigned to more services tended to be disproportionately high-risk categories—at least in Alameda County: minorities, clients from nonnuclear families, clients with more priors, pure status offenders, and clients with more than one status offense as part of their instants. Counseling only—a term included only because it is implied by the significant interaction term of MULTSTAT / COUNSEL—is associated with fewer subsequents, but this is to be expected since clients referred to this service are disproportionately nonminority, low in priors, and had instant offenses other than runaway or ungovernable. All of these factors are associated with fewer subsequents in Alameda County.

Connecticut

The only variables that predict outcome in the Connecticut site are priors, age, and an instant offense of runaway. As usual, priors and runaway are positively correlated with subsequents. Age, on the other hand, is negatively related—that is, the older the client, the less likely he or she is to have subsequents. The fact that after age 16 juvenile records are not kept in this state may account for this relationship. SERVNUM, although not significant, shows the same pattern as before, that is, more services are associated with more subsequent offenses. But, as usual, clients with more services are higher-risk clients. In Connecticut they were disproportionately pure status offenders, had priors, and were from nonnuclear families. After taking into account all of these background variables, no services or combinations of services were related to outcome. The total R^2 for this equation is only .08, the lowest in the analysis. This may be related to the fact that only court referrals could be measured; police records were not made available to the researchers at this site.

Delaware

While combinations and interactions were inconsequential in the prediction of subsequents here, there did appear to be some impact attributable to single services. As a group, the single services applicable in Delaware were significant. The strongest effect is seen in residential services, but they differ by the type of residential placement. The pattern seems to be that the longer-term residential placements (group homes and foster homes) predict fewer subsequents, while the short-term placements (shelter care) predict more subsequents. For this reason, a new term, "LONGTERM," was constructed for test in the final equation. LONGTERM consists of clients assigned to group or foster homes. The effect described here has stood up to several tests of its stability and strength. Clients assigned to this type of service were not materially different from those assigned to other types of services as had been the case in other sites where apparent "effects" were found. About 40 clients in Delaware were assigned to long-term residential care and even more were assigned to shelter care, thereby providing a reasonably stable estimate of their effects and strengthening the conclusion for Delaware that longer-term residential placement had an ameliorative effect.

Another possible service impact seen in this site is associated with assignments to counseling only. The apparent effect is in the direction of fewer subsequents. We cannot be as sure of this as we were about the LONGTERM effect, because clients assigned to counseling were "easier" clients than those sent to some other services. They were disproportionately low in priors and were from nuclear families. To be fair, though, ungovernables were also overrepresented and this is a high-risk group in Delaware.

One other service effect should be mentioned. We are used to seeing SERVNUM positively related to subsequents and then discounting the effect by virtue of the fact that the more difficult clients are usually assigned to more services. Here, the effect of number of services is quite strong but the assignment biases are not severe. The biases in assignment are among nonnuclear family clients (a relatively high-risk group) and runaways (a low-risk group in this site). We are inclined, therefore, to consider more seriously the possibility that increasing numbers of services may actually have led to more subsequents in the Delaware program.

The remaining variables in the final equation for Delaware are only control variables, but they show similar effects in this site as elsewhere.

Priors had a very substantial impact on subsequents, as did age, although the age relationship seems to be more complicated here than elsewhere. In addition, there seemed to be stronger seasonal effects in this site than were shown by the sites described so far.

Illinois

This is a site where some of the more severe problems of skewness occur. Almost all (99 percent) clients received diversion/evaluation. Almost half received residential care (47 percent), and 25 percent received outreach services. Few clients received the rest of the services. As noted earlier, this program was designed to provide temporary community detention only. Interestingly, few assignment biases were evidenced in this site, and there were no significant service effects either singly or in combination. Similarly, no types of services were particularly beneficial or harmful to particular client types. Even number of services does not predict subsequent offenses. Only priors, ethnicity, and age predict subsequents here, and they are all in the expected direction. Together they explain 13 percent of the variance in subsequent arrests.

South Carolina

This is another site where skewness was a problem, with 97 percent of the group receiving counseling services. As a group, individual services proved significant. This was largely due to counseling (received by 97 percent of the clients), followed by outreach (received by only 4 percent of the clients), which did not reach significance individually. Consequently, the strongest effects are seen in services containing 97 percent and 4 percent of the clients, respectively. Since counseling reached significance individually, it will be included in the final equation in spite of the heavily skewed distribution. To the extent that we can trust the effect, it was ameliorative, that is, clients at this site who were assigned to counseling were less likely to have subsequent offenses than clients who did not receive counseling.

Types of services as applied to clients with priors proved significant as a group. That is, some services seemed more effective for clients with prior offenses than other services, or some services were more effective than others with clients who had no priors. In particular, the most effective combination is residential service for clients with priors. This can be interpreted in two ways: (1) among clients with priors, residential services are most effective or (2) residential services are most effective on clients with priors. While this is an interesting finding, we must still be cautious since very few clients are represented by this combination ($N = 11$).

Another set of interactions proved significant. It concerned the assignment of services to runaways. Within this group of terms, the combinations of RUNAWAY /RESIDENTIAL and RUNAWAY /OTHER showed themselves to be significant individually. The interpretations are similar to those applied to the L2PRIORS interactions, except that in the case of RUNAWAY /OTHER the relationship is detrimental. That is, runaways assigned to "other" services had higher subsequents than runaways assigned to alternative types of services. (In this site, "other" refers to contract referrals to private psychologists or psychiatrists.) On the other hand, runaways assigned to residential services were better in terms of subsequents than were runaways assigned to alternative types of services. We have the problem of small numbers with this finding as well, but it does at least correspond to the finding concerning clients with priors and residential treatments, and is buttressed by the fact that assignment biases are minimal in this site.

If we trust the coefficients based on such skewed distributions, we would conclude that, overall, counseling was a better approach for status offenders in South Carolina but that residential placement was more effective for runaways and clients with priors—a believable finding.

Among the control, or base model, variables there are some familiar patterns as well as some differences compared to other sites. Priors, as usual, is significantly related to more subsequents, indicating difficulty in dealing with clients with prior records. Also, SERVNUM is related to subsequents in the usual (increased subsequents) manner; and, as in Delaware, it is not so plagued by assignment biases as to render it uninterpretable. Anglo clients are somewhat overrepresented in larger numbers of services, and this is, in South Carolina, a higher-risk group than minorities, but this is the only bias problem we face here. This is one more small piece of evidence that a plethora of services may not produce expected benefits.

Unusual in this site are the negative (reduced subsequents) relationships of maleness and runaway with subsequent offenses. In most sites these are high-probability groups where subsequents are concerned, but the opposite is true in South Carolina.

Clark County

The only service effects seen in the Clark County site, as individual services or combinations, with or without specification of client type, were associated with COUNSELING and SERVNUM. Unfortunately, COUNSELING and SERVNUM are highly correlated (.71) making it impossible to separate the effects of one from the other. Almost everyone in this site received diversion /evaluation, with little left to decide but whether or not to send the client to counseling. The impact, whether due to counseling, number of services, or something else (counseled clients are more likely to be young and therefore prone to subsequent offenses), the relation is detrimental; that is, more subsequent arrests follow. The only control variables necessary in this equation were age (several versions) and whether or not the client was from a nuclear family. As always, clients from nuclear families are less likely to get into subsequent trouble than are other clients.

Spokane County

The individual service terms in Spokane County did not show significance, nor did they as combinations. However, one set of client-service interactions was demonstrated to contribute to explained variance; these had to do with runaways. According to the final equation, runaways who were assigned to multiservice centers or to counseling only were arrested more frequently than others. We were told that many Spokane youths referred to these services had drug-related problems. This finding could be seen as complementing the finding from South Carolina that runaways (and clients with priors) do better in residential treatment than other types of treatment. In addition, long-term residential treatment seemed more beneficial in general in Delaware.

The effect of SERVNUM is, as usual, in the direction of more subsequents, but is not significant in this site. However, two high-risk categories (runaways and Anglo clients) are overrepresented in higher numbers of services, leading us to expect more subsequents from clients receiving more services anyway. (In Spokane, Anglos were slightly more arrest prone.)

All other variables in the equation are there for control purposes. Those with priors and those brought to the program for running away are, overall, more likely to recidivate. AGE, RUNAWAY, and MULTSTAT, on the other hand, are related to fewer subsequents. Seasonal and program duration effects are stronger in this site than in most other sites as well. The model finally explains about 12 percent of the variance in subsequents.

Summary of the First Half of the Six-Month Analysis

Few strong service effects were observed, and those that were often were based on small numbers or were riddled with assignment bias problems. There are a few hints, however. Primarily, residential services, especially longer-term care (as shown in Delaware), may be more effective than other types of programs, especially for the most difficult clients— runaways and clients with priors. In one site, runaways did particularly badly with counseling and multiservice center referrals. There is some equivocal evidence that more services may be somewhat harmful. In most sites this comparison was impossible because it was confounded with a more difficult clientele. However, the relationship held up in two sites where this was not an obvious problem.

The more solid findings of this analysis did not concern the effectiveness of services. Rather, they identified rather consistently across sites the more difficult types of clients faced by practitioners. They include runaways, pure status offenders (that is, offenders with no delinquent offenses on their records), males, and, most certainly, clients with prior records.

A Search for Patterns

In the preceding analysis we were careful to ignore all effects that were not statistically significant individually and as groups of variables. Effects were discussed with considerable caution due to assignment biases and skewed distributions. It could also be argued that the number of variables found significant means little since they were few among a very large number of significance tests. A more reasonable approach is to rely on *patterns* observable across sites and situations. The following analysis searches for patterns that hold across sites regardless of statistical significance. For simplicity and because few service combinations have more than a few cases representing them, only single services will be considered. Finally, only the direction of the effects will be included in the analysis.

Table 9.9 displays the data relevant to this analysis. There are two rows for each service type, excluding the outreach and "other" categories, which are too diverse across sites to be meaningful. The first row of each section of the table indicates the direction and degree of assignment bias for the service in each site. Where there is a bias that would predispose the clientele to recidivism, one or more plus signs appear. Where the bias indicates a tendency away from recidivism (a negative relationship to subsequents) one or more minus signs appear. The number of signs for each site is determined by (1) the number of categories overrepresented in the services that are associated with recidivism (and their strength of association), and (2) an adjustment for biases that predict the opposite direction. The signs are not meant to be precise, but to reflect in a general way the degree to which programs are working with or against probabilities. For instance, residential programs in Alameda County (see the first row, second column of Table 9.9) received clients who were disproportionately minority, from nonnuclear families, had longer prior records, were pure status offenders, and were runaways. Each of these biasing factors would predict further involvement in the system in Alameda County. Together, they present a formidable obstacle for any program practitioner.

The second row of each section of Table 9.9 indicates the sign of the regression coefficient representing the service type in each site. The coefficients represent the effects of the services after controlling statistically for assignment biases to the extent possible. All service variables were included simultaneously in the equation. It is, of course, not possible to control perfectly for assignment biases using statistical methods; they

TABLE 9.9   Direction of Single-Service Regression Coefficients After Controlling for Assignment Bias and Showing Assignment Biases: Six-Month Follow-Up

	Pima County	Alameda County	Connecticut	Delaware	Illinois	South Carolina	Clark County	Spokane County
Residential								
Assignment biases (sign of relation with subsequents)	+	+++ +++	++	++	++	0	+	+++
Sign of service relation with subsequents[a]	−	+	−	−	−	−	−	+
Counseling								
Assignment biases (sign of relation with subsequents)	0	−−	−−	−	NA	0	+0	0
Sign of service relation with subsequents[a]	+	+	+	−	NA	−	+	−
Diversion/Evaluation								
Assignment biases (sign of relation with subsequents)	++	+++ +++	++ ++	+++	0	0	0	NA
Sign of service relation with subsequents[a]	+	+	−	+	−	+	+	NA
Multiservice								
Assignment biases (sign of relation with subsequents)	−	−	NA	NA	NA	0	NA	0
Sign of service relation with subsequents[a]	−	+	NA	NA	NA	−	NA	−
Outreach (too variable)								

a. Minus sign indicates fewer subsequent offenses; plus sign indicates more subsequent offenses.

251

must be borne in mind while interpreting results of any analysis involving effects possibly confounded by such biases.

The first section of the table pertains to residential services. The hints of the relative success of residential services that were seen in the earlier analysis receive support here. All eight sites offered residential services for some of their clients. Out of the eight sites, six produced lower subsequents for clients receiving these services. More impressive, in most of the six sites showing reduced subsequents, the effects were achieved in spite of difficult clientele compared to clientele assigned to other services. The two sites showing increased subsequents had even more difficult clients than was usual for residential services. This is the strongest pattern that we will see in either the six- or the twelve-month analysis.

Counseling programs fare less well in this analysis. Out of seven sites offering counseling programs to their clients, four yielded increased subsequents. In two sites, Alameda and Connecticut, the increased subsequents effect was in the face of particularly arrest-resistent clients. In another two sites, the effect was shown on an unbiased or nearly unbiased clientele. Three sites showed reduced subsequents effects. In two cases, the reduction effect was seen on an unbiased clientele, while in the third, the clients of the programs were biased against subsequents, thereby making the achievement less noteworthy. The pattern would have to be seen as mixed, but the weight of the evidence is against counseling. It is difficult to find explanations for the variation in the kinds of counseling programs found in the various sites. Some were privately run, and others were run by probation departments or by departments of corrections, but these factors seem unrelated to the direction of the effects.

Diversion/evaluation programs, more appropriately called crisis intervention programs, were offered in seven sites. Of the seven, four resulted in more subsequents. Most programs, though, were working against probabilities. Three of the increased subsequents effects are seen in sites where the clientele was very difficult, while two are seen in programs with apparently unbiased types of clientele. There were, however, two sites where the coefficients predicted fewer subsequents. One such effect was accomplished on an unbiased clientele while the other was attained in the face of a high-risk group. It is interesting to note that the two apparently successful crisis intervention programs were run by nonjustice organizations. One program was in Illinois, where interventions were by youth advocates; the other, in Connecticut, was staffed and run by a welfare department. All of the programs producing increased subsequents effects were based in the juvenile justice system. This is hardly conclusive evidence against programs based in the system, but it is a pattern worth noting. Overall however, the findings for counseling and crisis intervention approaches are discouraging. They are not, however, surprising (except, presumably, to practitioners who cling tenaciously to these modalities). As Coates (1981: 94) has noted in another context, interventions based on individual change or limited to short durations cannot effec-tively deal with the potent social networks and environments in which youngsters play out their daily behavior.

The final service type subjected to this analysis is multiservice center programs. Four sites assigned clients to these types of programs. Most of these programs were of the standard type, such as YMCAs, Boys Clubs, and so on. The Pima County program offered a number of services fall-ing into this category; some were of the usual type and others were quite unusual, such as the Young Women's Center and the YMCA's minibike program. The Alameda County program was unusual in that the services in many of their multiservice centers (Youth Service Bureaus) were ori-ented toward youth advocacy. In three of the four sites the services coded as multiservice centers yielded fewer subsequents. However, their clien-tele was not of a difficult sort; most were biased against subsequent of-fenses. Only one site offered unbiased clients to multiservice centers. Here (in South Carolina) the effect still predicted fewer subsequents. Only in Alameda County was there an increase in subsequents, and this was produced on a very arrest-resistant group of clients. The real pattern, though, is for multiservice centers to receive low-arrest-probability cli-ents and to produce low levels of recidivism among their clients.

Summary of the Search for Patterns

The most impressive performance, based on this simple analysis, seems to come from residential services. The clientele referred to these services is more consistently difficult and arrest prone. In spite of this, the record of these programs is to produce lower-recidivating clients. The most discouraging picture comes from the counseling programs, where clients are typically not difficult and yet four out of seven programs showed increased subsequents. The picture is mixed, however: Counsel-ing programs in two sites resulted in negative coefficients (reduced subse-quents) based on nonbiased clientele. Diversion /evaluation (crisis inter-vention) and multiservice programs present very mixed results. By and large, their coefficients match the direction of the client bias, with crisis intervention programs receiving difficult clients and multiservice centers receiving "easy" clients.

Overall Six-Month Arrest Data Summary

Strong and consistent service effects are hard to identify in a data set of this type, and none were found. The strongest effect we have seen in this analysis comes from residential services, and this is far from unequivocal. However, it may well be that residential programs result in lower recidi-vism in more difficult and arrest-prone clients. This proved to be the case in Delaware, and in at least one site it was particularly true for runaways and clients with arrest histories. The same types of clients were particularly recidivistic when assigned to multiservice and counseling programs in another site. Finally, in the analysis of the directions of effects, residential programs show the most consistent pattern of low recidivism, even though the clients of these programs would be expected to recidivate more on the average. Although the residential service findings are not unequivocal, they are bolstered by findings in other studies. For instance, both Empey and Lubeck (1971) and Murray et al. (1978) find residential treatment more effective than other kinds of treatment. In these cases the clients were far more serious offenders than we find in this sample, but the similarities in findings are worth noting. Other effects are variable and difficult to interpret.

Finally, the issue of number of services assigned is an interesting but difficult one. Number of services is consistently related to higher subsequents, but often the clients who receive multiple services are the more difficult clients. From this we would assume that the causal direction is from difficult clients to multiple services rather than the other way. However, in two sites where clients referred to multiple services were not noticeably different from clients referred to one service, the positive effect of number of services remained. It is, at least, a relationship worth pursuing in other studies, as indeed it was in the National Evaluation of Diversion Projects (Dunford et al., 1982). That analysis, with the advantage of random assignment of cases to experimental and control situations, found *no* relationships between level of service and either recidivism or cognitive changes.

Analysis of Twelve-Month Sample

The twelve-month group is considerably smaller than the six-month group, and, of course, it is an earlier sample. The purpose of the twelve-month analysis was to test the stability of the findings from the six-month analysis. Toward this end, the final equations from the six-month analysis were tested on the twelve-month group. However, two sites—Connecticut and Clark County—did not operate programs or evaluations long enough to make a twelve-month follow-up possible. In addition, since the sample sizes were considerably smaller in the remaining sites, some terms had to be dropped from the equations as there were not enough cases represented by them. With these reservations, we proceed to the comparison.

Table 9.10 lists the terms of each equation used in the six-month analysis for each site available for the twelve-month analysis. Opposite each term in the table are regression coefficients for the twelve-month equation and, in parentheses, the corresponding coefficients for the six-month analysis. This is followed by the standard errors, F ratios, and probabilities for each term for each of the two analyses. In addition, the R^2 for each equation is shown opposite the names of the sites.

Overall, the twelve-month equations are very similar to the six-month

TABLE 9.10   Regression Equations for Twelve-Month Follow-Up

Variable	Regression Coefficient 12-month (6-month)		Standard Error 12-month (6-month)	F 12-month (6-month)
Pima County ($R^2 = .19$)				
L2PRIORS	.41	(.26)	.04(.03)	**88.60(88.20)**
PURESTAT	.22	(.25)	.16(.10)	1.88 (6.26)*
RUNAWAY	.09	(.13)	.10(.06)	.80 (4.46)*
MULTSTAT	.04	(−.12)	.14(.09)	.07 (2.05)
SERVNUM	.10	(.09)	.06(.04)	3.01 (4.46)*
DIVERSION	.09	(.09)	.10(.06)	.79 (1.85)
OTHER	.09	(.13)	.15(.11)	.38 (1.33)
DIVER/OTHER	−.46	(−.54)	.29(.22)	2.55 (5.95)*
Constant	.03	(.01)		
Alameda County ($R^2 = .22$)				
L2PRIORS	.39	(.25)	.06(.04)	**35.76(41.01)**
MULTSTAT	.37	(.52)	.25(.19)	2.12 (7.21)**
SERVNUM	.08	(.20)	.12(.07)	.43 (8.18)**
COUNSELING	−.11	(−.06)	.15(.09)	.55 (.43)
MULTOFF/COUNSEL	NA	(−.60)	NA(.28)	NA (4.53)*
Constant	.31	(.03)		
Delaware ($R^2 = .22$)				
L2PRIORS	.22	(.20)	.08(.04)	**7.65(24.47)**
AGE	.24	(.16)	.12(.06)	3.81 (6.19)*
AGE13UN	.87	(.46)	.34(.18)	**6.72 (6.44)*
AGE16UP	−.83	(−.60)	.29(.15)	**8.04(16.57)**
SERVNUM	.31	(.19)	.11(.06)	**7.44(12.42)**
LONGTERM	−.79	(−.49)	.27(.16)	**8.54 (9.62)**
COUNSELING	−.44	(−.17)	.17(.09)	**6.73 (3.50)
SPRING	NA	(−.21)	NA(.11)	NA (3.91)*
SUMMER	NA	(−.24)	NA(.09)	NA (6.56)*
Constant	−2.77	(−1.78)		
Illinois ($R^2 = .21$)				
L2PRIORS	.37	(.27)	.05(.03)	**64.84(92.59)**
ANGLO	−.19	(−.21)	.12(.07)	2.59 (9.45)**
AGE	−.15	(−.07)	.04(.02)	**15.49(10.05)**
Constant	2.91	(1.62)		
South Carolina ($R^2 = .14$)				
L2PRIORS	.17	(.22)	.10(.07)	2.94(10.74)**
MALE	−.21	(−.12)	.08(.05)	*6.60 (6.92)**
RUNAWAY	−.13	(−.11)	.12(.08)	1.18 (2.28)
SERVNUM	.13	(.12)	.06(.04)	*4.72 (7.46)**
COUNSELING	−.51	(−.39)	.20(.14)	*4.58 (7.60)**
OTHER	−.05	(−.14)	.13(.09)	.18 (2.73)
RESIDEN	NA	(.14)	NA(.09)	NA (2.18)
RUNAWAY/OTHER	.36	(.45)	.23(.15)	2.38 (9.37)**
RUNAWAY/RES	NA	(−.50)	NA(.16)	NA (9.63)**

(continued)

TABLE 9.10   (Continued)

Variable	Regression Coefficient 12-month (6-month)		Standard Error 12-month (6-month)	F 12-month (6-month)
PRIORS/RES	NA	(−.30)	NA(.12)	NA (5.74)*
Constant	.61	(.41)		
Spokane County ($R^2 = .16$)				
L2PRIORS	.25	(.17)	.06(.04)	**16.84(14.72)**
MALE	.33	(.21)	.10(.07)	**10.32 (8.78)**
AGE	−.11	(−.06)	.03(.02)	**11.83 (8.27)**
RUNAWAY	−.14	(−.10)	.13(.08)	1.14 (1.34)
MULTSTAT	−.12	(−.05)	.17(.11)	.53 (.23)
TIME	−.09	(−.03)	.03(.01)	**6.75(11.70)**
SUMMER	−.31	(−.19)	.17(.07)	3.28 (7.56)**
SERVNUM	−.00	(.06)	.11(.07)	0.00 (.69)
MULTISERVICE	−.17	(−.30)	.23(.16)	.55 (3.68)
COUNSELING	−.03	(−.18)	.19(.13)	.03 (2.12)
RUNAWAY/MULTISERV	.30	(.36)	.26(.18)	1.30 (3.91)*
RUNAWAY/COUNSEL	.55	(.31)	.22(.15)	*6.01 (4.23)*
Constant	2.46	(1.44)		

*$p < .05$.
**$p < .01$.

equations. A number of terms that were statistically significant with the six-month group are not statistically significant for the twelve-month group. However, the regression coefficients are of similar magnitude and always (with two exceptions) of the same sign (direction). The two instances of sign reversal were for terms that were not significant in the first analysis. The first is seen in Arizona for the term MULTSTAT, included only as a companion to RUNAWAY since the two were highly related. The second instance is found in Spokane, where the coefficient for the term SERVNUM was reduced from .06 to −.00.

There were four effects that seemed worthy of note in the six-month analysis. The first was in Delaware, where long-term residential care produced a strong negative (subsequents-reducing) coefficient. The twelve-month follow-up shows an even stronger coefficient, which remains statistically significant.

The second effect occurred in South Carolina, where the combinations of RUNAWAY and RESIDEN, as well as PRIORS and RESIDEN, showed strong negative, statistically significant coefficients. Unfortunately, neither of these terms represented enough cases to appear in the twelve-month equation and therefore cannot be tested for stability.

The third set of effects noted in the earlier analysis came from Spokane. They were interaction effects from the combinations of RUNAWAY with MULTISERV and with COUNSELING. Both terms were positively (detrimentally) related to subsequent offenses. This seemed complementary to the South Carolina finding that runaways are best treated with residential care. In the twelve-month group the same effects appear, and both are significant. The interaction term including MULTISERV decreased slightly in strength (.36 to .30) but remained significant, while the other term including COUNSELING increased in strength (.31 to .55) and also remained significant.

The final trend noted in the earlier analysis was the consistency with which SERVNUM or number of services assigned predicted more subsequent offenses. It remains unclear what the causal direction of this effect is since the more difficult cases are usually assigned to more services, but whatever the direction, the effect remains stable in all sites but Spokane, as noted earlier. The two sites (South Carolina and Delaware) where the SERVNUM effect seemed relatively uncontaminated by assignment biases and multicollinearity again produce positive coefficients that are statistically significant.

Summary of Arrest Data Analysis

In each case where previous findings were testable on the twelve-month sample, the findings were confirmed. In one critical case the findings were not testable. These concerned the apparently beneficial (subsequent-reducing) effect of residential care for runaways and for clients with priors in South Carolina. All other effects concerning the subsequent-reducing impact of residential services were supported, as was the subsequent-increasing effect of counseling and multiservice centers for runaways in Spokane. Finally, to the extent that there seemed to be a deleterious impact of number of services on subsequents, or an impact of difficult clients on number of services, it remains true in the twelve-month analysis. It is, however, still impossible to be sure of the causal direction of the effect in this analysis. It is instructive to note, however, that the experimentally more controlled study of the National Diversion Project (Dunford et al., 1982) yields so few differences that concerns for causal directions are minimized. In that evaluation, a few intersite differences and a negative finding for recreational services are overwhelmed by the overall *failure* of the various treatments and levels of service provided to yield group differences of any value. Neither that national evaluation nor ours makes one sanguine about the diversion /treatment process. It is worth repeating, as well, that both studies are multisite replications of programs, not single programs for which the findings can be readily dismissed on the basis of low external validity.

Analysis of Self-Reported Delinquency

The use of self-reported delinquency data in this report has some advantages and some disadvantages. The disadvantages have to do with the fact that self-report requires interviews with clients, and thereby inevitably reduces sample size through attrition. The advantages all relate to the fact that offenders engage in more potentially chargeable activity than that for which they were arrested, so frequencies and distributions are more favorable for analytic purposes. Specifically, in this analysis, important *dimensions* of delinquent behavior can be acknowledged and attended to with use of self-report data, while this was not possible with arrest data.

The disadvantage of smaller sample size ($N = 951$) will be offset somewhat by doing an aggregate analysis, bringing sites into the analysis as a series of dummy variables in an attempt to "partial out" jurisdiction effects rather than treating each site separately.

The availability of more offenses per person will permit several types of analyses beyond those for the simple effect of services upon subsequent offenses. The first analysis will examine the dimensions of self-reported delinquency and the potential specialization of offenders. In a much simpler manner, this will be done with arrest data as well in preparation for the comparison of official and self-reported offending.

The second set of analyses will explore the relationship between arrests and behavior, using the dimensions established in the first analysis.

The third set of analyses will be the most rigorous possible with this data set and pertains to the effect of service types on subsequent offenses.

Finally, an analysis will be made of the relationships among prior offenses (official and self-report), service types (taken individually), and subsequent offenses. This analysis will take into account the strength and sign of these relationships relative to each other. Statistical significance will not be a prominent feature of this particular analysis.

The Variables

The client background variables used in this analysis will be familiar from preceding chapters. They are: AGE, MALE, ANGLO, and NUCLEAR. Similarly, the services in question have all appeared in previous analyses: DIVERSION /EVALUATION, SHELTER, GROUP, FOSTER, LONGTERM, RESIDEN, MULTISERV, COUNSELING, and SERVNUM.

The variables unique to this analysis are those measuring offense behavior of the clients both before and after service intervention and as reflected by arrests (probation referrals for Connecticut) and self-reports. (It should be noted here that Clark County does not appear in this analysis. Because clients were not interviewed until six months after intervention, there are no self-report measures of prior behavior.)

Hindelang et al. (1979) have pointed out that offense behavior is not unidimensional and that treating it as such is likely to mask important effects, especially in comparing self-reports to official records. A series of

factor analyses was therefore undertaken on the self-report data to identify dimensions of behavior. In the light of space limitations, only the final
result will be reported here. [8]

Before proceeding to the factors, the reader should be reminded that
the self-report information was gathered twice on each client. The first
(Wave 1) interview was administered after service assignment and covered the six-month period prior to program intervention. The second
administration (Wave 2) took place approximately six months after service assignment, and represents postservice behavior. Each wave is
treated separately and then is compared to the other.

A preliminary step in the factor analyses was inspection of the distributions of the variables. Not surprisingly, there were problems. The more
serious offenses showed the familiar highly skewed distribution, with the
majority of cases at 0. The less serious offenses were more evenly distributed but heavier (in terms of frequency) at both ends of the distribution.
In addition, the means and variances were quite diverse. There was little
that could be done for the skewness (since it differed by offense) by using
transformations. However, the means and variances problems were resolved by standardizing the responses (at mean of 0 and unit variance).
Consequently, all that follows reflects standardized rather than raw
scores.

Arrest data were treated as before, that is, the number of charges plus
1 transformed to the log base 2. The only difference is that for this analysis they are also divided into status offenses and nonstatus offenses yielding the following variables:

L2SUB6STAT
L2SUB6NONSTAT
L2PRIORSTAT
L2PRIORNONSTAT

Dimensions of Self-Report

The factor analyses consistently produced three strong factors and one
independent item, RUNAWAY. On the basis of these factors, four self-
report indices were constructed as simple summations of subsets of the
self-report items, with each item treated as a standard score (mean of 0,
unit variance). Shown below are the indices, their estimated reliability
(based on standardized items), and their component items.

Dimensions	Reliability (Alpha)	Items
1 DRUGSR1 (Wave 1)	.83	Use and sale of pills
DRUGSR1 (Wave 2)	.82	Driving under influence
		Use and sale of hard drugs

Dimensions	Reliability (Alpha)	Items
		Use and sale of marijuana
		Drinking
		Getting drunk
		Sniffing glue
2 PREDSR1	.82	Burglary
PREDSR2	.83	Shoplifting
		Misdemeanor theft
		Felony theft
		Breaking and entering
		Joyriding
		Vandalism
		Receiving stolen goods
		Robbery
		Concealed weapon
		Assult
3 ADOLSR1	.77	Truancy
ADOLSR2	.81	Disobeying parents
		Disobeying school rules
		Curfew
4 RUNSR1	NA	Runaway (single item)
RUNSR2	NA	Runaway (single item)

In the above list, the acronyms are used as follows: DRUGSR1 stands for the report of a drug (or alcohol) offense (DRUG), self-reported (SR), on the WAVE 1 interview (1), and so on.

The factors divided quite well into (1) drug and alcohol behavior, (2) predatory behavior, (3) fairly typical adolescent misconduct, or rebellion against authority, and (4) running away. Interestingly, runaway did not relate well to any dimension or item. It always remains independent. This may address the popular notion that running away necessitates other law violations and therefore leads to a more serious involvement in crime. This may be true in some cases but does not seem to be the rule. In addition, this finding may give some credence to the notion held by many practitioners that the act of running away is, in some cases, therapeutic. Also note that the second factor, predatory behavior, corresponds very well to the general delinquency factor noted in most prior research as supporting the nonspecialization pattern of delinquency.

A comparison of Wave 1 behavior with Wave 2 behavior for the same individuals was the next analysis undertaken. The purpose was to determine the stability of behavior over time regardless of services. Figure 9.1 displays the statistically significant path coefficients among the four sub-indices of self-report. It is clear that, in each case, the Wave 1 measure of a subindex is considerably more related to its Wave 2 counterpart than it

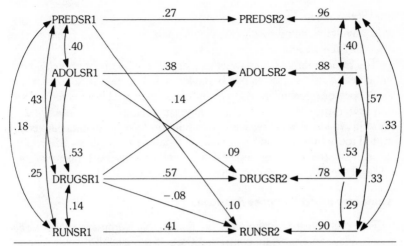

FIGURE 9.1   A Simple Path Analysis of Relationships Between Wave 1 and
            Wave 2 Self-Report Indices

is to any other Wave 2 subindex. We interpret this to indicate some stability in the dimensions of behavior. Note that runaway emerges as separate from other offense types.

Table 9.11 addresses a similar question for official offenses. This table is a simple correlation matrix, made possible by the relative simplicity of the dimensions used with official offenses. The evidence for stable dimensions using arrest data is not as compelling as that using self-report data, but the same pattern is visible. The two highest correlations in the table are between (1) nonstatus priors and nonstatus subsequents and (2) prior status and subsequent status offenses.

This analysis raises the question of the relationship between self-reported delinquency and official delinquency. Table 9.12 addresses this question. In general it can be said that status offenses are considerably more at risk of official notice than are predatory or drug offenses. This is particularly true for runaway, which, not surprisingly, results in more arrests for status offenses than for nonstatus offenses. Youngsters who engage in rebellious behavior other than running away are arrest prone for both status offenses and nonstatus offenses. The same pattern holds for both six-month periods shown in the table. Both drug and predatory behavior are lower risk offenses, especially drugs. These data would seem to buttress the point made by Hindelang et al. (1979), that is, it may be less useful to compare total arrests with total self-report behaviors. In this data set there are several dimensions to delinquent behavior and they relate differently to arrest data.[9] Of course, we cannot be sure that the differential risk of arrest for the various offense categories is not a reflection of the particular sample we are working with. These are all youth who have committed status offenses for which they have come to the attention of authorities.

The final preliminary analysis concerns the relationship between client characteristics and offense behavior. The question is, who commits what type of offense? Table 9.13 indicates that predatory offenses are committed more by males and younger juveniles than by females and older juveniles. Both adolescent rebellious and drug behaviors are committed more by Anglo and older youth. Finally, runaways are disproportionately minority and young. We suspect that these patterns reflect arrest and status offender program referral criteria.

Summary of Preliminary Analyses

The preceding analyses can be reasonably summarized by three points. First, an important component of self-reported behavior, insofar

TABLE 9.11   Correlation Matrix for Official Offenses: Prior and Subsequent Offenses

	L2PRIOR NONSTAT	L2PRIOR STAT	L2SUB6 NONSTAT	L2SUB6 STAT
L2PRIOR NONSTAT	1.0			
L2PRIOR STAT	.26*	1.0		
L2SUB6 NONSTAT	.31*	.09*	1.0	
L2SUB6 STAT	.04	.31*	.23*	1.0

*p ≤ .05.

TABLE 9.12   Correlations for Official Versus Self-Report Offenses

Self-Reported Offenses	Official Offenses			
	L2PRIOR STAT	L2PRIOR NONSTAT	L2SUB6 STAT	L2SUB6 NONSTAT
PREDSR1	.03	.10*		
DRUGSR1	.05	.003		
ADOLSR1	.10*	.10*		
RUNSR1	.32*	−.03		
PREDSR2			.05	.09*
DRUGSR2			.07*	.05
ADOLSR2			.07*	.05
RUNSR2			.30*	−.000

*p ≤ .05.

as it relates to official offending, is the single offense, runaway, which has little in common with the rest of the self-report variation. This may be unique to a status offender program sample, but it speaks to the methodological issue of the use of overall summations versus subindices in self-report, especially when comparing self-report to official delinquency.

Second, there are several dimensions of offense behavior that are not highly related to one another, one of which is a large, general delinquency factor. This point is best made by self-report data but also receives some support from arrest data.

Third, the status offender program sample is a unique one, so that traditional relationships cannot be assumed. Specifically, Anglos and younger youth report more substance abuse, while boys and younger youth report more predatory offenses than others.

Service Effect Analysis—Multiple Regression

This will be the first of two analyses of service effects on self-reported behaviors and arrests. It will represent the more severe test of services because service effects on subsequent arrests is tested only after controlling for (1) all site terms, (2) all Wave 1 self-report dimensions (if significant), and (3) both dimensions (status and nonstatus) of official arrests (if significant). Service effects on arrests are not calculated directly in this analysis (this was done in an earlier section of this chapter). Rather, Wave 2 self-reported behavior is controlled before assessing effects on arrests. Any effects of service on arrests, then, would be interpreted as system response effects over and above behavior. That is, if a service type predicts arrests, or explains variation in arrests beyond what is explained by behavior, we can only assume that something about the service itself makes the client disproportionately vulnerable to arrest (beyond what is expected on the basis of behavior). Tables are not shown for this analysis since there are so few service effects identified. The services tested in this manner are: diversion, shelter, group, foster, long-term residence (combination of group and

TABLE 9.13 Correlation Matrix for Client Characteristics and Self-Report

	Male	Anglo	Age
PREDSRI	.19*	.06	−.09*
ADOLSR1	.02	.17*	.14*
DRUGSR1	−.04	.24*	.19*
RUNSR1	−.20*	−.06	−.01
PREDSR2	.12*	.06	−.09*
ADOLSR2	.01	.13*	.05
DRUGSR2	.0001	.25*	.17*
RUNSR2	−.11*	−.06*	−.13*

*$p \le .05$.

foster), residential care (combination of group, foster, and shelter), multi-service center, outreach, counseling, and number of services. The services were tested against the rest of the equation serially.

A total of three statistically significant service effects were seen among all of these tests. The first is an effect of shelter care producing arrests beyond the expectations from self-reported runaway. The second is the effect of foster care on reducing arrests for "adolescent rebellion" (as measured by ADOLSR2) below that expected from self-reported behavior. The third effect is that of counseling in reducing official nonstatus offenses.

Briefly, a few effects were seen in the arrest analysis that are not seen in this first analysis. In addition, any effects seem to be unpatterned and therefore difficult to interpret. It may be that including as many control variables (especially site variables) as we did may have been too rigorous a test. For instance, if site variables are correlated with residential services (they are) and if residential care is correlated with subsequent behavior, the service-behavior correlation is likely to be "absorbed" by the site variables entered earlier in the equation. This danger implies the need for another, more liberal, analysis.

Service Effect Analysis—Correlations

This correlational analysis looks at the differences between the correlation of Wave 1 self-report dimensions with service types (reflecting the behavior of the clients before entering or early in service) and the correlation of the Wave 2 behaviors with services. For instance, the first section of Figure 9.2 shows that predatory offending before the program was correlated at +.01 with diversion /evaluation or crisis intervention. However, Wave 2 predatory behaviors are correlated at −.03 with this service. This would be interpreted as a slight recidivism-decreasing effect of crisis intervention on predatory offenses. Three situations would qualify as a beneficial effect in this analysis: (1) a positive correlation with the service for offenses occurring prior to the program intervention and a negative correlation with the service for offenses occurring after the intervention; (2) a positive correlation for prior offenses and a smaller positive correlation for offenses after intervention; and (3) a negative correlation for offenses occurring before the program and a larger negative correlation for offenses occurring after the intervention. A deleterious effect, of course, would be defined by the opposite condition.

The comparisons shown in Figure 9.2 can be analyzed in at least two ways. The first focuses on the service and the second focuses on the offender type.

Close inspection of Figure 9.2 reveals that some services are generally more effective than others. The services that show at least some beneficial effect (very small in some cases) on all categories of offenders are

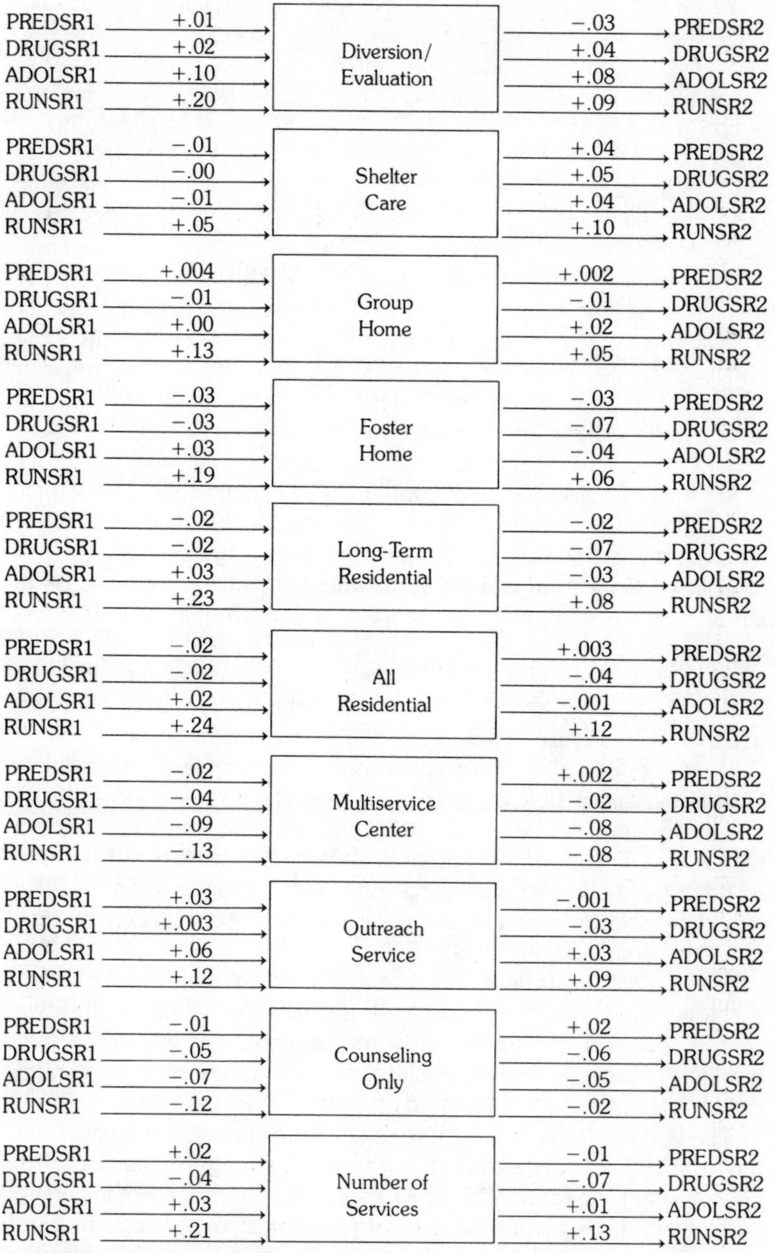

FIGURE 9.2 Wave 1 and Wave 2 Correlations with Services for
Self-Report Dimensions

outreach and large numbers of services (the latter is a direct contradiction to the results of the arrest data analysis). Those services that have a beneficial effect on three offender types and do not have a deleterious effect on the fourth are foster care and long-term residential care (combination of group and foster). Clearly, the LONGTERM effect is largely due to foster care.

Overall, the least beneficial (in terms of offense reduction) are multiservice centers, counseling, and shelter care. These three services show deleterious effects for almost all offender types.

Among those services that were generally beneficial, group homes appear to be especially effective with adolescent rebellion behaviors (largely status offenses) and runaways. The combination of group homes and foster homes (long-term residential) are more effective for drug users and runaways than for others. Foster homes are most effective for runaways, and the same effect on runaways is seen by residential services in general. A large number of services seem to be best for runaways.

On the other side of the coin, multiservice centers appear least effective with runaways, as do counseling services. Shelter care is least effective with status offender clients of all types, including runaways.

The second way of looking at the data in this figure is based on offender types. For instance, predatory offenders seem to be best served by outreach programs, group homes, crisis intervention, and a large number of services. However, they seem to do worst with multiservice centers, counseling, and shelter care. All effects for predatory offenders, whether they increase or reduce recidivism, are small.

Drug offenders also are affected in only small degrees by the services. On the beneficial side are outreach, counseling, group homes, foster homes, residential services generally, and especially long-term residential services. Finally, number of services (larger) shows a beneficial effect on this type of offender. On the harmful side for drug users are multiservice centers, crisis intervention, and shelter care. Again, all effects mentioned for drug users are small.

Status offenders (referred to here as adolescent rebellious behavior), excluding runaways, show positive but small effects from multiservice centers, outreach programs, crisis intervention, residential care, large numbers of services, and especially foster care. Counseling, shelter, and the group homes do not appear to do well for these offenders.

The largest effects in the entire data set are seen for runaways. Here the beneficial services are listed in order of the strength of their beneficial effects: long-term residential care, foster care, residential care in general, crisis intervention, group homes, larger number of services, and outreach. Deleterious effects are also stronger for runaways than for other types of offenders. They include, in order of the strength of their effects: counseling, multiservice centers, and shelter care.

Summary of Self-Report Analysis

The self-report analysis has yielded several findings of interest. Offending behavior has been shown to be composed of several categories; in addition to a large predatory factor, these include drug, adolescent rebellion, and runaway behaviors. Runaway behavior is quite independent of other types of offender behavior. Further, the major link of self-report to arrest data is in status offenses, particularly runaways—that is, runaway is the highest arrest-risk behavior. It has also been shown that in this sample of offenders predatory offenses are committed more by males and younger juveniles, status and drug offenses by Anglos and older youth, and runaway by females—all this judged by the juveniles' self-reports.

After controlling for client characteristics and site effects, as well as prior self-reported behavior and arrests, very few services showed statistically significant effects on any behavior type or arrest frequencies. The few that did occur were not patterned and are therefore not very informative.

A comparison of behavior before and after service interventions yielded a few effect patterns that seem worth summarizing. On the basis of this analysis, there is evidence that some services are generally more effective than others. Those showing consistent, although small, beneficial effects are outreach programs, larger numbers of services, and longer-term residential treatment. Residential treatments showed the strongest effects, thereby supporting a similar finding based on arrest data. Showing effects of increased recidivism generally are multiservice centers, counseling, and shelter care.

Offenders most amenable to service seemed to be runaways. They were best served by long-term residential placements and crisis intervention. The offenders least well served overall seemed to be offenders with predatory offense backgrounds. This is not surprising in a program designed for status offenders. Drug offenders showed their strongest beneficial effect in long-term residential placements.

All these effects must be treated with caution, unless seen consistently over many differing situations, since biases cannot be adequately controlled to be sure effects are real and not artifacts of program assignment.

CHAPTER SUMMARY

There were three major findings based on the arrest data analysis that can be compared to the self-report analysis findings:

(1) Residential treatment showed the most consistently beneficial effects in the arrest data analysis. More specifically, long-term residential placement received support from one site, Delaware. The self-report

analysis supports both aspects of this finding. Foster care and group homes show consistent offense-reduction relationships. Shelter care, on the other hand, did not show the same effect, but an opposite one. The policy implications of this finding are unclear. The most obvious interpretation is that since long-term residential care is beneficial, its use should be expanded. On the other side of the issue is the fact that the finding is based on a very small proportion of the total sample. Indeed, some practitioners felt that residential care was needed in a surprisingly small number of cases. If their inclinations were accurate, the beneficial effect of residential placement may apply only to the few most difficult cases. It is also true, however, that our juvenile justice system and related practitioners (system and private) usually start from the premise or assumption that children are better off in their own families if there is any way this can be worked out. If this assumption is inappropriately strong, it may be that residential care is underutilized in view of its apparent benefits. Only a systematic test of residential care treating a variety of client types would yield an answer to this ambiguity.

(2) In the arrest analysis, runaways seemed to benefit most from residential placements. This is also the case in the self-report analysis, so that we gain confidence in this finding as well.

(3) There was some evidence in the earlier analysis that providing a larger number of services was harmful to clients. However, this finding was consistently contradicted by the self-report analysis. Two interpretations of these contradictory findings seem possible. First, they may well be simply unstable results that should be dismissed. Second, there may be a beneficial effect in terms of behavior but a harmful effect in terms of the official response to the youths' behavior. It is impossible to know which is correct, if either. The diversion analysis of Dunford et al. (1982) found impact in neither arrest nor self-report delinquency.

Finally, a factor analysis on this status offender cohort revealed that runaways were the most distinct group. They are also the most treatable according to the self-report data analysis, especially by long-term residential care. Perhaps, then, service delivery for runaways should be considered separately from those for other youths. Certainly this is also the implication of Little's findings, referred to in Chapter 3, that the runaway act has some qualitatively unique aspects to it, both in terms of underlying motivations and in terms of the responses of officials. Within the DSO data set, Rojek and Erickson (1982: 16) have undertaken an intensive analysis of the Pima County offense patterns and, quite independently, come to a very similar conclusion: "It would appear that the act of running away is qualitatively different from other delinquent offenses by virtue of the fact that runaways tend to be arrested for the same offense or else move to the state of desistance." Little's (1981) fourfold typology suggests the need for carefully differentiated responses for the categories of runaways she characterizes as (1) self-emancipated minors, (2) forced emancipated minors, (3) parented children, and (4) victimized children. But additional caution is in order: A bibliographic review undertaken in 1975, prior to Little's research and ours, lists *sixteen* other studies with various typologies of runaway children (U.S. Department of Health, Education and Welfare, 1975). The issue of the "true" and special nature of runaways has not yet been resolved.

NOTES

1. Illinois's limitation of DSO programming to monitoring during the prehearing period may reflect a more pervasive failure of the Cook County court system to provide full service to its juvenile clients (see Reed et al., 1981).

2. This same pattern of limited service delivery is also reported in the national evaluation of OJJDP's prevention programs (see National Council on Crime and Delinquency, 1981).

3. The total number of clients included in this analysis is drastically reduced from the total number recorded as entering the program. In Delaware, clients received at court intake by the family court intake unit were not recorded as receiving services unless they appeared at one of the community agencies to which they were referred for additional services. In South Carolina, the missing cases are attributable to missing data.

4. Number of prior offenses is the total number of *charges* that appear on all *arrests* prior to the referral date. The analogue to this measure applies for "number of subsequent offenses."

5. The term "bias" here refers to a statistical over- or underrepresentation. It in no way implies unfair selection or discrimination, but merely the results of both bureaucratic and professional assignment judgements.

6. This would seem to confirm our assignment of highest seriousness to the runaway category, as noted earlier.

7. Throughout the discussion, where the term "significant" is used, "statistical significance" (at the .05 level) is meant. The next eight sections will be analyses of the results of this process in each site.

8. The reader may want to review the comments early in Chapter 4 concerning studies of offense specialization as a context for judging the factor-analysis results reported here.

9. Still, it must be kept in mind that our category of "predatory" behaviors includes the bulk of what are generally categorized as delinquent offenses. Only drug and status offenses yielded separate factors.

chapter 10

Progress Toward Deinstitutionalization

by Frank R. Hellum

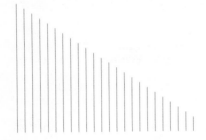

T*his report examines the pro-* gress of the eight DSO programs in achieving the goal of deinstitutionalization as defined in Section 223(a) (12) of the Juvenile Justice and Delinquency Prevention (JJDP) Act of 1974. At the inception of these programs in 1976, this JJDP section required that eligibility for formula grants to participating states must be conditioned on the acceptance of a

---

Authors' Note: This chapter is excerpted from a larger, more detailed 122-page report, which appeared as Chapter XXII in the full final report on the national DSO evaluation. Readers are referred to the original material for more detail.

plan that would commit a state to "provide within two years after submission of the plan that juveniles who are charged with or who have committed offenses that would not be criminal if committed by an adult, shall not be placed in juvenile detention or correctional facilities." During June of 1976, the Administrator of the Law Enforcement Assistance Administration, in concurrence with Senator Birch Bayh, chairman of the Senate Subcommittee to Investigate Juvenile Delinquency, established a substantial compliance standard allowing acceptance of a 75 percent reduction in detention and correctional placements for states that were unable to achieve full compliance within the initial two-year period. Although the terms of Section 223 (a) (12) were expanded by the 1977 amendments to the JJDP Act, this Chapter is limited to a concern with deinstitutionalization as defined in the original legislation. It does so without reference to the shifting definitions of secure detention and secure facilities (Zatz, 1982b: 52). Table 10.1 provides an initial view of the extent to which the DSO programs achieved deinstitutionalization by means of blocking or preventing the secure placement of status offenders. This table offers a comparison between the numbers of detained and institutionalized status offenders in the program period with the figures available during a pre-program period of equal duration.

Throughout this discussion, and especially because of our dependence upon aggregated official statistics, the reader is reminded that the meanings of "secure detention" and institutionalization are problematic. For instance, we have seen a juvenile detention center made nonsecure by the removal of locks, while perimeter fencing remained intact. In another instance, a detention center wing was turned into a "crash pad" for runaways to and from which they could come and go at will. When counselors (actually county probation officers) felt their control slipping, they arranged that runaways would don county-issue clothing, and then reminded clients that to leave with county property constituted a delinquent act for which detention might be appropriate! Finally, there are the many stories of temporary detention employed by frustrated police officers: locked police vehicles, stations with handcuffs attached to radiators, and so on.

Also, these data cannot speak to the issue of "relabeling," recognized by many as another route to getting around detention prohibition (see Handler and Zatz, 1982: 10). A series of analyses on California data reported in Van Dusen and Klein (1981) revealed at least three routes by which status offenders, no longer detainable, could be relabeled so as to make detention possible: (a) In cases where police charges included both status and delinquent offenses, police often used the delinquent charge to obtain detention far more than was the case prior to the DSO legislation; (b) similarly, data are presented showing more status offenders being handled as dependent /neglected children (and thus detainable); fi-

TABLE 10.1 Summary of Detention and Institutional Commitments, Comparing Preprogram and Program Periods of Equal Duration for All Evaluated DSO Programs

Program Site	Months Compared[a] N	Percentage of Program Period	Institutions			Detention				
			Preprogram N	Program N	Change N	Preprogram N	Program N	Change N	Total N	Change %
Pima County	15	83	0	8	+ 8	690	317	− 373	− 365	−53
Alameda County	6	33	missing information			1100[b]	834	− 266	− 266	−24
Connecticut	12	92	126	73	− 53	442	540	+ 98	+ 45	+ 8
Delaware	12	67	51	9	− 42	647	702	+ 55	+ 13	+ 2
Illinois	12	67	statutory prohibition			1783	824	− 959	− 959	−54
South Carolina	4.8[c]	20	missing information			182	214	+ 32	+ 32	+18
Clark County	12	67	8	2	− 6	666	440	− 226	− 232	−34
Spokane County	18	86	21	7	− 14	621	330	− 291	− 305	−48
Totals	91.8	62	206	99	− 107	6131	4201	−1930	−2037	−32

a. The number of months used for comparison was determined by the availability of information during the program period. For example, Pima County data were for 15 months of the program (July 1976 through September 1977) and were used in a comparison with a 15 months preprogram period (April 1975 through June 1976).

b. Figures for Alameda County are estimates representing 50 percent of the 1975 preprogram detentions and 50 percent of the 1976 program period detentions. After six months of program operation in the latter half of 1976, the detention of status offenders was prohibited by state statute.

c. Comparable detention figures were available for only two of the five evaluated counties in South Carolina, and were limited to the first year of program operation. While twelve-month comparisons were made in these two counties, the available data represents only two-fifths of the counties for one-half of the two-year preprogram period (i.e., 40 percent of twelve months).

nally (c) there was evidence of some increased use of public and private mental health commitments for status offense behavior.

More generally, Smith et al. (1979: 12) have concluded that there is a dearth of policies among intake officials about the application of such terms as dependent, status, and delinquent: "What policy does exist does not appear to significantly influence the decisions officials make."

Examination of the column totals in Table 10.1 reveals the aggregate level of achievement in reduced detention for all DSO programs. The first column indicates that comparative data were available covering 62 percent of the period in which DSO programs were fully operational prior to the termination of evaluation efforts on January 1, 1978. This figure is weighted toward the earliest months of operation and translates into an average for the DSO programs of 11.5 months' activity out of a total of 18.5 operational months. The combined accomplishment of all programs in reducing the number of detained and institutionalized status offenders is shown in the final columns of Table 10.1. In the preprogram period, 6337 status offenders were placed in secure facilities—6131 in detention and 206 committed to institutions. During a period of equal length in which the DSO programs were operational there were 4300 secure placements—4201 detained and 99 institutionalized. The net decrease of 2037 secure placements during the program period amounts to a 32 percent reduction from the number of such placements occurring in the preprogram period. In summary, the overall DSO effort can be seen as having achieved a 32 percent level of deinstitutionalization of status offenders during an average of 11.5 months of program activity. If this rate of reduction were maintained for a two-year period, the programs would have attained about a 67 percent reduction, or slightly less than the 75 percent substantial compliance standard set by LEAA and almost exactly that attained *nationally* between 1975 and 1979 (Krisberg and Schwartz, 1982: 12).

The results from an alternative method of assessing the impact of the programs on the detention of status offenders can be seen in Table 10.2. In contrast to the previous table, which showed the absolute change in detention, these results take into account the trend in detention at each site before the program and allow a measure of change relative to the preprogram experience. If the assumption is made that past performance provides an accurate estimate of future attainment, then the predicted figures in Table 10.2 represent estimates of what would have occurred in the absence of the DSO programs. The difference between predicted and actual detentions is a measure that attempts to separate the effect of the programs from other factors influencing the detention of status offenders.

This analysis offers a somewhat altered view of the impact of specific programs. In Pima County, for instance, there was an existing trend toward reduced detention before the DSO program that would have

TABLE 10.2   Predicted and Actual Detention of Status Offenders During the
Program Periods in All Evaluated DSO Program Sites

Program Site	Program Months N	Predicted Detention[a] N	Actual Detention N	Difference Between Predicted and Actual N	%
Pima County	15	445	317	− 128	− 29
Alameda County	6	1014	834	− 180	− 18
Connecticut	12	385	529	+ 144	+ 37
District 1	12	117	114	− 3	− 3
District 2	12	240	331	+ 91	+ 38
District 3	10	28	84	+ 56	+200
Delaware	12	758	702	− 56	− 7
Illinois	18	2922	1234	−1679	− 57
Cook County	18	2509	923	−1586	− 63
Macon County	18	237	124	− 113	− 48
LaSalle/McLean counties	17	176	196	+ 20	+ 11
South Carolina	12	182	214	+ 32	+ 18
Anderson County	12	79	78	− 1	− 1
Spartanburg County	12	103	136	+ 33	+ 32
Clark County	12	751	440	− 311	− 41
Spokane County	18	445	330	− 115	− 26
Totals	105	6902	4609	−2293	− 33

a. With two exceptions the predicted program figures were obtained by continuing the preprogram detention trend throughout the program period. For Alameda County the predicted figure represents the annual change in 1974-1975 applied to one-half the 1975 figure (as an estimate for the six months of program operation in 1976 prior to an effective change in legislation preventing detention of status offenders). The predicted figure for South Carolina represents actual detentions in 1975. Both exceptions were due to the unavailability of monthly detention figures during the preprogram period.

yielded an expected figure of 445 detained status offenders during the first 15 months of the program period. When the 317 actual detentions are compared to expected detentions (instead of the preprogram total of 690—see Table 10.1) the percentage change drops from a 53 percent to a 29 percent reduction. In other words, almost half of the change in detention for Pima County could be the result of policies that were already in effect before the start of the DSO program. In Connecticut there was also a declining trend before the program that would have yielded an expected figure representing a 19 percent reduction from the preprogram level. In two of the three districts in Connecticut there was a reversal of the previously established trend, which amounted to a 37 percent *increase* in statewide detention during the program period. In comparison to Table 10.1, the analysis of relative change affects the magnitude but not the direction of program impact at specific sites. The overall reduction in detention shown in Table 10.1 amounts to a 31 percent decrease, from 6131 to 4201, and is comparable to the relative reduction of 33 percent shown in Table 10.2, where a slightly longer period of program operation is represented in the data.

Finally, it should be noted that reform legislation across the country was contributing independently to a reduction of status offender detentions by virtue of reductions in status offense arrests (Krisberg and Schwartz, 1982; see also Teilmann and Klein, 1980, who cite a 45 percent drop in status offense arrests following the new nondetention law [AB3121] in California). Krisberg and Schwartz find insignificant correlations between the expenditure of OJJDP funds and rates of change in detention and use of training schools.

DATA COLLECTION

The attempt to document program accomplishments in deinstitutionalizing status offenders involved two separate data collection efforts. As originally designed, the evaluation of DSO programs did not include a study of deinstitutionalization. Rather, it was agreed that this information would be forthcoming from monitoring reports required of the participating jurisdictions. Although the submission of these reports was a seemingly automatic feature of the terms under which program funds were allocated, it became apparent during the second year of evaluation that the anticipated level of information would be unavailable. This development necessitated a revision in plans for the national evaluation, involving an independent effort to obtain data at the local level.

This section will review the progress of both data collection efforts and will specifically focus on the following: (1) the difficulties and shortcomings of the original federally mandated data collection procedures; and (2) the level of success in obtaining information under the revised procedures. These efforts offer valuable insights into the major problems of data access that should be considered in any future effort of a similar nature. We feel it is important to point out the various lessons that have been learned in attempting to assess deinstitutionalization, and to familiarize the reader with the quality of the data on deinstitutionalization available in a heterogeneous collection of local juvenile justice systems.

The Original Design

In planning the national evaluation of DSO programs, decisions were made *not* to provide measures of program impact in reducing the rates of detention and correctional commitment for status violations. This omission resulted from neither an oversignt in designing the research nor a judgment to devalue detention and correctional experiences as evaluation measures. Rather, the reason was an early assumption, shared by the evaluators and the Office of Juvenile Justice and Delinquency Prevention, that the necessary information would be obtainable from monitoring reports generated at the state level. Unfortunately, this assumption proved to be unwarranted.

The requirement for state monitoring of compliance in deinstitutionalizing status offenders is found in Section 223(a)(14) of the JJDP Act of 1974 (U.S. Department of Justice, 1974). Under this provision participating states were to submit annual reports of the number of status offenders placed in secure detention and correctional facilities. In June 1976, the Law Enforcement Assistance Administration provided further specification of the need for baseline comparison data and the methods to be utilized in measuring compliance. During the summer of 1977, in the final months of the national evaluation, the National Institute for Juvenile Justice and Delinquency Prevention informed the national evaluators of problems encountered in obtaining monitoring data. After requesting from NIJJDP all currently available data for the eight evaluated DSO sites, the following major problems were discovered.

Reporting periods. Consistently reported data for both program and preprogram periods would not be available for states in which DSO programs had been funded. This presented two types of difficulties. First, comparison between program sites required measures of performance over similar periods of time, but the baseline monitoring information varied among sites from 1973 to 1975 and precluded this type of analysis. Second, even within-site comparisons would have been of questionable value where the baseline data left a gap of as much as two years prior to the program period.

Reporting methods. Another barrier to uniform comparison involved the use of alternative reporting methods in compiling the monitoring reports. The three major alternatives (aggregate annual totals, average monthly figures, and daily census results) would have prevented any meaningful contrast between sites using different reporting methods.

Aggregation of data. While program activities were generally confined to specific counties or districts, monitoring reports offered information aggregated at the statewide level. Without disaggregated reporting for jurisdictions where DSO programs were operating, it would not have been possible to assess deinstitutionalization in relation to program efforts.

Definitional variation. Although attempts were made to foster the use of common definitions for federal monitoring, it was not clear that state data had been generated on the basis of similar definitions of key terms. In fact, analyses such as those undertaken by Saari (1978) make it clear that one should *not* expect comparable definitions. The national evaluation had frequently encountered definitional variation among programs in differing states over terms closely related to the monitoring effort, such as in distinguishing between secure and nonsecure facilities, and in designating a juvenile violation as a status offense. If these variations also existed in the monitoring data, then it could lead to substantial underreporting of detained and institutionalized status offenders by some jurisdictions and would further undermine the potential for comparative analysis.

Descriptive characteristics. State monitoring reports only provided an enumeration of status offenders placed in secure facilities and did not include information necessary for an analysis of possible changes in the demographic characteristics of institutionalized populations or of shifts in the duration of confinement. Added descriptive data would allow at least a preliminary examination of the manner in which deinstitutionalization was implemented.

Accuracy of reported data. The difficulties of obtaining accurate data from state and local records had previously been established in other areas of the national evaluation. Here it had been found that even in jurisdictions with computerized systems, the identification and tracking of status offenders could be frustrated by a variety of factors. Some systems might not have been operational long enough to include the information from past years necessary in providing baseline statistics. Also, the coding categories in these systems were designed for retrieval of information relevant to the jurisdiction and might not include status offense codes. Finally, local requirements for purging juvenile records at age of majority may involve the deletion of computerized records as well as destruction of case files. In jurisdictions relying on manually assembled records, the data collection task can be extremely burdensome and the resulting statistics may reflect a multitude of errors and omissions. Against this background it could be anticipated that at least a portion of the monitoring information would be highly suspect as an accurate accounting of detention and institutional commitments.

Interpretive background. Reliance on secondary data such as that offered in monitoring reports involves a high degree of isolation from events that may have had a significant influence in determining a statistical outcome. For example, in attempting to attribute a decline in institutional commitments to the activities of a DSO program, it would be useful to know if a statutory revision had been enacted that effectively prohibited such commitments. Adequate interpretation of data on deinstitutionalization as measures of program impact would require an additional level of information beyond that planned as part of the original monitoring effort.

Some of these concerns can be discerned through an examination of Figure 10.1, which presents the trend lines for the number of status offenders detained in Connecticut for the years 1975 through 1977. During

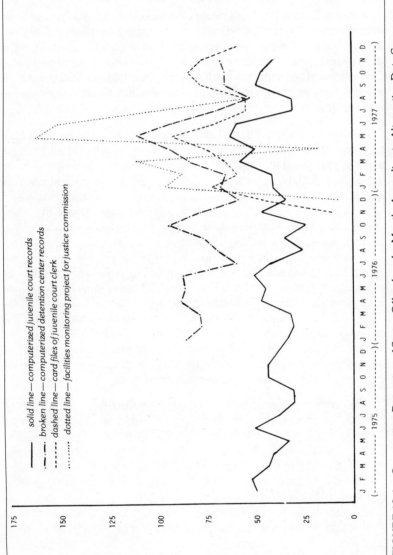

FIGURE 10.1   Connecticut Detention of Status Offenders, by Month, According to Alternative Data Sources

the evaluation, the State of Connecticut was eventually found to have *four* separate data sources recording the monthly detention figures for status violations. The earliest system, represented by the solid line, is a computerized record maintained by the juvenile court, which provided detention figures for the full three-year period. A second computerized system, marked by the broken line, was developed from intake records at the four state detention centers beginning with calendar year 1976. The third system was established by the chief clerk of the juvenile court as a screening procedure for the DSO program and is represented by the dashed line. The dotted line represents a final version of statewide detention compiled for the State Justice Commission in its effort to fulfill the monitoring requirement. There are obvious disparities among these systems in their reported numbers of detained status offenders. In the order presented above, the average monthly figures for the data sources are 41, 77, 64, and 78, respectively.

While these variations suggest the use of different definitions for status offenses, there is also the possibility of serious error in the data. For instance, the version developed for the State Justice Commission monitoring is extremely erratic in reporting 110 detentions for April 1977, a decline to 18 in May, and an increase during June to 166. While the organizational processes involved in arrest, court action, and incarceration normally produce some variation in the flow of cases over time, fluctuations of the magnitude reported in the monitoring effort raise immediate questions concerning the accuracy of the data.

In addition to the disparities that can be seen in Figure 10.1, there is also an interesting type of convergence in the figures of the four data reporting systems. In each system there is a peak level of detention reported for the summer of 1977, with a uniform decline continuing through the month of August. Although the trends over previous years indicate a seasonal decline in detention during the summer months, the 1977 experience is more pronounced and points to the possibility that the fully operational DSO effort may have successfully affected statewide detention of status offenders. This interpretation loses some of its credibility, however, when it is noted that the detention center with the highest volume of admissions was closed during this period due to problems concerning fire regulations.

Having considered the types of problems that could be expected in the data obtained from the monitoring reports, the evaluation staff assessed a number of alternatives in approaching the issue of documenting progress toward deinstitutionalization. First, would it be worth the effort to pursue the original design and utilize whatever information the monitoring reports might provide? Had this been attempted, a comparative analysis of the DSO sites would not have been possible and, furthermore, the effort would have been based on sources such as those depicted in Figure 10.1 but without any opportunity to assess the quality of the data.

Second, since the Office of Juvenile Justice was in the process of revising procedures for monitoring deinstitutionalization, would it be possible to await the results of later monitoring reports? Unfortunately, the time constraints of the national evaluation precluded this option.

Third, would it be acceptable simply to abandon the attempt to assess program effects on detention and correctional placements? This option would have created the unenviable prospect of having to produce an evaluation on deinstitutionalization without the capacity to examine one of the major objectives of the DSO programs. In rejecting each of these alternatives, the only remaining choice lay in the direction of developing a revised strategy for obtaining deinstitutionalization data.

The Revised Strategy

As an initial step in developing an alternative data set, an agreement was reached with NIJJDP that contacts would be made with each of the local evaluation grantees to determine the feasibility of gaining detention and correctional data directly from the program sites during the remaining months of the evaluation period. If feasible, the national evaluation would undertake a special study of the DSO program impact in reducing the number of status offenders confined in secure facilities. The following describes the data elements and sources of information eventually relied upon in assessing deinstitutionalization and discusses the extent to which the revised strategy yielded the desired level of information.

Data Elements

The general objective in pursuing a revised strategy was to document, as fully as possible, any alteration in patterns of detention and correctional commitments that might reasonably be attributed to the DSO programs. Toward this end an attempt was made to obtain serial data over a sufficient number of points in time to allow an assessment of changes at the various stages of program development. Furthermore, the request for data also called for detailed information that would permit an examination of differential shifts among subgroups within the institutionalized populations. Essentially, the request for information was focused on the following types of data.

Number of status offenders entering secure facilities. These data were requested on a monthly basis for each separate facility serving the program site. The time frame was set for at least one year of the preprogram period and the entire program period. Separate reporting was requested on admissions to detention within the program site, and on commitments to correctional institutions originating from the program jurisdiction.

Duration of secure placement. In the case of detention this called for the average number of days for admissions in a given month, with any portion of a 24-hour period being counted as a full day. Since institutional commitments can be rather lengthy, and in some instances might extend beyond the data collection period, an alternative measure was specified that called for a count of the number of commitments from the program jurisdiction remaining in the institution during each month following original placement.

Gender and ethnic characteristics of secure placements. This was requested on a quarterly basis for both detention and correctional placements.

Total versus program-eligible status offenders. While all DSO programs generally excluded transient youths as out-of-jurisdiction runaways, some of the programs (most notably Connecticut and Clark County) imposed more restrictive eligibility requirements that could have left large numbers of ineligible youth subject to detention or correctional commitment. Interest in the effects of varying eligibility requirements led to a request for separate data on the total status offender population as well as the smaller group of "program eligibles."

Data Sources

The early assumption underlying the revised data collection strategy was that the local evaluators at each program site would be involved in compiling the available information on detention and institutional placements. Various problems such as the timing of the data request, previous commitment of resources, and competing interests of the local evaluators resulted in their participation in only five of the eight sites. While alternative sources were eventually located, the inability to secure the cooperation of all the local evaluators affected the quantity of information gathered from the different program jurisdictions. The final sources of detention and institutional data from each site are described below.

Pima County. The data on detained status offenders were compiled by the local evaluators from a computer tape provided by the juvenile court staff. Information on institutional commitments was obtained from the research and evaluation unit of the court. Since the Pima County court routinely destroys juvenile records at age of majority, a retrospective tabulation is likely to yield an underestimate of actual cases. For example, files no longer existed for 35 percent of the correctional commitments during the period of 1974 through 1977, and it is possible that some of these missing cases may have been adjudicated for status violations.

Alameda County. The limited information from this site was provided by the Office of Criminal Justice Planning for Alameda County. Detention figures were obtained from a computerized master file maintained by the juvenile probation department and reflected the number of status offender "book-ins" to the Juvenile Hall detention facility. Alcohol possession offenses were not included in the count of status violations. The only available institutional data were obtained from a previous study that only provided partial information for the calendar year of 1974.

Connecticut. Of the four data sets on detention of status offenders, a decision was made to rely on the computerized system maintained by the juvenile court. While it is thought that this system may underestimate the number of detained youth, there is no evidence that the downward bias changed through time. The Connecticut data, therefore, can be taken as an accurate indicator of through-time changes or trends, but cannot be viewed as an exact record of actual detentions. The figures in this report were obtained by the local evaluator from the computerized court records.

Delaware. The detention and institutional data were compiled from records available to the Delaware State Planning Agency, the Governor's Commission on Criminal Justice. The figures represent in-state residents who had been charged only with a status violation at the time of incarceration.

Illinois. The detention figures for three of the program sites were obtained directly from facility records by the local evaluators. The data from Cook County represent a 16 percent random sample and not a total population. For the purposes of this report the Cook County sample is treated as the population of detained youth. Estimation of the actual population can be obtained by increasing the reported figures by a factor of 6.25. There are no figures on correctional placements due to the statutory prohibition that has existed in Illinois since 1974.

South Carolina. The data on institutional commitments in the five evaluated counties were obtained from the South Carolina Department of Youth Services. This information covered the two years of the program operation, 1976 and 1977, but was not available for the period prior to program funding. Partial detention information for the five counties was obtained from a report prepared for the Office of Criminal Justice Programs (Stephen Carter & Associates, 1977). These data were available for only the year immediately preceding the program, 1975, and the first year of program operation, 1976. A study by the local evaluators reports on the statewide experience regarding detention and institutional placement. This latter report included areas in which the program was not in operation and did not provide separate reporting for the evaluated counties. With regard to institutionalization, the evaluated counties where the program was known to have been operational did not replicate the statewide experience; no appreciable change was noted in the number of detained status offenders (Banks and Deutsch, 1979).

Clark and Spokane counties. The local evaluator responsible for both of these sites provided detention and institutional data obtained from computerized court records in each county. In Washington the possession of alcohol by a minor was considered a delinquent offense and does not appear in the status offense data.

Data Availability

The request for detention and institutional data was aimed at securing measures on a number of items over a sufficient period of time to allow an adequate assessment of change. As seen in Figure 10.2, it was not possible to obtain data for uniform time measures across all the sites. Here the x's represent availability of data in preprogram months, and the o's indicate data for the program period. Delaware, for instance, provided preprogram detention data for only twelve months in 1974-1975 and program information for calendar year 1977. The last column indicates availability of information on a monthly or annual basis. Since institutional commitments occurred at a relatively low frequency, the issue of monthly or annual data was not of major significance. With detentions, however, the lack of monthly figures reduced considerably the potential for analyzing changes that may have resulted from the establishment of the DSO programs.

The time periods for which information was available can be seen in Table 10.3. In the eight programs there are two states, Connecticut and Illinois, with separately analyzed data on jurisdictions within the program site. South Carolina is also represented by five evaluated counties, but the lack of detailed information led to the consideration of all counties as a single site. Overall, the data can be seen as covering 12 specific DSO program sites. The total number of months, both before and after the program starting dates, are shown in separate columns for the available detention and institutional data. For detention information there was an average of 37.6 months of coverage, and for institutions there was an average of 35 months of available data over all the sites (excluding Illinois, which did not institutionalize status offenders).

Table 10.4 summarizes the availability of information by specifically requested items for the eight major site groupings. The compliance figures represent simple percentages of the number of sites supplying the minimal level of information requested by the national evaluation. There was considerable variation between the program sites in providing data. Only in Illinois was it possible to obtain information for all the relevant items, which, because of statutory prohibitions, were limited to detention of status offenders. Clark and Spokane counties provided virtually all of the requested detention data, but none of the descriptive information on the number of institutionalized status offenders. The least successful data collection efforts were in Alameda County and South Carolina.

	1974	1975	1976	1977	1978	Type of Reporting
	J FMAMJ J ASOND	J FMAMJ J ASOND	J FMAMJ J ASOND	J FMAMJ J ASOND	J FMAM J J	
Detention Data						
Arizona—Pima County	x x x x x x x x x x x x	x x x x x x x x x x x x	x x x x x x o o o o o o	o o o o o o o o o o o o	o o o o o o o	monthly
California—Alameda County	x x x x x x x x x x x x	x x x x x x x x x x x x	x x x x x x x x x o o o	o o o o o o o o o o o o	o o o o o o o	annual
Connecticut—District 1		x x x x x x x x x x x x	x x x x x x x x x x x x	o o o o o o o o o o o o	o o o o o o o	monthly
Connecticut—District 2		x x x x x x x x x x x x	x x x x x x x x x x x x	o o o o o o o o o o o o	o o o o o o o	monthly
Connecticut—District 3		x x x x x x x x x x x x	x x x x x x x x x x x x	o o o o o o o o o o o o	o o o o o o o	monthly
Delaware		x x x x x x x x x	x x x x x x x x x o o o	o o o o o o o o o o o o	o o o o o o o	monthly
Illinois—Cook County		x x x x x x x x x x x x	x x x x x x x x x o o o	o o o o o o o o o o o o	o o o o o o o	monthly
Illinois—LaSalle/MacClean counties		x x x x x x x x x x x x	x x x x x x x x x x x x	o o o o o o o o o o o o	o o o o o o o	monthly
Illinois—Macon County		x x x x x x x x x x x x	x x x x x x x x o o o o	o o o o o o o o o o o o	o o o o o o o	monthly
South Carolina		x x x x x x x x x x x x	x x x x x x o o o o o o	o o o o o o o o o o o o		annual
Washington—Clark County	x x x x x x x x x x x x	x x x x x x x x x x x x	x x x x x o o o o o o o	o o o o o o o o o o o o	o o o o o o o	monthly
Washington—Spokane County	x x x x x x x x x x x x	x x x x x x x x x x x x	x x x x x x x x x o o o	o o o o o o o o o o o o	o o o o o o o	monthly
Institutional Commitment Data[a]						
Arizona—Pima County	J FMAMJ J ASOND	x x x x x x x x x x x x	x x x x x x x x x x x x	J FMAMJ J ASOND J FMAM J J	annual
California—Alameda County	x x x x x x x x x x x x	x x x x x x x x x x x x	x x x x x o o o o o o o	o o o o o o o o o o o o		annual
Connecticut		x x x x x x x x x x x x	x x x x x x x x x x x x	o o o o o o o o o o o o	o o o o o o o	monthly
Delaware		x x x x x x x x x x	o o o o o o o o o o o o	o o o o o o o o o o o o	o o o o o o o	annual
South Carolina		x x x x x x x x x x x x	x x x x x x x x x x o o	o o o o o o o o o o o o		annual
Washington—Clark County	x x x x x x x x x x x x	x x x x x x x x x x x x	o o o o o o o o o o o o			monthly
Washington—Spokane County	x x x x x x x x x x x x	x x x x x x x x x x x x	x x x x x o o o o o o o	o o o o o o o o o o o o		monthly

FIGURE 10.2 Comparison of Periods Covered and Type of Reporting for Detention and Institutional Commitment Data in All Program Sites

NOTE: x indicates preprogram month; o indicates program month.
a. Illinois statute prohibits institutional commitment of status offenders.

TABLE 10.3 Program Starting Dates and Periods Covered by Detention and Institutional Commitment Data

| | Program Starting Date | Availability of Detention Data | | Availability of Institutional Data | |
		Period Covered	# of Months	Period Covered	# of Months
Arizona—Pima County	6/76	1/74-9/77	45	1/74-9/77	45
California—Alameda County	7/76	1/74-12/77	48	1/74-12/74	12
Connecticut—District 1	12/76	1/75-11/77	35	1/75-11/77	35[a]
Connecticut—District 2	12/76	1/75-11/77	35	1/75-11/77	35[a]
Connecticut—District 3	2/77	1/75-11/77	35	1/75-11/77	35[a]
Delaware	6/76	8/74-7/75 & 1/77-12/77	24	1/74-12/75 & 8/76-12/77	41
Illinois—Cook County	7/76	7/75-7/78	37	— —	—[b]
Illinois—LaSalle/McLean Counties	9/76	1/75-7/78	43	— —	—[b]
Illinois—Macon County	7/76	7/75-7/78	37	— —	—[b]
South Carolina	1/76	1/75-12/76	24	1/76-12/77	24
Washington—Clark County	7/76	1/74-6/77	42	1/74-6/77	42
Washington—Spokane County	4/76	1/74-10/77	46	1/74-10/77	46

a. Connecticut institutional data were available as state totals only, not reported by district.
b. Illinois statute prohibits institutional commitment of status offenders.

The final column of Table 10.4 indicates the level of success in securing information on specific data items. The institutionalized population proved to be the most difficult on which to obtain detailed information. This is because in most sites the institutional commitments are recorded at a state facility that does not provide detailed information on commitments from local jurisdictions. Even among the detained population it was relatively more difficult to obtain descriptive information that would permit subgroup comparisons. In some of the sites it was maintained that status offenders entering detention in the program period were largely ineligible for alternative treatment because of current probation status on a prior offense or because they were nonresidents of the jurisdiction. The inability to provide a separate count for eligible youth made it impossible to verify the claims regarding the detained population. There was also a lack of information on the gender and ethnic composition of incarcerated status offenders. Of the eight sites, four could not provide data on gender and five were unable to specify the ethnic characteristics of the detained population. For institutional commitments, only one site had separate counts for males and females, and none of the sites could provide detailed ethnic information.

Since the request for this information was delayed until very late in the evaluation data collection period, it was encouraging to find that at least some statistics could be gathered for all the DSO program sites. The local evaluators and others who participated in this task can be credited with

TABLE 10.4 Availability of Detention and Institutional Commitment Data for DSO Programs

Type of Data Requested	Type of Data Received								Percentage of Compliance
	Pima	Alameda	Connecticut	Delaware	Illinois	South Carolina	Clark	Spokane	
Detention Data									
monthly detention	month	year	month	month	month	year	month	month	75
one-year preprogram period	2.5	2	2	1	1	1	2.5	2	100
full program period (%)	83	100	92	67	100	50	67	86	79
total status offenders	yes	yes	yes	no	yes	yes	yes[a]	yes[a]	88
eligible status offenders	no	no	no	yes	yes	no	N.A.[b]	N.A.[b]	50
facility or region specified	N.A.[b]	N.A.[b]	yes	yes	yes	yes	no	yes	100
average detention days	no	yes[c]	no	no	yes	no	yes	yes	50
gender specified	yes	no	no	yes	yes	no	yes	yes	50
ethnicity specified	no	no	no	no	yes	no	yes	yes	38
Institutional Data									
monthly commitments	year[c]	year[c]	month	year	N.A.	year	month	month	43
one-year preprogram period	2	1	2	1	N.A.	0	2.5	2	86
full program period (%)	83	0	92	67	N.A.	100	67	86	67
total status offenders	yes	yes	yes	yes	N.A.	yes	yes	yes	100
eligible status offenders	no	no	no	no	N.A.	no	no	no	0
facility or region specified	no	no	no	yes	N.A.	yes	no	no	29
number remaining	no	no	no	no	N.A.	no	no	no	0
gender specified	no	no	no	yes	N.A.	no	yes	no	14
ethnicity specified	no	no	no	no	N.A.	no	yes	no	0
Percentage of full compliance	35	24	39	50	100	33	47	53	

a. Available for program period only.
b. Item is not applicable to this program site.
c. Reporting of partial or incomplete data.

accomplishing a monumental eleventh-hour task. Their success, however, should not be taken as evidence of the adequacy of local information systems in providing juvenile justice data. Even where evaluators could obtain access to computerized data, it was not possible to obtain uniformly recorded information across program sites. The experience in gathering the information for this report points to the need for development of information systems that can be used as a basis for deciding policy on a range of issues in juvenile justice, including, but not limited to, the treatment of status violations.

SUMMARY OF FINDINGS

While the nationally evaluated DSO effort represented eight county or statewide program sites, there were divisions within two of the states, Connecticut and Illinois, that resulted in the reporting of detention and institutional commitment data for twelve separate program locations. Previous sections examined the influence of these programs. This summary section presents the findings, from the programs for which information was available, relative to six measures of deinstitutionalization—number of detentions, institutional commitments, detention of nonresidents, length of detention, gender differences, and ethnic characteristics.

Number of Detained Status Offenders

Among the DSO programs there was no single pattern with respect to change in the number of detained status offenders. The summary data in Table 10.5 compare the average monthly detention figures for the total program and six-month interim periods to the monthly average of the entire preprogram period. In the ten programs reporting interim figures, the most common pattern involved initial declines followed by a higher percentage reduction in the later interim periods. Compared to the preprogram average, the final interim period reductions for these programs were −83 percent (Pima County), −35 percent (District 1 in Connecticut), −44 percent (Macon County), −47 percent (Clark County), and −63 percent (Spokane County). Cook County was unique in that the highest decline occurred in the first six months, −65 percent, and leveled off at −57 percent in the remaining months of the program. The remaining sites showed an increase in detention for at least one if not all of the interim periods. These increases contributed to the following total program period changes: +40 percent (District 2, Connecticut), +29 percent (District 3, Connecticut), +9 percent (Delaware), and +16 percent (LaSalle and McLean counties, Illinois). The two sites for which interim data could not be obtained recorded estimated changes in the program

TABLE 10.5 Change in Total and Interim Program Detention, Compared to Average Monthly Detention During the Preprogram Period for All DSO Program Sites

	Preprogram Detention		First 6 Months		Second 6 Months		Third 6 Months		Total Program Detention		
	N	Monthly Average	Monthly Average	% Change	Monthly Average	% Change	Monthly Average	% Change	N	Monthly Average	% Change
Arizona—Pima County	1733	57.8	30.2	−48	17.7	−69	10.0	−83	317	21.1	−63
California—Alameda County	4583	191.0							834	139.0	−27[a]
Connecticut—District 1	292	12.7	10.8	−15	8.2	−35			114	9.5	−25
Connecticut—District 2	454	19.7	29.8	+51	25.3	+29			331	27.6	+40
Connecticut—District 3	162	6.5	8.0	+23	9.0	+38			84	8.4	+29
Delaware	647	53.9			59.3	+10	57.6	+7	702	58.5	+9
Illinois—Cook County	1526	127.2	44.5	−65	54.5	−57	54.8	−57	923	51.3	−60
Illinois—Macon County	134	11.2	9.3	−17	5.0	−55	6.3	−44	124	6.9	−38
Illinois—LaSalle/McLean counties	219	11.0	9.5	−14	14.2	+29	9.0	−18	178	12.7	+16
South Carolina	182	15.2							214	17.8	+18[b]
Washington—Clark County	1665	55.5	44.0	−21	29.3	−47			440	36.7	−34
Washington—Spokane County	1048	38.8	24.7	−36	16.0	−59	14.3	−63	330	18.3	−53
Totals	12,645	50.6	23.4	−54	24.4	−52	27.9	−45	4,591	28.9	−43

NOTE: Interim period may be less than six months depending on availability of data.
a. Estimated number of program detentions.
b. Based on two of the five evaluated counties.

period of −27 percent (Alameda County) and +18 percent (South Carolina). For the twelve jurisdictions, seven showed a reduction during the period of the DSO program, and five recorded increased levels of status offender detentions. The aggregate level of change for all sites as compared to the preprogram monthly average amounted to a 43 percent decline in detention.[1] A similar, mixed picture is reported for the seven states surveyed by Handler and Zatz (1982).

Institutional Commitments

The comparative figures on institutional commitments for status violations were available in five of the eight basic program sites. As shown in Table 10.6, there were substantial reductions in four program sites, with ranges from −50 percent to −86 percent change in commitments. This contrasts somewhat with the "virtually eliminated" result reported for seven states by Handler and Zatz (1982: 88). The increase for Pima County is misleading in that it is based on a very small number of commitments during the program, compared to an even smaller number in the preprogram period. Comparison of commitment rates based on population provide more of a perspective on the issue of correctional placement for status violations. In the preprogram period these rates varied from less than 1 to as high as 11 commitments per 100,000 total population in the specific program sites. For the sites in which data were available for both periods, the program rates shifted to between 1 and 4 commitments per 100,000 population. The program rate for South Carolina is obviously much higher than the other sites and in the absence of preprogram data cannot be assessed as an indication of change. Statutory prohibition in Illinois (and to a partial extent in Alameda County) eliminated the consideration of institutional commitments.

Detention of Nonresidents

In all the DSO sites, nonresident status offenders were generally ineligible for program services and it could be assumed that the detention of these youths would be unaffected by DSO activities. The Cook County, Illinois, site provided the information needed to test this assumption. As expected, the rate of nonresident detentions remained constant throughout a period of substantial change in the numbers of detained resident status violators. So, also, did detentions of delinquents (Spergel et al., 1981). In fact, this lack of variation, combined with the volume of such cases, points to the existence of a relatively large number of noncriminal youth who did not benefit from the DSO effort. The average monthly detention of nonresidents was maintained at approximately 40 cases in the program and preprogram periods. Since the Cook County data represented a 16 percent sample of all detention, the actual number of de-

TABLE 10.6 Change in Average Monthly Institutional Commitments and Rates per 100,000 Total Population Between the Preprogram and Program Periods for all DSO Programs

	Preprogram Period			Program Period			Percentage of Change
	N	Monthly Average	Annual Rate per 100,000[a]	N	Monthly Average	Annual Rate per 100,000[a]	
Pima County	6	0.20	0.54	8	0.53	1.43	+165
Alameda County	129	10.75	10.08		not available		N.A.
Connecticut	308	13.39	5.18	73	6.08	2.35	− 55
Delaware	154	5.31	11.00	14	0.74	1.53	− 86
Illinois		statutory prohibition			statutory prohibition		N.A.
South Carolina		not available		189	7.88	10.08[b]	N.A.
Clark County	30	1.00	7.76	6	0.50	3.88	− 50
Spokane County	32	1.19	4.66	5	0.28	1.10	− 76
Totals	656	4.36		295	3.28		

a. Based on total estimated 1975 population.
b. Computed for five evaluated counties only.

tained nonresidents in the county can be estimated at 250 per month, or 3000 annually. In the preprogram period, nonresidents represented about 24 percent of all detentions, but with the decline in resident detentions in the program period, the stable nonresident population achieved a 48 percent representation among total detentions. These findings suggest that in urban areas similar to Cook County consideration should be given to deinstitutionalization efforts aimed at the issue of nonresident status offenders.

Length of Detention

The analysis of length of detention for status offenders focused on two issues: (a) the extent to which programs may have achieved a reduction in the number of detained youth by diverting only the less difficult cases and detaining a core group for extended periods of time, and (b) whether programs that failed to reduce the number of detentions may have succeeded in limiting the length of status offense placements. On the first issue there were four sites that had reduced the number of detained youth and also provided information on the length of detention. An attempt was made to test the relationship between average length of detention and number detained in each month of the program. The finding of a negative relationship would indicate that few status offenders (a core group) were being detained for extended periods of time. In three of the sites—Pima County, Macon County, and Spokane County—there was no significant relationship. For Cook County, however, the average length of detention was inversely related to the number of detentions and represented an overall increase of 32 percent, compared to the preprogram length of detention figures. This suggests the possibility that the marked rate of initial program period reduction in Cook County involved an element of "creaming" in which only the less difficult cases were diverted from detention. The leveling off of detention in the later program months could represent an unwillingness to divert the more difficult types of status offense cases from detention.

On the second issue, there were two sites that failed to reduce the number of detentions in which it was possible to obtain length of detention information. In both programs there was an effect on the average number of days that status offenders remained in detention. The Delaware program reduced the length of detention during the program period by about 50 percent. In the LaSalle /McLean area the average period of detention declined by 24 percent during the program.

Gender Differences

Among the six jurisdictions reporting the gender characteristics of detained status offenders there was no uniform influence on the percent-

ages of female and male detentions. Before the DSO effort the proportion of females in the detained population ranged from 50 percent to 70
percent. In two sites there was *no change* associated with the program
period. In Clark County, females were a 60 percent majority before the
program and remained at the same level in the six months of the program
for which data were available. In Spokane County, the disparity had
been reduced from a high of 70 percent female in the earliest preprogram
months to approximately 50 percent female just before the start of the
program. The percentage stayed at this lower level throughout the program period.

In two of the Illinois programs there was an *increase* in the percentages
of female detentions. Cook County recorded a shift from 50 percent before DSO to 60 percent female detention in the program months. This
was accomplished by diverting more males than females from detention
in the program period. In the LaSalle /McLean area there was an increase in detention during the program that primarily involved female
status offenders. This resulted in a shift from 60 percent to 70 percent
female detentions after the start of the DSO effort.

The jurisdictions showing a *decrease* in the percentage of female detainees exhibited a pattern of diverting more females than males in the
program period. In Macon County, Illinois, female detention dropped from
65 percent to 55 percent in the program period. In Pima County, Arizona,
there was a decline in female detention from 50 percent to 35 percent
during the program. This was the only instance in which the program percentage of females constituted a minority of the detained population.

With the exception of Pima County, none of the DSO programs attempted to deal specifically with the needs of female status offenders.
The changing percentages of female detainees at the other sites were
probably the result of contextual factors external to the program models.

This mixed picture contrasts rather sharply with the conclusions drawn
for the nation as a whole (Krisberg and Schwartz, 1982), where female
detention reductions were observed to constitute the bulk of the decrease. Reasons for this disparity are not at all clear.

Ethnic Differences

In the five programs providing this information there was little or no
evidence of a racial or ethnic bias in diverting status offenders from detention. During the first year of the Macon County program the reduction
in detention largely involved Anglo youth. However, the number of detained minority youth remained at a low level, about two per month, and
the program is reported as having eventually removed all status offenders from detention. In Cook, LaSalle /McClean, Clark, and Spokane
counties the percentage of detained minority youth was approximately

the same in both the preprogram and the program periods. With the exception of Cook County, however, these jurisdictions contained a small minority population to begin with and would be expected to show little variation in this regard. The Cook County data did reveal that minority youth, mostly Black, were a majority of all detained status offenders and seem to be overrepresented in comparison to their number in the general population.

NOTE

1. The differences between the figures shown in this section and those presented elsewhere are due to the use of the full preprogram data and adjustments related to variations in program starting dates that have been included for this summary section.

chapter 11

DSO Realities and Implications

A Summary Statement

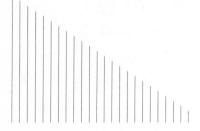

$$I_{n \text{ the preceding chapters, we}}$$

have attempted to elucidate the bases for determining the level of "success" achieved in DSO. The picture is, at best, mixed. A press release from OJJDP inadvertently revealed how such a mixed picture may lead to widely discrepant interpretations of this success; here are examples of headlines used on newspaper articles emanating from the release:

Counseling Cuts Confinement, Not Juvenile Arrests, Study Says [*The Cincinnati Enquirer*, 10/12/82]

Counseling Helps Juveniles, Study Finds [*Wilmington* (NC) *Star*, 10/4/82]

Counseling, Home Programs Can't Cut Re-Arrests [*Butler* (PA) *Eagle,* 10/7/82]

Home Placement, Counseling Helps Some Juveniles [*Kirkland* (WA) *Journal American,* 10/4/82]

Juvenile Re-Arrest Rates Remain High [*Rome* (NY) *Sentinel,* 10/4/82]

Community Aid Found Effective in Curbing Teen Crime [*Tyler* (TX) *Telegraph,* 10/4/82]

Plan For Juvenile Offenders Studied [*San Jose* (CA) *Mercury,* 10/4/82]

The DSO program, like many of its forerunners in delinquency policy initiation and evaluation, stands as a media Rorschach, to be interpreted as much from readers' values as from the program's demonstrable outcomes. In this final chapter, we attempt our own interpretation, using a multitude of the facets of our DSO inkblot. To some of these facets we give greater priority than to others. We have tried to be explicit about these priorities; readers applying different weights to various facets are of course well within their rights, but we challenge such readers to be equally explicit.

CONTEXT AND CONSTRAINTS

The Experience Base

Both the DSO program and the national evaluation were limited in achieving their goals by elements of their natural context and by the constraints placed upon them. Some of these limitations were unavoidable and represent the types of limitations to which most social programs may expect to be subject (National Council on Crime and Delinquency, 1981). Others, while understandable, might well have been avoided and certainly should be thoroughly considered in the design of similar programmatic and evaluative attempts in the future.

To begin with, DSO was a "guinea pig" in delinquency programming. Although large projects had been attempted in earlier years, most notably during the Kennedy and Johnson eras, DSO was the first to be launched under the 1974 Delinquency Act, the first to consist of coordinated projects in various sites across the nation, and the first of many to be launched by the Office of Juvenile Justice and Delinquency Prevention. For the administration and staff of OJJDP, this was unexplored territory; the mounting of such a coordinated effort was based on no prior experience. This was as true of the program phase as it was of the evaluation phase; the national evaluation staff had never before been involved in such a massive, complex exercise. For example, so many staff memos had to be written (over 150 of them) that four "memos on memos" were needed simply for updating purposes. So much data collection took place that, for example, 60,250 data forms were shipped to one site alone; there were eight evaluation sites.

There are many kinds of evidence to show just how much of a guinea pig DSO was. Inadequate provision was made for program start-up time, and, because many programs failed to begin operations on schedule, the organization and timing of data collection were thrown out of phase. Procedures for obtaining and guaranteeing the cooperation of local justice and community agency officials were piecemeal, misleading, and, as it turned out in some sites, inadequate. Criteria for program selection were oriented largely to indications of the organizational and administrative competence of program proponents, the weights assigned to them determined as much by group process as by prior knowledge. Created initially to obtain uniform data across all program sites, evaluation instrumentation and computer software design required repeated modification to accommodate the differences among sites in the content and availability of their data sources. The effort to create a data system sensitive to variation in site data and responsive to the needs of site evaluators as well as to evaluation research needs overreached itself in complexity and led to serious difficulties in providing feedback to site evaluators and program directors.

Finally, and most pronounced during the early stages of the enterprise, relations between the program and research staffs of OJJDP were marked by disagreements concerning the level of priority to be accorded evaluation aims, with drastic consequences for collaboration. This was a classic instance of the suspicion and conflict that frequently characterizes relations between the program and the research establishments. The ill feeling was translated into the program/research relations in many of the sites, and produced such a baroque communication structure among OJJDP staffs, local staffs, and the national evaluation staff that serious rifts in viewpoint and sense of priorities could not be entirely surmounted. Among other more positive things, DSO became an exercise in interpersonal and interorganizational frustration and aggression. The program and the worth of the evaluation suffered equally.

Mixed Messages

Partly because DSO was an enterprise based on so little experience and partly because the legislation leading to it was far from informative as to goals and rationale, much room for interpretation existed. The OJJDP guidelines specified that status offenders were to be removed from incarceration, that alternatives to secure detention were to be established, and that procedures for accomplishing these goals were to be tested as models for future programs. The guidelines stressed community-based services, heterogeneity of services, and "per child" accountability. Beyond this, however, great latitude was left to program proponents in terms of goals, rationales, and specific practices. OJJDP was not itself of a single mind with respect to these matters.[1] Logan and Rausch (1980: 40) commenting on the Connecticut results, put it this way: "Lacking a coherent and consistent philosophy of the legal status of juveniles, we do not have a clear enough focus on what constitutes the *problem* of 'status offenses,' let alone what would constitute a solution and how to achieve it."

The same was true of the evaluation design. Research and program staffs within OJJDP differed fundamentally on the appropriate level of research input in program planning and project selection. They differed on the degree to which DSO was to experiment, demonstrate, control, explore, or document procedures developed in the field. They differed on the uses to which evaluation data were to be put, whether in the form of experimental, process, or formative evaluation. Even within the OJJDP program staff, there was a wide range of tolerance for research inputs and program accommodations to evaluation needs. Overall, however, evaluation needs were given low priority.

The most immediate result of this ambiguity in program and evaluation elements was the delivery of mixed and inconsistent messages to *local* program and evaluation staffs. Coupled with the wide latitude in goals and practices elicited in program proposals, this resulted not in a set of deinstitutionalization programs the evaluation of which could provide clear guidelines for future deinstitutionalization programming, but in a dozen community intervention programs with uncoordinated mixes of prevention, diversion, and decarceration that would sorely test the establishment of *any* generalizations for future programming.

Site Selection

Of several hundred preliminary proposals submitted to OJJDP under the DSO initiative, approximately seventy were selected by OJJDP staff as having most promise. The national evaluation staff was asked to judge these for their evaluability so that program awards would enhance the likelihood of obtaining reasonable evaluations. It was noted earlier that the evaluation needs were accorded a subordinate position in the OJJDP strategy. Nowhere did this become more obvious than in the use made of the recommendations of national evaluation staff. Of the twelve projects eventually funded, only one was in the recommended group of eleven sites, with a second funded project being the one suggested by the evaluators as a substitute for the first if the first could not, for some reason, be funded. Two sites were selected from a group of nine poor alternatives and one from a group judged barely acceptable. The remaining seven projects eventually funded included five that were rejected outright by the evaluation staff, and two that had not even been included in the first cut of seventy program-acceptable projects.

It was with the announcement of these final funding decisions that the national evaluation group and the NIJJDP research staff realized the full scope of the evaluative limitations within which they would be working. Of the twelve funded programs, one with strong political overtones in its selection was excluded from the evaluation (it was evaluated separately), two more were excluded later for the very reasons they had not been recommended earlier, and a fourth was eliminated after the first year because its local evaluation inadequacies proved in time to be insurmountable.

Added to low influence of evaluation considerations in site selection was the unwillingness of OJJDP program staff to argue for any of a number of alternative research designs. These were provided to the staff at its request but had little impact on either site selection or contractual relationships within the funded projects. The alternatives suggested to staff by the evaluators represented a truly wide range of possibilities, but it became clear that little encouragement of their consideration actually followed. Site visits to the finalists in the competition often included assurances from OJJDP program staff that evaluation design considerations were not to stand in the way of implementing approved program procedures. And so, indeed, they did not. (Although one site did agree to a randomly assigned control group, program staff at that site failed to maintain the randomization procedure.)

The problems that accompanied the site selection process and the downgrading of alternative research designs should not be dismissed lightly. They affected the attitudes of national evaluation staff and its monitors in NIJJDP, deepened the already existing rift within OJJDP, put a pall on the relationships between national and local evaluators, and sorely limited the level of accommodation between program and research groups both nationally and locally.

Hoped-for levels of cooperation were not legitimized, and a series of compromises emerged that inevitably detracted from the value of the final evaluation. Research controls were abandoned. Collection of social adjustment data immediately following program referral was in many instances not facilitated, resulting in a serious loss of the very data so greatly desired by OJJDP program staff. As is so often the case, the short-term detriment in such situations is to the research teams. In the long run, however, the damage to the evaluation process is clearly most harmful to program staffs, who are deprived of useful measures of effectiveness, and to program clients in years to come, whose services received will benefit minimally from the assessment of their greatest utility.

Gaps in the Data Base

A program such as DSO is based on a mixture of myths, assumptions, accumulated experiences, and sharable data. In the case of DSO, assumptions and accumulated experiences predominated where reliable data either did not exist or were not employed.

In a number of sites, the actual numbers of status offenders who had been institutionalized and detained prior to the inception of the program simply could not be assessed, given the state of the local data systems. This had a detrimental impact on careful planning in those sites. Another obstacle revolved around the very definition of "status offender" as judged by state code and local practice. Since an operational definition was not supplied by the OJJDP guidelines, local programs had to struggle with the problem in a series of unique situations, each of which tended to yield unique (and evaluation-defying) solutions. The decisions on what behaviors would be considered status *offenses*, what incidents of mixed status and delinquent *charges* would be included, and what patterns of prior offenses would yield status *offenders* were made locally, idiosyncratically, and, to some extent, arbitrarily. The situation has been well summarized by Zatz (1982b: 44):

> these behaviors are subsumed in state statutes under such categories as truancy, incorrigibility, runaway, beyond control, and variations on the phrase "in need of supervision." However, the definitional task is compounded by several factors, including: (1) different jurisdictions join different actions under the rubric of a status offense; (2) many jurisdictions do not have a separate classification for youth who have committed status offenses, preferring to label them as delinquent, or dependent or neglected children; and (3) social science data and the experience of many juvenile justice professionals call into question the premise that the status offender is in real life any different from the delinquent offender. All of these matters serve to complicate the process of definition. [2]

This last point is one of considerable significance; the 1974 act assumed the existence of a *type* of youth known as a status *offender*. Although the OJJDP guidelines specifically questioned this assumption on the basis of the review of prior studies, and although some research throws into question the existence of status offenders as a discriminable category of youths, the DSO program assumed the existence of status *offenders*, youths separable from, and therefore different from, delinquent offenders. This, of course, is also the assumption in many juvenile courts where final dispositions are often based on the reification of the status offender concept (Carter, 1979).

What would happen if the assumption were incorrect, if today's status offender is tomorrow's delinquent and vice versa? If this interchangeability of offenses were to be the rule, then an antidetention or deinstitutionalization program based on one set of behaviors alone could be meaningless, an arbitrary response to an occasional symptom of a broader syndrome. One would have to reorient programming to a status *offense*, not a status offender program, a program rationalized primarily on legal grounds rather than humanitarian or treatment philosophies. These latter grounds, however, were the foundation of DSO. Our own analysis of this issue suggests on the contrary that a relatively small proportion of youth cited for a status offense are of a special status offender "type." Thus it cannot be assumed that the treatment rationales applied to them have been altogether appropriate, a fact to be taken into account in assessing the impact of the program on client recidivism.

Taking that point yet one step further, it may be recalled that our analysis in Chapter 9 suggested that runaways, in particular, may represent a discriminable group within the status offending population, and may therefore be considered for some form of offense-specific treatment. An interesting analysis of early Pima County data reported by Rojek (1978) reports on the "match" between the offense recorded for each youngster by the referring and recipient agencies (that is, matches between the referral form and the entry form). In over one-third of the cases, the offenses did not match, despite the fact that there were only five status offense categories available and two of them (runaway and ungovernability) accounted for half the cases. Thus, as Rojek (1978: 8) indicates, "in over one-third of the cases, juvenile offenders were receiving services or treatment for an offense they may not have committed."

This concern with the definition of status offenders is of course typical of the approach to social problems often found among academics, but it is often a source of frustration for social practitioners. Thus one of the topics for serious dispute in the joint DSO national meetings was just this. A minor revolt among program administrators—"There's too much emphasis on definitions of status offender"—was met by an LEAA administrator with a forthright rebuttal that unfortunately, was never adequately translated into the local programs. The LEAA official noted:

> We *must* have a "crisp" definition of status offender or we will end up with mush. This program cannot be all things to all people. I do not want to see any kids taken into the program who are not status offenders and would not have been detained if the DSO program were not in operation. There will be other programs on prevention, violence, drugs, etc. Unless we stick to a strict definition of status offender, the evaluation will be meaningless.

Every evaluator would prefer a setting conducive to the effective management of a carefully conceptualized evaluation design with cooperative relations between program and research staffs. Such situations have existed, of course, although they are less common than one would hope. DSO was not one of those. DSO was characterized by ambivalence, frustration, time and resource limitations, inadequacies in thought and design, and constant accommodations to the context and constraints of its implementation. To understand what the evaluation had to offer, it is necessary to understand the context and constraints we have described. To maximize its contribution to future enterprises of this sort, the DSO evaluation *as a process* must be described in terms such as the foregoing. Other OJJDP national evaluations—of diversion, of prevention, of school violence, of restitution programs—have already benefited from the DSO experience; the guinea pig has served its purpose for those who would listen. We move now to a brief discussion of the basis on which program proposals were selected for funding, examining the problem of convergence between the selection criteria and the DSO program rationale.

ADEQUACY OF RATIONALE FOR
PROGRAM PROPOSAL SELECTION

Ideally, a social program is based upon and guided by elements of a logically sound conceptual framework. It is to be hoped that it is also informed by relevant prior research and experience so that action options will not be weighted and chosen in accordance with arbitrary or simply convenient criteria. The absence of such a framework invites program inconsistency, inconclusive results, and capricious adoptions of inadequate alternative rationales.

DSO was loosely based on labeling theory, and, to a far smaller extent, differential association theory. It was also infused by a spirit of humaneness in that the incarceration of noncriminal juveniles was felt to be unwarranted and potentially damaging to them.

Neither the legislation nor the program guidelines provided by OJJDP offered anything but the most cursory analysis of the structure or propositions of labeling theory. Program proposals, understandably, did not therefore reflect action programs based on theory, nor were they selected in terms of their theoretical articulations. Instead, a series of twelve mixed criteria were employed in site selection,[3] in three stages as follows:

(1) *first cut*
    (a) agreements with justice agencies
    (b) agreements with community agencies
(2) *second cut*
    (c) allocation of local funds
    (d) likelihood of program continuation following termination of federal support.
    (e) number and quality of service agencies
    (f) program quality; for example, administrative acumen and sophistication of leadership
    (g) provision for accountability of program funds

      (h) likelihood of obtaining public support
      (i) evaluability
  (3) *third cut*
      (j) number of status offenders likely to be benefited
      (k) likelihood of changing justice system procedures and policies favorable to deinstitutionalization
      (l) likelihood of affecting the jurisdiction's disadvantaged youth population

It would be hard to argue that these are inappropriate site selection criteria. Indeed, they represent a good deal of experiential evidence for variables related to success or failure of program implementation. But it would be equally hard to argue that they represent a consistent conceptual framework. If program designs met only the above criteria—no matter how adequately—they could not be expected to shed much light on our understanding of delinquency, status offenders or offense behavior, organizational response to program interventions, or the value of alternative treatment approaches. And, because the OJJDP guidelines demanded no consistent conceptual framework, the programs on site yielded none. Instead, they provided a series of relatively uncoordinated beliefs about juveniles, juvenile offenders, and treatment modalities, and values concerning humaneness, family life, community responsibility, and equity. From its very inception, therefore, the DSO program was flawed by its failure to provide the kind of sound conceptual underpinning that could generate, in its field test sites, useful knowledge about the effects of deinstitutionalization on status offense behavior.

LEVEL OF IMPLEMENTATION

The extent to which the eight evaluated programs achieved adequate levels of implementation varies considerably, but overall a set of quite active programs eventually emerged that provided services to about 16,000 youth during the two-year federal support period. Did DSO "pass" the test of program implementation? In terms of activity level, overcoming some rather formidable obstacles, and establishing viable program structures, the answer is clearly yes. In terms of achieving some intermediate goals of program acceptance, the answer again is yes, but with some significant qualifications. In terms of applying program activities to the appropriate population of youngsters, the answer is far more mixed. There is considerable evidence for "net widening" and "creaming," that is, many of the juveniles served by the program probably were not those for whom the programs were funded or the legislative provisions enacted. Application of "treatments" to a clientele not demonstrably in need of help cannot be credited in favor of implementation.

Let us look briefly at those factors that detract from the otherwise successful picture of implementation.[4]

Net Widening

Perhaps most significant with respect to program implementation is the matter of client targeting. Each of the eight programs established its own criteria regarding the eligibility of status offending youth to receive program services, usually though not uniformly in response to court-imposed restrictions. These criteria ranged at one extreme from the acceptance of anyone who committed a status offense without regard to other offense characteristics (Pima County), to excluding all except "pure" status offenders sufficiently chronic to warrant actual detention under prevailing court practices. Between these extremes, eligibility requirements variously excluded those on probation for a prior status offense, those arrested for combined status and criminal offenses, and those with extensive records of prior criminal offenses. Such eligibility restrictions inevitably biased the DSO program population in the direction of the less intractable offenders, probably including many who would not have been caught up in the referral network had the program services not been available.

Further evidence of probable net widening and creaming was found in comparing evaluated program clients to a group of clients from a preprogram period when, in many of the sites, status offenders were in principle if not always in practice subject to detention in locked facilities. The comparison indicated that the program clients constituted a less serious set of cases. Compared with the preprogram group, they were more likely to be female, more likely to come from intact parental situations, less likely to have delinquency charges included in their instant offense, and, most important, less likely to have had serious prior offense records. The mean number of prior offenses recorded by the police for the preprogram group was 1.88, while for program clients it was 1.33.[5]

In only one site was there a mean prior record that strongly suggested compliance with the selection from the appropriate population and, even in that site, evidence for substantial net widening has been reported independently by the site evaluator (Spergel et al., 1981). The seven other sites reveal a less serious set of clients than the mean of the preprogram group. Several of them evidence a balance of detainable and nondetainable offenders that yields strikingly low prior offense means. These problems speak to the difficulty of identifying an appropriate target population of status offenders for deinstitutionalization, a matter of serious neglect in the conceptualization and planning of the DSO program. This significant lack of clarity is mirrored in one writer's characterization of such programs: "Decarceration, deinstitutionalization, diversion—under whatever name the process masquerades" (Scull, 1977: 41).[6]

Receptivity to Deinstitutionalizing Objectives

The DSO program achieved very real gains in this respect among court personnel, primarily by demonstrating the feasibility of eliminating the use of preadjudication detention as a means of assuring the subsequent appearance of the youth to further case processing. The gain was particularly notable in the program jurisdictions that had been least receptive to deinstitutionalizing objectives. This achievement was limited, however, by a general insistence on the part of court personnel to retain jurisdiction in status offense cases, largely frustrating the destigmatization aims of the DSO program.

Cooperation of Juvenile Justice Agencies

While it was possible to obtain some level of cooperation from court personnel at each site, this was not the case generally for police agencies. With few exceptions, the police viewed the status offender program as undermining the deterrent effect of their work. In the planning phase of each program, it was possible to obtain initial agreements of cooperation from juvenile justice agencies during the period of program proposal development. In many instances, however, these agreements were not fully honored in practice, impeding planned and expected forms of implementation.

Development of Alternative
Youth Service Networks

Over the two-year period of its life, the DSO program succeeded in developing some very effective service networks. However, implementation of this objective was hampered by failure to provide sufficient time for program start-up. In some instances, contracting arrangements were protracted by difficulties in resolving disagreements about the choice of clients for referral. Where local government units were the program proponents, delays were caused by the extensive technical requirements imposed by fiscal regulation. Still, this limited achievement contrasts well with situations in which no resource development took place. One example is provided by Gordon's (1980) description of California's failure to develop new referrals for status offenders, but see also Coates et al. (1978) for the Massachusetts experience.

Range of Services Provided

A substantial volume of services was provided by the eight funded programs. However, their variety was extraordinarily narrow. They were restricted almost entirely to individual and family counseling and to residential placement, despite rather strong urging by OJJDP that youth advocacy be included in the repertoire of services. In only two of the eight sites was youth advocacy included. One form of advocacy was the centerpiece of the Cook County segment of the Illinois program, and a number of youth service bureaus in the Alameda County program emphasized this service approach. The restricted range of services is particularly regrettable, since this offered little opportunity to evaluate possible differences in behavior outcome in relation to differences in services.[7] It is not clear that service breadth was determined by client needs, as opposed to organizational habits and vested interest (see Spergel et al., 1981, on the Illinois program).

Program Models for Deinstitutionalization

A subordinate but important objective of the DSO program was to test the capacity of various program designs to achieve progress in the face of field realities. On the basis of the descriptive materials presented in Chapter 5 and 6, attention is directed to features both positive and negative for progress in status offender deinstitutionalization.

(a) Community support for the program is most effectively mobilized by enlisting the participation of those public officials in the jurisdiction who are identified as leaders in the informal power structure of the community. Their commitment to the support of the program becomes real to the extent that they themselves rather than their subordinate surrogates take an active part in program planning and continue their activity by accepting membership in an organization created specifically to promote and monitor the program. Such commitment endows the program with a public and visible legitimacy. This design feature was notably exemplified in the Spokane County program.

(b) In jurisdictions without deinstitutionalizing legislation, courts may nominally accept the value of status offender deinstitutionalization, but insist on retaining their discretion in selecting cases for diversion from detention and institutional commitment. In such jurisdictions, programs designed to exercise influence close to the "front end" of status offender entry in the juvenile justice system tended to be relatively more effective in implementing their objectives. This is the case as well in jurisdictions that deinstitutionalize status offenders on the basis of administrative practice in the absence of a compelling statute. The critical decision point is most commonly at court intake. In several of the court-sponsored programs (Almeda, Pima, and Clark counties), as well as in the single non-court-sponsored program that positioned program personnel in the court (Delaware), special court intake units were established with court-granted authority to divert status offenders from detention. A contrasting case is represented by the South Carolina program, where DSO program staff had access only to a locked diagnostic facility that served the entire state.

(c) Extremely innovative programs that took a "grass-roots" approach in providing alternative youth services paid a heavy price in lost credibility and support from juvenile justice personnel and the highly professionalized youth service agencies. Such programs attempted to reduce the social distance between clients and service providers, or to engage local residents in the task of normalizing the behavior of status offenders. Problems of eroded credibility arose in the programs funded in Pima County and in the Cook County Detention Alternatives program in Illinois. There is clearly a need either to balance the requirements of program innovation with those of professional competence or to locate innovative programs to the extent possible in the "main-line" youth service agencies.

(d) The designs represented in the DSO program illuminate a central dilemma in efforts to deinstitutionalize status offenders. If it is assumed that the two major objectives of this effort are their decarceration and destigmatization, the DSO experience suggests that the first objective can be achieved at some sacrifice of the second. The diversion of status offenders from secure detention and from institutional commitment was on the whole most fully effected in programs centered in and sponsored by juvenile justice agencies, principally courts. However, this inevitably entailed substantial exposure to preadjudication processing, first by the police and subsequently by court intake staff. Subsequent outright release or referral to a youth service agency cannot be expected to counteract completely the stigmatizing experience of "front end" formal processing, even though the admittedly more severe experience of actual detention is avoided. So far, then, as jurisdiction in status offense cases is retained in the juvenile court, progress in decarceration in these cases may be expected to outstrip progress in destigmatization. If the aim of the decarceration objective is the destigmatization of status offenders, their retention under the jurisdiction of the court becomes problematic.

OUTCOME ACHIEVEMENT

Three major sets of outcome measures were planned by the national evaluators. One of these, changes in social adjustment as measured by a variety of individual-level scales, was invalidated by the delayed interview schedules used in a number of sites. Due to program staff resistance, fears of "contaminating" crisis intervention procedures in particular, and the extremely short-term and low-level service given to many clients, interviews often occurred after treatment or service had been terminated. Thus no "before-treatment" measure was obtained in many instances, and it became impossible to develop a satisfactory program-related social adjustment change measure.

Two other forms of outcome measurement are available—recidivism and decarceration levels. Since removing status offenders from secure placement was central to the legislative intent that led to DSO, program success in achieving their removal from detention and from institutions is obviously a pivotal issue. Two approaches were taken to evaluating this form of outcome. In both cases, problems of the data bases available at the sites enormously complicated the task, while site selection by OJJDP has made it impossible to draw an overall definitive conclusion.

The reason for this latter comment is rather simple. Legislation often reflects, rather than initiates, social change. In the case of the 1974 Juvenile Delinquency Act, the DSO provisions reflect a trend already in place in many states. By the time of DSO implementation in 1976, 15 states had already prohibited postadjudication commitment of status offenders, and another 21 did so during the program period. In addition, 5 had prohibited all or some preadjudication detention prior to program initiation, and another 14 did so during the program period. The challenge to OJJDP was to locate program sites in light of this dominant trend. Of the 8 selected sites, 6 were placed where the trend had already been initiated either by legislative act or by administrative practice. For example, the laudable Spokane program was implemented after status offender referrals "had been declining for more than two years . . . and most of the indicators of penetration would have declined to the same low levels even without the federally-funded DSO project" (Schneider et al., 1978).

OJJDP had the choice of locating programs in amenable sites, where the trend was well under way and additional funds were most likely to yield salutary effects, or locating them where the trend was not visible and the need as well as the obstacles were greatest. Perhaps because the focus in site selection was on the organizational and administrative competence of project proponents and on their expressed enthusiasm for the undertaking, the choice fell on sites representing the full range of advancement toward deinstitutionalization.

The first approach to outcome measurement on this issue was to perform a "system rates" analysis (Carter, 1981). The basic rationale underlying this approach is that the juvenile justice system is just that, a *system*, such that major changes in one of its components would result in adjustment in other, adjacent or dependent, components. Thus if status offenders were removed from institutions (and if their number were substantial), one should see changes in offender flow and perhaps length of stay in those institutions. If status offenders were no longer detained, the same should be true in the case of juvenile detention centers, police holding tanks, and so on. There might also be reductions in arrest rates as a police reaction to the loss of the detention "hammer." Finally, if diversion of detainable status offenders to community facilities is achieved, then one could expect adjustment in rates of arrest, petitioning to court, and other local processing alternatives.

The national evaluators sought from each local evaluator a system diagram (following a specified generic model) and rate data associated with each major processing point in the system for two points in time, one prior to and one during the program period. The request, in time, caused considerable consternation as it was discovered that a number of sites did not have data systems capable of reflecting case inventories. This mirrors the complaint of Arthur D. Little, Inc. (1977) in the attempt to assess costs of deinstitutionalization in ten states. This was especially true at the "front end" of the system, in rates of referral to the police, rates of police dispositions, and characteristics of these offenders. In a word, the sites chosen for program funding reflected the low priority given to evaluation criteria, being unable to provide sufficiently reliable data to allow a useful analysis of program impact on system rates.

With the data that were obtainable, it seemed that there were as many sites with an increase of offenders associated with the program as there were sites with a decrease. This general trend characterized each investigated point in the system, referrals to enforcement *and* initial detention *and* court intake *and* probation as a disposition *and* institutionalization as a disposition. Although the data systems were often inadequate to the task and the procedure yielded inventories at two points in time rather than cohort flows, one might have expected DSO to have resulted in some consistent pattern of rate change. It did not, and the implication is that rate changes were not of sufficient magnitude (given the initial preprogram levels) to be reflected by a system rates methodology that is ordinarily quite sensitive to change. A similar level of ambiguity has been reported for client flows in the National Evaluation of Diversion Projects (Dunford et al., 1982).

The second approach to assessing success in decarceration is provided by a separate study of total numbers of status offenders detained and institutionalized during the program and the comparable preprogram periods. The data were supplied in different ways and from different sources in the various sites. In several instances, counties within program sites presented separate tallies, so that our data are for a larger number of units than our eight composite sites.

With respect to status offender detention, we found seven jurisdictions with detention reductions and five jurisdictions with an increase. The aggregated level of reduction was 43 percent of the preprogram period, lower than one would anticipate given special funding and legislative mandates. Comparable data were available for institutional rates in only five sites. One of these showed no effective change, but this was on a base of only six cases so that nothing can be made of this. The other four sites showed reductions ranging from 50 percent to 86 percent. In at least four sites, then, success with respect to reduction in institutionalization was considerably greater (67 percent) than it was for detention (43 percent). This difference favoring reduction in institutional rates over detention rates makes a great deal of sense in terms of the acceptability of the two forms of decarceration in the minds of the public and of the juvenile justice professionals. Handler et al. (1982: 107-108) state the case effectively:

> The response to detention may be contrasted with that to incarceration. The mandate of each is in similar form; that is, a negative prohibition for which implementation and monitoring are relatively straightforward—not completely without difficulty, but somewhat so. Yet detention has had a different history at the state level. Only four out of the seven states in our study forbid its use for status offenders. There was and still is decidedly less agreement about both the wisdom and the feasibility of abolishing secure detention for status offenders. There is a strong feeling, by no means restricted to law enforcement, that there must be a way to hold ungovernable and runaway youth—at least for a short period—until parents, courts, or some other agency can take over. This need is especially felt in the rural areas, where there are only jails and no other facilities, secure or nonsecure. There is a high level of frustration and strong feelings about this point in the process; bewildered, anxious, and angry parents call on the police for help and want them to respond. There is also the feeling that secure detention, as a short, snappy, informal punishment, is a needed sanction for troublesome youth. It is a good lesson of what the future holds if certain conduct continues. In all of the states we studied, there was a strong local feeling in favor of some form of secure detention for status offenders; this was clearly different from feelings about the wisdom of prohibiting incarceration. Detention is much closer to home than incarceration.

A similar conclusion was reached in a conceptual analysis of California's deinstitutionalization legislation (later confirmed empirically):

> We would expect a great deal of resistance and some unintended consequences as a result of attempts to implement deinstitutionalization of status offenders. The provision is not philosophically resonant with most of the practitioners who must implement it; it decreases the discretion of police, probation, and courts; nevertheless it is unequivocally mandated. It is not surprising, therefore, to find frustration, efforts to circumvent the law, and a tendency to ignore status offenders coming up as a continuing theme [Van Dusen and Klein, 1981: 11].

Readers should also review, on relative rates of decreasing detention and incarceration, the ten-state report by Arthur D. Little, Inc. (1977).

Still, taking our sets of data together, it seems clear that a reduction in secure placement of status offenders did take place during the program period. Although this does not constitute proof that the programs *caused* the reduction, since such reductions were part of the larger national trend in any case (Krisberg and Schwartz, 1982), knowledge of particular program activities makes us confident that a portion of the reductions can be credited to the DSO program. But it remains uncertain whether or not the reductions obtained fell short of the levels presumably attainable. Further, it remains unknown whether other forms of institutionalization may have absorbed some DSO clients. Such a possibility is clearly demonstrated by Krisberg and Schwartz (1982), Lerman (1980), and Guttridge (1981) with respect to the use of private and mental health facilities for detention and institutionalization of status offending youth.

Outcome achievement was also assessed by a third procedure, the comparison of official recidivism rates (number of police charges) of the evaluated program sample with a comparison group of preprogram status offenders identified in each site. While the two groups were designed to be comparable in their characteristics, the tendency of DSO program staffs to select less serious cases yielded a client cohort that should have yielded lower recidivism rates even in the absence of the program. Nonetheless, when the records of program and preprogram cohorts were compared with prior offenses and client background variables statistically controlled, both six months and twelve months after the charge for which they were selected, program clients showed a slight but statistically significant higher recidivism rate than the preprogram groups.

This higher recidivism rate results from aggregating the data across all eight sites. For each site separately, the difference in recidivism rates between the preprogram and the evaluated program groups was not statistically significant in most of the sites. However, on the basis of the data aggregated for all sites, the DSO program did not appear to have a beneficial effect with respect to client recidivism.

There are two rather different implications of this overall result. First, since there is not all that much difference between results for program clients and the preprogram groups, many of whom *were* more subject to secure confinement, there is no support here for retaining secure detention or placement of status offenders. This is especially true in view of a cost analysis (Peat, Marwick, and Mitchell, & Co., 1981) that shows lower costs associated with DSO than with justice system processing.

Second, however, is the less satisfactory implication that DSO failed to reduce recidivism rates despite all the time, concern, and funds that went into the development of its various community services. Most DSO funds did not go into the process of deinstitutionalizing clients, the area of greater positive impact. They went into what can best be described as diversion and prevention activities in the majority of sites. That these activities had so little effect on recidivism rates, especially in the face of considerable evidence of net widening, which yields a more "amenable" client group, means that we must look quite closely at the relationship of the program to both its intent and its outcome. If something "went wrong" above and beyond the constraints mentioned earlier, we may best seek it in these relationships. The two following sections deal with these issues.

PROGRAM INTEGRITY

A central question that must be raised in program evaluation is the program's achievement in integrating its activities with its rationale. To achieve integrity, program activities must articulate with the rationale, the utility of which may than be assessed by examining how well it was represented operationally by actual program content.

We know from earlier sections of this volume that the DSO program rationale was itself not well explicated. [8] Our expectations for its articulation in activities at the eight sites must therefore be tempered. The underlying rationale of labeling theory was not explicated well in the federal legislation. Neither was it fully elaborated in OJJDP's program guidelines, nor actively solicited in the OJJDP guidance and monitoring of program applications and grant awards. Hence it is not too surprising that program staffs on site did not mount programs clearly and explicitly based on the premises of labeling theory.

However, it must also be acknowledged that labeling theory itself does not readily yield an obvious paradigm of implementation guidelines. Its propositional structure is ambiguous, its scope arguable, and its implications for action more proscriptive than prescriptive. Nonetheless, labeling theory offers several central tenets that might have been selected to promulgate program activities in the sites selected for OJJDP support. If we look at these, we can, to some extent, gauge the potential for program integrity and thereby permit judgments of actual versus possible achievement.

For instance, labeling theorists consistently suggest that stigmatizing labels are disproportionately applied to disadvantaged groups by the agents of social control. We should therefore expect greater levels of detention and institutionalization for members of ethnic minority groups, the poor, and perhaps females, and statistics have generally supported these expectations. DSO, one might expect, would therefore concentrate its efforts disproportionately on serving these groups. Aggregating over all sites, there is no evidence that this was done. The program tended to be applied in greater proportions than found in the preprogram groups to females, but also to whites, and those from intact nuclear families. Such a program directed by labeling theory proponents would have reversed this comparison.

Another prominent feature of the labeling approach is its attention to the role of the agents of social control, in this case the police, courts, and agencies closely aligned with them. Labeling theory would dictate (1) the emptying of detention halls and institutions in a manner to minimize the involvement of control agencies; (2) the diversion of status offenders to agencies or services not associated with the justice system; (3) care in avoiding other stigmatizing labels available through mental health services, and (4) care in avoiding the spread of stigmatizing labels from one agency to others.

Clearly, DSO did not consistently employ these dictates. Some of the programs were in fact run by the court system, under court control. While not uniformly the case in all court-controlled programs, in some instances probation officials (Pima County) or employees of correctional units (South Carolina) were primary contact personnel with the clients. Collaboration between public and private agencies was actively sought (although *not* always achieved) and feedback on client progress at some sites given to the justice agencies.[9] Finally, most DSO programs stressed individual and family counseling as the treatment of choice, which could in many cases lead to the substitution of a negative mental health label for the negative justice label.

Obviously, the eight sites differed considerably in their adherence to labeling theory dictates, both by accident and by design. But equally obviously, in the absence of clearly drawn and clearly mandated guidelines derived from labeling theory, they did not as a group implement central labeling propositions. We can confirm the comments made so far by reference to a third major tenet of labeling theory, which states that the labels applied to the "clients" of a stigmatizing system come to be incorporated in the self-identity of the clients whose behaviors then validate the new identity. In the DSO case, recidivism may result from the acceptance of labels attached to, and accepted by, status offenders. Such labels would fall into two domains, one suggesting delinquency and one suggesting emotional disturbance. DSO programs, overall, did not materialize in a form to prevent this progression, as indicated by the following observations:

(1) Potentially stigmatizing treatments, counseling in various forms, clearly predominated over less stigmatizing alternatives such as advocacy programs, opportunity enhancement, skills development, and the like.

(2) The minimal service provision actually achieved (most DSO clients were seen only briefly and seldom were referred for other forms of nonstigmatizing aid) could not have been designed for the effective inculcation of conforming, deviance-resistant self-identities.

(3) Net widening, the drawing into the DSO network of youngsters whose behavior did not justify their inclusion, was reported by many site evaluators and is clearly evident in the aggregated national analysis. Net widening is anathema to labeling theorists, who would see it as the first

step in the self-fulfilling prophecy that leads from first label application to eventual development of a deviant career.

Summarizing briefly the situation of the labeling rationale, it is clear that DSO programs were not formulated principally to elaborate that approach, nor did they achieve its activation inadvertently. This reflects a comparatively low priority given to such implementation (but *not* to the rationale, it should be noted) by OJJDP staff.

By way of contrast, more emphasis was given to the humane rationale, which said simply that the incarceration of youngsters for noncriminal activities, and their exposure to the ills of detention facilities, is bad per se. It is bad for youngsters and morally unacceptable. [10] Logan and Rausch (1980: 43-44) state the case well as a result of their experience with the frustrations of the Connecticut DSO program:

> From this point of view, Connecticut's 1.6 million dollars might better have been spent to hire a few lawyers to "spring" the status offenders who were incarcerated, to challenge the constitutionality of status offenses, and to lobby for their statutory removal from juvenile court jurisdiction. This would have been less expensive and possibly more effective by virtue of being aimed at the legal heart of the problem.

This humane rationale, far simpler in conception and given higher priority by OJJDP in its monitoring activities, led more directly to appropriate program activities. Policies were promulgated, edicts written, and a number of status offenders were removed from secure placement while many others were diverted prior to such placements. The data on changes in institutional and detention levels show clearly that substantial progress was made. Yet it is surprising that federally mandated levels were not achieved overall. The experiences in Massachusetts, Vermont, California, Washington, and even Pima County prior to DSO make it clear that almost total deinstitutionalization can be achieved, and rather quickly, where there is the will to do so. DSO proved that the humane rationale can be approached at a reasonable pace with available programmatic steps. It also proves that program integrity is not the only requirement; other elements are needed.

One of these is desire. DSO sites did not lack the desire to deinstitutionalize in most cases, but they did lack the will for full and rapid achievement. They faced other problems as well. Data were collected in each site from judges, police, and various community leaders nominated by local program directors as important to the DSO enterprise. In particular, information was sought from these respondents on what they *felt* DSO should achieve, reflecting one would suppose both their rationales and their preferred program activities and outcomes. Analysis of these data (Gardiner, 1981) revealed that there was a general lack of consensus about DSO criteria, on what they wanted to see from DSO. Not only were there differences *between* practitioner groups (such as judges and police) but there was no consensus *within* these groups. Thus DSO program managers were faced with the implementation of program activities that would raise resistance no matter what choices were made. Concerted effort for change would expectably be hampered under these conditions.

Finally, under this heading, we should note that OJJDP and the sites placed considerable emphasis on the development of interagency service networks, understanding that DSO goals required more than a simple array of alternative services. Coordination and collaboration were seen as necessary for successful deinstitutionalization and diversion. We have already noted that the labeling rationale would argue against certain forms of public /private agency collaboration, but such is not true of the humane rationale.

Separate analyses have been undertaken of the interorganizational aspects of the DSO programs in the various sites (Miller, Gordon, and Heck, 1981; Gordon, 1980). It was noted in one of these that the coordination task seemed formidable:

> Many of the problems that were encountered can be traced to the fact that most of the programs were funded and implemented with only indistinctly drawn organizational features. New projects were combined with or superimposed upon ongoing ones and formerly independent agencies were tied into networks of service delivery with other agencies, both public and private. Methods of coordination, spheres of responsibility, and the division of labor among the parts of these complicated systems were not always apparent. An argument could certainly be made that a flexibly structured approach to the delivery of human services is preferable to one that requires precisely defined organizational features, on the grounds that such flexibility will have a payoff in performance that a more bureaucratic approach would sacrifice. However, indistinctly defined boundaries and responsibilities are not synonymous with the flexibility this argument has in mind. The lack of clarity encountered in the DSO programs meant that their activity often took place in an atmosphere of turbulence and uncertainty, a fact that should definitely influence the way the findings are read. The idea of conducting an organizational evaluation was sometimes conceptually out of phase with the somewhat unorganized state of the programs [Miller, Gordon, and Heck, 1981].

Yet, despite the very inauspicious start described above, the data from the organizational study suggest that effective interagency networks did, indeed, get established, and staff morale levels were relatively good. To the extent that DSO programs developed strategies to optimize their interorganizational relationships, they fostered community contacts, activism on behalf of their status offender clients, and perceived effectiveness. Once again, then, we have evidence of considerable activity at the eight sites, considerable evidence of overcoming constraints against program implementation, large numbers of clients served—in fact, considerable overall accomplishment of intermediate goals. Had program integrity been higher—that is, had activities articulated rationales—then perhaps program achievement might also have been higher. As it is, we are faced again, as we are so often in areas of human service delivery, with a heavy investment of human resources whose accomplishments are partially, ambiguously, or not at all related to the guiding ideas or intentions that initiated the program. Consider, in light of the low impact and significant net widening of the Spokane program, this description offered by the site evaluators:

> Youth Alternatives was a well-managed, highly competent organization with a dedicated staff. They handled more than 50 status offender referrals per month, and almost all of these were referred to them from legitimate juvenile justice system authorities. Program personnel were on-call at all hours of the day or night to handle crises, find temporary shelter for the youngsters, settle disputes that would permit the youth to return home, and so on [Schneider et al., 1978].

But of course, the most beautifully mounted attack is of little more than aesthetic value if it has not first correctly identified and located its target. One function of theory in social programming is to improve such target identification and location; this was manifestly lacking in DSO.

OUTCOME INTEGRITY

As a final and crucial mode of program assessment, the intended effects of program activities on program outcome require examination. To the extent that program activities are designed to lead to intended outcomes, we may speak of a program's outcome integrity. We have noted that in addition to enhancing humaneness and equity by reducing the use of secure confinement in status offense cases, the control and prevention of delinquency represented the second major, if implicit, goal of the DSO program. In this discussion, the outcome integrity of the program is assessed with respect to the articulation of program activities with a delinquency control outcome. Here, we suspend the issues related to program integrity, the articulation of program rationale with program activity, and instead take the program at face value.

We have already noted, of course, that outcome levels of delinquency reduction were disappointing. Overall, the program was associated with a consistent, statistically significant, if small, increase in recidivism in comparison with preprogram groups. Obviously, a significant decrease could have been reasonably expected. However, this statement is about a mean, an average outcome, so that there must in fact have been a number of successes as well as failures. If we can discern components of the program related to each, we will increase the instructive value of the program experience.

Two approaches to outcome integrity were selected. The first deals with the levels of variables that might relate to outcome, because some of these are more amendable to program manipulation than are others. The second approach looks specifically at *types of services* offered to clients to ascertain their relative impact on recidivism, if differences exist.

The first analysis pitted four levels of variables against each other as determinants of the variance in recidivism. *Site*, a "variable" of obviously complex nature, was compared with a large number of *client characteristics*, along with the eight categories of *services* employed throughout the project, and finally with nineteen descriptions of the *facilities* that delivered the services. A series of regression analyses were utilized to assess the relative contribution of these four categories of variables to the subsequent offenses of program clients.

With all other levels held constant, client characteristics emerged as the most potent set of variables. This necessarily increases our concern with the issues of proper client targeting, net widening, and so on. Next in order came site and facility levels, the ordering dependent upon the form of regression analysis taken. Site, of course, is a given, once a program has been launched, and speaks importantly to issues in the initial selection of projects to be funded. Facility variables, on the other hand, represent many factors that can be manipulated by both selection and organization of functions; thus both funders and monitors on the one hand and program organizers on the other have some leverage in affecting outcome through attention to service deliverers.

Showing the least effect on the subsequent offenses of program clients were the service variables. The significance of this seems great to us. Most practitioners place great weight on service modalities—types of treatments, strategies of intervention, and so on. Within DSO (and in many other programs evaluated in the past), the type of service delivered was apparently of minor importance in affecting the offense behavior of clients.[11] Yet type of service probably occupies more practitioner time and attention than any of the other categories of variables.

Perhaps the low contribution of service categories is a function of having many clients in no demonstrable need of service. Perhaps it reflects the low level of diversity between the services actually delivered; most of them turned out to be counseling services in which conceptual distinctions were likely to be less notable than their similarities. Perhaps these services were too minimal to manifest differential effects. Or it may be that the services we generally offer are simply not powerful. Our data do not permit one to select among such alternatives; they merely highlight the problem and stand as a warning about the appropriateness of concentrating planning efforts on types of service rather than on types of clients in particular.[12]

The second approach to assessing outcome integrity concentrated on the services delivered, because of the great weight assigned to these variables by the practitioner community. As we have just seen, service is not a variable category of much moment, but within it our analysis might yet have found some modalities to be more effective than others. In particular, we sought interactions between *type of service* and *type of client*; in other words, what works for whom? In this analysis, unlike all the others, we were able to look at recidivism measured both by official offense data and by self-report delinquency.

Unfortunately, due to the absence of control groups or random assignment to different forms of service, the analysis has been unable to disentangle important client selection and assignment biases from treatment effects. For instance larger numbers of services are associated with higher than expected recidivism rates. But this could well be due to the assignment of more serious offenders to more services. The analysis was also hampered by the fact that many sites offered only a few of the service categories. Finally, as we have noted, the absence of strong service effects overall militated against finding many differential relationships.

Two or three interesting trends did emerge, nonetheless. One of these is that foster care may be particularly beneficial for runaways and for the very small number of program clients from families so demoralized and conflict ridden that the clients could not be returned home. We note, in this regard, the conclusion of Handler and Zatz (1982) that foster care is a burgeoning approach to status offender treatment. A second trend is that long-term residential placement may be beneficial for more serious offenders, those with more extensive prior records. Finally, it appears that standard counseling services may be detrimental overall. None of the effects were overly strong, but these three were of sufficient consistency to merit close attention in the future. Within the constraints of the analysis problems we have described, they provide beacons, however weak, to guide controlled experimentation in future status offender programming where such programming proves justifiable.

SELECTED IMPLICATIONS

A project as large and complex as the DSO program naturally yields many implications and suggestions, both minor and major. Some of the more obvious implications to be drawn from the national evaluation are subsumable under the three headings below.

On Status Offender Deinstitutionalization

(a) Our data, along with those from prior studies, strongly suggest that the "pure" status offender is a relatively uncommon youngster; most offenders evidence a mixed status/delinquent offense pattern. Future programs must either aim at the *child* as target, regardless of the "accidental" charge lodged against him or her, or respond to the act alone without assumptions that the act signifies special child characteristics.

(b) The paternalistic stamp of most treatment programs conflicts somewhat with the liberationist thrust of the children's rights movement of which DSO is a forerunner. Policymakers must consider more fully that if deinstitutionalization is appropriate for youth charged with a status offense, then perhaps their removal from juvenile court jurisdiction is also appropriate. This is certainly the implication of labeling theory, the conceptual framework avowedly underlying the federal legislation. It is also the conclusion of the site evaluators of the Connecticut DSO program (Logan and Rausch, 1980). Policymakers should also consider more fully the precise objective to be served in status offender deinstitutionalization. If the aim is humaneness and equity, programs are perhaps best centered in the courts, where the critical disposition decisions can be made to avoid secure confinement as a response to a noncriminal offense. In the light of this aim, the removal of status offense cases from court jurisdiction may not only be unwarranted, but might well impede the achievement of this objective. This may be the emerging position of the National Council on Crime and Delinquency, to judge from the recent policy statement stressing the view that the failure of "reform" programs to date implies that we should let crime and the justice system find their own "natural" accommodations (Doleschal, 1982).

On the other hand, if delinquency control is the aim, care must be exercised to base a status offender program on soundly validated knowledge about the processes that may foster a juvenile career of multiple offenses. Labeling theory is clearly a weak reed to support the expectation that simple avoidance of juvenile justice processing will effectively prevent delinquency, and is hardly sufficient grounds on which to base a movement to divest the courts of jurisdiction in status offense cases. As seen in the experience of the DSO program, in the current "state of the art" neither juvenile justice processing nor deinstitutionalization in status offense cases offers delinquency control advantages over the other, although the latter may afford some cost reduction. While it is not possible in these cases to justify the use of secure confinement as a delinquency control expedient, claims for decarceration appear equally unwarranted. With respect to the problems of delinquency control, this remains an important finding in the evaluation of the DSO program, and points firmly to the need for well-designed field tests of program approaches to the treatment of status offending youth based on a thorough assessment of the research in support of existing delinquency theory.

(c) The data indicate that alternative services for youth identified, however uncertainly, as status offenders are not necessarily productive. This is especially true of various forms of counseling service. Other projects on delinquency treatment, over many decades, have yielded substantially similar results. Policymakers *and* treaters must be willing to face and test seriously the proposition that early offenders are not amenable to the treatments in our standard repertoire and may best be left alone. It remains true that half of those arrested for the first time are never arrested again. As Murray and Rubin (1982: 84) note, "Courts and social service agencies need to carefully examine the range and focus of their programs keeping in mind a canon of the helping professions: 'First, do no harm.' "

(d) One tentative, positive finding of DSO is that residential treatment programs may be effective with higher-risk offenders. This suggestion fits with data reported for serious-offender projects in Utah, Los Angeles, and Chicago (Empey and Lubeck, 1971; Empey, 1982; Murray and Cox, 1979). Serious attention to restricting our rehabilitative services to this type, and for high-risk offenders only, may be in order.

(e) DSO was a two-year-plus program, lodged in many instances in highly amenable sites. Yet the level of deinstitutionalization achieved, while substantial, was not up to the standards required. In other settings—Massachusetts, Vermont, California, Pima County—far more complete deinstitutionalization has been achieved *far* more rapidly by *edict*, administrative or legislative. For this type of goal, care and caution may have proved less effective than swift, legally mandated action. Policymakers need to consider the price of "going slow" in jurisdictions prepared to bar secure confinement as a response to status offenses. On the other hand, in jurisdictions not ready to take this step, as was the case in two of the DSO program sites (Delaware and South Carolina), the program apparently paved the way for legislative action promoting the deinstitutionalization of status offenders immediately following termination of federal funding.

On Program Constraints

(a) Treading on unknown territory entails exploration. Lead time for program development is essential both for local program developers and for funding organizations, the latter to develop adequate conceptual guidelines, and the former to develop adequate operational procedures. DSO had some lead time, but not enough for the task.

(b) Agreements with local authorities, police, and courts, in the case of DSO, need to be hammered out in greater detail and with greater assurance against backsliding. The tendency is for project applicants to ob-

tain minimal, nonbinding letters of cooperation where genuine commitments are really needed. Funders must be willing to test the levels of
commitment among collaborating agencies prior to program awards.

(c) Prior analysis of the critical decision points in an operating system
would have benefited several DSO projects. The political "clout" of the
court and the potential for effective resistance by police proved in some
sites to have been underestimated. The administration of a major program should take into account these critical decision-making points in the
system. To be effective in diverting status offenders from secure confinement, programs must be so structured as to exert influence on the crucial
case disposition points in the justice system. DSO programs with direct
access to the police and to court intake units, whether structurally (as in
the case of Delaware) or informally (as in the Spokane County program),
were more successful in diverting status offenders from secure confinement. Where such access was much reduced, as in the South Carolina
program, there was little diversion from placement in detention facilities.
In the seven states they surveyed, Handler et al. (1982: 90) found the
stance of the juvenile court judge to be the most crucial factor.

(d) The "disinterested" and questioning stance of independent evaluators, while often disconcerting to program planners, is nonetheless perhaps the best guarantee that untested assumptions will not guide program development. *Genuine* program and evaluation staff interaction
should be required from the very beginning stages of program development, with evaluators as close-to-equal partners, rather than as consultants. Site selection, goals, success criteria, and guidelines for project applicants may all benefit where the program and evaluation inputs are
seen as having potentially equal merit.

On External Validity

One must assume that programs such as DSO are not designed principally to benefit only the clients involved in the brief two- or three-year life
span of the program. Rather, they are designed for the long-term benefit
of all the clients to follow. The 16,000 youths benefited or harmed by
their participation in DSO are but a small portion of the youths across the
country who are yet to be served by virtue of committing a status offense.
The importance of DSO, then, is as a *demonstration* of service potentials.

(a) Demonstrations cannot prove their worth beyond their own limited time and clientele in the absence of concrete evaluability. DSO had a
far lower level of evaluability than was potentially available to it. Elements of reasonable evaluation *must* be built into social programs of this
sort earlier, with greater criterion weight in funding decisions. Issues of
comparative designs, data systems, lead time, guarantees of data access,
and site selection to maximize generalizability are not extraneous but ba-

sic components of the ultimate utility of program efforts. The limitations of the value of DSO should be ample witness to this conclusion.

(b) The five tests of adequacy of rationale, level of implementation, outcome achievement, program integrity, and outcome integrity, if considered carefully during planning rather than after program termination, could provide program staffs with a major head start in mounting operations for which outcomes, of whatever sort, will have greater utility. In particular, far greater attention to adequacy of rationale and program integrity seem pivotal to the successful demonstration of what we can and cannot yet accomplish in social programming.

NOTES

1. Unfortunately, this same pattern was later manifested, with frightening redundancy, in OJJDP's national delinquency prevention initiative. See the National Council on Crime and Delinquency report (1981).

2. OJJDP did commission a separate study that developed a uniform and consistent definition of "status offender." The problem of persuading jurisdictions with diverse views of this category was regarded as too formidable to overcome (see White, 1976).

3. These were the explicit criteria. Political considerations were involved in several of the choices, and the need for regionalization affected some other choices.

4. The evaluators of the Pima County program have added a somewhat more cynical note about the motivations of net-widening agencies. They note:

[There was] intense competition for clients and for agency survival in the community-based sector. Many of these community agencies refused to see themselves in terms of a two-year demonstration project. Within a short time of their initial funding, each agency set out to procure a more stable funding source and began to orient themselves toward the program dictates of local funding agencies. The size and diversity of the client list became a sine qua non for future funding. The temporary nature of this diversion experiment became translated into a permanent enterprise. Those programmatic expectations and mandates emanating from the federal funding agency became co-opted by local funding agencies. The locus of control dissipated into survival techniques, vying for scarce resources and community attention [Rojek and Erickson, 1981].

5. In the case of South Carolina, some irregularities in data collection by the local evaluator may have distorted the picture, but not enough to invalidate that state's admitted approach to selecting very minor offenders.

6. The DSO experiences with net widening are far from unique. Indeed, a rather substantial amount of literature on this issue is now available, most recently summarized by Blomberg (1980). The latest analysis emanates from the Status Offender Service Unit in St. Louis, where the evaluator concludes, "It is apparent that the existence of this program, rather than diverting youths from the pool of referred youth, simply contributed to it" (Decker, 1982: 6).

7. Interestingly, the same narrowness has been noted in the OJJDP prevention programs, in which funded agencies continued to offer the services they had traditionally offered

without accommodating the program requirements. In this case, however, the dominant modality was recreation, not counseling (National Council on Crime and Delinquency, 1981).

8. For an alternative example, see Lloyd (1980: 42-56), in which definitive principles of treatment for DSO clients are set forth on the basis of a family system approach. These principles are largely unconnected to the empirical realities of a status offending population.

9. Miller, Gordon, and Heck (1981) have provided an independent demonstration of network centrality achieved in the various DSO sites. Gordon, employing a combination of our data and those of Miller et al., has tested the validity of two competing propositions, one suggesting that effective interagency connections would lead to label spread and greater recidivism and the other suggesting that such connections would lead to lower recidivism by reason of appropriate client selection, referral, and resource acquisition. The data support the label spread proposition, perhaps, as Gordon (1980) suggests, "simply as a result of the referral process." Such a finding, Gordon (1980: 92-93) continues, "emphasizes the need to consider the extent to which the agency itself is involved in the creation or proliferation of delinquency by virtue of its own actions."

10. Readers finding this humane rationale quite acceptable at face value might want to review Scull's (1977: 1-2) rather sardonic statement of its underlying assumptions and implications.

11. The data base supporting this finding was in part limited by less than full access to the differentiating detail that would have been desirable regarding variations in duration of treatment, and in the competence, experience, and specific intervention approach of the service provider, any or all of which might have identified successful treatment approaches. Confidence in the finding is nonetheless warranted by its congruence with findings on treatment outcome in numerous other studies (see Lipton et al., 1975; Wright and Dixon, 1977; Romig, 1978).

12. The client characteristics consistently most positively correlated with recidivism levels were prior offenses, male gender, age, and the instant offense of alcohol possession.

APPENDIX:
DSO PUBLICATIONS AND DISSERTATIONS

Doctoral Dissertations[1]

Davis, Sharon Kantarowski (1980) "Interaction processes in large-scale evaluation research." University of Southern California.

Heck, Carl L. (1980) "Facility effects on status offender recidivism." University of Southern California.

Lynch, James P. (1983) "Community organization and the delivery of police services." University of Chicago.

Rausch, Sharla P. (1982) "Perception of sanctions, informal controls, and deterrence: a longitudinal analysis." University of Connecticut.

Reamer, Frederic G. (1978) "Response bias in research interviews with clients of a social welfare program." University of Chicago.

Journal Articles and Book Chapters

Datesman, Susan (1982) "The impact of official and self-reported delinquency on adolescent attitudes and self-images: a longitudinal assessment," in V. L. Swigert (ed.) Law and the Legal Process. Beverly Hills, CA: Sage.

Klein, Malcolm W. (1979) "Deinstitutionalization and diversion of juvenile offenders: a litany of impediments," in N. Morris and M. Tonry (eds.) Crime and Justice: An Annual Review of Research, Vol. I. Chicago: University of Chicago Press.

Kobrin, Solomon, Frank R. Hellum, and John W. Peterson (1980) "Offense patterns of status offenders," in D. Shichor and D. H. Kelly (eds.) Critical Issues in Juvenile Delinquency. Lexington, MA: D.C. Heath.

Lincoln, James R., Suzanne B. Lincoln, and Douglas Smith (1982) "Analyzing agency effects on juvenile offenders: methods and applications" in J. Hagan (ed.) Deterrence Reconsidered: Methodological Innovations. Beverly Hills, CA: Sage.

Miller, Jon (1980) "Access to interorganizational networks as a professional resource." American Sociological Review 45: 479-496.

Miller, Jon, James R. Lincoln, and Jon Olson (1981) "Rationality and equity in professional networks: gender and race as factors in the stratification of interorganizational systems." American Journal of Sociology 87: 308-335.

Rausch, Sharla P. (forthcoming) "Court processing vs. diversion of status offenders: a test of deterrence and labelling theories." Journal of Research in Crime and Delinquency.

Rausch, Sharla P. and Charles Logan (1983) "Diversion from juvenile court: panacea or Pandora's box?" in J. Kluegel (ed.) Evaluating Contemporary Juvenile Justice. Beverly Hills, CA: Sage.

Reamer, Frederic G. (1979) "Protecting research subjects and unintended consequences: the effects of guarantees of confidentiality." Public Opinion Quarterly 43: 497-506.

Rojek, Dean G. (1982) "Juvenile diversion: a study of community cooptation," in D. G. Rojek and G. F. Jenson (eds.) Readings in Juvenile Delinquency. Lexington, MA: D. C. Heath.

Rojek, Dean G. and Maynard L. Erickson (1981) "Reforming the juvenile justice system: the diversion of status offenders." Law and Society Review 16: 241-264.

Rojek, Dean G. and Maynard L. Erickson (1982) "Delinquent careers: a test of the career escalation model." Criminology 20: 5-28.

Schneider, Anne (1981) "Effects of status offender deinstitutionalization," in R. Roesch and R. R. Carrado (eds.) Evaluation and Criminal Justice Policy. Beverly Hills, CA: Sage.

Spergel, Irving A. (1982) "The role of the social developer," in D. S. Sanders (ed.) The Developmental Perspective in Social Work. Honolulu: University of Hawaii Press.

Spergel, Irving A., Frederic G. Reamer, and James P. Lynch (1981) "Deinstitutionalization of status offenders: individual outcome and system effects." Journal of Research in Crime and Delinquency 18: 4-33.

Spergel, Irving A., James P. Lynch, Frederic G. Reamer, and John Korbelik (1982) "Response of organization and community to a deinstitutionalization strategy." Crime and Delinquency 28: 426-449.

Teilmann, Katherine S. and Pierre H. Landry, Jr. (1981) "Gender bias in juvenile justice." Journal of Research in Crime and Delinquency 18: 47-80.

NOTE

1. All available through University of Michigan dissertation microfilms.

REFERENCES

ALLINSON, R. [ed.] (1978) Status Offenders and the Juvenile Justice System: An Anthology. Hackensack, NJ: National Council on Crime and Delinquency.

Arthur D. Little, Inc. (1977) Cost and Service Impacts of Deinstitutionalization of Status Offenders in Ten States: "Responses to Angry Youth." Washington, DC: Author.

BANKS, J. and S. J. DEUTSCH (1979) Effectiveness of Deinstitutionalization in South Carolina. Atlanta, GA: Technology Institute, Inc.

BARKER, G. H. (1940) "Family factors in the ecology of juvenile delinquency." Journal of Criminal Law and Criminology.

BECKER, H. S. (1963) Outsiders: Studies in the Sociology of Deviance. New York: Free Press.

BLOMBERG, T. G. (1980) "Widening the net: an anomaly in the evaluation of diversion programs," in M. W. Klein and K. S. Teilmann (eds.) Handbook of Criminal Justice Evaluation. Beverly Hills, CA: Sage.

BURKHART, K. W. (1975) The Child and the Law: Helping the Status Offender. New York: Public Affairs Committee, Inc.

California Youth Authority (1974) A Comparison of Admission Characteristics of Youth Authority Wards: 1965-1973. Sacramento: Author.

CARTER, R. M. (1981) "Evaluation of the deinstitutionalization of status offenders project through the system rated methodology," in S. Kobrin and M. W. Klein, National Evaluation of the Deinstitutionalization of Status Offender Programs, Final Report, Vol. II. Washington, DC: U.S. Department of Justice.

CARTER, T. J. (1979) "Juvenile court dispositions: a comparison of status and nonstatus offenders." Criminology 17: 341-359

CLARKE, S. H. (1975) "Some implications for North Carolina of recent research in juvenile delinquency." Journal of Research in Crime and Delinquency 12 (January): 51-60.

CLOWARD, R. A. and L. E. OHLIN (1960). Delinquency and Opportunity: A Theory of Delinquent Gangs. New York: Free Press.

COATES, R. B. (1981) "Community-based services for juvenile delinquents: concept and implications for practice." Journal of Social Issues 37: 87-101.

———— A. D. MILLER, and L. OHLIN (1978) Diversity in a Youth Correctional System: Handling Delinquents in Massachusetts. Cambridge, MA: Ballinger.

COHEN, A. K. (1966) Deviance and Control. Englewood Cliffs, NJ: Prentice-Hall.

———— (1955) Delinquent Boys: The Culture of the Gang. New York: Free Press.

COHEN, J. and P. COHEN (1975) Applied Multiple Regression/Correlation Analysis for the Behavioral Sciences. Hillsdale, NJ: Erlbaum.

DECKER, S. H. (1982) "A systemic analysis of diversion: net-widening and beyond." University of Missouri—St. Louis. (mimeo)

DOLESCHAL, E. (1982) "The dangers of criminal justice reform." Criminal Justice Abstracts 14: 133-152.

DUNFORD, F. W., D. W. OSGOOD, and H. F. WEICHSELBAUM (1982) National Evaluation of Diversion Projects. Washington, DC: NCJRS, U.S. Department of Justice.

ELLIOTT, D. S. (1966) "Delinquency, school attendance and dropout." Social Problems 13 (Winter): 307-324.

EMPEY, L. T. (1982) American Delinquency: Its Meaning and Construction (2nd ed.). Homewood, IL: Dorsey.

———— (1978) American Delinquency: Its Meaning and Construction. Homewood, IL: Dorsey.

———— and S. LUBECK (1971) The Silverlake Experiment: Testing Delinquency Theory and Community Intervention. Chicago: Aldine.

_____ (1968) "Conformity and deviance in the 'situation of company.'" American Sociological Review 33 (October): 761-774.

ERICKSON, M. L. (1979) "Some empirical questions concerning the current revolution in juvenile justice," in L. T. Empey (ed.) The Future of Childhood and Juvenile Justice. Charlottesville: University of Virginia Press.

FOX, V. (1977) Community-Based Corrections. Englewood Cliffs, NJ: Prentice-Hall.

GARDINER, P. C. (1981) "Evaluation of the deinstitutionalization of status offender programs through the application of multi-attribute utility measurement," in S. Kobrin and M. W. Klein, National Evaluation of the Deinstitutionalization of Status Offender Programs, Final Report, Vol. II. Washington, DC: U.S. Department of Justice.

GLASER, B. G. and A. L. STRAUSS (1967) The Discovery of Grounded Theory. Chicago: Aldine.

GLUECK, S. and E. GLUECK (1940) Juvenile Delinquents Grown Up. New York: Commonwealth Fund.

GORDON, M. A. (1981) "The impact of juvenile justice reform law on community service providers," in K. T. Van Dusen and M. W. Klein (eds.) Implications of California's 1977 Juvenile Justice Reform Law. Washington, DC: U.S. Department of Justice /NIJJDP.

_____ (1980) "The relationship of agency network centrality to client recidivism." University of Southern California, Department of Sociology. (mimeo)

GOTTFREDSON, M. R., M. J. HINDELANG, and N. PARISI (1977) Sourcebook of Criminal Justice Statistics. Washington, DC: Government Printing Office.

GUTTRIDGE, P. (1981) "Psychiatric and non-psychiatric factors in the hospitalization of adolescents." Ph.D. dissertation, University of Southern California.

HANDLER, J. F. and J. ZATZ [eds.] (1982) Neither Angels nor Thieves: Studies in Deinstitutionalization of Status Offenders. Washington, DC: National Academy Press.

HANDLER, J. F., M. SOSIN, J. A. STOOCKEY, and J. ZATZ (1982) "Deinstitutionalization in seven states: principal findings," in J. F. Handler and J. Zatz (eds.) Neither Angels nor Thieves: Studies in Deinstitutionalization of Status Offenders. Washington, DC: National Academy Press.

HICKEY, W. L. (1977) "Status offenses and the juvenile court." Criminal Justice Abstracts 9 (March): 91-122.

HINDELANG, M. J., T. HIRSCHI, and J. G. WEIS (1979) "Correlates of delinquency." American Sociological Review 44 (December): 995-1014.

HIRSCHI, T. (1969) Causes of Delinquency. Berkeley: University of California Press.

HODGKISS, M. (1933) "The influence of broken homes and working mothers." Smith College Studies in Social Work.

Institute for Juvenile Research (1972) Juvenile Delinquency in Illinois. Chicago: Illinois Department of Mental Health.

JOHNS, D. and J. BOTTCHER (1980) AB 3121 Impact Evaluation: Final Report. Sacramento: California Youth Authority.

Joint Commission on Correctional Manpower and Training (1970) Perspectives on Correctional Manpower and Training. Washington, DC: Government Printing Office.

KLEIN, M. W. (1983) "Offense specialization and versatility among juveniles." British Journal of Criminology.

_____ (1979) "Deinstitutionalization and diversion: a litany of impediments," in N. Morris and M. Tonry (eds.) Crime and Justice: An Annual Review of Research, Vol. I. Chicago: University of Chicago Press.

_____ (1971) Street Gangs and Street Workers. Englewood Cliffs, NJ: Prentice-Hall.

KOBRIN, S. (1959) "The Chicago Area Project—a 25-year assessment." Annals of the American Academy of Political and Social Science 332: 19-29.

KORNEGAY, S. A. and J. L. WOLFLE (1982) "Services for status offenders under the LEAA, OJJDP, and Runaway Youth Programs," in J. F. Handler and J. Zatz (eds.) Neither Angels nor Thieves: Studies in Deinstitutionalization of Status Offenders. Washington, DC: National Academy Press.

KRISBERG, B. and I. SCHWARTZ (1982) Rethinking Juvenile Justice. San Francisco: National Council on Crime and Delinquency.

Law Enforcement Assistance Administration [LEAA] (1975) Program Announcement: Deinstitutionalization of Status Offenders. Washington, DC: Government Printing Office.

———— (1974) Children in Custody: A Report on the Juvenile Detention and Correctional Facility Census of 1971. Washington, DC: Government Printing Office.

LEMERT, E. M. (1951) Social Pathology. New York: McGraw-Hill.

LERMAN, P. (1980) "Trends and issues in deinstitutionalization of youths in trouble." Crime and Delinquency 26 (July): 281-298.

———— (1975) Community Treatment and Social Control. Chicago: University of Chicago Press.

———— (1974) "The New Jersey Training School for Girls: a study of alternatives." New Jersey Department of Institutions and Agencies. (mimeo)

LEVINE, T. (1977) "Community-based treatment for adolescents: myths and realities." Social Work 22: 144-147.

LIPTON, D., R. MARTINSON, and J. WILKS (1975) The Effectiveness of Correctional Treatment: A Survey of Treatment and Evaluation Studies. New York: Praeger.

LITTLE, M. A. (1981) "Police and runaway perceptions of the runaway act." Ph.D. dissertation, University of Southern California.

LLOYD, L. (1980) D.S.O. Handbook: A Guide to Effective Services for Status Offenders. San Francisco: Social Advocates for Youth.

LOGAN, C. H. and S. P. RAUSCH (1980) "An evaluation of Connecticut's DSO project." Presented at the annual meeting of the American Society of Criminology, Storrs, Connecticut.

MANNHEIM, H. and L. T. WILKINS (1955) Prediction Methods in Relation to Borstal Training. London: Her Majesty's Stationery Office.

MARRIS, P. and M. REIN (1973) Dilemmas of Social Reform. Chicago: Aldine.

MERTON, R. K. (1968) Social Theory and Social Structure. New York: Free Press.

MILLER, J. (1980) "Access to interorganizational networks as a professional resource." American Sociological Review 45: 479-496.

———— A. GORDON, and C. L. HECK (1981) "The organizational properties of seven programs for the deinstitutionalization of status offenders," in S. Kobrin and M. W. Klein, National Evaluation of the Deinstitutionalization of Status Offenders Programs, Final Report, Vol. II. Washington, DC: U.S. Department of Justice.

MILLER, J., J. R. LINCOLN, and J. OLSON (1981) "Rationality and equity in professional networks: gender and race as factors in the stratification of interorganizational systems." American Journal of Sociology 87: 308-335.

MONAHAN, T. P. (1957) "Family status and the delinquent child." Social Forces 35: 250-258.

MULVEY, E. P. and J. T. SAUNDERS (1982) "Juvenile detention criteria: state of the art and guidelines for change." Criminal Justice Abstracts 14 (June): 261-289.

MURPHY, P. T. (1974) Our Kindly Parent—The State: The Juvenile Justice System and How It Works. New York: Viking.

MURRAY, C. A. and L. A. COX, Jr. (1979) Beyond Probation: Juvenile Corrections and the Chronic Delinquent. Beverly Hills, CA: Sage.

MURRAY, C. A., D. THOMPSON, and C. B. ISRAEL (1978) UDIS: Deinstitutionalizing the

Chronic Juvenile Offenders. Washington, DC: American Institutes for Research.

MURRAY, J. P. and H. T. RUBIN (1983) Status Offenders: A Sourcebook. Boys Town, NE: Boys Town Center.

National Council on Crime and Delinquency (1981) The National Evaluation of Delinquency Prevention. San Francisco: Author.

———— (1961) Standards and Guides for Detention of Children and Youth (2nd ed.). New York: Author.

National Opinion Research Center (1975) Appendix F of the 1975 NORC General Survey of Social Issues. Chicago: Author.

NEJELSKI, P. (1976) "Diversion: the promise and the danger." Crime and Delinquency 22: 393-410.

NYE, F. I. (1958) Family Relationships and Delinquent Behavior. New York: John Wiley.

OHLIN, L. E., A. D. MILLER, and R. COATES (1975) "Analyzing reform in human services: a case study of Massachusetts youth corrections." Presented at the meetings of the Society for the Study of Social Problems, Cambridge, Massachusetts.

PAPPENFORT, D. M. (1970) "Detention facilities." A Census of Children's Residential Institutions in the United States, Puerto Rico and the Virgin Islands, Vol. 7. Chicago: University of Chicago Press.

Peat, Marwick, and Mitchell, & Co. (1981) "Comparative cost analysis of deinstitutionalization programs," in S. Kobrin and M. W. Klein (eds.) National Evaluation of the Deinstitutionalization of Status Offender Programs, Final Report, Vol. II. Washington, DC: U.S. Department of Justice.

POLK, K. and D. S. HALFERTY (1966) "Adolescence, commitment and delinquency." Journal of Research in Crime and Delinquency 4 (July): 82-96.

POLK, K. and S. KOBRIN (1972) Delinquency Prevention Through Youth Development. Washington, DC: U.S. Department of Health, Education and Welfare (YDDPA).

POLK, K. and W. E. SCHAFER [eds.] (1972) School and Delinquency. Englewood Cliffs, NJ: Prentice-Hall.

President's Commission on Law Enforcement and Administration of Justice (1967) Task Force Report: Juvenile Delinquency. Washington, DC: Government Printing Office.

RECTOR, J. (1975) "The juvenile justice and delinquency prevention act of 1974." Los Angeles Bar Bulletin (February): 151-154.

REED, D., H. MEYER, K. ZALENT, and J. LINN (1981) Promises, Promises—Does the Juvenile Court Deliver for Status Offenders? The Record in Cook County, Illinois. Chicago: Chicago Law Enforcement Study Group.

ROJEK, D. G. (1982) "Juvenile diversion: a study of community cooptation," in D. G. Rojek and G. F. Jenson (eds.) Readings in Juvenile Delinquency. Lexington, MA: D. C. Heath.

———— (1978) "Quarterly progress report, evaluation of Status Offender Project, Pima County, Arizona." University of Arizona—Tucson. (mimeo)

———— and M. L. ERICKSON (1982) "Delinquent careers: a test of the career escalation model." Criminology 20: 5-28.

———— (1981) "Reforming the juvenile justice system: the diversion of status offenders." Law and Society Review 16: 241-264.

ROMIG, D. A. (1978) Justice for Our Children. Lexington, MA: D.C. Heath.

RUTHERFORD, A. and O. BENGUR (1976) Community-Based Alternatives to Juvenile Incarceration. Washington, DC: U.S. Department of Justice.

SAARI, R. (1981) "The effectiveness paradox: institutional vs. community placement of offenders." Journal of Social Issues 37: 34-50.

———— (1978) "Status offenders: their fate in the juvenile justice system," in R. Allinson (ed.) Status Offenders and the Juvenile Justice System: An Anthology. Hackensack, NJ: National Council on Crime and Delinquency.

_____ and R. VINTER (1976) "Justice for whom? Varieties of juvenile correctional approaches," in M. W. Klein (ed.) The Juvenile Justice System. Beverly Hills, CA: Sage.

SCHNEIDER, A. L. (1982) "Relabeling and net-widening: the Washington (State) experience with divestiture of court jurisdiction over status offenders." Presented at the meetings of the American Society of Criminology, Portland, Oregon.

_____ C. M. CLEARY, and P. D. REITER (1978) Executive Summary: Final Evaluation Report on the Spokane Project to Deinstitutionalize Status Offenders. Portland, OR: Institute of Policy Analysis.

SCHUR, E. M. (1973) Radical Nonintervention. Englewood Cliffs, NJ: Prentice-Hall.

_____ (1971) Labeling Deviant Behavior. New York: Harper & Row.

SCULL, A. T. (1977) Decarceration—Community Treatment and the Deviant: A Radical View. Englewood Cliffs, NJ: Prentice-Hall.

SELLIN, T. (1958) "Recidivism and maturation." National Probation and Parole Association Journal 4: 241-250.

SHANNON, L. (1963) "Types and patterns of delinquency referral in a middle-sized city." British Journal of Criminology 4: 24-36.

SHAW, C. R. and H. D. McKAY (1969) Juvenile Delinquency and Urban Areas. Chicago: University of Chicago Press.

SMITH, C. P., T. E. BLACK, and F. R. CAMPBELL (1979) A National Assessment of Case Disposition and Classification in the Juvenile Justice System: Inconsistent Labeling, Vol. I. Washington, DC: U.S. Department of Justice.

SMITH, C. P., D. J. BERKMAN, W. N. FRASER, and J. SUTTON (1980) A Preliminary National Assessment of the Status Offender and Juvenile Justice System: Role Conflicts, Constraints, and Information Gaps. Washington, DC: U.S. Department of Justice.

South Carolina Department of Youth Services (1975) Special Analysis. Columbia: Author.

SPERGEL, I. A. (1975) "Community-based delinquency-prevention programs: an overview," in G. R. Perlstein and T. R. Phelps (eds.) Alternatives to Prison: Community-Based Corrections, a Reader. Pacific Palisades, CA: Goodyear.

_____ J. KORBELIK, F. G. REAMER, and J. P. LYNCH (1981) "Interactions between juvenile justice system and community structure in the deinstitutionalization of status offenders." Presented at the International Symposium on Sociological Perspectives in Delinquency Prevention, Wuppertal, West Germany.

Stephen Carter & Associates (1977) Comprehensive Statewide Juvenile Detention Study. Columbia, SC: Author.

TANNENBAUM, F. (1938) Crime and Community. New York: Columbia University Press.

TEILMANN, K. S. and M. W. KLEIN (1980) "Juvenile justice legislation: a framework for legislation," in D. Schichor and D. H. Kelly (eds.) Critical Issues in Juvenile Delinquency. Lexington MA: D. C. Heath.

_____ (1979) Summary of Interim Findings of the Assessment of California's 1977 Juvenile Justice Legislation (AB 3121). Los Angeles: University of Southern California.

THOMAS, C. W. (1976) "Are status offenders really so different?" Crime and Delinquency 22: 438-455.

THORNBERRY, T. (1973) "Race, socioeconomic status, and sentencing in the juvenile justice system." Journal of Criminal Law and Criminology 64 (March): 90-98.

TOBY, J. (1957a) "The differential impact of family disorganization." American Sociological Review 22 (October): 505-512.

_____ (1957b) "Social disorganization and stake in conformity." Journal of Criminal Law, Criminology and Police Science 48 (May /June): 12-17.

U.S. Department of Health, Education and Welfare, Office of the Assistant Secretary for Planning and Evaluation (1975) Runaway Youth: Annotated Bibliography and Literature Overview. Washington, DC: Department of Commerce, National Technical Information Service.

U.S. Department of Justice, Office of General Counsel, LEAA (1974) Indexed Legislative History of the Juvenile Justice and Delinquency Prevention Act of 1974. Washington, DC: Government Printing Office.

VINTER, R. D. [ed.] (1976) Time Out: A National Study of Juvenile Correctional Programs. Ann Arbor: University of Michigan.

VAN DUSEN, K. T. (1981) "Changes in status offender handling," in K. T. Van Dusen and M. W. Klein (eds.) Implications of California's 1977 Juvenile Justice Reform Law. Washington, DC: U.S. Department of Justice /NIJJDP.

—— and M. W. KLEIN (1981) Executive Summary: Assessment of the Impact of California's 1977 Juvenile Justice Reform Law. Washington, DC: U.S. Department of Justice/ NIJJDP.

WARREN, C. A. B. [ed.] (1981) New Forms of Social Control: The Myth of Deinstitutionalization. American Behavioral Scientist 24: special issue.

WATKIN, E. (1975) Children Without Justice: A Report by the National Council of Jewish Women. New York: National Council of Jewish Women, Inc.

WEISBROD, J. A. (1981) Family Court Disposition Study. New York: Vera Institute of Justice.

WHITE, J. L. (1976) "Status offenders: which side of the road?" Criminal Justice Review 1 (Spring): 23-43.

WOLFGANG, M. E., R. M. FIGLIO, and T. SELLIN (1972) Delinquency in a Birth Cohort. Chicago: University of Chicago Press.

WRIGHT, W. E. and M. C. DIXON (1977) "Community prevention and treatment of juvenile delinquency." Journal of Research in Crime and Delinquency 14: 35-67.

YOUNG, T. M. and D. M. PAPPENFORT (1977) Secure Detention of Juveniles and Alternatives to Its Use. Washington, DC: U.S. Department of Justice.

ZATZ, J. (1982a) "Problems and issues in deinstitutionalization: historical overview and current attitudes," in J. F. Handler and J. Zatz (eds.), Neither Thieves nor Angels: Studies in Deinstitutionalization of Status Offenders. Washington, DC: National Academy Press.

—— (1982b) "Problems and issues in deinstitutionalization: laws, concepts, and goals," in J. F. Handler and J. Zatz (eds.), Neither Angels nor Thieves: Studies in Deinstitutionalization of Status Offenders. Washington, DC: National Academy Press.

AUTHOR INDEX

SUBJECT INDEX

active federalism, 24-29, 34

advocacy, 37, 114, 117, 122, 125, 128-129, 140-143, 152-153, 155, 171, 183, 185, 187n, 217-220, 252, 253, 305, 312

age, 172, 182, 185, 195, 196, 207-209, 213n, 227, 229, 230, 245-249, 258, 262, 263, 267, 322n; at first offense, 186n

Alameda County, 14, 44, 171, 197, 202, 210, 213n, 217-222, 227, 229, 230, 235, 250, 252, 253, 281, 283, 289, 305; effectiveness of services, 245

Alaska, delinquency legislation, 20, 35

alcohol, minor in possession of, 65, 67, 86, 182, 194, 195, 212n, 227, 260, 282, 283, 322n

Alston Wilkes Society, 219

Arizona Supreme Court, 121

Arkansas, 35, 44, 52

attachment, school and family, 172

Bayh, Birch, 32, 271

birth cohort, Philadelphia, 86, 87

"cafeteria-style" delinquency, 86

California, 213n, 214n; delinquency legislation (AB3121), 13n, 37, 271, 275, 304, 309, 313, 319

California Youth Authority, 126, 214n

Chicago, 28, 138; Police Department, 140; see also Cook County

chronic offenders, 86

Clark County, 14, 44, 137, 171, 193, 196, 197, 200, 202, 210, 217-222, 227, 229, 235, 242, 254, 258, 281, 283, 287, 292, 305; effectiveness of services, 248, 249

Cleveland, 28

client characteristics, as predictors, 170-188, 203, 316

"come-back" statutes. See violation, court order.

comingling of status, delinquent, adult offenders, 10, 29, 33, 85

community agencies, 13n

community-based treatment, services, programs, 11, 12, 20-22, 29, 31, 33, 35, 36, 40-42, 46, 47, 49, 51, 110, 111, 114, 115, 117, 119, 121, 123, 127-130, 134, 135, 138-144, 146, 147, 150-152, 157, 161, 165, 173, 174, 177, 183, 187n, 188n, 218, 296; defined, 110

community tolerance, 40, 41, 114, 123, 131, 136, 144, 151, 159, 172, 182

community treatment, 9

Connecticut, 14, 22, 44, 136, 170, 171, 175, 193, 196, 202, 209, 213n, 217, 218, 220-222, 227, 229, 234, 235, 239, 252, 254, 258, 274, 279, 281-283, 287, 297, 313, 318; program description, 144-151; effectiveness of services, 245, 246

control groups, 93, 196, 213n

Cook County, 138-141, 143, 144, 208, 211n, 269n, 282, 287, 289, 291-293, 305, 306

cost effectiveness, benefit, 191, 212n, 310

counseling: general, 121, 123, 134, 152, 156, 157, 161, 162, 173, 217-221, 234, 235, 242, 245-249, 252-254, 256-258, 264, 266, 267, 316, 317, 319, 322; crisis, 115, 126-130, 132, 133, 152, 154, 156, 183, 185, 217, 221; family, 121, 125, 126, 128-130, 132-134, 153, 172, 186n, 187n, 217, 221, 304, 312, 322; individual, 125, 137, 153, 187n, 221, 304, 312

"creaming," 291, 302, 303

crisis intervention, 111, 122, 127-130, 132-135, 156, 161, 165, 173, 216-219, 221, 242, 252, 253, 264, 266, 267, 306

crisis receiving homes, 127, 128, 130

curfew violation, 65, 67, 194, 195, 212n, 227, 235

customary household. See family.

decarceration, 21, 22

decriminalization, 20

335

ABOUT THE AUTHORS

Solomon Kobrin is a Senior Research Associate at the Social Science Research Institute and Professor Emeritus in the Sociology Department at the University of Southern California. Prior to his 20 years at USC, he was for 25 years a senior staff member of the Institute for Juvenile Research in Chicago, where he worked with such outstanding scholars of the "Chicago School" of Sociology as Clifford Shaw and Henry McKay. Dr. Kobrin has served as an officer of numerous professional associations and as consultant to such federal agencies as the U.S. Children's Bureau, various branches of the Law Enforcement Assistance Administration, the National Institute of Juvenile Justice and Delinquency Prevention, the Department of Health, Education and Welfare, and the President's Committee on Law Enforcement and the Administration of Justice. He has been the recipient of the prestigious Sutherland Award from the American Society of Criminology. In addition to DSO, Dr. Kobrin has most recently directed major research projects on neighborhood changes and crime rates, crime indicators, the criminal behavior of mental health patients, and the recidivistic violent behaviors of a major cohort of juvenile probationers.

Malcolm W. Klein is Professor of Sociology at the University of Southern California and has served as Department Chair since 1971. He initiated the establishment of USC's Social Science Research Institute in 1972 and continues to carry out his research there. Among his publications are *Juvenile Gangs in Context, Street Gangs and Street Workers, Back on the Street: The Diversion of Juvenile Offenders, The Juvenile Justice System, The Handbook of Criminal Justice Evaluation,* and the forthcoming *Western Systems of Juvenile Justice.* Dr. Klein has conducted basic and applied studies on gangs, police programs, community treatment of juvenile offenders, and juvenile law reform. In addition to consultations for various public and private agencies, he has served on peer review panels for the National Institute of Mental Health and National Institute of Justice. Among other professional involvements, he currently serves on the Board of the American Society of Criminology.